S0-CFN-886

COLLECTION

Eli, Eli, lamma sabacthani?

Volume III

ANIMUS INJURIANDI - II

(Desire to Offend)

Atila Sinke Guimarães

Copyright 2011 © by Atila Sinke Guimarães

All rights reserved. No part of this book may be reproduced or transmitted in any form or by any means whatsover, including the Internet, without permission in writing from the author, except that brief selections may be quoted or copied for non-profit use without permission, provided full credit is given.

ISBN-13: 978-0-9819793-3-5

Library of the Congress Number: 2011936174

First edition 2011 by Tradition in Action, Inc.

Printed and bound in the United States of America

The front cover is a reproduction of *Christ before Caiaphas* by Giotto in the Cappella degli Scrovegni, Padua

Cover by the TIA art desk

Tradition in Action, Inc.
P.O. Box 23135
Los Angeles, CA 90023
www.TraditionInAction.org

OTHER BOOKS BY THE SAME AUTHOR

From the Collection *Lamma Sabacthani*

In The Murky Waters of Vatican II - Volume I - Demonstration of the ambiguity in the official texts of Vatican II

Animus Injuriandi I (Desire to Offend I) - Volume II - The spirit of Vatican II reflected in the desire to offend the Church

Animus Delendi I (Desire to Destroy I) - Volume IV - The spirit of Vatican II, and the consequent desire to destroy the Church

Animus Delendi II (Desire to Destroy II) - Volume V - How Secularization and Ecumenism express the spirit of Vatican II and act to destroy the Church

Will He Find Faith? (Inveniet Fidem?) - Volume VI - How the foundations of the Catholic Faith changed radically after the Council

Ecclesia (The Church) - Volume XI - The new ecclesiology inspired by Progressivism, completly at variance with Catholic doctrine

Special Editions to the Collection

Quo Vadis, Petre? (Where are you going, Peter?) – An analysis of the ecumenical initiatives planned for the passing of the Millennium

Vatican II, Homosexuality & Pedophilia – First published as an appendix of *In the Murky Waters*, the work was expanded to cover the devastating effects of these vices on the clergy, mainly in the U.S.

Previews of the New Papacy (co-author) – A photographic confirmation of the desire to destroy the Papacy.

Other Works of Interest

We Resist You to the Face (co-author)

War, Just War

An Urgent Plea: Do Not Change the Papacy (co-author)

Booklets

The Universal Republic Blessed by the Conciliar Popes
The Biblical Commission on the Jews
Curious Affinities between the Thinking of JP II and Marxism
Petrine Primacy Challenged
The Return of the Muslin Threat
The End of the Galileo Myth
A Cordial Invitation to 171 Rabbis and Jewish Scholars
Resistance versus Sede-Vacantism
We Are Church: Radical Aims, Dangerous Errors

These works can be purchased from
Tradition in Action, Inc. * PO Box 23135 * Los Angeles, CA 90023
Phone: 323-725-0219 * Fax: 323-725-0019
www.TraditionInAction.org

TABLE OF CONTENTS

*   *   *

INTRODUCTION

§ 1   Continuing the analysis of the spirit of Vatican Council II, as we explained in Volume II, we will dedicate this Volume III to studying the *animus injuriandi* turned against Catholic Doctrine that took place under the eyes – or at least with the tolerance – of those ecclesiastical authorities charged with interpreting and applying Vatican II.

§ 2   After studying the offenses made against the Holy Catholic Church in *Animus Injuriandi I*, it seems to us that the next step is to present the offenses made against Faith and Morals. In so doing, we will present a wide picture of the progressivist *desire to offend*.

Were such examples to encompass almost all the characteristics of the Church and countless points of her doctrine, the picture still would not be complete without considering the praise lavished by conciliar leaders on heretics, schismatics and Jews. Although such praise is not a direct insult, it entails grave indirect outrages to the honor of the Church, who has always condemned those heretics, and to the honor due those points of the Catholic Faith denied by heretics. This is why the first Chapter of this Volume studies these affronts.

§ 3   Chapter I is, therefore, a link joining two sets of offenses. The first bloc is constituted of the offenses against the Holy Church presented in Volume II. The second is the ensemble of offenses made against the honor of Catholic Doctrine and is found in this Volume from Chapter II onward.

*

§ 4   As in Volume II, in each Chapter we will first present a general outline explaining the doctrine advocated by the progressivists. Such outlines are intended to provide our Reader with a summary of aspects of Catholic Doctrine denied by Progressivism. This facilitates assessing the gravity of the offenses.

A Reader could possibly have uncertainties about some progressivist doctrine that we expound. Accordingly, when needed, we will present texts that are not directly offensive but

---

[1] Cf. Vol. II, *Animus Injuriandi I, passim.*

confirm our analysis. Such texts are, therefore, collateral apologetic additions that would not be part of the demonstration of the progressivist *animus injuriandi* if this work were addressed exclusively to scholars and specialists.

*　　*　　*

Chapter I

PRAISE OF HERETICS, SCHISMATICS & JEWS

§ 1   Indirect insults can be made to the honor of the Catholic Religion. Though indirect, they are still most grave offenses.

       This is the case of the excerpts analyzed in this Chapter.

§ 2   The praises that Catholic Hierarchs and theologians have been lavishing upon heretics are indicative of an *animus* opposed to the *sentire cum Ecclesia*. They reveal complicity with the doctrinal errors of the heretics they praise, and tacitly "absolve" the moral decadence and crimes that followed those heresies.[1] Finally, such praises are indirect censures of the con-

---

[1] Worthy of note, for example, is the extreme moral degeneration that was a product of the Pseudo-Reformation. Martin Luther and his followers were the first to recognize the depravation into which they had plunged:

- In 1529 the heresiarch stated: "The [Lutheran] Gospelers are seven times worse than before. For, after the preaching of our doctrine, men have given themselves over to stealing, lying, cheating, drinking and every kind of iniquity. ... Princes, lords, noblemen, bourgeois and peasants have all lost their fear of God" (Martin Luther, *Werke*, Weimar: Kritische Gesamtausgabe, 1883, vol. 28, p. 763, *apud* Leonel Franca, *A Igreja, a reforma e a civilização*, Rio de Janeiro: Livraria Catholica, 1928, p. 440).

- In 1542, Luther wrote his disciple Nicolaus von Amsdorf about the general ambience created by Protestantism: "The increase of vice, avarice, usury, licentiousness, hatred, perfidy, envy, pride, impiety and blasphemy is ... so out of bounds that it is unlikely God will still have mercy on Germany" (Wilhelm Martin Leberecht de Wette, *Briefe, Sendschreiben und Bedenken: vollständig gesammelt*, Berlin, 1825-1828, vol. 5, p. 462, *apud ibid.*, p. 441).

- The following year, he wrote to the same accomplice: "It was thus with the world before the deluge, before the Babylon captivity, before the destruction of Jerusalem and the fall of Rome, and before the calamities in Greece and Hungary; thus it will be, and now is, before the ruin of Germany" (De Wette, *Briefe,* vol. 5, pp. 600-601, *apud ibid.*, p. 441).

- In 1538, he stated: "Who among us would have dared to preach if he could have foreseen that the result of our preaching would be so much disgrace, so much scandal, so much ... perversity? But now that we have reached this state, let us bear its consequences" (J. G. Walch, *Sämtliche Werke,* Halle, 1740-1753, vol. 7, p. 564, *apud ibid.*, p. 443).

- By abolishing celibacy of clergymen, allowing divorce and approving polygamy, Protestantism inundated Germany and the Nordic countries with a moral mudslide. In 1522, Prior Johann von Staupitz wrote Luther, his former novice, complaining that his doctrine had been adopted only by those who frequented the brothels (cf. De Wette, *Briefe,* vol. 2, p. 315, *apud ibid.,* p. 453).

- By doing away with the Sacrament of Matrimony, Luther tore apart the institution of the family and inaugurated an era of unbridled pagan sensuality. In 1562, former Lutheran Fr. Friedrich Staphylus wrote: "When matrimony was considered a Sacrament, chastity and honesty in marital life were cherished and loved; but when the people read in Luther's books that the marital state was an invention of men ... his counsels were soon so accepted that, as far as marriage is concerned, there is almost more honesty and dignity in Turkey than among our evangelized Christians in Germany" (*Nachdruck zur Verfechtung des Buchs vom rechten wahren Verstandt des goettichen Worts,* Ingolstadt, 1562, fol. 202b., *apud ibid.,* p. 449).

- Fr. Leonel Franca comments: "With the degeneration of matrimony, women fell into scorn and ignominy. More than anyone else, Luther contributed to this with unspeakable indignity. To the reformer, a woman was nothing but "a stupid animal" (Weinar, *Werke,* vol. 15, p. 420), a mere instrument to satisfy man's sexual desires. In his vulgar language, he goes as far as to compare her to a pregnant cow: 'Also, women get tired and blow up during pregnancy; no problem letting them blow up, that is what they are for'" (M. Luther, *Saemtliche Werke,* Erlangen, 1826, vol. 20, p. 84, *apud ibid.,* p. 449).

On the moral decadence of German youths of both sexes following the introduction of Protestantism, there are copious authoritative testimonies:

- Waldner states: "As far as licentiousness is concerned, a 10-year-old boy or girl today knows more than a man of 60 used to know" (*Bericht etlicher Stücke den jüngsten Tag betreffend,* Regensburg, 1565, fl. E., *apud ibid.,* p. 453).

- In 1562 the well known Danish theologian Nicolau Hemming made this accusation: "Modesty used to be the most precious treasure of virgins; today, they display in their dress and customs a complete lack of shame" (in Döllinger, *Die Reformation,* vol. 2, p. 674, *apud ibid.,* p. 453).

- In 1561, Andre Muskulus, one of the most fiery champions of Lutheranism, wrote: "We all speak out loudly and deplore that never since the world began have the youth been more scandalous and perverted than now, and certainly they could not become worse" (*Von des Teufels Tyrannei,* in *Theatrum diabolorum,* p. 160, *apud ibid.,* p. 453).

demnations the Church once promulgated against those who are now eulogized.

§ 3   It would seem that the authors of such praises would fall under the strong condemnations found in the Canons of the Pius-Benedictine *Code of Canon Law*, which placed under suspicion of heresy anyone who praised a heretic or took up his defense.[2]

---

[2] In December 1967, the Brazilian monthly *Catolicismo* published a work by Arnaldo Xavier da Silveira titled "Actions, Gestures, Attitudes and Omissions that Characterize a Heretic," which examines infractions that raise the suspicion of heresy according to the Pius-Benedictine *Code of Canon Law*. We selected some paragraphs referring to those who praise heretics or defend them:

"The *Code of Canon Law* enumerates various actions whose nature causes the one who practices them to become suspect of heresy. ... Let us analyze the infractions that, according to the *Code of Canon Law*, create a suspicion of heresy: ...

"7. To assist spontaneously and knowingly, in any way, in the propagation of heresy (can. 2316);

"8. To assist actively at the religious services of non-Catholics or take part in them, unless one is present only passively by virtue of his civil office or a social necessity, or for some grave reason, and provided that there be no danger of scandal (can. 2316). ...

"These [nine] instances that raise suspicion of heresy are those set out in the *Code of Canon Law*. Nevertheless, as theologians note, there are also non-canonical cases of suspicion of heresy. ...

"There are several other types of actions connected with heresy that used to be punished by the Old Law and do not appear, at least explicitly, in the Pius-Benedictine *Code*. These include believing the heretic, promoting him, receiving him and defending him. ...

"**Those who believe or are disposed to believe the heretic** 'are ones who, in bad faith, accept by a judgment of their intelligence at least one heretical doctrine proposed by the heretic even though they are not members of his sect' (Francisco Xavier Wernz and Pedro Vidal, *Ius Canonicum*, Rome: Gregorian University, 1927, p. 450) ...

"**Promoters of heresy** 'are those who, by some action or omission, favor the heretic in a way that results in promoting the heretical doctrine' (*ibid.*, p. 450) ...

"**Those who receive or harbor heretics** are 'ones who hide or welcome heretics in their own or other abodes so that they can escape a judicial investigation and the penalties they would deserve' (*ibid.*, pp. 450-451) ...

"**Defenders of heretics** are 'those who do not adhere interiorly to the heretical doctrine but nonetheless defend it with words or writings

Respected theologians and canon lawyers have commented on these canons.[3]

§ 4   The goal of this Volume, however, is not to **judge** what has been perpetrated against Catholic Doctrine,[4] but rather to **report** the affronts and blasphemies made against Catholic Faith and Morals. This will make it possible for the competent authorities to judge what is happening. At the same time it will provide the common faithful with elements to know the *animus injuriandi* of conciliar Progressivism and understand the spirit of tolerance established in the Church at Vatican Council II.

Our approach here is to expound rather than to judge. Our intention is to provide the necessary elements for the first

---

against those who impugn it. In this genre are also included those who protect heretics, either by force or any other unjust means, in the face of a legitimate campaign waged against the heresy' (*ibid.*)" (A.X. da Silveira, "Actions, Gestures, Attitudes and Omissions that Characterize a Heretic," pp. 5-6).

[3] **On canonical cases of suspicion of heresy**, see: F. X. Wernz and P. Vidal, *Ius Canonicum*, vol. 7, pp. 451-452; Adolphe Tanquerey, *Brevior Synopsis Theologiae Moralis* (Paris-Tornai-Rome: Desclée, 1946), p. 386; Arthur Vermeersch and Joseph Creusen, *Epitome Iuris Canonici* (Milan-Rome: Dessain, 1946), vol. 3, p. 316; Felice Cappello, *Summa Iuris Canonici* (Rome: Universitas Gregoriana, 1955), vol. 3, pp. 552-553; Iohannaes Ferrere and Alfredus Mondria, *Compendium Theologiae Moralis* (Barcelona: Subirana, 1953), vol. 2, p. 743; Stephanus Sipos, *Enchiridion Iuris Canonici* (Rome: Herder, 1954), p. 609; Eduardus F. Regatillo, *Institutiones Iuris Canonici* (Santander: Sal Terrae, 1961), vol. 2, p. 573; Thomas Iorio, *Theologia Moralis* (Naples: D'Auria, 1960), vol. 2, pp. 253-254., 260-261.

On infractions connected with heresy in the old Canon Law, see: Franciscus Suarez, *De Fide - Opera Omnia*, vol. 12, disp. 24, sect. I; Joannis de Lugo, *De Virtute Fidei Divinae - Disputationes Scholasticae et Morales,*(Paris: Vivés, 1858), vol. 2, disp. 25, sect. I; Francis Schmalzgrueber, *Jus Eclesiasticum Universum* (Rome: Typ. Rev. Cam. Apostolicae, 1845), vol. 5, part 1, tit. 7, vol. 10, § 91-92; Josephus D'Annibale, *Summula Theologiae Moralis* (Milan: Ex Typ. S. Josephi, 1882), part 2, p. 8; F. X. Wernz and P. Vidal, *Ius Canonicum*, pp. 450-451; A. Michel, entry *Herésie, hérétique* [Heresy, heretic], in *Dictionnaire de Théologie Catholique* (Paris: Letouzey et Ané, 1920), vol. 6, col. 2244.

[4] Volumes VI, VII, VIII, IX, X and XI of this Collection will analyze in detail what has been done and taught by the Council and the post-conciliar Church that conflict with Catholic doctrine.

phase of the Thomistic method of seeing, judging, acting. As we describe the gravity of an action and of its consequences, however, we will at times point out its similarities with errors or heresies. This will be a contribution to the second phase. In these cases, we will avoid making express judgments and present only hypotheses or questions.

Nonetheless, in some instances the exposition of the facts and their comparison with Catholic doctrine will almost inexorably lead to a judgment. This results not from an express transgression of our goal to expound the facts, but because the infraction committed is judged of itself.

§ 5   Thus, adopting this method of exposition we avoid classifying canonically those who praise heretics; we avoid the discussion about the validity of applying these canons against the heretics, since several of these canons no longer appear in the *Code of Canon Law* of John Paul II.[5] We also avoid analyzing the legitimacy of abolishing such canons, essential to the under-

---

[5] In comparison with the 1917 *Code of Canon Law*, the *New Code* eliminated, among others, the following canons related to heretics and the suspicion of heresy:

- Can. 167, §1, n. 4, which established that the heretic or schismatic cannot vote in ecclesiastical elections, such as the election of a Pope;

- Can. 1240, which prohibited Church burials for heretics, schismatics, apostates or those belonging to Masonic sects;

- Can. 2315, which prescribed suspension *a divinis* of clergy who were suspected of heresy, and ordered that if the accused did not amend within six months, he would be named a heretic;

- Can. 2316, which set down that anyone who spontaneously or consciously assisted a heresy in any way would be under suspicion of heresy;

- Can. 2317, which ordered that the priest who publicly or privately taught or defended condemned doctrines, even those not formally heretical, should be removed from the ministries of teaching, preaching and hearing confessions;

- Can. 2318, which prescribed that publishers of apostate, heretical or schismatic books which spread apostasy, heresy and schism – as well as those who read or keep them without due permission – should incur excommunication *ipso facto*;

- Can. 2372, which ordered the suspension *a divinis*, reserved to the Holy See, of anyone who received [sacramental] orders from one who was excommunicated, suspended or under interdict, or from a known apostate, heretic or schismatic.

standing of the Church Militant. Finally, we avoid entering the broader discussion of whether a *Code of Canon Law* that virtually abolished the notion of heretic in the Church is legitimate.[6]

§ 6   The analysis of texts and actions of high dignitaries of the Holy See – even of John Paul II and Benedict XVI who have opened their arms to the Protestant heresy, the Eastern schismatics and Judaism – is not intended to stimulate an attitude of insubordination against the Vatican. The position of this Work toward these ecumenical initiatives,[7] which unfortunately have become increasingly frequent after the Council, is similar to that taken by Prof. Plinio Corrêa de Oliveira in 1974 in the public *Manifesto of Resistance* against the trumpeted Vatican policy of *détente* with Communist regimes.[8]

§ 7   In other words, it is an attitude of respectful resistance, duly defined and approved by renowned theologians who studied the topic.[9] It is the application of the principle: "A Pope who

---

[6] *The New Code of Canon Law*, in force since November 1983, avoids defining what is a heretic, apostate or schismatic, contrary to the former *Pius-Benedictine Code* (cf. can. 1325, §2).

Explaining canon 751, Fr. Jesus S. Hortal, S.J., the commentator of the new *Code*'s official translation published by the CNBB [National Council of Brazilian Bishops], writes:

"The new *Code* no longer defines the concepts of heretic, apostate and schismatic, as in the old *Code*, but rather the terms *heresy, apostasy* and *schism*. Fundamental to the concept of heresy is the notion of pertinaciousness, that is, the clear and continual consciousness of culpability for negating or denying a truth of the faith. Accordingly, the Decree *Unitatis redintegratio* of Vatican Council II states in item 3 that those who were born into communities separated from the Catholic Church and who are imbued with faith in Christ 'cannot be accused of the sin involved in separation, and the Catholic Church embraces them as brothers, with respect and affection'" (J. Hortal, *Comentários ao Código de Direito Canônico de 1983,* in John Paul II, *Código de Direito Canônico,* São Paulo: Loyola, 1983, p. 347, note 751).

[7] What we say here about ecumenism will apply to other fields also, as the Reader will see in other places in this Collection.

[8] Cf. General Introduction to the Collection, Vol. I, *In the Murky Waters of Vatican II*, Note 16a-b, pp. 49-51.

[9] For excerpts from authoritative authors, among them St. Thomas Aquinas, St. Augustine and St. Robert Bellarmine, who hold that the faithful have the right and duty to resist authority, see my article ,"The Duty to Resist" in *We Resist You to the Face* (Los Angeles: Tradition in Action, Inc., 2000), pp. 151-156; see also General Introduction to the

publicly destroys the Church must be resisted." [10]

It is important to note that the position of resistance against certain actions of a Pontiff is not a novelty in the History of the Church. Even though such instances are exceptions, the path trodden by the Church is dotted with Catholics who have taken this stance.[11]

§ 8   The following examples are taken from the first 12 centuries of the History of the Church, when Popes who took equivocal positions regarding the Faith, Liturgy and Canon Law faced the resistance of great Saints or even the simple faithful.

§ 9   • This was the case of St. Peter (33-67), who was causing perplexity among the first Christians because he wanted the Gentiles to follow the old Judaic laws for food and fasting. For this reason, he was reprimanded by St. Paul (Gal. 2:11-14).

§ 10   • In an analogous instance, Pope St. Anicetus (155-168) wanted to regularize the rites of the Church and date of Easter. He met firm resistance from St. Polycarp of Smyrna who opposed that uniformization.[12]

§ 11   • Because of his adherence to Arianism, Pope Liberius (352-366) was directly criticized by St. Athanasius and St. Hilary of Poitiers, and later by St. Jerome, who did not hesitate to call him a heretic: "Liberius, vanquished by the tediousness of exile and subscribing to heretic perversity [to the semi-Arian profession of faith], entered Rome as a conqueror."[13]

Collection, Vol. I, *In the Murky Waters of Vatican II*, Note 3, pp. 36-39; § 18, pp.53-55.

[10] Francisco de Vitoria, *Obras de Francisco de Vitoria* (Madid: BAC, 1960), pp. 486-488; cf. Robert Bellarmine, *De Romano Pontifice*, in *Opera omnia* (Palermo-Naples-Paris: Pedone Lauriel, 1871), vol. 1, lib. 2, c. 29; Francisco Suarez, *De Fide*, in *Opera omnia*, disp. 10, sec, 6, p. 16. For the texts of these authors, see *In the Murky Waters of Vatican II*, Note 3, pp. 36-39.

[11] For more historical examples of resistance against Popes, see *We Resist You to the Face*, (Los Angeles: Tradition in Action, 2000), Chap. V, Item 4, pp. 56-58; see also my articles "Resistance: Historical Precedents" and "Lessons from the Past," in *ibid.*, pp. 157-167.

[12] Cf. Jules Lebreton, *Les Pères Apostoliques et leur époque*, in Augustin Fliche and Victor Martin, *Histoire de l'Eglise* (Paris: Bloud & Gay), vol. 1, pp. 341-342; J. Lebreton, *La réaction catholique, in ibid.*, vol. 2, pp. 87-88.

[13] St. Jérome, *De viris illustribus*, 97; *Quae gesta sunt inter Liberium*

§ 12

• Such was also the case of Pope St. Zozimus (417-418), who for a time supported the heretics Pelagius and Celestius and met with firm resistance from St. Augustine, St. Aurelius and other African Bishops.[14]

§ 13

• Later came the sad and pusillanimous pontificate of Pope Vigilius (537-555), who, under strong pressure from Empress Theodora, ratified Emperor Justinian's edict condemning the "Three Chapters." This action, equivalent to condemning the Council of Chalcedon and approving Monophysitism, raised a strong resistance in various parts of Christendom.[15]

§ 14

• Also Pope Honorius I (625-638), faced with Monothelism, "by sacrilegious treason, allowed the immaculate Faith to be stained," in the words of Pope St. Leo II (682-3), who censured him.[16] He was also condemned by the VI Ecumenical Council of Constantinople (680-681).[17]

That same Pope was severely reprimanded in a letter from St. Braulio of Saragossa when he learned that baptized Hebrews had received permission from Rome to return to their Jewish superstitions. Addressing himself directly to the Pope, St. Braulio said he could not believe that "the astuteness of the serpent had been able to leave traces of his passing over the stone of the Apostolic See." [18]

§ 15

• St. Columban did not hesitate to write Pope St. Boniface IV (608-615), warning him not to succumb to Nestorianism. [19]

---

et Felicem, in *Collectio Avellana*, I, *apud* Gustave Bardy, *Les origines de l'arianisme et le Concile de Nicée, in ibid.*, vol. 3, p. 154.

[14] G. de Plinval, "Les luttes pélagiennes," *in ibid.*, vol. 4, pp. 108-109. For more details of St. Augustine's resistance, see Vol. I, *In the Murky Waters of Vatican II*, § 18, notes 17-21, pp. 53-54.

[15] Cf. Louis Bréhier, "La politique religieuse de Justinien," Fliche-Martin, *Histoire de l'Eglise*, vol. 4, pp. 457-458; L. Bréhier, "Le Concile de Constantinople et la fin du règne de Justinien," *in ibid.*, pp. 476-477.

[16] Cf. DS 563.19.

[17] Cf. DS 552.

[18] Cf. René Aigrain, 'L'Espagne chrétienne,' in Fliche-Martin, *Histoire de l'Eglise* , vol. 5, p. 246. He also cites the letter of St. Braulio (PL 80, 668).

[19] Cf. René Aigrain, Les Papes et l'Italie de 604 a 757, *in ibid.*, vol. 5, p. 396.

§ 16   • In the Masses celebrated in the imperial chapels, Emperor Charlemagne maintained the Creed containing the *Filioque*, thus resisting Pope St. Leo III (795-816), who did not want to offend the Emperors of Byzantium who were opposed to the dogma of the double procession of the Holy Ghost from the Father and the Son.[20]

§ 17   • The ascension of Pope Formosus (891-896), who as a Cardinal had been excommunicated by John VIII (872-882) and whose election was, according to many, irregular, gave rise to a celebrated canonical *imbroglio*. After his death and burial, the body of Formosus was exhumed, and he was judged and "deposed" by the Cadaveric Synod in 897,[21] provoking more years of struggle in the Church between the two papal factions. For the next 15 years, Boniface VI (896), Stephen VI (896-897), Romanus (897), Theodore (897), John IX (898-900), Sergius III (904-911), etc., who succeeded one another in the Pontifical Chair, would each excommunicate his predecessor and annul his pontificate, among other acts of hostility. [22]

§ 18   • Paschal II (1099-1118), pressured by Emperor Henry V, granted him the privilege of naming or investing Bishops. This concession aroused a general protest in Christendom. The people called on the Pontiff to revoke his act for being opposed to tradition. It should be noted that the act could be called null and void since it was extracted by force.[23]

§ 19   We present this short list of examples, which continues in the History of the Church until today, only to clearly demonstrate that there have been innumerable cases of legitimate resistance in the past – be they doctrinal, liturgical or canonical. With regard to canonical positions of resistance, which were numerous, our list only broached the epoch of Pope Formosus.

§ 20   One can see, therefore, that neither Saints, Doctors nor theologians exclude in their studies the possibility that authori-

---

[20] Cf. Émile Amman, 'Les transformations de la Chrétienté au début du IX siècle,' *in ibid.*, vol. 6, p. 183.

[21] Cf. E. Amann, *Les tribulations du Siège Apostolique (885-962), in ibid.*, vol. 7, pp. 19-20.

[22] *Ibid.*, pp. 24-25., 30-31.

[23] Cf. Augustin Fliche, *La Réforme grégorienne et la Reconquête chrétienne (1057-1123)*, in Fliche-Martin, *Histoire de l'Eglise*, vol. 8, pp. 362-363.

ties should be publicly resisted and contested by the faithful. Nor does History teach that such resistance amounts to a diminution of love for the Church, the Papacy and the principle of authority.

With this said, the Author of this Volume goes on to deal with the painful question of the official praise bestowed by the Vatican and John Paul II on the religiosity, mission and person of Martin Luther.

1. Numerous Eulogies of the Protestant Heresy

A. Official Church Sources Praise Luther's 'Religiosity' and 'Mission'

§ 21   The first action that clashes with the Catholic sense is the participation of high-ranking dignitaries of the Church, notably Cardinal Johannes Willebrands, then President of the Secretariat for the Union of Christians, in a ceremony held by the Protestants to commemorate the 500th year anniversary of the German heresiarch's birth.

The post-conciliar Church thus celebrated the birth of one of her worst enemies of the last four centuries... Willebrands went so far as to state that Luther did not break unity with Christ by apostatizing from the Catholic Church. Also astounding is the praise the Holy See's representative lavished on Luther, whom he called a "religious genius."

This report is from *L'Osservatore Romano*, the official daily of the Holy See:

"With a solemn ceremony in St. Thomas Church in Leipzig in the German Democratic Republic, celebrations commemorating the 500th anniversary of Martin Luther's birthday started yesterday evening, Friday, November 11 [1983].

"Participating at the inaugural ceremony were Cardinal Johannes Willebrands, President of the Secretariat for the Union of Christians, along with Msgr. Klein of the same Secretariat; Cardinal Joachim Meisner, Bishop of Berlin; and Msgrs. Schaffran and Dissemond, secretary of the Bishops' Conference of Berlin. ...

"During the celebration Cardinal Willebrands delivered a long speech offering a testimony of the Catholic Church on the religious personality of Martin Luther. '**Through baptism**,' said the Cardinal, '**Luther was united to the body of Our Lord Jesus Christ in the concrete form of his Church. He**

thus became our brother in Christ. Although he later failed to remain in full ecclesiastical communion, this fraternity in Christ was not destroyed.

"Belonging to Jesus Christ and fraternity in Him, which baptism gives us as a foundation of our Christian existence," the Cardinal continued, "was taken up by Vatican Council II as one of the touchstones for the official entrance of the Church into the global movement of Christendom, turned toward promoting the reestablishment of her unity in faith and sacramental communion. In this regard we call to mind with gratitude the essential contribution made by Cardinal Bea. ...

"Luther's theological heritage was studied in its multi-faceted aspects," Cardinal Willebrands continued, concluding that **Luther "was a 'religious genius,' although not completely understood in his essential aspects**. It should cause no surprise that many questions have not been unequivocally answered in the research made by Catholics and Evangelicals. This is all the more reason for us to proceed with our efforts in the theological terrain."[24]

§ 22   One year later, Cardinal Willebrands exonerated the heresiarch, shifting the blame for the rupture of Christendom to the Catholic Church. In a "passionate speech"[25] at the Ecumenical Institute of Bari in February 1984, he stated that to be healed from the "wounds of the past," the Church would need to make a "more just and honest portrait of Luther." *L'Osservatore Romano* reported his speech:

"It cannot be denied that Luther is present in Western Christendom. His name is a sign of the division in it. Hence the question: 'But why?' We can sketch a quick response, but the essential question remains: Which is the deeper meaning of what happened? Is it enough for us to take refuge in the impenetrable mystery of Divine Providence? Or should we instead ask ourselves: **What can we do today to heal the wounds of the past and how should we do it? Making a more just and honest**

---

[24] "Celebrato a Lipsia il centenario della nascita di Martin Lutero," *L'Osservatore Romano*, November 13, 1983, p. 7.

[25] In the words of Fr. Salvatore Manna, "the passionate speech given by Cardinal Willebrands in a hall of the State University of Bari was attended by a large crowd" ("Il Card. Willebrands inaugura il corso dell'Instituto S. Nicola," *L'Osservatore Romano*, February 5, 1984, p. 6).

portrait of Martin Luther also will serve to heal the wounds of the Body of Christ." [26]

Such statements by Willebrands apparently suppose that the "wounds of the past" were not caused by the apostasy of the cantankerous German friar, but resulted from some "fault" of the Church, who supposedly painted an unjust and dishonest portrait of him. This supposition, which completely reverses the question, is insulting in itself, especially when uttered by a Cardinal officially representing the Holy See.

§ 23

Unfortunately, Willebrands' praises of Luther are not rare. In his official speech in Evian in 1970, at the Fifth Plenary Assembly of the World Lutheran Federation, the Prelate paid homage to the heresiarch by calling him "Common Master." Until that moment, the Church had always reserved this title exclusively for St. Thomas Aquinas, who was deservedly bestowed with this honor indicating that he should be followed by all the schools of theology in the Church. These were the Cardinal's words:

"Who does not recognize that a more just assessment of the person and work of Martin Luther is imperative?"

"Over the last few centuries, **the person of Martin Luther has not always been duly respected by Catholics,** and his theology has not always been correctly expounded. This has served neither truth nor love and, therefore, has not served the unity that we strive to achieve between ourselves and the Catholic Church.[27] On the other hand, **we can affirm with joy that in the last few decades many Catholic scholars have been striving for a more precise understanding of the figure of Martin Luther and his theology**. ...

"Who today could deny that **Martin Luther was a profoundly religious personality who sought the message of the Gospel honestly and with abnegation**? Who could deny that despite the torments he inflicted upon the Catholic Church and the Holy See – truth demands we admit this – he conserved a considerable measure of the riches of the ancient faith? **Did not Vatican Council II approve demands that had been formulated by Martin Luther which have allowed many aspects of**

---

[26] *Ibid.*

[27] In this phrase it is curious that Willebrands includes himself in the number of the Lutherans, situating himself outside the Catholic Church.

the Christian faith and life to be better expressed today than in the past? To say this ... is cause for great joy and hope.

"In an extraordinary way for his time, Martin Luther made the Bible the starting point of theology and the Christian life. In your churches, the Bible has since enjoyed a privileged place and been studied with great zeal. For its part, with a profundity never before attained, **Vatican Council II inserted the Holy Scripture** – which has always been a treasure in the Catholic Church – **more fully into the life of the Church** and her members and made it more fruitful for the latter. ...

"**In Martin Luther, one word continuously comes to mind, the great word 'faith.' Luther profoundly recognized its value and many men – both inside and outside your churches – have learned to live from it until today**. If there seems to have been a certain exclusiveness on this point, which might justly be derived from the emphasis that Luther gave it in his talks, **the joint research** by Catholic and Protestant scholars on this matter **shows that the word 'faith,' in the sense that Luther attributed to it, does not exclude works, charity and hope**. One can rightly say that, as a whole, Luther's notion of faith means nothing but what the Church calls charity.

"It is neither necessary nor possible to expound here the essential points of Luther's theology. Many things would have to be said about **his theology of the cross, his Christology, his insistence on the divinity of Christ, questions that today make us feel particularly united with him**. Both Catholic and Protestant scholars, however, draw our attention to still another aspect: the difficulty of presenting the thinking of Luther precisely, exhaustively and, above all, proportionately, giving full justice to many of his formulations that he did not express in a systematic way. It pleases me to think that **in this regard we are in accord with your feelings** ...

"In a session whose theme is 'Sent to the World,' it is good to reflect upon a man for whom the doctrine of justification[28] was the *articulus stantis et cadentis Ecclesiae* [the article

---

[28] Treating the Protestant doctrine of justification, praised here by Willebrands, the Council of Trent sets out Catholic doctrine on the matter and anathematized the errors of Luther and his followers in 33 canons (session VI, the *Decretum de justification* of January 13, 1547). See, for example, the Lutheran theses condemned by canons 9 to 12:

• "Canon 9: If anyone says that the sinner is justified by faith alone, meaning that nothing else is required to cooperate in order to ob-

upon which the Church stands or falls]. He can be our **common master** in this field when he affirms that God must continuously remain the Lord and that our most essential human response must continue to be an absolute confidence in and worship of God." [29]

Willebrands' praise of the heretic of Wittenberg is an enormous offense against the Church. The latter, as suggested by Willebrands, should consider the revolted, impure, apostate and heretical friar as a fountain from which her children can draw the pure water of good doctrine. Furthermore, his statement is an affront to St. Thomas Aquinas, the authentic "Common Master" of the Church.

§ 24   Willebrands' comparison of Luther to the Angelic Doctor could not fail to raise eulogies of progressivist leaders like the German Fr. August Hasler,[30] author of a book critical of Pius IX and papal infallibility:

"In an official speech at the Fifth Plenary Assembly of the Lutheran World Alliance held in Evian in 1970, **Cardinal Willebrands**, president of the Vatican Secretariat for the Union

---

tain the grace of justification, and that it is not in any way necessary that he be prepared and disposed by the action of his will, let him be anathema" (DS 1559).

- "Canon 10: If anyone says that men are justified without the justice of Christ, whereby He atoned for us, or that it is by this justice itself they are formally just, let him be anathema" (DS 1560).

- "Canon 11: If anyone says that men are justified either by the sole imputation of the justice of Christ or by the sole remission of sins, to the exclusion of the grace and the charity that the Holy Ghost instills in their hearts and dwells in them, or also that the grace by which we are justified is only the good will of God, let him be anathema" (DS 1561).

- "Canon 12: If anyone should say that the faith that justifies is nothing other than confidence in divine mercy, which remits sins for Christ's sake, or that it is this confidence alone that justifies us, let him be anathema" (DS 1562).

[29] Johannes Willebrands, Lecture delivered at the Fifth Assembly of the Lutheran World Federation, June 15, 1970, *La Documentation Catholique*, 1569, September 6, 1970, pp. 765-766.

[30] Fr. August Bernhard Hasler worked at the Secretariat for the Union of Christians from 1967 to 1971. As its representative he participated as one of four Catholic observers present at the Fifth Assembly of the Lutheran World Federation.

of Christians, **undoubtedly took a courageous step forward in the rehabilitation of Luther and the Reformation**. He stated that he could 'happily verify that a scholarly and more precise understanding of Martin Luther and his theology has been developing among many Catholic scholars over the last few decades.' **Regarding the doctrine of justification, Willebrands went so far as to call Luther the 'common master.'**"[31]

§ 25   Otto Hermann Pesch,[32] a progressivist *ardito*, thought that Willebrands should have gone much further. His words in fact confirm the gravity of the position taken by the Cardinal:

"The words dedicated to Luther in the speech Cardinal Willebrands gave at the World Lutheran Assembly in the city of Evian near Geneva in September 1970 were not as extraordinary as they might appear to many. **Yes, they were words of praise for the great researcher of the Gospel's truth,** but no real concessions were made in those fields where Luther's theology would have really caused discomfort: his conception of the sacraments, the ministry, Church, Scripture and the Magisterium. ...

"**He called Luther the 'Common Doctor' of Christendom (an honorific title until then reserved for Thomas Aquinas!)** but not in the sense of a *quaestio juris* (he should teach us all what must be taught) but only as a *quaestio facti* (**Luther should teach us all** on those points where he did not manifestly abandon Catholic tradition: **the concept of faith, the relationship between faith and charity, the confession of the divinity of Christ, etc.**)."[33]

§ 26   If Pesch, who made these "complaints" about the "moderation" of Willebrands' stance toward the Protestants, could have seen the future, perhaps he would be surprised. Fourteen years after Willebrands called Luther the "common master" and less than 10 years after Pesch's critique, that same Prelate admitted many such concessions of the Catholic Church toward

---

[31] August Hasler, "Lutero nei testi scolastici di teologia cattolica," *Concilium*, 1976/8, p. 150.

[32] A theology major who studied at the University of Munich, Otto Pesch was the first Catholic to become a professor in a Protestant institute. In 1975 he began to teach at the evangelical Institute of Theology of Hamburg University. He was a staff member of *Concilium* magazine, specializing in ecumenism.

[33] Otto Hermann Pesch, "Lo stato attuale di comprensione e di intesa su Lutero," *Concilium* 1976/8, p. 185.

Protestantism during the commemorations of the 500th anniversary of the heretic held in Bari. His speech seemed a response to the complaints of Pesch and other *arditi* of the time. Was it a coincidence? A natural "evolution" of the times? Or the result of a concerted effort by the "moderates" and the *arditi* to execute a prepared plan?

To analyze tactical collusions made to advance progressivist goals would exceed the limits of this Volume.[34] But nothing prevents us from raising the question in passing.

§ 27

In his Bari speech, transcribed by *L'Osservatore Romano*, Cardinal Willebrands reveals the Catholic post-conciliar policy of adaptation to Protestantism:

"In addition to recovering the central role of Scripture in the Church and in the lives of the faithful, since Vatican II Catholics have been increasingly willing to reassess the common priesthood of the faithful and the co-responsibility of laymen in the whole life of the Church; to recognize the character of the Pilgrim Church on earth; to reevaluate the local churches; to accept liturgical reform with the introduction of national languages; to concede to having communion under the two species, and to adopt the declaration on religious liberty." [35]

These statements by Cardinal Willebrands, who held the office of president of the Secretariat for the Union of Christians, presuppose the at least implicit acquiescence of John Paul II. If the Pontiff had disagreed with the stands of the Prelate, he would certainly have admonished him. This papal silence suffices for it to be said that the Pope agreed with these policies and eulogies. This silence is an indirect but cogent proof.

§ 28

More than this indirect proof, however, there is a direct and undisputable proof. It is a personal letter from the Pontiff to Cardinal Willebrands dated October 31, 1983, encouraging and directing him to participate in the commemorations for Luther. The letter was published in *L'Osservatore Romano*.

At the beginning of the letter, John Paul II pays homage to the heresiarch by calling him "Doctor," recalling the title

---

[34] The collaboration between the moderates and the *arditi* will be analyzed with regard to the condemnations of Fr. Marie-Dominique Chenu and Fr. Hans Küng in Vol. IV, *Animus Delendi I,* Chap. III,1, §§ 1-73.

[35] S. Manna, "Il Card. Willebrands inaugura il corso," p. 6.

of "common doctor" or "common master" that Willebrands had used before. He writes:

"November 10 is the 500th anniversary of the birth of **Doctor Martin Luther** of Eisleben. On this occasion, numerous Christians ... remember that theologian who, at the threshold of modern times, contributed substantially to the radical change of the ecclesiastical and secular reality in the West. Until today our world experiences his great impact on History." [36]

The directives at the end of the John Paul II's letter take on an imperative tone:

"**I trust,** therefore, **Cardinal, that** on these foundations and in this spirit, **the Secretariat for the Union [of Christians]**, under your direction, **will carry forward this dialogue** that began with great seriousness in Germany even before Vatican Council II, **and that you will do so with fidelity to the Faith freely given**, which implies a penitence and a readiness to learn by listening." [37]

§ 29

The "foundations" and "spirit" that the Pontiff indicates as goals to Cardinal Willebrands are acknowledging the "fraternity" between Catholics and Protestants and the affirmation of Luther's "profound religiosity" and "ardent passion" for eternal salvation. This can be verified in the following paragraphs from the letter of John Paul II:

"Well-known personalities and institutions of **Lutheran Christendom** have expressed the wish that the year dedicated to Luther be marked by a genuine ecumenical spirit and that reflections about Luther may contribute to the unity of Christians. **I welcome this intention with satisfaction, seeing it as a fraternal invitation to achieve, through a common effort, a more profound and complete vision of historical events and a critical analysis of Luther's multifarious heritage**.

"Indeed, **the scientific research of Evangelical and Catholic scholars, which has already achieved many points of convergence, has led to the sketching of a more complete and nuanced picture of Luther's personality as well as a more complex schema of the historical, political and eccle-**

---

[36] John Paul II, Letter to Cardinal Willebrands of October 31, 1983, published under the title "La verItá storica du Lutero alimenti il dialogo per l'unitá," *L'Osservatore Romano*, June 11, 1983, p. 4.

[37] *Ibid.*

siastical reality in the first half of the 16th century. These results have provided visible proof of the profound religiosity
of Luther, who was moved by an ardent passion for the question of eternal salvation."[38]

One cannot but be confused to find John Paul II extending a "fraternal invitation" to Protestants "with satisfaction" and
overemphasizing historical and psychological conditions of the
past in order to find "points of convergence" between the Catholic Church and the Protestant heresy.[39]

§ 30   Regarding the errors of Luther, all involving matters of
Faith, the sketching of "a more complete and nuanced picture of
his personality as well as a more complex picture of the historical reality" does nothing to change the solemn condemnations
of the heresiarch's theses made by Pope Leo X in the Bull *Ex-*

---

[38] *Ibid.*

[39] Although further on John Paul II gives some importance to the doctrinal controversy in the "dialogue" with Protestants, in this excerpt he
appears to subordinate the understanding of truth to historical conditions.

In contrast with this tendency, consider the clear teaching of St. Pius
X condemning the Modernist errors in apologetics: "**Hence that common axiom of the Modernist school that in the new apologetics,
religious controversies must be determined by historical and
psychological research**" (Encyclical *Pascendi Dominici gregis* of
July 3, 1907, Vozes: Petrópolis, 1959, n. 35).

Further, the Decree *Lamentabili* of the Roman and Universal Holy Inquisition of July 3, 1907 presents a *Syllabus* of condemned Modernist
propositions, some of which can be indirectly likened to the position of
John Paul II. They include the following:

"III. From the ecclesiastical sentences and censures passed against
free and more advanced exegesis, one can conclude that **the faith
proposed by the Church contradicts History** and that Catholic dogmas cannot really be harmonized with the true origins of the Christian
religion. ...

"XXII. **The dogmas**, which the Church holds as revealed, are not
truths that have come from heaven; they **are a certain interpretation
of religious facts** that the human mind has acquired at the cost of
laborious efforts. ...

"LIV. **The dogmas, sacraments and hierarchy, both in concept
and reality, are nothing but interpretations and evolutions of
Christian thinking**, which have developed and been perfected by an
external series of additions to the small germ latent in the Gospel" (DS
3403, 3422, 3454).

surge Domine of June 15, 1520. He summarizes this teaching with these strong words:

"We condemn, reprove and entirely reject each and all of the aforementioned articles or errors [of Luther] as heretical, scandalous, false, offensive to pious ears, seductive of simple minds and opposed to Catholic truth."[40]

Thus it is perplexing to see John Paul II call Luther a man gifted with a "profound religiosity" and an "ardent passion" for eternal salvation, in contradiction with the constant teaching of the Church!

§ 31   Are such statements not offensive to the honor of Catholic Faith, the reverence and obedience due the teaching of the Magisterium through the course of History, the merit of the many Saints who fought against Protestantism and the martyrs who died under its wrath?

One sees that Cardinal Willebrands, whose statements and participation in the ceremonies commemorating the birth of the heresiarch cause astonishment, was in fact only following the orientation of John Paul II, clearly laid out in the letter we just analyzed.

*

§ 32   Unfortunately, however, John Paul II's expressions of sympathy for the Protestant heresy were not limited to this one letter. He took the initiative to participate in a Lutheran service in Rome, thus violating the centuries-old condemnation of the Church against those who participate in heretical services.[41]

---

[40] Leo X, Bull *Exsurge Domine* of June 15, 1520, DS 1492.

[41] a. We are well aware that, from the juridical standpoint, a Pontiff stands above the provisions of the *Code of Canon Law* and thus in exceptional cases may dispense persons from them; therefore, he may also dispense himself.

We are also aware that, supposing the Pontiff's legitimacy, the *Pius-Benedictine Code* had ceased to be in force 15 days before his visit to the Lutheran temple in Rome.

Nevertheless, leaving aside the juridical sphere to consider the doctrinal one, it should be noted that a Pontiff may not contradict the perennial teaching of the ordinary and extraordinary Magisterium in matters of Faith and Morals. If he does so, he is judged *ipso facto* by the previous teaching of the Church.

b. As a consequence, the faithful have the right and the duty to resist, question, warn or admonish that Pope. This has been demonstrated by the teaching of great Doctors of the Church (cf. Vol. I, *In the Murky Waters of Vatican II*, General Introduction, Note 3, pp. 36-39) and the historical examples of courageous Saints (see in this Chapter, §§ 7-20). Therefore, by taking such an attitude, the faithful are not setting themselves up as judges of the Pope.

c. Pius IX condemned the thesis that Protestantism is a true form of the Christian religion. In the 18th proposition condemned by the *Syllabus*, one reads: "Protestantism is nothing but another form of the true Christian religion, in which one can please God in the same way as in the Catholic Church" (DS 2918). The idea contained in the condemned proposition appears to be the presupposition of the action of John Paul II, which we will analyze in the next text.

d. The disapproval of this action of John Paul II by the Magisterium of the Church is also confirmed by other papal condemnations:

• **Against religious indifferentism**:

Leo XIII, Encyclical *Ubi primum* of May 5, 1824 (DS 2720); Gregory XVI, Encyclical *Mirari vos* of August 15, 1832 (DS 2730-2731); Pius IX, Encyclical *Qui pluribus* of November 9, 1846 (DS 2875); Allocution *Singulari quadam* of December 9, 1854 (DS, note, p. 571; Letter *Gravissimas inter* of December 11, 1862 (DS 2860-2861); Epistle *Quanto conficiamur* of August 10, 1863 (DS 2865-2867); *Syllabus* of December 8, 1864 (DS 2921, 2977-2979).

• **Against those who admit salvation outside the Church**:

XVI Council of Toledo, *Symbolum*, May 2, 693 (DS 575); IV Lateran Council, November 11-30, 1215 (DS 802); Boniface VIII, Bull *Unam Sanctam* of November 18, 1302 (DS 870); XVI Council of Constance, decree confirmed by Pope Martin V on February 22, 1418 (DS 1191); Eugene IV at the Council of Florence, Bull *Cantate Domino* of November 4, 1442 (DS 1351); Pius IX, *Syllabus* (DS 2917); Apostolic Letter *Iam vos omnes*, of September 13, 1868 (DS 2997-2999); Leo XIII, Encyclical *Satis cognitum* of June 29, 1896 (DS 3304); Pius XII, Encyclical *Mystici Corporis* of June 29, 1943 (DS 3821-3822); Letter of the Holy Office to the Archbishop of Boston, August 8, 1949 (DS 3866-3867, 3871-3872).

e. It is, therefore, as an expression of the immutable doctrine of the Church that we cite the following canons of the *Pius-Benedictine Code*, in force only 15 days before John Paul II participated in the Lutheran service. These canons were removed from the 1983 Code:

"Can. 2316. **Anyone who spontaneously and consciously assists the propagation of heresy in any way, or who communicates *in divinis* with heretics, against the prescriptions of can. 1258, is suspected of heresy.** ...

"Can. 1258. **It is definitively prohibited for the faithful to assist in any active way at sacred ceremonies of non-Catholics or to**

By his action John Paul II stimulated the whole Church – the ensemble of Pastors and the faithful – to imitate him in the same practice, a practice wisely defined by the Church as suspicious of heresy. In addition, one would also say that he caused scandal to the good people who, only through heroism, manage to hold aloft the banner of the Faith in a neopagan world. Furthermore, by failing to ask the heretics for any abjuration of the errors they profess, he appears to have virtually "absolved" them.

§ 33   A report of John Paul II's visit to the Lutheran temple, as well as a transcript of his speech, was published in *L'Osservatore Romano*. Some excerpts follow:

"Yesterday, December 11, **John Paul II visited *Christuskirche*, the church of Rome's Evangelical Lutheran community**. During the meeting ... **the Pope participated in the liturgy of the word. During the service**, celebrated in German, … **the Holy Father delivered the following speech:**

"Esteemed brothers and sisters in Christ ...

"We are already at the threshold of the year 2000. 'We are also in a certain way in a season of a new Advent, a season of expectation.'[42*] For this reason, *I came to visit our neighbors*, so to speak, the citizens of this city '**who are united by a special**

---

take part in them" (*Codex Juris Canonici*, Rome: Tipografia Poliglotta Vaticana, 1917).

f. Serious and respected canonists have affirmed that anyone who disobeys those holding ecclesiastical offices who have become suspect of heresy is neither in rebellion nor schismatic: (F. X. Wernz and P. Vidal, *Ius Canonicum*, vol. 7, p. 439; Domenico Palmieri, *Tractatus de Romano Pontifice*, Rome, 1877, pp. 194-196).

g. Cardinal Cajetan, commenting on the adage '*Ubi Petrus ibi Ecclesia*' [Where the Pope is, there is the Church], nonetheless asserts that the Church is in the Pope when he behaves as Pope, that is, as head of the Church; however, should he not act as head of the Church, then the Church would not be found in him, nor he in the Church (cf. Charles Journet, *L'Eglise du Verbe Incarné*, Bruges: Desclée, 1962, vol. 2, pp. 839-840).

In the same sense, see: Francisco de Vitoria, *Obras de Francisco de Vitoria* (Madrid: BAC, 1960), pp. 486-487; Francisco Suarez, *De Fide: Opera Omnia* (Paris: Vivés, 1858), vol. 12, disp. 10, sect. 6, n. 16; Cornelio a Lapide, *Ad Gal.* 2:11; Antonio Peinador, *Cursus Brevior Theologiae Moralis*, vol. II/1, p. 287..

[42*] Encyclical *Redemptor hominis*, n.1.

affinity.'[43*] **I came here to commemorate with you, in prayer and meditation, the mystery of Faith of the Advent that is common to us,** its profound and multiple riches. **I came because the Spirit of God beckoned us in these days to seek the complete unity of Christians through ecumenical dialogue. We know the difficult history of this Evangelical-Lutheran community** in Rome, **its painful beginnings and the lights** and shadows **of its development in this city. ...**

"**Thus we find ourselves,** amid all the notorious divisions that still exist in doctrine and life, **profoundly united in the solidarity of all Christians at Advent.** We ardently desire unity and strive to achieve it, without letting ourselves become discouraged by the difficulties we may encounter along the way.[44*] Finally, **in this year that commemorates the birth of Martin Luther five centuries ago, there appears to rise from afar, like the dawn of the advent, a restoration of our unity and of our communion."** [45]

§ 34   John Paul II's sympathy for the Protestant heresy seems patent as he unites himself with the "pains" it suffered during the development of the Lutheran sect in the city of the Popes. The affection the Pontiff expresses is similar to that of a father speaking to his children...

Another singularity in his speech is a certain note of mysticism that John Paul II adopts with regard to the five hundred year anniversary of the heresiarch, relating the "dawn" of a universal religion with the half-millennium mark of the birth of the deplorable apostate monk. What is implied is that there would be no need for the conversion of the Protestants and the abjuration of their centuries-old errors for this unity to be achieved. Such a universal religion, however, would not be the Catholic Religion.

§ 35   In short, during his visit to the Lutheran temple of Rome, three fundamental positions of John Paul II toward heresy emerge:

First, he "spontaneously and consciously" participated

[43*] Vatican II, Decree on Ecumenism *Unitatis redintegratio*, n.19.

[44*] *Ibid.*, n. 6.

[45] John Paul II, "Il Papa invita a lavorare per l'unione senza lasciarsi scoraggiare dale difficoltà, *L'Osservatore Romano*, December 12-13, 1983, p. 4.

(cf. canon 2316 of the *Pius-Benedictine Code*) in a Protestant service;

Second, he supported, protected and encouraged heretics;

Third, he assumed that this unity with the Protestants does not require their conversion.

It seems to us that such actions – given the gravity of the matter involved as well as the august office of the one making them – are offensive to the Faith, opposed to the interests of the Holy Church and a cause of scandal for the faithful.

*

§ 36   Unfortunately, this public manifestation of affinity with Protestants and the consequent offense against the unicity of the Faith and of the Catholic Church are not exceptions in the pontificate of John Paul II. Another example is found in a speech he gave at a conference of the Geneva-based World Council of Churches. [46]

---

[46] As is known, divisions are rife in the Protestant religion. Nothing could be more consistent, since Luther's principles called for revolt against authority, which generate disciplinary divisions. They also demand free interpretation according to which each individual interprets Scripture and, consequently, Faith and Morals as he sees fit, thereby generating doctrinal divisions. Further, the heresiarch led a dissolute life, thus encouraging the eruption of new moral irregularities and scandals among his followers, depending on the lesser or greater degree of moral laxity adopted by them.

Founded in 1948 at the initiative of 147 Protestant sects, the World Council of Churches (WCC) is based in Geneva, Switzerland. Also present at the founding conference were some delegates from schismatic churches (of Constantinople, Greece and some emigrant colonies).

Nevertheless, from its very first meeting in Amsterdam, divisions arose among its participants, as evidenced by notes of the first proceedings: "We are not ignoring ... our divisions: They exist in matters of faith, ecclesiastical order and tradition; our national pride and our pride of class and race also play their part in them" (Amsterdam Meeting, Official Report published by W. A. Vissers't Hooft, Neuchâtel-Paris, *apud* Charles Boyer, entry "Oecuménisme Chrétien" in DTC., Tables, vol. 3, col. 3349).

It also became clear at the meeting of its Central Committee in Toronto (1950) that the WCC does not represent its member sects either in the realm of law or the field of facts. Its final document noted: "Here it

Before analyzing John Paul II's speech to the World Council of Churches, it seems opportune to set out the position of the Church on the "common ground" tactic the Pontiff employed there.

§ 37

In order to execute the maneuver of ecumenism, many progressivist sectors take the "common ground" tactic to its final consequences. Thus they underemphasize or even hide the points that separate the Catholic from the heretic, while overestimating the points that unite them.

Early on, modernist-progressivists introduced this tactic into Catholic Action to draw non-practicing Catholics and non-Catholics into its ranks.[47] Inspired by Maurice Thorez' "extended hand policy" (*politique de la main tendue*), which sought to justify alliances between Catholics and atheists and communists, Catholics assumed the role of "fellow travelers" of the left.

After the Council, this tactic became one of the presuppositions of ecumenism and inter-religious dialogue.

Whatever name it takes – dialogue, ecumenism, *politique de la main tendue*, common ground tactic or fellow travelers – the governing principles are always the same.

---

is stated that the Council is not a Church, a Super Church or the *Una Sancta*; that it has no authority over the Churches and does not have its own doctrine regarding the Church or unity" (cf. *ibid*). It is, therefore, nothing more than a forum for debate: "It is an institution that enables the Churches to confer among themselves and that acts in their name, in the measure that they so desire" (*ibid.*).

In order to promote "unity in one and the same faith, the Council can do no more than promote contact [among the members] ... It has no authority to give an orientation in a certain direction" (*ibid.*, col. 3353).

It is clear, therefore, that the WCC lacks any real substance. One could say that it is hardly more than a façade.

Nevertheless, the myth created by progressivist propaganda strives to present it to Catholics as a powerful giant that unites the large number of Protestant splinter sects, along with the Greek-schismatic churches, into a single bloc. Thus, the Catholic Church should treat this giant "representative" of the so-called Christian religions as an equal, dialogue with it and listen to its demands...

Even though this pretentious propaganda is far from reflecting the reality, it is an effective progressivist artifice to move conciliar ecumenism forward.

[47] Cf. Plinio Corrêa de Oliveira, *Em Defesa da Ação Católica* (São Paulo: Ed. Ave-Maria, 1943), pp. 240-260.

§ 38

In his book *In Defense of Catholic Action*, published in 1943,[48] Prof. Plinio Corrêa de Oliveira warned against the dangers of this tactic of systematically hiding from a sinner his true state:

"In short, when used not as an exception but in a frequent and habitual way, the so-called 'common ground tactic' is the canonization of human respect. To thus induce the faithful to dissimulate their Faith is an open violation of the words of the adorable Master:

"*You are the salt of the earth. But if the salt lose its savor, wherewith shall it be salted? It is good for nothing anymore, but to be cast out, and to be trodden on by men.*

"*You are the light of the world. A city seated on a mountain cannot be hid. Neither do men light a candle and put it under a bushel, but upon a candlestick, that it may shine to all that are in the house. So let your light shine before men, that they may see your good works, and glorify your Father who is in heaven*' (Mt. 5:13-16). ...

"In our days some souls are easily satisfied that any politician who speaks of God in one speech or another is an authentic and trustworthy Roman Catholic. This is the tactic of seeing only what unites us but not what separates us. Who would dare say to one of these vague 'deists' in certain liberal circles those terrible words of St. James: *You believe that there is one God. You do well: the devils also believe and tremble* (Jm 2:19). ... Yet this is the action of a Catholic, whose saintly and intrepid spirit should tolerate neither subterfuge nor sinuosity in matters of the Faith. How should we do apostolate? With the weapons of frankness: *But let your speech be, yea, yea: no, no; that you fall not under judgment* (Jm 5:12). ...

"Let us, therefore, flee from nothing, be ashamed of nothing: *For God has not given us the spirit of fear: but of power ... Be you not therefore ashamed of the testimony of Our Lord, nor of me his prisoner ...* (II Tim 1:7-8).

---

[48] The book was published with a preface by the Apostolic Nuncio to Brazil, later Cardinal Bento Aloisi Masela. In 1949, the author received a letter of praise from the Substitute Secretary of State, Msgr. Giovanni Baptista Montini, on behalf of Pope Pius XII. Msgr. Montini wrote: "The August Pontiff wishes with all his heart that this work may bring forth rich and seasoned fruits, and that from it you may reap great and many consolations."

"Does this attitude cause friction? No matter. We must live *with one mind laboring together for the faith of the Gospel; and in nothing be you terrified by the adversaries: which to them is a cause of perdition, but to you of salvation, and this from God*" (Phil 1:27-28).

"Any charity exercised to the detriment of that rule is false: *Let love be without dissimulation. Hating that which is evil, cleaving to that which is good* (1 Rom 12:9)." [49]

§ 39   In the early 20th century, the Sillon movement in France employed the common ground tactic, and this was one of the many errors Pope St. Pius X severely condemned in the movement. Referring to this Modernist error of the Sillon, the Saint wrote in his Encyclical *Notre Charge Apostolique*:

"For the construction of the city of the future, all workers from all religions and all sects were convoked. Nothing was asked of them but this: that they embrace the same social ideal, respect all creeds and bring with them a great supply of moral energy.

"Admittedly, it was proclaimed, 'The leaders of the Sillon ... ask everyone ... not to oppose each other on account of the philosophical or religious convictions that may separate them, but to march hand in hand, not renouncing their convictions, but trying to provide, on the ground of practical realities, the proof of the excellence of their personal convictions. Perhaps the union may come about on this ground of emulation among souls holding different religious or philosophical convictions.'[50*] ...

"Thus, a host of new groups – Catholic, Protestant, free-thinkers – now apparently autonomous, are invited to set to work: 'Catholic comrades will make an effort ... to instruct and educate themselves. Protestants and free-thinking democrats will do so on their side. Everyone, Catholics, Protestants and free-thinkers, will aim at arming the youth not for a fratricidal struggle, but for a disinterested emulation in the field of civic and social virtues.'[51*]

"These declarations and this new organization of Sillonist action call for very serious reflections. Here we have, founded

---

[49] Plinio Corrêa de Oliveira, *Em defesa da Ação Católica*, pp. 302-304.

[50*] Marc Sangnier, Speech in Rouen, 1907.

[51*] Marc Sangnier, Paris, May 1910.

by Catholics, an inter-denominational association that is to work for the reform of civilization, an eminently religious work ...

"**This being said, what should one think about the promiscuity** in which Catholic youths will be caught up with heterodox people and unbelievers of all kinds in a work of this nature? ... **What should one think of this respect for all errors and of this strange invitation made by a Catholic to all the dissidents to strengthen their convictions through study to give them ever more abundant sources of fresh forces?** ...

"Alas, yes, **the equivocation is revealed: The social action of Sillon is no longer Catholic.** The Sillonist as such does not work for a faction, and 'the Church,' he says, 'cannot in any sense benefit from the sympathies his action may stimulate.' A strange insinuation, indeed! ...

"**Even stranger, however, and at the same time unsettling and alarming, are the audacity and frivolity of men who call themselves Catholics and dream of re-shaping society under such conditions and of establishing on earth, over and above the Catholic Church, 'the kingdom of justice and love' with workers coming from everywhere, of all religions or no religion, with or without beliefs, as long as they set aside what might divide them. ...**

"**The end result of this promiscuity in process, the beneficiary of this cosmopolitan social action, can only be** a democracy that will be neither Catholic, nor Protestant, nor Jewish. It will be **a religion** (for Sillonism, as its leaders admit, is a religion) **more universal than the Catholic Church, uniting all men, who finally become brothers and comrades in the 'kingdom of God.'** [As they say,] '**We do not work for the Church, we work for mankind.'**

"And now, overwhelmed with the deepest sorrow, we ask ourselves, Venerable Brethren, what has become of the Catholicism of the Sillon? Alas! **this movement** that once offered such promising hopes ... and now **is no more than a miserable tributary of the great movement of apostasy being organized in all countries for the establishment of a One World Church, which will have neither dogmas nor hierarchy, neither discipline for the spirit nor curb for the passions,** and which, under the pretext of liberty and human dignity, would bring back to the world (should it triumph) the reign of legalized fraud and violence, and the oppression of the weak and all those who toil and suffer." [52]

What would be the reaction of St. Pius X today upon seeing this same method of religious promiscuity applied everywhere? But its aim is no longer just an inter-confessional union around temporal goals, as was the case of Sillon, but an inter-confessionalism around religious ideals, as is the case of the ecumenical dialogue carried out by Pontiffs like John XXIII, Paul VI, John Paul II and Benedict XVI? It is all the more appalling since this method is being applied to achieve the same goal of the Sillon, that is, the One World Religion that St. Pius X warned against as the modernist goal.

§ 40   Seeing the firm position of Holy Church on the "common ground tactic" and inter-confessionalism, a Catholic becomes perplexed in the face of the contradiction between the words of John Paul II and the teaching of St. Pius X.

Below we have placed in bold the passages where John Paul II praises the "common points" Catholics have with heretics, to conclude that Catholics have a "real communion" with Protestants. He is addressing the World Council of Churches:

"The Catholic Church and the member churches of the Word Council of Churches **have a long history in common: We share the painful memories of dramatic separations** and reciprocal polemics that have deeply wounded unity. It is a history during which **we have never ceased to have in common many elements or goods** by which the Church builds herself and is vivified.[53*]

"This history now becomes **the history of the rediscovery of an incomplete, but real, communion existing between us**; all of the elements that constitute or should constitute **this communion are progressively situated in their true perspectives, with all the consequences that this new perception brings to the collaboration between ourselves and our common testimony**." [54]

It seems impossible to use the tactic of "common ground" in a more heterodox way than what John Paul II has

---

[52] St. Pius X, Apostolic Letter *Notre Charge Apostolique* (Petrópolis: Vozes, 1953), nn. 30-33.

[53*] Cf. UR, n. 3.

[54] John Paul II, Speech to the World Council of Churches in Geneva on June 12, 1984, *L'Osservatore Romano*, June 14, 1984, p. 5.

done in this paragraph. No less alarming is the thinking that underlies his consideration that only after the "rediscovery' of a "real communion" with the Protestants will we situate ourselves in the "true perspectives" of this "communion." Such a statement would suppose that the perspective from which the Church viewed Protestants up until Vatican II was not the true one.

Considering either the statement that Catholics have a "real communion" with heretics or the hypothesis that the Holy Church has taken a false position toward the followers of Luther, it is very difficult to avoid the impression that we stand before an offense to the honor, purity and integrity of the Faith and an affront to the militancy of the Church.

§ 41   But this is not all that John Paul II said about "communion" with Protestants. In the same speech to the World Council of Churches in Geneva, he went on to state:

"'Baptism, therefore, establishes a sacramental bond of unity that links all who have been reborn by it.' [55*] Certainly, 'of itself it is only a beginning and a starting point, for it is directed wholly toward the fullness of life in Christ.' [56*] But, since we have all been baptized with a true baptism, **we are all a part of the one and same indivisible Spirit of God, incorporated to the only Son.** If we find ourselves divided, **we are nonetheless intertwined by the same embrace,** which St. Irenaeus called the 'two hands of the Father' (the Son and the Spirit). **This is what impels us to restore communion between ourselves.**" [57]

Here again, the words of John Paul II appear to frontally oppose the traditional teaching of the Church on the topic. [58]

[55*] UR, 22.

[56*] *Ibid.*

[57] John Paul II, Speech to the WCC in Geneva on June 12, 1984, *L'Osservatore Romano*, June 14, 1984, p. 5.

[58] In Note 41d of this Chapter, the Reader can find a list of papal documents that also apply to this topic. As an example, we point out the Apostolic Letter *Iam vos omnes* of September 13, 1868. On the occasion of the convening of Vatican Council I, Pope Pius IX invited those outside the Church to unite with her:

"No one can deny or doubt that this Jesus Christ, in order to apply the fruits of His Redemption to all generations of man, has built here on earth, upon Peter, His One, Holy, Catholic and Apostolic Church; and that He conferred upon her the power necessary to preserve whole and inviolate the deposit of Faith, and to transmit this same Faith to all

These words of John Paul II would also seem to be an offense against the Holy Church since they lead the faithful to place her on an equal footing with the Protestant heresy: Since we both are "involved in the one and same indivisible Spirit of God, incorporated to the only Son" and we both are "intertwined by the same embrace" in "the two hands of the Father."

§ 42

On his trip to Switzerland in June of 1984, John Paul II took part in an ecumenical prayer meeting of the Federation of Protestant Churches in Kehrsatz, where he referred to the alleged "zeal" of Zwingli and Calvin. In his address, he stated:

"This year **the memory of the zeal that animated two outstanding religious personalities in Swiss history is present in our mind**: *The first* is Huldrych Zwingli, whose five hundredth anniversary you are celebrating with various events honoring his person and his work; *the second* is John Calvin, who was born 475 years ago." [59]

Here as well, attributing zeal to Zwingli and Calvin can hardly be understood except as praise. Such praise implies an

---

peoples, tribes and nations, so that all men be united in her Mystical Body through Baptism ... Wherefore, this Church, which constitutes His Mystical Body, will persist and prosper in her stable and immutable nature until the end of time ...

"Whoever carefully considers and studies the situation of the various religious communities, divided among themselves and separated from the Catholic Church ... will be easily convinced that none of these associations – whether considered individually or taken as a whole – can in any way be seen as that One Catholic Church that Christ the Lord built and willed to exist. Neither can they in any way be considered members or part of this same Church, as long as they remain visibly separated from Catholic unity. It follows that such communities, lacking the living authority established by God to teach men – especially in Morals and matters of Faith and customs, directing and governing them in all that concerns eternal salvation – thus mutate in their doctrines and are constantly changing and unstable. ...

"For this reason, let all those who do not possess 'the communion and the truth of the Catholic Church' take advantage of this Council, in which she ... offers a further demonstration of her profound unity and impregnable vital force; and responding to the demands of their hearts, let them strive to leave this state that does not guarantee for them the security of salvation" (DS 2997-2999)."

[59] John Paul II, Speech to the Federation of Protestant Churches on June 14, 1984, *L'Osservatore Romano*, June 15, 1984, p. 8.

offense to the Church, which anathematized the two heretics.

§ 43   Similar comments could be made about the remainder of the speech, in which John Paul II reaffirmed his ecumenical commitment to "repair the damage" supposedly caused by the Catholic fight against the Protestants, whose leaders – in this case Zwingli and Calvin – would have been moved by the intention to "make the Church more faithful" to Our Lord Jesus Christ. John Paul II affirmed:

> **"Above all, the memory of events of the past should not stand in the way of our present efforts to repair the damage caused by those events**. Purifying the memory is an element of capital importance in ecumenical progress. It includes the frank recognition of reciprocal faults and errors committed in reactions of one to the other, when **each one had the intention to make the Church more faithful to the will of the Lord**."[60]

*

§ 44   The papal praise of the 16th century apostate Augustinian monk, Martin Luther, finds echo in lower echelons of the Church. In an interview to *L'Osservatore Romano*, Prior General of the Augustinian Order Fr. Martin Nolan celebrated the 500th year anniversary of Luther's birth as a "great event" and affirmed that his Order was striving to find points of unity with Protestants:

> "*Question*: This year another anniversary takes place: Luther's birthday. How does the Augustinian Order commemorate this date and what is its commitment in the ecumenical field?

> "*Answer*: **It is a great event that asks us to intensify our efforts to try to rebuild the unity of the Church. We will participate**, therefore, in the meetings held on the occasion of the centennial in Italy and abroad, endeavoring not only to study the reasons that led to the Reformation but also **to build bridges between ourselves, the Lutherans and other Protestant confessions** in order to favor ecumenism."[61]

It is symbolic and highly offensive to the Catholic Religion that the Prior General of the Order to which the German

---

[60] *Ibid.*

[61] Martin Nolan, interviewed by Piero Di Domenico on September 9, 1983, "Solo Dio può riempire il fuoto dell'uomo d'oggi come fu per S. Agostino, *L'Osservatore Romano*, September 21, 1983, p. 5.

heresiarch belonged should regard the celebrations of Luther with sympathy and total indifference toward the integrity of the Faith. Rather, he declared that his aim is to "build bridges" between heretics and the faithful.

With these eulogies of the Protestant sects made by John Paul II, the President of the Secretariat for the Union of Christians and the Prior General of the Augustinian Order, we believe to have presented expressive samples of indirect offenses against the honor of the Catholic Religion and the unicity of the Faith.

B. Cardinals & Bishops See Luther as a Charismatic-Prophetic Genius & Herald of Spiritual Renewal

§ 45   Since most of the praise of Luther transcribed above comes directly or indirectly from John Paul II, this Work, out of respect for the august post that he occupied, presented the Catholic Doctrine that conflicts with these offenses. Since the next group of offenses is from other ecclesiastics, the doctrinal explanations will be limited to an indispensable minimum. This is in keeping with the goal of this Volume, which is to present what clashes with the *sensus catholicus*.

Doing this, we offer the Reader a larger number of texts to help him realize the *animus injuriandi* of the conciliar spirit behind the ecumenical effort that generates such praise of heretics.

§ 46   Cardinal Joseph Höffner, then Archbishop of Cologne and president of the German Bishops' Conference, justified Luther's critique calling for a reform of the Church. He also endorsed Luther's thesis on penance and found no motive for division on the doctrine of justification. Speaking in the evangelical Lutheran church of Worms in 1983 at a celebration of the heresiarch's birth, the Cardinal went so far as to admit that criticizing the Church was legitimate and necessary and affirmed that the apostate monk was a charismatic-prophetic genius.

He concluded his shocking statements by saying that Catholics have much to learn from Luther and can be more faithful to him than the Lutherans themselves. Each assertion, in itself, is an offense against the Catholic Religion and an attack against the Faith. These were Cardinal Höffner's words:

"It was not from mere courtesy that I accepted the invitation to attend this commemoration. **I am filled with joy and** gratitude that we can celebrate this day without polemics, in an ecumenical openness ...

"The person and work of Martin Luther are of interest also to us ... Above all, **we Catholics are perplexed because Martin Luther's appeal for reform in our Church had widespread repercussions, but was heeded neither immediately nor conscientiously by the authorities.**

"'When Our Lord Jesus Christ said, *Do penance!* He wanted the whole life of the Christian to be one of penance.' This, **the first of Luther's *95 Theses*** of October 31, 1517, signals the beginning of the Reformation. In that time it was an appeal to an undivided Christendom. Today it **poses a question to Catholics and Evangelical Christians: Will we allow ourselves to be moved by this message and change ourselves interiorly?** ...

"Today, it is clearer to us than it was in the past that **the doctrine of justification is not necessarily a motive for ecclesial division.**[62] **In the struggle against many theologians and religious practices that** – in the words of Joseph Lortz – **presented Catholicism insufficiently, Luther expressed himself as a true Catholic. ... Indeed, it is legitimate and necessary to criticize the Church because she always falls short of what she should be.** ...

"We do have a question about Martin Luther, which he addressed to himself during a painful crisis of conscience: Did he strive hard enough to prevent the division of Western Christendom – a separation that during the time of the discoveries spread throughout the world? **This question, although critical of the reformer, does not signify that we, as Catholic Christians, do not have much to learn from Luther. This question does not prevent us from seeing Luther as a religious, a great man of prayer, a charismatic-prophetic genius. Luther knew that he was called to proclaim God and his salvific action.** ...

"Believing in the divinity of Jesus Christ, in his Resurrection, in the sacrament of baptism and in the supper, **the Catholic Christian is on Luther's side today even against many of**

---

[62] This statement of the Cardinal-Archbishop of Cologne is in clear opposition to the Church's Magisterium. The Lutheran doctrine of justification, the foundation of the Protestant errors, was solemnly condemned in the Seventh Session of the Council of Trent (cf. *Decretum de justificatione* of January 13, 1547, cited in Note 28 of this Chapter).

those [Protestants] who think that only they can be affiliated with the reformer."[63]

§ 47   Brazilian Cardinal Aloisio Lorscheider, a member of the Sacred Congregation for the Clergy, the Sacred Congregation for the Religious and Secular Institutes and the Secretariat for Non-Christian Religions, believes that if Luther had lived in the time of Vatican II, he would not have been excommunicated. The Cardinal defends the heresiarch and calls for his rehabilitation and the restoration of his good name since what moved Luther to wage war on the Church and the Catholic Faith was his "good intention." Each of Cardinal Lorscheider's statements that follow can be seen as an offense:

"The Church should not condemn persons, and excommunication is already disappearing. **Luther was excommunicated** because of the mentality of that time and **because the information on his writings that we have today was lacking then**. Now we read them without passion and **we are motivated to restore the figure of Luther. ... If Luther had lived in our time, he would not have been excommunicated, for at depth his intentions were good. ... He was misunderstood in his time."**[64]

§ 48   For Cardinal Julius Döpfner, then Archbishop of Munich and one of the Moderators at Vatican II, the Church would be "a petty Church," "coarse" and "narrow-minded" were she not to accept a moderate inter-confessionalism with heretics. These are no longer indirect offenses, as in the case of praising heretics, but direct affronts. Döpfner states:

"There is a second position that goes to the opposite extreme. It is either complete union or nothing at all. Whoever lacks any element of unity whatsoever is absolutely not part of her [the Church]. Either one belongs to the one and only Church of Christ and follows everything said in the second letter to the Ephesians, or one is not a part of the Church ... he is outside of the only single body [of Christ], and the Lord is not a Redeemer, but rather a judge who reproves. In this case, there is no more hope! **"There is only one choice: to be either a heretic or a member of the true Church! This crude mentality**[65] **did not**

---

[63] Joseph Höffner, Speech in Worms, *Deutsche Tagespost*, November 4-5, 1983, p. 4.

[64] Aloisio Lorscheider, Interview in *O Povo* (Fortaleza, Brazil), November 15, 1983, p. 5.

[65] It appears that the Cardinal Moderator of the Council considers the

condemnations of the Church against heretics as reflecting a "crude mentality." Would he also find the mentality of the Savior "crude" when He commanded: "And if your eye scandalize you, pluck it out, and cast it from you" (Mt 18:9), the evangelical precept upon which anathemas are based? Following this logic, Our Lord's condemnation of the wicked would also be "crude": "Depart from me, you cursed, into the everlasting fire" (M. 25:41).

Every manifestation of execrating evil would apparently be "crude" for Cardinal Döpfner. This would also be the spirit expressed in the *Pontifical Romano*. which establishes the solemn rite of excommunication and prescribes the following anathema, to be pronounced by the Bishop:

• "[Name person], led by the Devil, having abandoned through apostasy the promise he had made at his Baptism, has not feared to ravage the Church of God, steal Church goods and violently oppress the poor of Christ. In our concern over this, we do not desire that he perish because of any pastoral neglect of our own. For before the dread Judgment seat, we will have to render an account to the Prince of Shepherds, Our Lord Jesus Christ, in accordance with the terrible warning the Lord Himself addresses to us with these words: *If you do not speak to warn the wicked from his wicked way, to save his life; the same wicked man shall die in his iniquity; but his blood will I require at your hand* (Ez 3: 18). Therefore, we have canonically warned him once, twice, a third and yet a fourth time so that he might conquer his malice, inviting him to amend himself, make reparation and penance, and reprehending him with paternal affection. But he – o woe! – despising the salutary admonitions of the Church of God, which he has offended, and led by the spirit of pride, has not wanted to make any reparation.

"The precepts of the Lord and of the Apostles speak clearly about what to do with such prevaricators. For the Lord says: *Wherefore if your hand or your foot offends you, cut them off and cast them from you* (Mt 8:18). And the Apostle advises: *If any man that is called a brother be a fornicator, or covetous, or a server of idols, or a railer, or a drunkard or an extortioner: with such a one, do not so much as to eat.* (1 Cor 5:11) And John, the favorite disciple of Christ, forbids that one should even greet one who is wicked: *If any one comes to you and brings not this doctrine, do not receive him into the house, and greet him not* (2 Jn 1:10).

"Therefore, carrying out the precepts of the Lord and of the Apostles, let us take from the body of the Church with the iron tongs of excommunication this putrid and incurable member who refuses to accept the remedy, so that the rest of the members of the body may not be poisoned by such a pestiferous disease. He has despised our admonitions and our repeated exhortations; having been warned three times,

appear only among Catholics – nor does it now. ...

"Finally, there is a third position, which is that of the Council ... In the post-conciliar era, it can never be proclaimed enough ... that we can only properly understand and live the Council if we accept its gift of discernment. **Only thus will we be saved from an ecumenical euphoria that is equally as wrong as a narrow-minded confessionalism**. From these reflections, the authentic ecumenical position develops. ...

---

according to the precept of the Lord, he would not amend himself and do penance; he has not reflected upon his guilt, nor has he confessed it; neither has he presented any excuse through a third party, nor did he ask for pardon. But, with his heart hardened by the Devil, he continues to persevere in the same evil as before, according to the words of the Apostle: *The impenitent heart stores up to itself wrath for the day of wrath* (Rom 2:5).

"Wherefore by the judgment of God Almighty, the Father, the Son and Holy Ghost, of St. Peter, the Prince of the Apostles, and of all the Saints, and by virtue of the power which has been given us of binding and loosing in Heaven and on earth that which was divinely entrusted to us, we deprive him [the person is named] with all his accomplices and all his abettors of the Communion of the Body and Blood of Our Lord; we separate him from the society of all Christians; we exclude him from the bosom of our Holy Mother the Church in Heaven and on earth; and we declare him excommunicated and anathematized, as well as judge him condemned to eternal fire with Satan and his angels and all the reprobates. So long as he will not burst the fetters of the Devil, amend himself and do penance and make reparation to the Church, which he has offended, we deliver him to Satan for the perdition of his flesh, so that his soul may be saved on the day of judgment.

"To this, all the assistants answer: "*Fiat, fiat, fiat*" [so be it, so be it, so be it].

"The Bishop and the assisting priests then cast to the ground the lighted candles they have been carrying. Notice is sent in writing to all the priests in the neighboring parishes, as well as to the Bishops, of the name of the one who has been excommunicated and the cause of his excommunication in order that they may have no communication with him, thus removing them from any occasion of excommunication" (in *Catolicismo*, December 1952).

By denying that the Holy Church should apply penalties to heretics, Cardinal Döpfner makes himself their defender. In their work *Ius Canonicum*, the known Jesuits Francisco Xavier Wernz and Pedro Vidal describe the defenders of heretics as "those who, although not interiorly adhering to heretical doctrine, defend it with words or writings against those who impugn it; those who protect heretics – either by force or by unjust means – from a legitimate persecution waged against the heresy" (vol. 7, p. 78).

"The first ecumenical appeal of our time is for us to grow in the Church, and precisely in that Church presented to us in the Epistle to the Ephesians. But **it is not necessary to grow in a petty Church positioned in parallel to Christ, but rather to grow through the head, which is Jesus Christ. ... It is necessary to take advantage of all the profound forces of unity of which the Apostle speaks, but not in a unilateral way.** ... We see what the Catholic Church is in herself, but **we also want to know how the grace of Christ, the fullness of his Spirit, works in other churches and Christian communities.**"[66]

§ 49   Also expressive of the conciliar spirit of many Prelates is the Declaration of the Catholic-Lutheran Joint Commission, signed by its co-president, Bishop Hans Martensen of Copenhagen, in 1964. The document, published in *SEDOC* magazine, abounds with praise of Luther and insults to Holy Mother Church:

"At the beginning of this century, a rediscovery of the figure of Luther began to take place in the churches and the theology of Reformation. Soon afterward we saw, on the part of Catholics, an ever-growing interest in the person and work of Luther. This study has offered a remarkable scientific contribution about the Reformation and Luther, and, with regard to **the progress of ecumenical understanding,** it **has paved the way for a more positive Catholic view of Luther.** For this reason, the traditional perceptions of Luther, marked by a strong polemical note, are starting to collapse on both sides. At the same time, **he is beginning to be recognized as a witness of the Gospel, as a master of the faith, as a herald of spiritual renewal.**

"**Luther's appeal to reform the Church,** which was an appeal to penance, **still resonates in our ears. It continues to invite us to listen again to the Good News, to recognize our own infidelities to it, and to render it a testimony worthy of faith. This cannot be done today without taking into account the other church [Protestantism] and its testimony, without trying to reconcile ourselves with it and without renouncing traditional polemical perceptions.**"[67]

---

[66] Julius Döpfner, *La Chiesa vivente ogg* (Bari: Paoline, 1972), pp. 439-441.

[67] George A. Lindbeck, "Declaration of the Catholic/Lutheran Joint Commission on the Fifth Centennial of Martin Luther," *SEDOC* 16, Petrópolis, March 1964, cols. 839-840.

§ 50

After these statements, the Bishop of Copenhagen goes on to address the doctrinal field, declaring that Catholics should accept Luther's heretical theses. Bishop Martensen thus seems to incur the aforementioned condemnations of the Holy Church[68] and offends against the honor and integrity of the Catholic Faith.

"Today Protestant and Catholic studies on Luther, as well as **biblical studies have opened the way for an agreement** in the two churches **about the central aspiration of the Lutheran Reform. Taking into account the historical conditions of our forms of expression and thinking has also helped to make Luther's thinking amply recognized in Catholic circles as a legitimate form of Christian theology, especially in regard to his doctrine on justification**.

"Considering what had been admitted in common agreement between Catholic and Lutheran theologians since 1972 (*The Gospel and the Church*), the Catholic-Lutheran Declaration says this about the Augsburg Confession: 'A full consensus begins to take shape on the doctrine of justification, which was decisively important to the Reformation: **Only through grace and faith in the salvific action of Christ, and not on the basis of our merits, are we accepted by God** and received by the Holy Spirit, who enables and invites us to do good works.' ...

"Luther's concept of justification by faith and his proclamation of it clashed with the forms of piety of his time, which purposely concealed the gratuity of God's justice. For Luther, **his contestation was not only in accordance with the doctrine of the Church, but it even seemed to him a defense of the Church herself. He did not want to consider the idea of separation from the Church**: He even rejected it forcefully. Consequently, **what he intended to do was not understood by the theological and ecclesiastical authorities of Germany, nor later by Rome**."[69]

§ 51

Perhaps sensing the doctrinal weakness of his position, Bishop Martensen invokes the authority of Cardinal Willebrands and Vatican II:

"This new attitude toward Luther, who was in earlier times chastised with excommunication, is reflected in the words of Cardinal Willebrands at the Fifth Plenary Assembly of the World Lutheran Federation: '**Who can deny today that Mar-**

---

[68] See Note 28 of this Chapter.

[69] H. Martensen and G. Lindbeck, "Declaration of the Catholic-Lutheran Joint Commission,' cols. 840-841.

**tin Luther was a profoundly religious person who honestly
sought the message of the Gospel with abnegation? Who
can deny that ... Martin Luther conserved an appreciable
amount of the riches of the old Catholic Faith?** Did not **Vatican Council II accept demands which, among others, had
been expressed by Martin Luther and which express many
aspects of the Christian faith and life better than in times
past? To say this**, despite all the differences, **is a cause for
great joy and much hope.'**

"Among the ideas of the Vatican Council, where one can
see an acceptance of Luther's demands, one finds, for example,
the following:

- "An emphasis on the decisive importance of Sacred
  Scripture for the life and doctrine of the Church;[70*]
- "The description of the Church as the 'People of God';[71*]
- "The affirmation of the need for a permanent reform in
  the Church on her historical pilgrimage;[72*]
- "The understanding of ecclesiastical ministries as service oriented; [73*]
- "The emphasis on the priesthood of all who are baptized; [74*]
- "The commitment to the rights of the person and liberty
  in religious matters.[75*]

**"Other demands made by Luther in his time that can
be considered as satisfied in the theology and pastoral action
of the Catholic Church of our days include the use of the
vernacular in the Liturgy, the possibility of receiving communion under two species, the renewal of theology and the
celebration of the Eucharist."[76]**

[70*] Dogmatic Constitution on Divine Revelation (*Dei Verbum*).

[71*] Dogmatic Constitution on the Church (*Lumen gentium*), chap. 2.

[72*] *Ibid.*, n. 8; Decree on Ecumenism (*Unitatis redintegratio*), n. 6.

[73*] Decree on the Pastoral Office of the Bishops (*Christus Dominus*),
n.16; Decree on the Ministry and Life of Priests (*Presbyterorum ordinis*).

[74*] Dogmatic Constitution on the Church (LG), nn. 10,11; Decree on
the Apostolate of the Laity (*Apostolicam actuositatem*), nn. 2, 4.

[75*] Declaration on Religious Liberty (*Dignitatis humanae).*

[76] H. Martensen and G. Lindbeck, "Declaration of the Catholic-Lutheran Joint Commission," cols. 843-844.

§ 52   To these satisfactions the Council made to the demands of Luther, Hans Küng adds others:

- The abolishment of Latin;[77]
- The overemphasis given to the announcement of the word;
- The participation of the faithful in the liturgy;[78]
- The diminution of private Masses;[79]
- The attenuation of the Roman character of the Catholic Church; [80]
- The independence of the national Episcopates;
- The decentralization of the Roman Curia;
- Liturgical inculturation.[81]

§ 53   Along these same lines, in an interview with a German paper, Bishop Karl Lehman augured that Luther should no longer be considered a heretic since he is a "great personage of faith in the choir of witnesses of the Gospel." He further declared that today we must "understand the necessity of Luther's mission." Such statements constitute offenses against the Church and the Faith.

In that German paper, we find this report of the Bishop's words:

"The new Bishop of Mainz, Lehmann, described the state of Catholic research on Luther and ended by asking, '**Is Luther still a heretic?**' This word indicates a controversy over the true faith, said Lehmann.

"He continued: '**Perhaps one day we could abandon the word heretic, if we were able to see Martin Luther as an unquestionable and great personage of faith in the polyphonic choir of the witnesses of the Gospel, and thus un-**

---

[77]   Hans Küng, "La riforma liturgica del Concilio Vaticano II e la riunione con I cristiani separati," in V.A., *I grandi temi del Concilio* (Rome: Paoline, 1965), pp. 110-111, 115-116.

[78]   *Ibid.*

[79]   *Ibid.*, pp. 112-113.

[80]   *Ibid.*, pp. 113-114.

[81]   *Ibid.*

derstand under a new light the need for his mission and its grandeur.'"[82]

Bishop Lehmann was a theological adviser to Cardinal Döpfner and a member of the International Theological Commission. He was also a consultant on dogma for *Concilium* magazine.[83] From 1987 to 2009 he was president of the German Bishops Conference, the highest representative post of the Catholic Church in Germany. In 2001 John Paul II made him a Cardinal.

§ 54   Joseph Ratzinger, today Benedict XVI, affirms that in a certain way there is not much difference between the Catholic Church and Protestantism:

"Today, 400 years after the Reform, we can declare that in the opposition dividing Luther and the Council of Trent **... the dilemma that tore apart Western Christendom in a certain way has already disappeared."** [84]

Further on, Ratzinger praises Luther's teaching on Scripture as legitimate:

"One could say that something like a specific autonomy of Scripture exists as an objective norm which, from many points of view, **clarifies the ecclesiastical Magisterium. This was, undoubtedly, a legitimate demand of Luther that still was not duly accepted in the Catholic Church and her Magisterium."**[85]

These are statements of Prelates praising Luther and his heresy that exemplify the spirit of the Council.

C. Important Theologians Express Admiration for Luther and Other Heretics

§ 55   We have already mentioned the important role played by Fr. Yves Congar in preparing the conciliar documents and the good standing he enjoyed with the Pontiffs John XXIII, Paul

---

[82] "Nachdenken über eine neue Synode der Bistümer in der Bundesrepullik," *Frankfurter Allgemeine Zeitung*, November 12, 1983, p. 4.

[83] Cf. "La sorpresa Lehmann, *Il Regno*, 1987/18, p. 477.

[84] Joseph Ratzinger, "Exame do problema do conceito de Tradição," in V.A., *Revelação e Tradição*, pp. 19-20.

[85] *Ibid.*, p. 38.

VI and John Paul II.[86] He was also praised by the Vatican organ *L'Osservatore Romano* when the Franciscan Friars of the Atone-ment[87] presented him the Christian Unity Award, declaring that "Fr. Congar's original and patient research was always animated by keen intuitions." [88]

§ 56   In his work *The Catholic Church and Modern France*, Fr. Congar establishes general principles on dealing with the enemies of the Church based on the premise of respecting and loving heretics:

"Today there is not only respect for the other, but also interest in the other *as the other*. We are almost reaching the point of saying that what is in one's own house is completely worthless: 'The grass is always greener on the neighbor's lawn.' **The modern mind has a favorable bias toward the heretic: subverting the received ideas in every field, it opens the way for progress. The heretic brings novelty, even in the realm of truth.**

"Is it a matter of loving men? Jacques Maritain has shown that in former times the others were loved for what they could become, that is, they would meet with us and become as-similated to us. **Today they are loved for what they already are, precisely because of their difference.**" [89]

§ 57   The excerpt below is expressive of Congar's love for the heretics:

"In a lively conversation I had with Cardinal Baudril-lart in February 1939 ... he attacked me harshly: 'How can you explain that **you Dominicans, who were once the Order of the Inquisition, have now become friends with the Protestants and others**?'I responded with the deep conviction I have always had: 'It is in the name of the same love for the truth, but applied in a different way.'

---

[86] Cf. Vol. II, *Animus Injuriandi I*, Introduction, Note 14c, l, m, o, r; Chap. VI, Note 2.

[87] The Franciscan Friars of the Atonement were founded in New York State in 1898. Its ministry emphasizes ecumenism and the unity of all men. It also has communities in Canada, England, Ireland, Italy, Ja-pan, Brazil and Jamaica (cf. "Conferito a padre Yves Congar il premío per l'unitâ dei cristiani, *L'Osservatore Romano*, November 28, 1984, p. 5).

[88] *Ibid.*

[89] Yves Congar, *L'Église Catholique et France Moderne* (Paris: Ha-chette, 1978), p. 140.

"Then they [Catholics] thought they possessed it [the truth] entirely, and anything that did not conform to their rigid, defined orthodoxy should be eliminated (*ex-terminated*, in the sense of being banished). **I want to gather up every particle of truth, wherever it may be found, with the same care I would have in picking up a particle of a consecrated host**. This is the theological or doctrinal aspect of ecumenism."[90]

§ 58   Love for the heretics as heretics finds an even more radical development in the writings of Fr. Congar. In his view, attacking the Church "makes the intelligence more acute." For this reason "Satan perhaps has a more profound vision of God." He states:

"The 19th century saw the rise of the Positivism of Auguste Comte, the Anti-Theism of Feuerbach, the Materialism of Marx, and the Evolutionism of Lamarck and Darwin and Scientificism. Only later Nietzsche would find an audience, unmasking the falseness of a morality and a Christianity as if it were a 'Platonism for the people.' Then, he would make a subversion of values and would proclaim the 'death of God.' His work, he wrote, comes from 'a school of suspicion.'

"Since then, the name 'masters of suspicion' was given by Paul Ricoeur to those who denounced – behind religious speeches or behaviors – something completely different from what those speeches were intended to translate: the alienation of man (Marx), the cultivation of weakness opposed to the instinct of power (Nietzsche), the maintaining of childish attitudes and illusions (Freud). **It seems that attacking Christianity makes the intelligence more acute. 'Satan perhaps has a more profound vision of God.'**"[91]

These general principles, set out by Congar to promote love for the heretic and admiration for the enemies of the Church (including Satan…) were probably not absent from his important collaboration at Vatican II.

§ 59   Other factors also played a role in developing the ecumenism of Fr. Congar. This can be inferred from the statements below:

"I came to know Germany by means of my studies, above all in the person of Luther. **This man exerted the strongest possible influence on my research.** Obviously I saw what

---

[90] Y. Congar, *La crisi nella Chiesa e Mons. Lefèbvre* (Brescia: Queriniana, 1976), pp. 47-48.

[91] Y. Congar, *L'Église Catholique et France Moderne*, p. 29.

could be censured in his character, his doctrine and the role – undoubtedly unwillingly – that he played in the terrible division of Churches. Nevertheless, **this man is one of the greatest religious geniuses in all of history.**

"In this regard, I place him on the same plane as St. Augustine, St. Thomas Aquinas or Pascal. In a certain way he is even greater. He rethought all of Christianity. He gave it a new synthesis, a new interpretation. This man, rooted in the Middle Ages, lifted the medieval world. Contrary to Calvin, who was principally a humanist and a jurist, Luther was a man of the Church; he had a theological formation, he had a very profound Catholic spiritual background. All this **was pervaded and impelled by an immense creative energy.** ...

"I have studied Luther intensely. Not a month goes by without my returning to his writings. I am not afraid to say it: **I have admiration for him.** They are going to censure me, but I am ready to stand behind what I have said."[92]

§ 60   Knowing that Fr. Congar worked on 14 of the 16 final documents of the Council[93] and aware of his great admiration for Luther, one should not be surprised that he acknowledges that Vatican II assimilated elements of the work of the German heresiarch. Congar admits this freely:

"Today certain Protestants ... say that **if Luther had lived after Vatican II, he would not have separated from Rome.** Numerous points of his reform have been assimilated: the role of the Word of God, the role of the laity, and even practical things like communion of the chalice."[94]

§ 61   Corroborating this statement by Congar is a Protestant author who says: **"Luther would have considered Vatican II as his own council."**[95]

---

[92] Jean Puyo interroge le Père Congar (Paris:Centurion,1975), p. 59.

[93] Cf. *Informations Catholiques Internationales*, May 15, 1969, p. 9.

[94] *Jean Puyo interroge le Père Congar*, p. 62.
• More eulogies of Luther and Protestants made by Congar can be found in *La Parole et le Souffle* (Paris: Desclée, 1984), pp. 85-87; *Un peuple messianique* (Paris: Cerf, 1975), p. 120; *Jean Puyo interroge le Père Congar*, pp. 63, 151; *Theology's Tasks after Vatican II*, in V.A., *Theology of Renewal - Renewal of Religious Thought* (Montreal: Palm Publishers, 1968), vol. 1, p. 50.

[95] Albert Branderburg, "Martin Luther gegemwürtig," *Katolische Lutherstudien*, Paderborn, 1969, p. 146, *apud* Otto Pesch, "Lo stato attuale di comprensione e de intesa su Lutero," *Concilium*, 1976/8, p. 193.

Fr. Hans Urs von Balthasar places Luther side by side with St. Ignatius of Loyola as one who promoted the "theology of the Cross":

"The golden epoch of the theology of the Passion runs from 1300 to 1700. ... **A new impulse came from St. Ignatius of Loyola**'s meditation on the Passion. ... **In addition to Ignatius of Loyola**, who did not explicate his theology of the cross himself, **we find Luther, the Augustinian who** from his early days as a Catholic ... to his last years, **never stopped elaborating his whole theology** specifically **based on the events of the Passion.**"[96]

§ 62   Fr. Hans Küng is normally considered a radical progressivist who cannot be controlled by the official "moderate" leaders. That he is a radical, there is no doubt; that he is out of control is a point open to discussion.

What Küng said 40 years ago is today endorsed by "moderates" in general. Then, for example, in a conversation between Paul VI and Congar, the latter disparagingly deemed Küng "a Protestant to some extent."[97] Later, however, John Paul II and Benedict XVI, Cardinal Willebrands and Fr. Congar himself, as well as a large part of the Episcopate, would take the same positions – or even more radical ones – as the ones Küng had adopted earlier. This fact disproves the notion that the theologian from Tübingen is a breakaway schooner unconnected to the fleet of progressivist ships. Instead, he seems to be a reconnaissance vessel, who is not afraid to expose himself to the censures of public opinion in order to prepare it for the convoy that is trailing behind.

§ 63   The eulogies of Luther we have presented thus far were made by "moderates." If we compare those comments to what Küng said about Luther years earlier, we will see that today's moderates are animated by the same spirit as yesterday's *arditi*.

Notwithstanding such essential concordance, we emphasize here the offensive character of both.

---

[96] Hans Urs von Balthasar, *Mysterium Paschale*, in V.A., *Mysterium Salutis - Compêndio de dogmática*, ed. by Johannes Feiner and Magnus Löhrer (Petrópolis: Vozes, 1974), vol. III/6, p. 28.

[97] Speaking about his conversation with Paul VI about Hans Küng, Congar said: "For Küng, to be faithful is to be faithful to the Gospel, to Scripture, considered, in my opinion, in a somewhat Protestant way – that is, without taking into account Church tradition and all of ecclesial life" (*Jean Puyo interroge le Père Congar,* pp. 160-161).

§ 64   Below are some excerpts from works of Küng praising heretics:

• **"What would the Church be without** Origen, Augustine and Thomas Aquinas, but also without **Luther and Calvin** and all the other doctors, great and small?"[98]

• "**Luther can be excused,** since a new church was something that he did not want. At the beginning of the debate **he was already excluded, excommunicated by those who lived in another world** (the Renaissance) **and who notoriously understood little about its theological problems**; thus the unfortunate separation was unleashed." [99]

• **"Luther's protest ... was more than well-founded."**[100]

• "**Not so rarely 'Catholicism' – when compared to 'Protestantism' – leaves a very poor impression from a spiritual standpoint. There are also actual theological reasons for this.** According to the most frequently quoted text on this matter (Eph 1:19), **the Church is not**, of herself, **the plenitude; the Church does not know any type of plenitude that belongs by right to her by virtue of which** – of herself and without danger – **she would be universal, perfect and 'Catholic.'"**[101]

§ 65   Like Congar, Küng does not restrict his praise solely to Luther. The following excerpts reveal the admiration of the conciliar *perito* for various heretics and require no commentary:

• "After Simon Magus, the Church Fathers consider **Marcion** the great heretic: 'the firstborn son of Satan' (St. Polycarp). **The rich, cultured and intelligent orator of Synope in Pontus did not want to initiate any heresy, but simply meant to reform the Church.**" [102]

• "It is extraordinary how often one reads about the **Marcionite martyrs**. It was not the pagan State but rather the

---

[98] H. Küng, *A Igreja* (Lisbon: Moraes, 1970), vol. 2, p. 260.

[99] H. Küng, *Veracidade - O futuro da Igreja* (São Paulo: Herder, 1969), p. 160.

[100] H. Küng, *A Igreja*, vol. 2, p. 121.

[101] *Ibid.*, pp. 80-81.

[102] *Ibid.*, vol. 1, pp. 350-351. Marcion of Pontus (85-160) was one of the most dangerous heretics in early Christianity. His belief that there are two distinct deities of the Old and the New Testament was denounced by the Church Fathers and he was excommunicated.

Church, that is, the Christian State that condemned them to death. **Among the heretics there are countless martyrs** who were tortured and killed not only by the pagans but also by the Church! **Among these there is an even larger number of small and great confessors. How many of them, like Marcion – or Arius and Pelagius, Gottschalk and Eriugena, Wycliffe and Hus, Giordano Bruno and Blaise Pascal – were deeply imbued with the sense of God and marked by the Message of the Gospel?**" [103]

• "**What would the Church be without** a Francis of Assisi, or without **so many other great and small holy prophets, including the heretics?**" [104]

• "**The great heretics** did not have an easy life. They **dedicated themselves completely to their task**; they did not fear the consequences and subjected everything to what they believed. **They sacrificed everything**; thus they developed an unusual capacity to withstand shock. **In this the heretics were similar to the great saints!**" [105]

• "**There is one thing that should never be denied to them [the heretics], to those who indirectly also enriched the Church with their rich creative instincts, with their courage and refusal to compromise, with their heroism and absolute fidelity to their truth**; who set whole generations on fire with their enthusiasm. ... **What cannot be taken from them is their good faith!**" [106]

• "**The list of points on which the heretics were later vindicated is truly long: It extends from practical demands such as the use of the living language in the liturgy or allowing lay people to share the chalice – which heretics of the Middle Ages had already called for – all the way to some doctrinal statements** that were later accepted by the Church, although often in another context, with different wording or some other emphasis.

"**It is not simple ... to clearly establish the boundaries between truth and error, the Church and heresy** in the

---

[103] *Ibid.*, vol. 1, p. 358.

[104] *Ibid.*, vol. 2, p. 258

[105] *Ibid.*, vol. 1, p. 358.

[106] *Ibid.*, vol. 1, p. 359.

dynamics of history. **This should serve ... as a warning for the Church to be prudent with the heretics but, at the same time, to welcome them.**"[107]

§ 66   In his book *Veracity*, Hans Küng shows how Vatican II accepted several errors of the 16th century pseudo-reformers, confirming in general lines the affirmations of Bishop Martensen of Copenhagen presented above.[108] According to Küng, these are the main points introduced by the Council that draw the Church closer to Protestantism:

"a. A 'biblical spirit' in the liturgy, Church life and theology;

"b. A liturgy of the people: the participation of the community in prayer, song and receiving the Body of the Lord; the introduction of the vernacular; the adaptation of the liturgy to the different nations; the simplification of the rites; the reform of the sacramental rites; allowing lay people to share the chalice;

"c. 'The valorization of the laity;'

"d. An emphasis on the 'importance' of the local church as well as the particular churches (dioceses, nations); the decentralization and the internationalization of the Roman Curia;

"e. The 'reform' of popular piety: the end of indulgences; the 'reform' of the fast; **'unmasking' the danger of a spurious Marianism**, flawed with regard to biblical immediacy and Christocentrism."[109]

§ 67   Küng then asks this revealing question: **"What would Martin Luther do, had he been born in today's Catholic Church? Some would say, smiling – and not without reason – that he would be a conciliar *perito*: Many of his demands have in great part been met by this Council.**[110]

In addition to these famous theologians, there are many others who are less known who added their voices to the choir of praise for Protestant heretics. A few examples follow.

§ 68   Fr. Bernard Sesboué, S.J., a member of the International Theological Commission, writes:

"The great avatars, that is, the great transformations in Church life at the end of the Middle Ages, brought about a cer-

---

[107] *Ibid.*, vol. 1, p. 369.

[108] See § 51 of this Chapter.

[109] H. Küng, *Veracidade*, pp. 118-121.

[110] *Ibid.*

tain hardening of this dichotomy [between the Church as 'mystery,' pure and spiritual, and the institutional Church, stigmatized by sin] in the various reformers – **from Wycliff and John Hus to Luther and Calvin. From an Augustinian perspective, they spoke intelligently about the Church of the 'just' or the 'elect' which God alone knows and which, therefore, remains invisible and hidden to the eyes of man**.

"Undoubtedly this Church is present wherever the Word is announced with purity and the sacraments are duly ministered. But, in the final analysis, is God not the judge of the ecclesial reality of each community? **We must be careful not to simplify the extremely complex ecclesiological ideas of the great reformers**."[111]

§ 69   Sesboüé enthusiasm grows for Luther's "appeal to the Gospel":

"What was great about the cry launched by Luther in a Church fallen ill on account of the many deviations in the lives of her shepherds and the faithful **was his appeal to the Gospel: 'The Gospel before all else!'** In effect, **Luther made the Gospel a new experience.** Through a painful journey, **he had rediscovered the Gospel of grace and justification by faith** as it is proclaimed by St. Paul in the Epistles to the Galatians and the Romans. **Dazzled by this beam of light and moved by an incomparable Christian fervor, Luther then became an 'evangelist' and a confessor of the theology of the cross. ...**

"**Luther was right**, therefore, to ask those who would become his adversaries to enter into a discussion about the essentials, that is, the Gospel and faith in its existential dimension." [112]

§ 70   The next apologia for Luther comes from the pen of Otto Pesch, German professor of dogmatics and ecumenical theology:

"Finally, **the welcome of Luther by Catholics ... in the last few decades has made such progress, burying a bogged down polemic ... that the question appears on the horizon of whether there is still a reason for the existence of a specifically Lutheran church.**

---

[111] Bernard Sesboüé, *O Evangelho na Igreja - A tradição viva da Fé* (São Paulo: Paulinas, 1977), pp. 79-80.

[112] *Ibid.*, p. 72.

"1. **At Vatican Council II, the Catholic Church took up as her own Luther's demand for a constant penitential** *reform* **of the Church.**

"2. **The Lutheran doctrine of justification was recognized**, since **today no Catholic theologian or preacher still presents the salvation of man before God as dependent on his works and personal merit.** ...

"3. **Regarding the sacrificial character of the Mass and, consequently, the liturgical reform of the eucharistic celebration, theology – already long before Vatican II and, afterward, with the Council's liturgical reform – had looked at Luther's criticism with unanticipated seriousness and created an eucharistic celebration that, at the least, corresponds to Luther's demands** ...

"5. Also **the thorny problem of Scripture and Tradition has already been resolved in favor of a normative priority of the Scripture (as Luther advocated)**, in relation to which all posterior tradition can only have an explanatory, rather than a constitutive character.

"The extent of the convergences ... was also made possible by the collaboration of Catholic theologians in their research on Luther, which today has become normal on the international plane. ... In brief, **Luther is for Catholic theology today a witness of the common faith, serving as a guide for the past and the future: He is our 'common master,' as Cardinal Willebrands said** in Evian in 1970." [113]

§ 71 Fr. Daniel Olivier, a specialist on Lutheranism, is also the author of a work titled *Luther's Faith: The Cause of the Gospel in the Church.* He has taught courses on the Pseudo-Reformation in several European universities and written for *La Croix*, an organ of the French Episcopate. He also lavishes praise on the heresiarch and directs new offenses against the Catholic Religion:

"**In Worms**, before Charles V and the States of the Empire ... **the existence of the world in which we live depended only on the lucidity and courage of Luther, the last bastion of the Pauline principle of justification by faith alone [*sola fide*], without works.** ...

"The history of Protestantism demonstrates that **although the theses of Luther did not become the leaven of a renew-**

---

[113] Otto Hermann Pesch, "Comprensione di Lutero oggi," *Concilium* 1976/8 (It. ed.), pp. 181-182.

al of the Roman Church, they were nonetheless destined to have a long doctrinal and religious future. Advances in the ecumenical movement no longer permit the Church of Rome to reject and ignore this Christian current *en bloc*. ...

"Truthfully, it is the Protestants who must see if they understand Luther or not (and why). For our part, let us identify some of the facts that can explain the strange hostility of the Roman Church toward a Christian man whose intuitions are increasingly justified by the recent history of the Church herself."[114]

§ 72   These are some excerpts we deem opportune to bring to the attention of the Reader in this Item 1 so he can know another facet of the *animus injuriandi* that characterizes the spirit of the Council: the praise of heretics. These selections – from the official Vatican line, the "moderates" and the *arditi* – are samples of many that exist on this topic. We believe they express the various currents of conciliar Progressivism.[115]

2. The Greek Schismatics

§ 73   The ambition of the Patriarchs of Constantinople led them to claim the same dignity as the Sovereign Pontiff,[116] one of the motives for their break with Rome. From this error derives a "collegial" concept of Church government, a *sobornost*. This Russian word indicates the type of ecclesial government sought by the schismatics and corresponds to the collegiality advocated by the progressivists for the Catholic Church.[117] This is why the supreme body of the Schismatic Church is the so-called Holy

---

[114]   Daniel Olivier, "Perché Lutero non é stato capito?" *Concilium* 1976/8, pp. 31-32.

[115]   Most of the texts chosen for this Item were found during an early stage of the research undertaken to write the present Collection. We believe that if we were to make a specialized study on this topic today, we would have material for several volumes. The same can be said about the praise that has been lavished on Schismatics and Jews in the following Items 2 and 3. It is certain we would find many more quotes of this kind from the post-conciliar Popes, Vatican meetings, Bishops' conferences and works of theologians. We will not execute this extensive research, however. In this Chapter, we present only some illustrative samples sufficient to give the Reader an overall view of the topics studied in each Item.

[116]   Cf. M. Jugie, *Schisme byzantin*, in *DTC*, vol. 14, cols. 1317-1318.

[117]   See Note 134 of this Chapter.

Synod, in which the various patriarchs have a supposedly equal power in doctrinal decisions.

§ 74   To the patriarch of Constantinople, who adopted the title of "ecumenical patriarch," is conferred a small honorific distinction with the expression *primus inter pares*.[118] Therefore,

---

[118] Although schismatics try to present all the patriarchs in the "Holy Synod" as equals, with a merely honorific primacy conferred on the patriarch of Constantinople, the actuality is somewhat different.

The *first factor* in this difference is that the schismatic churches – since they preach Caesaropapism – are all, in principle and in practice, subordinate to the governments of their respective countries, and hence to their political interests. Therefore, the margin of religious independence they have is relatively small. It is exercised only in matters where the innumerable political interests of their respective governments are not prejudiced. Thus, the equality of the members of the "Holy Synod" is questionable in its very foundation, since the power of each ruling state is different.

The *second factor* that limits the supposed equality of the patriarchs in the "Holy Synod" derives from the first. Among the patriarchs who sit on the supreme council of the Schismatic Church, the most powerful – both because of the number of followers represented and the power of the government served – is the patriarch of Moscow. He is a puppet of the Communist leaders and represents 100 million believers, whereas the patriarch of Greece leads some 7.5 million, and the patriarch of Constantinople, some 2 million ("Eastern Orthodoxy," World Council of Churches website, 2011, p. 1805).

These data – generally ignored by the media – belie the myth that the members of the "Holy Synod" are equal, and raise the suspicion that schismatics cannot make use of their independence to combat Communism. It would seem that in practice its members follow the overall orientation of the powerful patriarch of Moscow, who could well be called *dominus inter servos* in relation to the other schismatic patriarchs, while the *primus inter pares* has only a preeminence of title and dignity.

Despite the celebrated policies of *glasnost* and *perestroika*, the fall of the Berlin Wall and the "iron curtain," we do not believe the situation in Russia has changed in its essence. Of the various republics that made up the USSR, those that abandoned Communism are returning to it "by the democratic way." In Russia Communism never lost its decisive role in the government and armed forces, despite the optimistic euphoria of the West. Thus, with regard to the Russian Schismatic Church, the situation remains much the same today, even after the many publicized changes.

We see, therefore, that the supposed equality of the schismatic pa-

the Schismatic Church has a collegial system of government in contrast with the monarchic regime of the Catholic Church, governed by the sole Vicar of Christ, the Pope.

§ 75   Thus, from the initial rebellion that caused the Eastern Schism other pernicious errors sprouted: the denial of the divine character of the Papal Monarchy and the claim that papal authority is subject to the decisions of a Synod or Council. With the Church's condemnation of Conciliarism and proclamation of the dogma of papal infallibility, such errors assumed the characteristics of heresy. That is to say, the Eastern Schism became heretical.[119]

---

triarchs is more myth than reality. It is, nonetheless, a myth accepted by the progressivists as an objective reality so that they can advance their plans for collegiality and ecumenism. To continue our analysis of Progressivism, we will therefore base ourselves on the reality of the schismatics' *sobornost.*

[119] The Church condemned a) the initial rebellion of the schismatics; b) the denial of the divine character of the papal monarchy; c) the supposed supremacy of the Synod over the Pope; and d) the denial of the dogma of papal infallibility.

These are the documents of the Church:

a. On the universal primacy of the Pope against the pretension of the Schismatics:

• Letter *Proposueramus quidem* by Pope St. Nicholas I (858-867) to Emperor Michael of September 28, 865: "Neither by Augustus, nor by all the clergy, nor by the kings, nor by the people will the judge be judged ... 'The supreme Seat will not be judged by anyone.'" (DS 638)

• IV Council of Constantinople, session X, February 28, 870, canon 21, *De primato romano inter sedes patriarchales*: "In the belief that the words 'He that receives you, receives me' (Mt. 10:40) 'and he that despises you, despises me' (Lk. 10:16), spoken by Christ to the Holy Apostles and His disciples, also refer to all who came after them and, like them, became Supreme Pontiffs and Princes of the shepherds in the Catholic Church, we hereby rule that absolutely none of the powerful of this world should attempt to dishonor or depose any of the five Patriarchs; rather they are to be held worthy of every honor and reverence, especially *first,* the Pope of Old Rome, *second*, the Patriarch of Constantinople, and then those of Alexandria, Antioch and Jerusalem. Nor shall anyone direct against the Pope of Old Rome any libelous and defamatory writings, as was done recently by Photius and earlier by Dioscorus" (DS 661).

"Therefore, whoever is so arrogant and bold as to hurl insults against the See of Peter, the Prince of Apostles, in writings or words, following the examples of Photius or Dioscorus, receives the same condemnation which they have incurred" (DS 662).

• XVII Ecumenical Council of Florence, Bull *Laetentur caeli* of July 6, 1439: "We define that the Holy Apostolic See, and the Roman Pontiff, have primacy over the whole world, and that the same Roman Pontiff is the successor of St. Peter, Prince of Apostles and true Vicar of Christ, superior to all as head of the whole Church, and father and teacher of all Christians; and that upon him, in St. Peter, Our Lord Jesus Christ conferred the full power of shepherding, ruling and governing the universal Church, as is also stated in the acts of the ecumenical councils and the sacred canons" (DS 1307).

• The Constitution *Super ad nos*, of March 16, 1743, by Pope Benedict XIV contains a profession of faith imposed on Simon Evadius, Archbishop of Damascus, when he was raised to the Maronite patriarchal seat of Antioch: "I venerate and accept all the universal councils legitimately held and confirmed by the authority of the Roman Pontiff, above all, the Council of Florence, and I profess that which was defined in it" (DS 2534).

b. The divine character of the Papal Monarchy

• Council Vatican I, in session IV, on July 18, 1870, promulgated the Dogmatic Constitution *Pastor Aeternus* defining papal infallibility. In chapter III one reads: "Wherefore we teach and declare that, by divine ordinance, the Roman Church possesses a preeminence of ordinary power over every other Church, and that this power of jurisdiction of the Roman Pontiff is both episcopal and immediate. Both clergy and faithful, of whatever tie and dignity, both singly and collectively, are bound to submit to this power by the duty of hierarchical subordination and true obedience, and this not only in matters concerning faith and morals, but also in those which regard the discipline and government of the Church throughout the world" (DS 3060).

* A joint statement by the German Bishops in January-February 1875 refutes the errors of a circular letter by the Prussian Chancellor Otto von Bismarck, who accused the Pope of becoming – with the dogma of Papal Infallibility – a monarch who is "totally absolutist, more than any absolute monarch on earth" (DS 3112). Refuting this error, the Bishops declare:

"According to these decrees, the Pope's power of ecclesiastical jurisdiction is a supreme, ordinary and immediate power, communicated to the Pope by Jesus Christ, the Son of God, in the person of St. Peter, and which is extended directly to the whole Church" (DS 3113).

Further on, the German Bishops wrote: "The Episcopate also exists by virtue of the same divine institution on which the office of the Supreme Pontiff is based" (DS 3115).

c. The alleged supremacy of the Synod over the Pope

• Pius II, in his Bull *Exsecrabilis* of January 18, 1460, condemns the conciliarist errors he professed in his youth before he became a priest:

"An execrable abuse, unheard of in past ages, has been propagated in our times: It is characterized by a spirit of rebellion and not by a desire to achieve a fair judgment, but rather to divert from some previous sin. Certain persons have dared to appeal to a future council against decisions by the Roman Pontiff, the Vicar of Jesus Christ, to whom was said, in the in the person of St. Peter, 'Feed My sheep' (Jo 21:17) and 'Whatever you shall bind on earth shall also be bound in Heaven (Mt 16:19).' ... Therefore, desiring to free the Church of Christ from this venom ... We condemn such appeals, as erroneous and detestable" (DS 1375).

• Pius IX, in union with Vatican Council I, states in the Dogmatic Constitution on the Church promulgated, on July 18, 1870: "Since the Roman Pontiff, by the divine right of the apostolic primacy, governs the universal Church, we likewise teach and declare that he is the supreme judge of the faithful and that he can be appealed to in all cases that fall under ecclesiastical jurisdiction. The sentence of the Apostolic See, whose authority is the highest, is not subject to revision by anyone, nor may anyone lawfully pass judgment thereupon. Hence, those who maintain that it is lawful to appeal from the judgments of the Roman Pontiffs to an ecumenical council, as if this were an authority superior to the Roman Pontiff, stray from the genuine path of truth.

"So then, if anyone says that the Roman Pontiff has merely an office of supervision and guidance, but lacks the full and supreme power of jurisdiction over the whole Church, and this not only in matters of Faith and Morals, but also in those which concern the discipline and government of the Church disseminated throughout the whole world, or that he has only the principal part but not the absolute fullness of this supreme power, or that this power of his is not ordinary and immediate both over all and each of the churches and over all and each of the pastors and faithful, let him be anathema" (D 1830-1831).

d. Papal Infallibility

• Pius IX, in union with Vatican Council I, teaches in the same Constitution on the Church, of July 18, 1870: "But since in this age when the salutary effectiveness of the apostolic office is most especially needed, many disparage its authority, we judge it absolutely necessary to affirm solemnly the prerogative which the only-begotten Son of God was pleased to attach to the supreme pastoral office:

"Therefore, faithfully adhering to the tradition received from the beginning of the Christian Faith, to the glory of God our Savior, for the exaltation of the Catholic Faith and the salvation of the Christian people, with the approval of the Sacred Council, we teach and define as a divinely revealed dogma that when the Roman Pontiff speaks *ex cathedra*, that is, when, in the exercise of his office as shepherd and teacher of all Christians, in virtue of his supreme apostolic authority, he defines a doctrine concerning Faith or Morals to be held by the whole Church, he possesses, by the divine assistance promised to

§ 76

In addition to the heresies already mentioned, there are two other grave doctrinal errors that constitute heresies to which the Greek Schismatics pertinaciously adhere. The *first* is the famous question of the *Filioque*: they do not admit that the Holy Spirit proceeds from the Father and the Son and claim that He proceeds from the Father alone. This is an error long opposed to the teaching of the Church.[120] The *second* is the negation of the

---

him in Blessed Peter, that infallibility that the Divine Redeemer willed His Church to enjoy in defining doctrine on Faith or Morals. Therefore, such definitions of the Roman Pontiff are of themselves, and not by the consent of the Church, irreformable.

"So then, should anyone, which God forbid, have the temerity to reject this definition of ours: let him be anathema" (D 1838-1840).

[120] Both of these errors clash with Catholic teaching:

a. **The Holy Ghost proceeds from the Two Persons of the Most Holy Trinity.** This can be verified in Sacred Scripture. St. Thomas Aquinas demonstrates that although Scriptures do not state verbally that the Holy Ghost proceeds from the Father and the Son, it is nonetheless affirmed in an equivalent way: Mt 10:20; Rom 8:9; Gal 4:6; Jo 14:16-26; 16:7; 16:13-15. His argumentation is developed in *De potentia*, q.10, a.5; *Contra gentiles*, IV, 24-25; *Contra errores Graecorum* (cf. M. Cuervo, "Introducciones al Tratado de la Santísima Trinidad," in St. Thomas Aquinas, *Summa Teologica*, Madrid: BAC, 1953, vol. 2, p. 224).

Further, the Church Magisterium has always taught that the Holy Ghost proceeds from the Father and the Son, and adopted the *Filioque* formula in various Councils, including the following:

• The XVII Ecumenical Council of Florence, in the Bull *Laetentur caeli* of July 6, 1439, confirming the Second Council of Lyons, expressly defined the procession of the Holy Ghost: "In the name of the Most Holy Trinity, Father, Son and Holy Ghost, with the approbation of this sacred and universal Council of Florence, we define – so that this truth of the faith be believed and accepted by all Christians, and that all likewise profess it – that the Holy Spirit comes eternally from the Father and the Son and has His essence and His subsistent being both from the Father and the Son, and proceeds eternally as from one principle and one spiration (cf. Second Council of Lyons).

"We declare that what the holy Doctors and Fathers say, namely, that the Holy Spirit proceeds from the Father through the Son, leads to the understanding that the Son also is the cause, according go the Greeks, and according to the Latins, the principle of the subsistence of the Holy Ghost, as is the Father also. And since all that the Father has, the Father himself in begetting has given to His Only-begotten Son, with the exception of Fatherhood, the very fact that the Holy Ghost proceeds from the Son, the Son himself has from the Father eternally,

dogma of the Immaculate Conception.[121]

Therefore, to the heresies that come from the conciliarism of the Greek Schismatics and their denial of Papal Infallibility, these two others that also constitute heresy should be added.

§ 77   In apparent disregard of these heresies and doctrinal and disciplinary errors, John Paul II preached unity with the Eastern Schismatics in words directed to Cardinal François Marty, who was returning from an ecumenical "pilgrimage" to the East, where he met with Dimitrios I, the schismatic patriarch of Constantinople. Applying the common ground tactic, the Pontiff would seem to incur the same errors of inter-confessionalism mentioned above.[122] He calls the Greek Schismatics "the second lung" of the Catholic Religion:

---

by Whom He is begotten eternally. We define, in addition, that the explanation of the expression *Filioque,* for the sake of declaring the truth and also because of imminent necessity, has been lawfully and reasonably added to the Creed" (DS 1300-1302; cf. DS 800, 850).

b. **The dogma of the Immaculate Conception** was defined by Pius IX in the Bull *Ineffabilis Deus* of December 8, 1854: "For the honor of the Holy and undivided Trinity, for the glory and adornment of the Virgin Mother of God, for the exaltation of the Catholic Faith, and for the furtherance of the Catholic Religion, by the authority of Jesus Christ Our Lord, of the Blessed Apostles Peter and Paul, and by our own authority, we declare, pronounce and define that the doctrine which holds that the most Blessed Virgin Mary, in the first instance of her conception, by a singular grace and privilege granted by Almighty God, in view of the merits of Jesus Christ, the Savior of the human race, was preserved free from all stain of original sin, is a doctrine revealed by God and, therefore, to be believed firmly and constantly by all the faithful.

"Hence, if anyone shall dare – God forbid – to think otherwise than as what has been defined by us, let him know and understand that he is condemned by his own judgment, that he has suffered shipwreck in the faith; that he has separated himself from the unity of the Church; and that, furthermore, by his own action he incurs the penalties established by law if he should dare to express in words or writing or by any other outward means the errors that he thinks in his heart" (D 1641).

[121] Cf. S. Vailhé, "Constantinople" (Église de), in *DTC.*, vol. 6, col. 1411.

[122] See §§ 37-39 of this Chapter.

"When I met with representatives of the other Churches in France at the Apostolic Nunciature in Paris during my pastoral trip of 1980, I spontaneously expressed this thought: '**My fraternal visit** to the ecumenical Patriarchate of Constantinople **gave me great hope. I found myself very comfortable in this atmosphere, in this milieu that**, evidently, **constitutes a great spiritual reality. It is a complementary reality: One cannot breathe as a Christian – I would say more, as a Catholic – with only one lung; it is necessary to have two lungs, that is, the Eastern and the Western.'** ... [123*]

"And so it is that **your ecumenical group** [on pilgrimage to the East, led by Cardinal Marty] ... also **had the grace to discover** not only the historic and artistic treasures of the Churches of the East, but also their soul, **their ardent faith in the resurrected Lord and, through Him, in the Holy Trinity; the special attention they pay to the work of the Holy Spirit in us, to the divine life in which our own lives are rooted,** above all through the sacraments, ... **their sense of Church.** ...

"Thus, **we Christians of the East and West must learn to love one another as brothers, in the complementarity of our spiritualities, of our faith that is practically the same, in our common apostolicity.** I am happy that you were able to meet again with **my brother, patriarch Dimitrios I.**" [124]

§ 78   Given the centuries-old condemnations of the Church against the Eastern Schism, it is hard to conceive how a Catholic, let alone a Pope, could feel comfortable in an atmosphere contaminated by such spiritual venom. It is quite difficult for a layman to understand how John Paul II could say this about himself, but it is more perplexing to see that he extends this feeling to every Catholic. In conscience, this is difficult to accept.

Indeed, he states: "One cannot breathe as a Christian – I would say more, as a Catholic – with only one lung; it is necessary to have two lungs, that is, the Eastern and the Western."[125]

[123*] *La Documentation Catholique*, 1980, p. 634.

[124] John Paul II, Audience to an ecumenical group on pilgrimage to the East led by Cardinal François Marty, in *L'Osservatore Romano*, 10-21-1983, p. 1.

[125] Although in thesis these statements by John Paul II could be interpreted as an allusion to Eastern spirituality prior to the Schism, in this concrete case they clearly refer to the present-day Greek Schismatics. What is more, the metaphor of the "two lungs" was repeated in *Re-*

demptoris Mater, Euntes in mundum and other papal documents. It has also been commented on by Prelates and official organs of the Vatican on various occasions. Albeit ambiguous in their application, Cardinal Franz König and *L'Osservatore Romano* interpreted it as referring to the Schismatic Church.

a. John Paul II in the Apostolic Letter *Euntes in mundum* of January 25, 1988 states: "Europe is Christian in its very roots. The two forms of the great tradition of the Church, the Eastern and the Western, the two forms of culture, complement each other like two 'lungs' of a single body (cf. Encyclical *Letter Redemptoris Mater*, 34, in AAS 79, 1987, p. 406). Such is the eloquence of the past; such is the inheritance of the peoples who live on our Continent. It could be said that the two currents, Eastern and Western, have become simultaneously the first great forms of inculturation of the faith, in whose ambit the one and undivided fullness entrusted by Christ to the Church, has found its historical expression" (*L'Osservatore Romano*, March 23,1988, Supplement, p. VI).

b. Cardinal König interprets the statements of John Paul II as referring to the Schismatic Church:

"I was really very impressed with the beginning of that Letter [*Euntes in mundum*]. The Pope made no criticisms, nor did he resort to an apologia, but he opened his heart without reservation or prejudice. ... John Paul II decidedly placed himself in the perspective of unity with the East, a unity which Christianity had lost with the Schism of 1054. The image most used by the Pope, the two lungs – the Western and Eastern, both necessary to the body – describes well the type of unity toward which we want to move" (Tommaso Ricci, "A Luz vem do Oriente, *30 Giorni*, June 1988, pp. 52-53).

c. *L'Osservatore Romano* applies the metaphor to the Catholic Church and the Schismatic Church on the occasion of the Millennium of the Baptism of Russia:

"The Millennium of the Baptism of Kievan Rus' is an event to which the Catholic Church paid great attention and attached great importance. The Holy Father himself recalled this great episode in the history of the Church and of Europe with two documents: The Apostolic Letter *Euntes in mundum* and the message *Magnum baptismi donum*, addressed to Ukrainian Catholics.

"In the first document John Paul II recalls that 'Europe is Christian in its very roots. The two forms of the great tradition of the Church, the Eastern and the Western, the two forms of culture, complement each other like two 'lungs' of a single body. Such is the eloquence of the past; such is the inheritance of the peoples living on our Continent.' The Holy Father calls to mind that 'at the same time, this heritage, in the last part of the 20th century, becomes a particularly pressing chal-

§ 79

These affirmations of John Paul II contradict the traditional position of the Catholic Church regarding the Eastern Schism in a way that clashes with the *sensus fidelium*:

1. **Dogmatically** he appears to acquiesce with the errors of the Schism by admitting that the Greek Schismatic Church is on an equal footing with the Holy Catholic Church: It is the "second lung," while the Catholic Church is the first.

Further, he seems to implicitly accept the theological error of the *Filioque* when he speaks, without any restriction, of the "ardent faith" of the Schismatics "in the Most Holy Trinity" and "the special attention they pay to the work of the Holy Spirit in us."

He also appears to accept indirectly the collegial distribution of power of the Schismatics when he unrestrictedly praises their "sense of Church."

One cannot see how all this can fail to profoundly offend

---

lenge to the unity of Christians. A sincere aspiration to unity is present among the people today, as a presupposition of that peaceful coexistence between the peoples in which the good of all lies.' ...

"And the kiss of peace sent by the Bishop of Rome to the millenarian sister Church manifests 'the ardent wish for that perfect communion desired by Christ and inscribed in the nature of the Church'" ("Aperte le celebrazioni per il millennio del battesimo della Rus' de Kiev," June 6-7,1988, p. 1).

d. The following commentary comes from an article titled "Cardinal Casaroli in Moscow for the Celebrations of the Millennium of Rus'" in *L'Osservatore Romano*:

"The Cardinal Secretary of State will assist at the celebrations of the Millennium of Christianity in the land of Rus' with the other members of the delegation sent by the Holy Father to participate in the rites and other public acts commemorating the great event that had so many consequences in the history of the Church and Europe.

"On accepting the invitation sent to him by the patriarch of Moscow Pimen, the Holy Father emphasized the importance that the Catholic Church attributes to this significant episode, for which he asked the attention and prayers of Catholics in the recent Apostolic Letter *Euntes in mundum*. In this document, John Paul II calls to mind that 'Europe is Christian in its very roots. The two forms of the great tradition of the Church, the Eastern and the Western, the two forms of culture, complement each other like two 'lungs' of a single body. Such is the eloquence of the past; such is the inheritance of the peoples living on our Continent'" (June 9, 1988, p. 1).

the *sensus fidelium* and, more importantly, the Catholic Faith. For a Catholic, it is difficult indeed to concur with the affirmation of John Paul II that the Greek Schismatic Church is a "second lung" that he needs in order to breathe.

§ 80   2. **Morally** it is also difficult to accept the apparently scandalous position of a Pontiff who seems to challenge the previous condemnations of the Church, notably against inter-confessionalism[126] and the Schism.[127]

Not only does his personal position cause scandal to the whole Church, but his words can be construed as an encouragement for all of the Hierarchy and the faithful to imitate him. Indeed, he says that "one cannot breathe as a Catholic with only one lung." This seems to imply that every Catholic should imitate the stance and spirituality of the Schismatics in order to "breathe well."

Further on, John Paul II indisputably confirms this encouragement: "We Christians of the East and West must learn to love one another as brothers, in the complementarity of our spiritualities, of our faith that is practically the same."

Likewise, his enthusiasm for the Schismatics appears clear when he says that he felt "very comfortable in this [schismatic] milieu," and later when he praises Cardinal Marty's ecumenical excursion and expresses his happiness that he could "again see my brother, patriarch Dimitrios I."

How can one fail to see in these words the opposite of the perennial teaching of the Church and a grave moral error? From the moral standpoint, it is very difficult to accept that the Schismatic confession constitutes a "second lung" for Catholics.

§ 81   3. **Historically**, John Paul II's affirmation that "one cannot breathe as a Catholic with only one lung" does not actually harmonize with the reality, since the Holy Church breathed perfectly well after the Eastern Schismatics separated themselves from her. One of most vigorous and healthy epochs in the history of the Church is found in the pontificate of St. Gregory VII, the high point in a series of pontificates of Gregorian Popes that preceded and followed his own. It was precisely at that time that the Schism occurred. It is understandable that this blossoming of

---

[126] See §§ 37-39 of this Chapter.

[127] See Note 118 of this Chapter.

health coincided with the separation of infected members – the Greek Schismatics.

In view of this historic reality, how can one accept John Paul II's statement that the Church "does not breathe well" without the Greek Schismatic "lung"?

§ 82   In view of the doubt his words cast in the minds of the faithful and their apparent opposition to the Catholic Faith, it is very difficult to avoid the impression that an offense was committed when he affirmed that the true Religion is equal – "another lung" – to a Greek Schismatic Church fraught with heresies and errors of all kind.

*

§ 83   Such interconfessional principles that appear in the speech of John Paul II to the ecumenical retinue of Cardinal Marty can be found in other actions of the same Pontiff. A notable example is the symbolic act he celebrated in Bari with the Greek Schismatic metropolite of Myra. On that occasion, the two lighted a single lamp at the same time to symbolize the "unity of faith of the sister Churches." In his homily that followed, John Paul II returned to the same idea, affirming that "without the genius gift" of the Schismatic Church, "the Church of Christ cannot manifest the full maturity of form received in the Cenacle." A report of this ecumenical event, published by *L'Osservatore Romano*, noted:

"Yesterday John Paul II visited for 13 hours the Province of Puglia. ... In the Basilica of St. Nicholas [in Bari] an ecumenical ceremony was held with the participation of the orthodox metropolite Konstantinidis and John Paul II. ... **Together they lighted a lamp with a single flame to symbolize the unity of faith between the sister Churches**."[128]

"The 'ecumenical vocation of the Church of Puglia' was emphasized by the Holy Father in Bari in the Basilica dedicated to St. Nicholas. Next to his tomb, **the Pope said, 'The Bishop of Rome comes here as a pilgrim and**, through him [St. Nicholas], **pays homage to the Eastern Church.'**...

"The ecumenical significance of this moment became evident with the 'ceremony of lighting the lamp with only one

---

[128] "La visita di Giovanni Paolo II a Bari terra d'incontro d'Oriente e Occidente," *L'Osservatore Romano*, February 27/28, 1984, p. 1.

flame, where the Holy Father and metropolite Konstantinidis of Myra filled the lamp with oil brought respectively from Rome and from the two vials that served to feed the one flame of the lamp."[129]

§ 84   John Paul II then delivered his speech: "**Today the two sister Churches of the East and the West understand that, without listening reciprocally to the profound reasons that sustain in each one the meaning of what characterizes it, without a reciprocal gift of the brilliant treasures that each one bears, the Church of Christ cannot manifest the full maturity of the form it received in the Cenacle at the beginning.**"[130]

The comments we made earlier on the Pontiff's words to Cardinal Marty can be applied equally to this speech. In them we find a similar praise of Schismatics and an offense against the Catholic Religion.

§ 85   It is not difficult to find other eulogies and expressions of sympathy for the Schism made by John Paul II and Benedict XVI. Among these, perhaps one of the more significant was John Paul II's participation in May of 1993 in a course of 12 classes of theology given by the Schismatic Church. According to reports, after the classes the Greek Schismatic theologians dined with the Pope. [131]

There is also the invitation of John Paul II to the patriarch of Constantinople Bartholomew I to write the meditations of the *Via Sacra*, which the Pontiff prayed during the solemn Good Friday ceremony of Holy Week in 1994, an act unparalleled in the History of the Church.[132]

§ 86   Similar expressions of praise for the Schismatics are expressed by Fr. Congar, "one of the pioneers of Catholic

---

[129] *Ibid.* p. 5.

[130] *Ibid.*

[131] Cf. Andrea Tornielli, "A moral se faz esperar," *30 Dias*, June 1993, p. 13.

[132] Cf. Lucio Brunelli," A via Sacra de Bartolomeu," *30 Dias*, March 1994, p. 24; Gianni Valente, "Bartolomeu I, a verdade está nos fatos," *30 Dias,* September 1994, p. 14.

ecumenism."[133] He advocates that the Catholic Church should shape her institution with small groups stripped of the monarchic principle and grouped together following the Eastern spirituality.[134] To justify such an assimilation, Congar describes receiving "the spiritual riches" of the Schismatics as an "immense grace":

"I repeat: small groups with an intense spiritual life and great liberty are most successful. This is what explains the attraction not only of the great Eastern spiritualities, but also of orthodox Christianity. ... Certainly in orthodoxy [the Schismatic Church] there is a spiritual depth and, at the same time, a sense of freedom that are quite extraordinary. From the ecumenical standpoint, **we have an immense interest – above all, an immense grace – in receiving the spiritual riches of orthodoxy [the Schismatic Church], in breathing in accordance with our Eastern tradition.**" [135]

§ 87   Earlier, Congar had already affirmed his unrestricted admiration for "orthodoxy": "**I admit that I love orthodoxy [that is, the Greek Schismatics] very much and feel a strong attraction to it.**"[136]

We believe that the ensemble of texts analyzed in this Item 2 constitutes an expressive sample of the eulogies of Schismatics that reflect indirect offenses to the honor of the Church and the Faith.

3. Regarding the Jews

§ 88   Comments similar to those made about interconfessional *rapprochement* with the Protestants and the Greek Schismatics could be made about the post-Conciliar relationship with Jews.

---

[133] Cf. Albert Michel, entry *Congar*, in *DTC*, Tables générales, vol. I, col. 791.

[134] Fr. Congar was the one who introduced the principle of collegiality into conciliar theology. Drawing his inspiration from the structure of the Schismatic Church, Congar translated the Russian expression *sobornost* as "collegiality" (cf. Olivier Rousseau, "La Constitution *Lumen gentium* dans le cadre des mouvements rénovateurs de théologie et de pastorale des dernières décades," in V.A., *L'Église de Vatican II*, Paris: Cerf, 1966, vol. 2, p. 44). The term was adopted by many conciliar Fathers and then entered into general usage
In the excerpt above, Congar refers indirectly to that principle, which also should govern the "small groups" that he admires.

[135] *Jean Puyo interroge le Père Congar*, p. 234.

[136] *Ibid.*, p. 51.

However, from the doctrinal standpoint in this case there are serious aggravating circumstances that imply a complete rejection of the Catholic Faith.

Indeed, it is known that the Jews peremptorily deny the divinity of Our Lord Jesus Christ[137] and also the Holy Trinity.

---

[137] The Jews' denial of Our Lord's divinity can be considered either in the Gospels or in the course of History:

a. **The Gospels** show with crystalline clarity the denial by the Jews of Our Lord's divinity. Here are two examples:

• "The Jews therefore answered, and said to him: Do not we say well that you are a Samaritan, and has a devil? Jesus answered: I have not a devil: but I honor my Father, and you have dishonored me. ... Amen, amen, I say to you: if any man keeps my word, he shall not see death for ever.

"The Jews therefore said: Now we know that you have a devil. Abraham is dead, and the prophets, and you say: If a man keeps my word, he shall not taste death for ever. Are you greater than our father Abraham, who is dead? and the prophets are dead? Who do you make yourself to be?

"Jesus answered: If I glorify myself, my glory is nothing. It is my Father that glorifies me, of whom you say that he is your God. And you have not known him, but I know him. And if I shall say that I know him not, I shall be like to you, a liar. But I do know him, and do keep his word. Abraham, your father rejoiced that he might see my day: he saw it, and was glad.

"The Jews therefore said to him: You are not yet fifty years old, and have you seen Abraham? Jesus said to them: Amen, amen I say to you, before Abraham was made, I am. They took up stones therefore to cast at him. But Jesus hid himself, and went out of the temple" (Jo 8:48-59).

• "And the high priest said to him: I adjure thee by the living God, that you tell us if you are the Christ the Son of God. Jesus said to him: You have said it. Nevertheless I say to you, hereafter you shall see the Son of man sitting on the right hand of the power of God, and coming in the clouds of heaven.

"Then the high priest rent his garments, saying: He has blasphemed; what further need have we of witnesses? Behold you have heard the blasphemy. What think you? But they answering, said: He is guilty of death. Then did they spit in his face, and buffeted him: and others struck his face with the palms of their hands, saying: Prophesy unto us, O Christ, who is he that struck you?" (Mt 26:63-68).

b. **In History**, the Jews sustained this deicidal hatred of Christ through the centuries (see §§ 113-143, Notes 138, 168 of this Chapter). In the

§ 89   Based on these fundamental points, the Jews accept nothing of the Catholic Religion: They repudiate the dogmas related to Our Lord such as the Redemption, the Resurrection and the Ascension, the institution of the Holy Church, the role of the Blessed Virgin Mary, sanctifying grace and, consequently, the Sacraments. Therefore, they deny almost every article of the Creed.

Given these fundamental reasons of a specifically religious nature, as well as the inexorable historic hostility that Judaism as a religion has always showed toward the Holy Catholic Church,[138] there is perhaps no greater enmity in History than the

---

Talmud, the central text of the Jewish religion since the second century, one finds an impressive array of blasphemies made against Our Lord (see Note 143), compiled in the infamous booklet *Toledot Iesu* (*The Life of Jesus* in Hebrew), called "the most abominable work ever to come from human hands" (cf. Charles Freppel, *Saint Justin*, Paris: 1869, p. 410, *apud* Felix Vernet, *Juifs et chrétiens*, in A. d'Alos, *Dictionnaire Apologétique de la Foi Catholique*, Paris: Gabriel Beauchesne, 1924, vol. 2, col. 1682).

Toledot Iesu, written in Germany around the ninth century, calls Jesus an illegitimate son, gravely insults the Blessed Virgin and "explains" that Our Lord was killed as punishment for his crimes of heresy and sorcery.

Isidore Loeb, a 19th century French Jewish scholar, attests to the blasphemous character of the *Talmud*: "Why is it surprising to find attacks against Jesus in the *Talmud*? It would be strange not to find them. If anything should cause surprise, it would be that it does not have many more" (*Revue des Études Juives*, vol. 1, p. 256, *apud* J. Bonsirven, entry *Talmud*, in *DTC*, vol. 15, col. 26).

About the insults against Our Lord Jesus Christ in the *Talmud*, see the works cited by F. Vernet, *Juifs et chrétiens*. col. 1690; G. Dalman, in H. Laible, *Jesus Christus im Thalmud* (Berlin: 1891), pp. 5*-9*, cf. 9-88; H. L. Strack, *Jesus, die Haeretiker und die Christen nach den ältesten jüdischen Angaben* (Leipzig, 1910), pp. 1-21, cf. 18*-47*; R. Travers Herford, *A Dictionary of Christ and the Gospels*, Rest, vol. 2, pp. 877-878.

According to the *Talmud,* God played "the role of a child or an imbecile" (cf. J. H. Pignot, *Histoire de l'ordre de Cluny*, Paris: 1868, vol. 3, p. 535; Giulio Bartolocci, *Bibliotheca magna rabbinica,* full citation of source, vol. 1, pp. 552-642).

[138] The militant hatred of the Jewish religion against the Holy Catholic Church and Christendom can be assessed in various texts in the *Talmud*. The *Talmud* is considered one of the most important books

of the Jewish religion. Wielding a great influence on Jews, it contains the doctrines, laws and commentaries made by the most expressive rabbis on the *Torah* – the work that contains the principal books of the Old Testament – throughout History.

Toward the end of the 19th century, Prof. August Rohling, German Catholic theologian and scholar of Hebrew archeology at the University of Prague, translated the *Talmud*. He published his translation in the book *Le juif selon le Talmud*. In his work *La conjuration antichrétienne*, Msgr. Henri Delassus quotes various excerpts from Rohling's book that demonstrate not only the hatred, but also the visceral opposition of Judaism to the true Religion and Catholics. Among them we selected the following:

"1. The souls of the Jews have the privilege of being part of God himself. The souls of other peoples on earth come from the devil and are like those of animals. ...

"5. As they await the coming of the messiah, the Jews live in a continual state of war with all the other peoples. When the victory is definitive, the others will accept the Jewish faith. Only the Christians will not participate in this grace; on the contrary, they will be completely annihilated, because they descend from the devil. ...

"8. Only Jews are men, the other peoples are nothing more than different types of animals. A dog is worth more than a non-Jew. The non-Jews are not only dogs, but asses. The souls of non-Jews come from the impure spirit, whereas the souls of Israel come from the spirit of God.

"9. The non-Jews were created only to serve the Jews night and day, without deviating from their service.

"10. It is forbidden for the Jew to praise the learning or virtue of a Christian.

"11. It is not just to show mercy toward one's enemies. ...

"14. A Jew may be hypocritical with a non-Jew. ...

"16. God granted all power over the goods and the blood of other peoples to the Jews.

"17. A non-Jew who steals from a Jew, even be it a pittance, should be killed. On the contrary, a Jew is allowed to do evil to a non-Jew. To despoil a pagan [i.e., a non-Jew] is permitted. ...

"19. You may deceive a stranger [a non-Jew] and practice usury against him. ...

"21. He who loves a Christian hates his own creator ...

"23. Annihilate the best of the non-Jews. Take the lives of the most honest of the idolaters.

"24. If a pagan falls into a pit, we should cover the pit with a stone and

one between the True Church and the False Synagogue – an enmity whose consequences mark the whole New Testament.

§ 90

    Just as in the Old Testament, Esau sold his rights as firstborn son for a bowl of lentils[139] and the Edomites – the people born of Esau – were hostile to the offspring of Jacob, so also analogously in the New Testament, the False Synagogue rejected its right as the first-born. Showing a supreme ingratitude toward God, it consummated its apostasy in the tribunal of Pilate and on the scaffold of the Cross, calling down on itself the consequences of that heinous crime.[140] And from its children – the new Edomites – a people would be born[141] who would pass

------

try to prevent him from getting out. When we see him fall into a river or in danger of death, we should not save him. Maimonides advises giving death wounds to every non-Jew when it lies in our power to do so. It is just to exterminate every heretic [i.e., non-Jew] with one's own hand; whoever sheds the blood of the impious offers a sacrifice to God. ... Those who deny the teaching of Israel, especially the followers of the Nazarene, should be killed, and to execute them is always a good work; if this is not possible, we should try to bring about their deaths. But whoever kills a soul of Israel will be judged as if he had killed the entire world" (*apud* H. Delassus, *La conjuration antichrétienne*, Lille: Desclée de Brouwer, 1910, vol. 3, pp. 1125-1128).

It should be noted that soon after Prof. Rohling published his work, which created a sensation by revealing these violent commandments of the *Talmud*, he publicly challenged anyone to demonstrate that his translation was not accurate. Although his findings gave rise to many protests, to this day they have not been disproved (cf. *ibid.*).

[139] Cf. Gen 25:31-33.

[140] "And Pilate seeing that he was accomplishing nothing, but that a tumult was being made; taking water washed his hands before the people, saying: I am innocent of the blood of this just man; look you to it. **And the whole people answering, said: His blood be upon us and upon our children**" (Mt 27:24-25).

[141] Here we do not speak against the Jewish people as a race, but only against the religion. For us, the expression Jewish people is equivalent to Judaism, the Jewish Synagogue or the Jewish religion.

Anyone who would interpret our writings as anti-Semitic with a racist or Nazi tone would be wrong, given the complete ideological aversion of the Author for Nazism, Fascism and their other variations of lesser import. The Author has adopted as his own the legendary combat of his mentor, Prof. Plinio Corrêa de Oliveira, against Nazism and Fascism that he had already taken up in the 1930s and '40s, when even some Catholics looked favorably on those movements.

through History combating the new spiritual offspring of Jacob, the Catholics.[142]

Homage to and eulogies of the Jews

§ 91   Disregarding the doctrinal and historic hostility the Jews have always had for our Religion, in the Declaration *Nostra aetate* Vatican II lamented the previous conduct of Holy Mother Church toward the Hebrew people. This was tantamount to asking pardon from the Jews.[143] At the same time, this Declaration laid the ground work for an "absolution" of the crime of Deicide, even though the Jews had never denied their responsibility for the crime.[144]

Prof. Corrêa de Oliveira's total disagreement with the philosophy and the political and social goals of the movements of Hitler and Mussolini was clearly stated in 447 articles published in the weekly newspaper of the Archdiocese of São Paulo, *O Legionário*. See, for example, the following: "Genealogy of Monsters," June 26, 1938; "What Road Is Fascism Taking?" August 7, 1938; "From Godesberg to Munich," October 2, 1938; "Twilight of the Devils," October 9, 1938; "Dawn of the Gods," October 23, 1938; "Still Fascism," January 8, 1939; "The Example of the White Russians," January 22, 1939; "Charity and Folly," May 14, 1939; "The Most Hateful of Despotisms," March 31, 1940; "Falsification," April 21, 1940).

After his collaboration with *Legionário* ended, Prof. Corrêa de Oliveira continued to fight the Nazi-Fascist errors in the monthly magazine *Catolicismo* and the daily newspaper *Folha de S. Paulo* (cf. *Um homem, uma obra, uma gesta - Homenagem das TFPs a Plinio Corrêa de Oliveira*, São Paulo: Edições Brasil de Amanhã, 1989, p. 39).

Further, the Author wants to register here his complete repudiation of the inhumane atrocities perpetrated by the Nazis against the Jews during the Second World War.

[142] Cf. St. Augustine, *Civitas Dei*, lib. 16, chap. 42; Tertullian, *Adversus Judaeos*, in PL 1, 636-637.

[143] *Nostra aetate* 4g; see text in Note 144b, below.

[144] a. The crime of Deicide is incontestably declared and condemned in various places in the New Testament, notably in the words of St. Peter to the Israelites after having received the Holy Ghost: "There-fore **let all the house of Israel know most certainly that God has made both Lord, and Christ, this same Jesus whom you have crucified**" (Acts 2:36).

In another speech, the Prince of Apostles says: "**Ye men of Israel ... The God of Abraham, and the God of Isaac, and the God of Jacob, the God of our fathers, has glorified his Son Jesus, whom you**

From *Nostra aetate* to this day, both Pontiffs and official representatives of the Holy See have demonstrated an increasing eagerness to have closer ties with the Jews without asking them to renounce their anti-Catholic perfidy.

§ 92   Such is the case of John Paul II, who, speaking to the leaders of the Jewish association B'nai B'rith, calls them "friends" and "brothers." He supposes the relationship between Catholics and Jews to be a "dialogue between the first and second part of the Bible" and pays "deep respect" to the Jewish identity, professing an ever increasing respect for the differences between Judaism and Holy Mother Church.

To justify such great respect for the enemies of the Church, John Paul II appeals to a "mysterious spiritual bond" which, through Abraham, supposedly links the Catholics and the Jews, without taking into account Our Lord Jesus Christ. In his address of March 2, 1984 to the B'nai B'rith members the Pontiff affirms:

---

indeed delivered up and denied before the face of Pilate, when he judged he should be released. But you denied the Holy One and the Just, and desired a murderer to be granted unto you. But the author of life you killed, whom God has raised from the dead, of which we are witnesses" (Acts 3:12-15).

The guilt of the whole people is declared also here: "And Pilate seeing that he was accomplishing nothing, but rather that a tumult was being made; taking water washed his hands before the people, saying: **I am innocent of the blood of this just man; look you to it. And the whole people answering, said: His blood be upon us and upon our children**" (Mt 27:24-25).

b. Despite these and many other texts that reveal the divine judgment on the whole Hebrew people, Vatican Council II approved the Declaration *Nostra aetate*, which reads: "Even though the Jewish authorities and those who followed their lead pressed for the death of Christ (cf. Jn 19:6), still, **what happened in His passion cannot be charged without distinction against all the Jews then alive, nor against the Jews of today**. Although the Church is the new people of God, **the Jews should not be presented as rejected or accursed by God, as if this followed from the Holy Scriptures**" (NA, n. 4G).

To characterize this text of *Nostra aetate* as an "indult" or "absolution" for the Deicide is far from imaginary. This idea has been disseminated in a large part of the progressivist literature dealing with Judaism. In some books it is even expressed peremptorily as, for example, by Fr. Federici, S.J.: "The accusation of Deicide, although in a contorted style [at Vatican II], is declared to be without foundation" (Tommaso Federici, "Religione e religioni oggi," in V.A., *Incontri tra le religioni*, Verona: Mondadori, 1969, p. 31).

"Because, **my dear friends**, as I have often said since the beginning of my pastoral service as Successor of Peter, the Galilean fisherman, **the encounter between Catholics and Jews is not a meeting of two ancient religions each going its own way, and not infrequently, in times past, in grievous and painful conflict. It is a meeting between 'brothers,' a dialogue**, as I said to the Representatives of the German Jewish Community in Mainz,[145*] **'between the first and second part of the Bible.'** And just as the two parts of the Bible are distinct but closely related, so are the Jewish people and the Catholic Church.

"**This closeness must be manifested in many ways. First of all, in a deep respect for each other's identity. The more we know each other, the more we will learn to assess and respect our differences**.

"But then, and this is the great challenge we are called to accept: **respect does not mean estrangement, nor is it tantamount to indifference. On the contrary, the respect we speak of is based on the mysterious spiritual bond** (cf. NA, 4) **that brings us close together, in Abraham and, through Abraham, in God who chose Israel and brought forth the Church from Israel**.

"This 'spiritual bond,' however, involves a great responsibility. **Closeness in respect implies trust and frankness, and totally excludes distrust and suspicion.**"[146]

§ 93   We find another striking example of the official Vatican orientation in Cardinal Johannes Willebrands' speech to the International Jewish Committee assembled in Rome in 1985. According to the Cardinal, the new relationship with Judaism is, for Catholics, a sign of "fidelity to our own vocation" and a "part of our response to God."

Further, he affirms that the two Testaments support this new relationship and invokes as argument the assistance of the Holy Spirit in the Declaration *Nostra aetate* of Vatican II. It is certainly curious to note the change of emphasis the Cardinal gives the conciliar document, first presenting it as a practical or pastoral initiative and afterwards acclaiming it as a dogmatic teaching.[147] Willebrands states:

[145*] November 11, 1980.

[146] Address of John Paul II to the international leaders of the Jewish Anti-Defamation League of B'nai B'rith of March 2, 1984, in *Insegnamenti di Giovanni Paolo II*, VII, 1, 1984, p. 741.

[147] On the ambiguity of the concepts of pastoral and dogmatic applied

"If in these past years the Jews have better appreciated the novelty and virtually **unique character of the text of *Nostra aetate*, we Catholics have come to better perceive how it actually accords with** a more profound layer of our tradition and even **with the Word of God in the two Testaments. It could not be otherwise, since it would later be approved by an Ecumenical Council. The conciliar documents**, as I am sure that all of you know, **are considered**, according to traditional Catholic teaching, **as coming ultimately from the Holy Spirit, who assists, illuminates and, if need be, corrects the human process of reflection and decision**.

"**Therefore, if God is behind the text of *Nostra aetate*,** and also *Lumen gentium* n. 6 (which should not be forgotten in this regard), **then the new relations with Judaism are not a question of a practical decision,** however noble and grand the alleged reasons may be. **It is for us, as Catholics, a question of fidelity to our own vocation, a part of our response to God.** ...

"Let us draw a first conclusion from all this: **Jewish-Catholic relations in the Catholic Church are here to stay, rooted, as they are,** not in any passing phenomenon and even less in any type of guilt complex ... but **in a renewed consciousness of the 'mystery' of the Church**, as *Nostra aetate* says from its beginning. **This is to say that they are rooted in theological convictions, which is essential for the Catholic Church. We cannot walk away from these convictions. Our own identity would be at stake here.**"[148]

So, according to Cardinal Willebrands, the relations between the Church and the Jews are no longer "a matter of practical decision," that is, a pastoral matter, but rather a clear-cut dogmatic question, a decision "assisted, illuminated and corrected" by the Holy Spirit; a profound and deeply-rooted "theological conviction" that involves the very "identity" of Catholics and "fidelity to their own vocation."

Disregarding the crime of Deicide and the militant hostility of Judaism against the Church, Willebrands presents the acceptation of Judaism by the Catholics as an imposition of the divine will. This is not a small leap. One could say that with one

---

to the Council, see Vol. I, *In the Murky Waters of Vatican II*, Chap. VI, §§ 52-59.

[148] Johannes Willebrands, Allocution au Comité international de liaison, in *La Documentation Catholique*, *Bilan du dialogue judéo-chrétien*, January 19, 1986, pp. 122-123.

bound he leaps over the deepest abyss that ever existed between two religions. How does he justify this transformation?

§ 94   Like John Paul II, as well as the document *Nostra aetate*, Willebrands offers no solid argument. He merely appeals to a confused notion of the "mystery of the Church." Based on this enigmatic concept and without any further clarification, he draws the most radical doctrinal consequences. Then he concludes with a kind of threat: If Catholics do not establish a new relationship with the Jews, they will be unfaithful to the actual vocation God has given them.

This sets up a supremely incoherent situation. After the Deicide the Jewish religion became the principal enemy of the Holy Church;[149] it denied the Catholic Faith and the divinity of Our Lord. Today, Judaism has not renounced any of its errors or crimes. The Conciliar Church, however, opens its arms to the Jews, abandoning the centuries-old Catholic position without the Jews taking any step in her direction. Is this a conversion of the Jews or a judaization of the Catholics? Then, a veil is thrown over the maneuver to try to conceal the abandonment of the Holy Faith. And this veil is called "mystery."

§ 95   If a random "mystery" implying a change of the Catholic Faith is to be taken seriously, then the early Catholics should have believed the heretics of their time who first applied the tactic of concealing their perfidious doctrines with the veil of a "mystery."[150] According to this suicidal reasoning, the last faith-

---

[149] See in this Chapter Notes 137, 138, 140, 144.

[150] St. Vincent of Lérins, a 5th century Father of the Church, in his well-known work *Commonitorium* describes the temptations suffered by Catholics in the first centuries with the constant eruption of heresies. He explains how the heretics, in their eagerness to introduce new doctrines fraught with errors and to lure the lukewarm and incautious, covered them with a veil of "mystery" known only to themselves:
"For if what is new must be avoided, then what is old must be preserved; and if what is novel is profane, what is ancient is sacred. ... In truth the doctrines of the heretics are falsely named, since, in order to deceive people, they adorn ignorance, soot and darkness with the name of learning, fresh air and light ... Hear, then, how they say, 'Come, you fools and miserable ones who are usually called Catholics, and learn the faith which no one understands but us, which was hidden for many centuries but was recently revealed and made known. However, learn it stealthily and secretly: it will please you.' And then: 'After you learn it, teach it secretly so the world does not hear you and the Church does not know about it. Indeed, only a few have been given [the privilege] to know the secret of such a great mystery'" (in *Joannis*

ful who will live at the time of the Antichrist also should believe in the latter-day heretics who will likewise hide their errors behind a "mystery."[151] Either case is an absurdity.

§ 96   Notwithstanding this inconsistency, the representative of the Holy See closes his salutation to the Jews calling for a union between the Catholics and the Jews "like that of Jacob and Esau," where Jacob "prostrated himself on the ground seven times" before approaching the representatives of Esau:

"Yet again ... I feel obliged to repeat what I have already said many times in this speech: In the field of Jewish-Christian relations, **we are not expected to do or to not do this or that based on opportunism or purely human convenience, but because we believe in the one God of Abraham**, Isaac and Jacob, and also of Jesus Christ, **and because, despite all our differences, we have finally been reunited ... like Jacob and Esau**, who one day embraced each other and were reconciled as brothers before God (as said in Gen 33:3-4). It is a text I would like to read as an appropriate conclusion for my talk but, at the same time, perhaps as the starting point for our next encounter:

"'And he himself [Jacob] went forward and bowed down with his face to the ground seven times until his brother came near. But Esau ran to meet his brother and embraced him: and clasping him fast about the neck, and kissing him, both wept.'"[152]

§ 97   As closer ties are being made between representatives of the Catholic Church and the Jews, which entails praise being lavished upon the Church's enemies and insults being tossed at her, it is worth pointing out a symbolic event that is highly expressive of the progressivists' intentions. It is the appointment of Msgr. Jean-Marie Lustiger, a well-known Jew-Catholic, as

---

Cassiani Opera Omnia, Paris: J.P. Migne, 1865, vol. 1, cols. 666-667).

[151] Referring to the apostasy at the end of the world, St. John describes it in the symbolic language of the Apocalypse:

"And there came one of the seven angels, who had the seven vials, and spoke with me, saying: Come, I will show you the condemnation of the great harlot ... with whom they who inhabit the earth have committed fornication with the wine of her whoredom. And he took me away in spirit into the desert. And I saw a woman sitting upon a scarlet colored beast, full of names of blasphemies, ... and on her forehead a name was written: Mystery" (Apoc 17:1-6).

[152] J. Willebrands, Allocution to the International Liason Committee, p. 125.

Archbishop of Paris in 1981. Lustiger was made Cardinal by John Paul II in 1993.

In an interview given to the *Jewish Telegraphic Agency*, Archbishop Lustiger unrestrictively states that even after he became a Catholic, he did not abandon Judaism:

"For me, the decision to become a Christian did not present itself as a denial of my Jewish identity, but as an affirmation of it taken up in Christianity. ... **I have always considered myself a Jew,** even though this is not the opinion of the rabbis. **I was born a Jew and will remain one, even if this is unacceptable to many."**[153]

§ 98   Asked by the reporter if he was favorable to the Catholic Church proselytizing in Jewish circles, Lustiger categorically answered, "No," which in effect signifies that the Jews do not need to convert:

"No, not proselytism, because this makes no sense; it would be an infidelity. The Jewish faith, like the Christian faith, is a call from God ... If to be Jewish is to respond to a call from God – not only personally but also by belonging to the people – in whose name can one raise obstacles to this call?" [154]

"*Question*: Is there nonetheless **an apostolic mission on the part of the Church**?

"*Answer*: I must say that **in relation to Israel, such [a mission] does not exist. ... Once again, proselytism as it is generally understood, no."** [155]

Further on, the then newly named Archbishop of Paris said: "**For me, the vocation of Israel is to take the light to the goyim [non-Jews]. This is my hope, and I believe that Christianity is a way to accomplish it.**"[156]

These statements by Cardinal Lustiger follow the same line as the declarations of John Paul II and Cardinal Willebrands. According to Lustiger, the Church is the one that should change

---

[153] Jean-Marie Lustiger, Interview to the *Bulletin de l'Agence télégraphique juive, apud La Documentation Catholique*, March 1, 1981 p. 239.

[154] *Ibid.*

[155] *Ibid.*

[156] *Ibid.*, pp. 239-240.

while Judaism should be considered the immutable and unattackable matrix...

§ 99

If the Archbishop of Paris was baptized, he did so because he considered the Church a part of Judaism. This is what he said in an interview with the *Tribune Juive*:

"My appointment and presence in Paris sharply emphasizes the part of Judaism that Christianity carries in itself. It is as if suddenly the crucifixes were to start to be displayed with the yellow star. ... Embracing Christianity, I finally discovered the values of Judaism instead of renouncing them."[157]

Since the aim of this Chapter is to offer examples of offenses against the Catholic Religion expressed in the praise that Prelates and theologians lavish upon the enemies of the Church, it presented only the bare minimum indispensable for the Reader to evaluate the ensemble of these insults and relate them to the spirit of the Council.

4. Symbolism of the Visit of John Paul II to the Synagogue of Rome

§ 100

John Paul II's visit to the Synagogue of Rome on April 13, 1986 was a spectacular and paradigmatic gesture in his *rapprochement* with the Jews. An analysis of this action, unprecedented in the History of the Church, seems indispensable to this Chapter. Although, in the wake of John Paul II, Benedict XVI has visited three more synagogues – Cologne, New York and Rome – the landmark remains the first visit by Pope Wojtyla. This visit offers the painful advantage of confirming for the Reader our comments on the praise made of the Jews. Furthermore, it reveals a worsening situation that implies, in our view, more grievous offenses against the honor of the Catholic Religion and Faith.

A. The Symbolic-Theological Character of the Visit

§ 101

John Paul II's visit to the Synagogue of Rome has a deep theological character and should not be viewed as a merely "pastoral" action, as some would like to present it in order to attenuate its gravity. Fr. Giuseppe de Rosa, S.J., affirmed its theologi-

---

[157] Jean-Marie Lustiger, Interview to the weekly *Tribune Juive*, *apud Le Monde*, September 5, 1981, p. 19.

cal importance in an article in *La Civiltà Cattolica* commenting on the event:

"The Pope's meeting with the Hebrew community of Rome – which at least symbolically represented all the Hebrew communities in the world, has not only a 'human' content but an actual 'theological' one. It was the recognition – or better, **the confirmation,** 20 years after Vatican II – **of the 'turnabout' worked by the Council in the Church's theological approach to Judaism.**"[158]

§ 102
With his symbolic-theological visit, John Paul II clearly broke with the tradition of the Church on her treatment of the Jewish religion. Quoting the Pontiff's speech delivered in the Hebrew temple, Fr. de Rosa says exactly this:

"As for the 'historical' character of the event, it lies in the fact that this gesture definitively closes one era in the relations between Christians and Jews and opens a new one.

"What is its real meaning? The Pontiff himself said it when he declared that 'coming after the pontificate of John XXIII and Vatican Council II, **this meeting** in some way **brings to an end a long period,**' upon which we must continue to reflect so that it may provide us with timely teachings. The 'long period' to which the Pope refers spans the centuries of reciprocal aversion between Jews and Christians ... This 'long period' of Christian anti-Semitism ... closed with the pontificate of John XXIII and Vatican Council II."[159]

§ 103
On the day of the visit, the Italian newspaper *Il Giornale* also emphasized the importance of the event: "No trip of this pilgrim Pope to any continent was as long as the one he made today: The short distance between the Vatican palaces and the synagogue of Rome took two thousand years to cover."[160]

Fr. Giovanni Caprile, S.J., a known chronicler of Vatican II, wrote: "It was a truly historic event, the first and so far the only such visit in the life of the Church and the Hebrew community since the time of St. Peter."[161]

---

[158] Giuseppe de Rosa, "Ebrei e cristiani `fratelli' nel `fratelo Gesù," *La Civiltà Cattolica*, May 3, 1986, p. 261.

[159] *Ibid.*, p. 260.

[160] *Il Giornale*, April 13, 1986, *apud* Giovanni Caprile, "Il Papa al tempio ebraico di Roma," *La Civiltà Cattolica*, May 3, 1986, p. 267.

[161] *Ibid.*, p. 264.

In Israel the pontifical gesture was seen as "an unprecedented opening." [162]

§ 104   Also, the rabbis who greeted John Paul II did not hide their joy at seeing the Pontiff abandon the two thousand-year-old doctrinal position of the Church. Speaking in the name of the Jews, Rabbi Giacomo Saban was the first to express his "satisfaction at seeing a Roman Pontiff cross the threshold of a synagogue for the first time." [163]

Elio Toaff, chief rabbi of the Israelites of Rome, manifested a similar pleasure: "As chief rabbi of this community ... I want to express my intense satisfaction with the gesture that you desired and today carried out by coming to visit a synagogue for the first time in the history of the Church, a gesture that will be recorded in History."[164]

Therefore, the general opinion was that the gesture of John Paul II characterized a symbolic rejection of the former position of the Church, which, based on profound historical and theological reasons, always viewed the Jewish religion as an enemy of the Catholic Faith.[165]

B. Outright Condemnation of the Church's Previous Conduct

§ 105   John Paul II did not stop, however, at the symbolic abandonment of Catholic tradition. He also severely condemned previous actions of the Holy Church, deliberately ignoring the doctrinal reasons that caused them. Doing this, he acted as if religious opposition between Catholics and Jews was nothing but an emotional phenomenon. This is what he solemnly and emphatically declared, raising the resounding applause of the Jews in attendance: [166]

---

[162] Broadcast of Radio Israel, *apud* G. Caprile, "Il Papa al tempio ebraico di Roma," p. 265.

[163] Giacomo Saban, Greeting, *L'Osservatore Romano*, April 14-15, 1986, p. 5.

[164] Elio Toaff, Speech addressed to John Paul II, *in ibid.*

[165] See Note 168 of this Chapter.

[166] John Paul II received a standing ovation when he alluded to the supposed guilt of the Church for the persecutions suffered by the Jews through the course of History (cf. Carlo de Lucia, "Cari amici e fratelli ebrei e cristiani," *L'Osservatore Romano*, April 14-15, 1986, p. 4).

"An evaluation of centuries-old cultural conditionings could not, however, prevent us from recognizing that **the acts of discrimination, of unjustified restrictions of religious liberty and of oppression against the Hebrews in the sphere of civil liberty were objectively deplorable.** Yes, once again, in my person, the Church, in the words of the well-known Decree *Nostra aetate* (n. 4) **'deplores the hatred, persecutions and all manifestations of anti-Semitism directed against the Hebrews at all times and by whomsoever.' I repeat, 'by whomsoever.'''**[167]

§ 106   To whom does John Paul's condemnation ultimately apply?

First of all, it takes in the innumerable Popes who justly condemned the Jews; then, it includes the numerous Councils that did the same. Following in their footsteps are the great number of Fathers, Doctors and Saints who combated Judaism or left writings condemning its errors.[168] Finally, it encompasses all the

---

[167] John Paul II, Allocution at the Synagogue of Rome, *L'Osservatore Romano*, April 14-15, 1986, p. 4.

[168] Over the centuries, the Church never changed her firm, wise stance on the Jewish question. On the one hand, she prevented the Jews from being mistreated and permitted them to practice their religion in private. On the other hand, in the face of the impossibility of converting them, she rebuked them for the crime of Deicide, exhorted them to repent and isolated them to prevent them from perverting Catholics.

Thus, regarding Judaism, numerous Popes, Councils, Catholic theologians and writers, as well as the old Canon Law, taught, condemned and prescribed the following:

a. Popes

• **St. Gregory the Great** (590-604), in *Epistulae* 8, 25, cf. 9, 55, wrote that the Jews should not be granted unrestricted liberty because of the frequent offenses they made against the Faith (cf. F. Vernet, *Dictionnaire apologétique de la foi catholique - DAFC*, col. 1726).

In a letter to the Frankish Kings Theodoricus and Theodebertus and to Queen Brunhilde, St. Gregory reminded them that Christians, the members of Christ, must not be trampled upon by Jews, the enemies of Christ (cf. *Epistula* 9, 109, 110, cf. 3, 38, *apud ibid*, col. 1744).

• **Honorius I** (625-638) urged the VI Council of Toledo, held in 638, to act forcefully in relation to the Jews (cf. René Aigrain, *L'Espagne chrétienne*, in Fliche-Martin, *Histoire de l'Eglise*, vol. 5, p. 246).

• **Leo VII** (936-939) authorized Archbishop Frederic of Moguncia to expel the Jews from the city because of the constant attacks they launched against the Catholics (cf. Auguste Dumas, *Le sentiment re-*

ligieux et ses aberrations, in ibid., vol. 7, p. 463).

• **Innocent III** (1198-1216), in a letter of January 17, 1208, addressed to the Count of Nevers, lamented the employment of Jews by feudal lords, calling them the "ministers of their extortions" because they exploited Christians through the practice of usury; see also his letters of January 16, 1205, to the King of France and of January 10, 1208, to the Bishop of Auxerre, (cf. A. Fliche, *La réforme de l'Eglise*, in Fliche-Martin, *Histoire de l'Eglise*, vol. 10, p. 142).

• **Gregory IX** (1227-1241), after receiving a report compiled by Nicolas Donin, a converted Jew from La Rochelle, that showed 35 articles in the *Talmud* insulting the Christian Faith, wrote to the Western Bishops and Sovereigns ordering all copies of the Jewish book to be confiscated. In 1239 he appointed William of Auvergne, Bishop of Paris, to make an investigation of the book. Once examined, the *Talmud* was condemned and copies of it were publicly burned in Paris in 1242. At the request of the Jews, the book was examined again in 1248 and was definitively condemned by William of Auvergne and the doctors of theology of the University of Paris, including St. Albert the Great (cf. F. Vernet, "Juifs et Chrétiens," in DAFC, col. 1691; Christine Thouzellier, *L'enseignement et les universités*, in Fliche-Martin, *Histoire de l'Eglise* vol. 10, pp. 379-380).

In the work *Excerpta talmudica* [*Excerpts from the Talmud*], written to justify this condemnation, one reads: "By a secret design of Providence, the errors, blasphemies and outrages contained in the *Talmud* had hitherto escaped the attention of the Doctors of the Church. Finally the wall has been breached; now one can clearly see these reptiles, these abominable idols that the House of Israel adores" (*apud*. F. Vernet, "Juifs et Chrétiens," *ibid*.).

• **Innocent IV** (1243-1254) ordered the *Talmud* to be burned because it was filled with errors and blasphemies (cf. *Registres d'Innocent IV*, vol. 1, n. 682, Potthast, 11376, *Chartularium*, n. 131, *ibid.*, vol. 1, nn. 173, 178; *Saint Louis et Innocent IV*, pp. 302-306, *apud* C. Thouzellier, *L'enseignement et les universités*, p. 380). In the Bull *Sicut tua nobis* of July 23, 1254, he authorized the Archbishop of Vienna to expel the Jews from his Diocese on account of their actions against the Catholic Faith and their disobedience of Church statutes (cf. F. Vernet, "Juifs et Chrétiens," col. 1739).

• **Clement IV** (1265-1268), in the Bull *Damnabili perfídia* of July 15, 1267, also condemned the *Talmud* (*ibid.*, col. 1692).

• **Honorius IV** (1285-1287), in the Bull *Nimis in partibus anglicanis* of November 18, 1285, repeated the condemnation of his predecessor (*ibid.*).

• **John XXII** (1316-1334) again censured the errors of the *Talmud* in the Bull *Dudum felicis recordationis* of September 4, 1320 (*ibid.*).

• **Eugene IV** (1431-1447), in the Bull *Dudum ad nostram* of August 8, 1442, prohibited the Jews not only from living with Christians, as the Third Lateran Council had already established (Decree V, VI, 5), but also from living among Christians, in view of the continuous blasphemies and attacks of the Jews against the Catholic Faith (*ibid.*, col. 1740).

• **Nicholas V** (1447-1455), **Calixtus III** (1455-1458) and **Paul II** (1464-1471) reissued or renewed the decisions of their predecessors (*ibid.*, 1728).

• **Sixtus IV** (1471-1484), in the Bull *Intenta semper salutis* of May 31, 1484, ordered that Jews and Muslims in Spanish lands should live separate from Christians, should wear distinctive clothing, and should not have Christian maids or servants in their houses, in addition to other measures aimed at protecting the faithful from dangers to the Faith resulting from living with Jews (cf. Bernardino Llorca, *Bulario Pontificio de la Inquisición Española*, Rome: Pontificia Università Gregoriana, 1949, pp. 106-108).

• **Leo X** (1513-1521) was known for his goodness toward the Jews, a fact recognized even by Hebrew historians of the time. Nevertheless, he was obliged on several occasions to take action against abuses practiced by them. When he learned that the Jews in Venice had published a book against the Catholic Faith, he reacted strongly in his Brief of May 25, 1518, addressed to the Nuncio in Venice (cf. *Arm.* 39, vol. 31, 1518, n. 48; and to the Doge, *Arm.* 40, vol. 3, n. 331, Vatican Secret Archives, *apud* L. Pastor, *Historia de los Papas*, vol. 8, p. 350).

• **Julius III** (1550-1555) approved the confiscation and burning of talmudic books by the Inquisition in 1553. He also authorized the Edict of the Inquisition of September 12, 1553, ordering all Princes, Bishops and Inquisitors to do the same. In the Bull *Cum sicut nuper* of May 29, l554, the Pope ordered the Jews to hand over all their books containing blasphemies or insults against Our Lord Jesus Christ (cf. *Bull.* 6, pp. 482-483, cf. *ibid,* vol. 13, p. 208).

• **Paul IV** (1555-1559) enacted strong measures to defend the integrity of the Faith and prevent the Jews from dominating Catholics. In the Bull *Cum nimis absurdum* of July 14, 1555, the Pope ordered the Hebrews of Rome and other cities in the Papal States to live separate from the Christians in their own section of the city. He established that there could not be more than one synagogue per city and that the Jews should wear a yellow cap; also he proscribed that Jews should have Catholic servants, work in public on Catholic feast days, write fraudulent contracts, use Hebrew in their accounting books, etc. (cf. *Bull.* 6, p. 498, cf. *ibid.*, vol. 14, pp. 234-235).

The Jews tried to bribe Paul IV by offering him 40,000 *escudos* to annul that Bull. (See a report on this topic in *Revue des Études Juives*, XX, 68, cf. Masio, *Letters*, 515, Berliner, II, 2, 7; Rodocanachi, 40-42; see also *Letters of Saint Ignatius*, 5, pp. 288-289, cf. L. Pastor, *Historia de los Papas*, vol. 14, p. 236).

Along with other measures, the Pontiff ordered the destruction of the talmudic and anti-Catholic books of the Jews (cf. Caracciolo, *Vita*, 4, 11; Erler, in the Archive of Canon Law, L III, 49; Reusch, I, 48; Vogelstein-Rieger, II, 156-157; Berliner, II, 2, 8-9; see also Caracciolo,

Censura y confisco de los libros judios en los Estados da la Iglesia, Frankfurt, 1891, cf. *ibid.*, vol. 14, p. 239).

• **Pius IV** (1560-1565) in 1564 placed the *Talmud* on the *Index librorum prohibitorum* [Index of Forbidden Books] and forbade books interpreting, expounding or commenting on it (cf. F. Vernet, "Juifs et Chrétiens," col. 1693).

• **St. Pius V** (1566-1572) in the Bull *Hebraeorum gens* of February 26, 1569, expressly condemned the Jews who dedicated themselves to the practice of "divination, sortilege, sorcery and witchcraft" (cf. *Bull. Rom.*7, p. 740, cf. L. Pastor, *Historia de los Papas*, vol. 17, p. 301). In that Bull, St. Pius V also accused the Jews of other crimes such as usury, theft, receiving stolen goods and exploiting prostitution. He closes the Bull with these words: "Finally, we consider as known and proven how vilely this perverse [Jewish] generation offends against the name of Christ, how hostile it is to those who bear the name of Christians, even making attempts against their lives" (*apud* F. Vernet, "Juifs et Chrétiens," col. 1712).

By a decree of February 26, 1569, the Saint expelled the Jews from the Papal States since, in addition to their crimes of usury and attempts to pervert Catholics, the Jews traitorously spied for the Muslims and supported their plans to conquer Christendom (cf. Brief of May 3, 1569, *apud* Laderchi, 1569, n 187). In this Brief, he says: "We know that this most perverse people have always been the cause and seed bag of almost all the heresies" (*apud* L. Pastor, *Historia de los Papas*, vol. 17, p. 306).

Along with this vigilant zeal against the Jewish perfidy, St. Pius V had an ardent desire for their salvation. Thus he was able to win the conversion of a good number of Hebrews, whom he baptized with his own hands. One of the most remarkable conversions he achieved was that of the chief rabbi of Rome, Elias, followed by the conversions of his three sons and one grandson. On the third day of Pentecost, June 4, 1566, they received Baptism with great solemnity at St. Peter's Basilica in the presence of the Sacred College of Cardinals and a multitude of the faithful (cf. *ibid.*, vol. 17, pp. 306-307).

• **Gregory XIII** (1572-1585), in his Brief of May 27, 1581, warned against converted Jews who returned to Judaism: "We have heard that many who recently converted from the Jewish perfidy to the Christian Faith, having repudiated Christ, have returned to Judaism like a dog to its vomit" (*apud ibid.*, vol. 19, p. 281).

In the Bull *Antiqua Judaeorum improbitas* of June 1, 1581, the Pontiff established these conditions when Jews should submit to the vigilance of Inquisitors: a) when they attack Catholic dogmas; b) when they invoke devils or offer sacrifices to them; c) when they teach Christians to do the same; d) when they utter blasphemies against Our Lord Jesus Christ and Our Lady, that is, "blasphemies considered heretical as such"; e) when they encourage Catholics to apostatize to Judaism or to abandon the Catholic Faith; f) when they prevent a Jew or an infidel from professing the Christian Faith; g) when they consciously favor apostates or heretics; h) when they keep or disseminate heretical, talmudic or other condemned Jewish books; i) when, out of scorn for the Holy Eucharist, Our Lord Jesus Christ and Christians, they crucify – especially on Good Friday – a lamb or a sheep, spit on it, or otherwise insult it; j) when they hire Christian nursemaids, in violation of the canons, or oblige Catholic wet nurses to pour their milk into the latrines and sewers after they have received Holy Communion (*apud* F. Vernet, "Juifs et Chrétiens," col. 1737).

In the Brief of February 28, 1581, Gregory XIII reaffirmed the prohibition against Jewish physicians tending Christian patients (cf. L. Pastor, *Historia de los Papas*, vol. 19, p. 282).

• **Clement VIII** (1592-1605), in the Bull *Cum Hebraeorum* of February 28, 1593 (cf. Reusch, I, 50, 333, 339, 534), proscribed talmudic and cabalistic books, as well as works written in Hebrew containing errors (See the list of books destroyed in Cremona reported by Sixtus of Siena, *Bibliotheca sancta*, Paris, 1610, pp. 310-311; cf. F. Vernet, "Juifs et Chrétiens," col. 1738). The prohibition contained in this Bull was included as a norm in the *Index* published on March 27, 1596.

In 1592 Clement VIII re-established the preaching of sermons aimed at the conversion of the Jews, and, in the Bull *Caeca et obdurata* of January 25, 1593, he reiterated the decrees of Paul IV and St. Pius V expelling them from the Papal States, with the exception of the cities of Rome, Ancona and Avignon (cf. L. Pastor, *Historia de los Papas*, vol. 24, pp. 111-112; F. Vernet, "Juifs et Chrétiens," col. 1731).

• **Urban VIII** (1623-1644) sent a Brief to the King of Spain on January 15, 1628, forbidding the crime of usury practiced by the Jews of Portugal (cf. *Epistula 5*, Secret Papal Archive, in L. Pastor, *Historia de los Papas*, vol. 28, p. 285).

• **Benedict XIV** (1740-1758) signed and promulgated a document on September 15, 1751, reaffirming the cautionary measures taken toward the *Talmud* by the Popes since Innocent IV (cf. F. Vernet, "Juifs et Chrétiens," col. 1694).

• **Pius VI** (1775-1799) published two edicts, one in October 1775 and another in January 1793, confirming the directives of Benedict XIV regarding the Jews (cf. *Analecta juris pontificii*, Rome, 1860, pp. 1422-1423; cf. F. Vernet, "Juifs et Chrétiens," col. 1694).

• **St. Pius X** (1903-1914), through a letter by his Secretary of State Cardinal Merry del Val, warmly praised the classic work by Msgr. Henri Delassus, *La conjuration antichrétienne*, which exposes the conspiracy of Judaism and Freemasonry against the Church and Christian Civilization (cf. Henri Delassus, *La conjuration antichrétienne*, vol. 1, p. V).

b. Councils

The following councils should also be included in the radical "anathema" issued by John Paul II at the Rome synagogue:

• The **Council of Elvira** (302), held at the end of Diocletian's persecution against the Christians, issued a canon that forbade Christians from giving their daughters in marriage to Jews; another canon prohibited Christians from sitting at the table with Hebrews (cf. H. Delassus, *La conjuration antichrétienne*, vol. 3, p. 1157).

• These prohibitions were reiterated by the **Councils of Laodicea** (4th century), **Vannes** (465), **Agda** (506) **Epaona** (517), as well as by the three **Councils of Orleans** (530, 533 and 541) (cf. *ibid.*).

In a canon repeated in the Decree of Gratian (III, D.IV, 93), the abovementioned Council of Agda established a series of precautions to be taken before baptizing Jews "who, because of their perfidy, often return to their vomit" (cf. F. Vernet, "Juifs et Chrétiens," col. 1734).

• The **Council of Mâcon** (581) enjoined Jews from holding posts allowing them to impose penalties on Christians (cf. H. Delassus, *La conjuration antichrétienne*, vol. 3, p. 1157).

• The **Council of Toledo** (589), in its canon 14, barred Jews from taking Christian women as wives (cf. R. Aigrain, *L'Espagne Chrétienne*, in Fliche-Martin, *Histoire de l'Eglise*, vol. 5, p. 238).

• The **Council of Paris** (614) sustained the prohibition against giving Jews public posts, whether civil or military (cf. H. Delassus, *La conjuration antichrétienne,* vol. 3, pp. 1157-1158).

• The **Fourth Council of Toledo** (633), in canon 59, determined that the sons of Jews who had falsely converted and then returned to Judaism should be educated in Catholic monasteries; it also ratified the measures adopted by King Sisenando regarding the Jews (cf. R. Aigrain, *L'Espagne Chrétienne*, in Fliche-Martin, *Histoire de l'Eglise*, vol. 5, p. 241).

• The **Sixth Council of Toledo** (638), in canon 3, issued stern words against the Jews (cf. *ibid.*, pp. 245-246.)

• The **Seventeenth Council of Toledo** (694) was held to analyze a plot aiming to install Judaism with the appearance of the Catholic Religion in Spain (cf. *ibid.*, p. 259).

• Other Councils also forbade Catholics from hiring Jewish physicians, servants and nursemaids. According to some Catholic moralists of the 18th century, depending on the circumstances, violating these prescriptions could constitute a mortal sin (cf. H. Delassus, *La conjuration antichrétienne,* vol. 3, p. 1158).

• The **Second Ecumenical Council of Nicaea** (787) denounced the false conversions of Jews (cf. Terminus, canon 8, in *Conciliorum Oecumenicorum Decreta*, Rome: Herder, 1962, pp. 121-122).

• The **Council of Metz** (888), reaffirming former canons, in canon 7 prohibited Christians from taking meals with Jews (cf. Mansi, vol. 18, col. 79, *apud* A. Dumas, *Le sentiment religieux et ses aberrations*, in Fliche-Martin, *Histoire de l'Eglise*, vol. 7, p. 463).

• The **Third Ecumenical Council of Lateran** (1179) forbade wealthy Hebrews from taking Christian wet nurses and slaves into their service (cf. Jean Rousset de Pina, *La politique italienne d'Alexandre III et la fin du schisme, in ibid.*, vol. 9/2, p. 167). It also anathematized those who, preferring Jews to Christians, received the testimonies of Jews against Christians and not that of Christians against Jews, since the latter "should be subjected to Christians" (Decret. II, XX, 21; cf. F. Vernet, "Juifs et Chrétiens," col. 1744).

• The **Fourth Council of Avignon** (1209) forbade Christians from dealing with Jews in any financial matters; canons 3 and 4 impose the threat of excommunication for such dealings (cf. A. Fliche, *La réforme de l'Eglise*, in Fliche-Martin, *Histoire de l'Eglise,* vol. 10, p. 174).

• The **Fourth Ecumenical Council of Lateran** (1215), in canon 67, condemned usurious Jewish money-lenders and prohibited Christians from engaging in commerce with them. Canon 68 ordered Jews to wear clothing that would distinguish them from Catholics and also forbade them to appear in public on Good Friday to prevent them from mocking Christians with their festive dress. Canon 69 reaffirmed the prohibition of the Council of Toledo against Jews holding public posts. Canon 70 condemned the Jews who claimed to have converted to the Catholic Faith but continued to practice rites of the Hebrew religion (cf. *Conciliorum Oecumenicorum Decreta*, pp. 241-243).

• The **Council of Narbonne** (1227) established that Jews should wear a distinguishing mark in the shape of a small circle. According to J. Levi (*Revue des Études Juives*, 1892, 1. 24), the circle symbolized the Host, habitually profaned by Jews. This emblem was adopted to be worn by the Jews everywhere except Spain. The Popes imposed such a symbol to distinguish Jews from Christians because, writes F. Vernet, "taking advantage of the confusion, the Jews have infiltrated Catholic ranks and committed crimes that would have been difficult or impossible to carry out had it been known or suspected that they were Jews" (F. Vernet, "Juifs et Chrétiens," col. 1741).

• The **Ecumenical Council of Basel** (1434), among other measures, required the Jews to hear Christian preachers and prohibited Catholics from participating in Jewish feasts (Session 20, *Decretum de Iudaeis et neophytis*, in *Conciliorum Oecumenicorum Decreta*, pp. 459-460).

Other Bulls & Decrees

There are still other Bulls of Popes and Decrees of Roman Congregations regarding the Jews, published in various collections and monographs, that number in the hundreds. In the entry "Juifs et Chrétiens" (cols. 1735s-1736), F. Vernet presents copious documentation on this topic. We transcribe it here for Readers who may be interested in learning more on the matter.

Corpus juris canonici, Decretalia V. 6; *Sextus Decretal,* V, 13; *Decreta Gratiani,* I^a, XLV, 3, 5, LIV, 12-18; II, XIV, VI, 2, XXVIII, I, 10-15, 17; IIIq, IV, 93, 94, 98 and *Septimus Decretal,* V, 1; A. Guerra, *Pontificiarum Constitutionum epitome* (Venice, 1772), vol. 1, pp. 191-196 (summarizes 38 Bulls published in the *Bullarium Romanum, Bullarium magnum,* and other works); L. Ferraris, *Prompta bibliotheca canonica* (Venice, 1782), vol. 4, pp. 208-237 (summarizes a large number of Constitutions of Popes and the Roman Congregations); E. Rodocanachi, *Le Saint Siège et les Juifs* (Paris, 1891), pp. 322-329 (gives an overall picture of the main Bulls relating to the Jews; F. Vernet in "Le Pape Martin V et les juifs," in *Revue des Questions Historiques* (Paris, 1892), vol. 51, pp. 410-423 (analyzes 84 documents), and in "Papes et Juifs au XIe. siècle," in *L'Université catholique,* Lyon, 1896, vol. 21, pp. 73-86, (analyzes documents from the *Formularium* of Marin d'Eboli regarding the Jews); M. Stern, *Urkundliche Beiträge über die Stellung der Päpste zu den Juden* (Kiel, 1893-1895), 2 vols. (The first volume contains the documents by Martin V and his successors; the second spans from Innocent III to Innocent IV); K. Eubel, "Zu dem Verhalten der Päpste gegen die Juden," in *Römische Quartalschrift* (Rome, 1899), vol. 13, pp. 29-43 (about the Popes who preceded Martin V); Constant, *Les Juifs devant l'Eglise et l'histoire* (Paris, n.d.), 2nd ed., pp. 267-323 (publishes 16 Bulls on the topic); Grégoire des Rives, *Epitome canonum conciliorum* (Lyons, 1663), pp. 264-268; A. Geiger, "Das Verhalten der Kirche gegen das Judenthum," in *Das Judenthum und seine Geschichte* (Breslau, 1870), vol. 2; F. Frank, *Dir Kirche und die Juden* (Regensburg, 1893).

About the Church and the Jews in the Papal States, see: F. Gregorovius, "Le ghetto et les Juifs de Rome," in *Promenades en Italie* (Paris, 1894), pp. 1-60; E. Natali, *Il ghetto di Roma* (Rome, 1887), vol. 1; E. Rodocanachi, *Le Saint Siége et les Juifs - Le ghetto à Rome* (Paris, 1891); A. Berliner, *Geschichte der Juden in Rom* (Frankfurt, 1893), 3 vols.; H. Vogelstein and P. Rieger, *Geschichte der Juden in Rom* (Berlin, 1895-1896), 2 vols.

On the Church and the Jews of Avignon, see: L. Bardinet, "Condition civile des Juifs du Comtat-Venaissin pendant le séjour des Papes à Avignon," *Revue Historique* (Paris, 1880), vol. 12, pp. 1-47; R. de Maulde, *Les Juifs dans les Etats français du Saint-Siège au Moyen Âge* (Paris, 1886), as well as numerous articles in *Revue des Études Juives.*

c. Church Fathers, Catholic Theologians & Writers

The following authors – including Doctors of the Church – criticized the Jewish onslaught against the Church and the Catholic Faith and are also supposedly included in John Paul II's "anathema":

• From the Early Christians to the Edict of Milan (313):

St. Justin, *Dialogus cum Tryphone*; Tertullian, *Adversus Judaeos*; St. Cyprian, *Testimonia ad Quirinus*; Pseudo-Cyprian, *De montibus Sina et Sion* and *Adversus Judaeos*; Novaciano, *De cibis judaicis*; Celsus, *Ad Vigilium episcopum de Judaica incredulitate*; *De solemnitatibus, sabbatis et neomeniis.* Also St. Irenaeus, Origen, Commodian, Ariston of Pella, Mistiades, St. Serapius of Antioch, Theodotus of Ancyra, Zophirus, Artapanus(cf. F. Vernet, *Juifs et Chrétiens,* in *DAFC,* col. 1749).

• **From 313 to 1100:**

In the East: Eusebius; St. Gregory of Nyssa, St. John Chrysostom, St. Basil of Seleucia, St. Anastasius of Sinai, St. Ephrem, St. Isidore of Pelusa, Theodore Abucara, Eusebius of Emesa, St. Cyril of Alexandria, Theodoretus of Cyrus, Jerome of Jerusalem, Leontius of Naples in Cyprus and Stephen of Bostra.

In the West: Evagrius, *Altercatio Simionis judaei et Theophili christiani*; *De altercatione ecclesiae et synagogae dialogus*; St. Augustine, *Sermo contra Judaeos paganos et arianos*; *Tractatus contra quinque haereses*; St. Isidore of Seville, *De Fide Catolica contra Judaeos*; Paulo Alvares de Cordoba; St. Agobard of Lyons, *De judaicis superstitionibus*, X; *De insolentia judaeorum*, IV; Amolon of Lyons, *Contra Judaeos.* Also St. Ambrose, St. Leo the Great, St. Sidonius Apollinarius, St. Jerome, Cassiodore, St. Gregory the Great, Severus of Minorca, St. Maximus of Turin, St. Ildefonso of Toledo, St. Julian of Toledo, Canon Henri, Rabano Mauro, Fulbert de Chartres, St. Peter Damian and St. Bruno of Würzburg.

• **From 1100 to 1500:**

Odon of Cambrai; Gilbert Crispin; Guibert de Nogent; Ruppert de Deutz; Peter the Venerable, *Adversus Judaeorum inveteratam duritiam*; Richard of Saint-Victor, *De Emmanuele*, book II; Inguetto Contard; Gautier de Chatillon and Baudouin de Valenciennes; Alain de Lille, *De Fide Catholica*; William of Auvergne; St. Albert the Great; St. Thomas Aquinas, *De regimine Judaeorum ad ducissam Brabantiae*; *Summa Theologiae*, III, q.47, a.5-6; Raymond Martin, *Pugio Fidei adversus Mauros et Judaeos*; Victor Porcheto de Selvatici; Nicolas de Lire; Lauterio de Batineis; Bernard Oliver; Jean de Baconthorpe; Paul of Venice; Stephan Bodiker, Bishop of Brandenburg; Cardinal Juan de Torquemada; Peter George Schwartz; St. Antoninus of Florence, *Dialogus discipulorum Emauntinorum cum peregrino*; Paulo Morosini, *De aeterna temporalique Christi generatione*; Pedro de Brutis, *Victoriae adversus Judaeos*; etc.

Several writers of Jewish origin who converted to the Catholic Faith have also pointed out the errors of the synagogue: R. Samuel de Fez, *De adventu Messiae* (PL 149, 337-368); Pedro Alfonso, *Dialogi* (PL 1.157, 535-572); Hermann (Judas of Colon), *De sua conversione* (PL 1.170, 805-836); Guillaume de Bourges, Paul Christiani and Jeronimo de Santa Fe, *Tractatus contra Judaeorum perfidiam*; Paul de Bonnefoy, *Liber fidei*; Paul de Bourges or de Santa Maria, *Scrutinium Scripturarum*; Alphonso de Spina, *Fortalitium fidei*; Pedro de la Caballeria, *Zelus Christi*; etc.

Catholics in the History of the Church who, in defense of the Faith, fought against Judaism. Therefore, John Paul II's "anathema" applies to the whole Church in over 2,000 years of her History – "whomsoever" and "at all times."

§ 107   When he cast the "anathema" in his Allocution, John Paul II invoked a very recent "tradition," as he himself noted. That is, he relied on the Council with its Declaration *Nostra aetate* and the example of John XXIII. Regarding the latter, he asserted:

"The legacy to which I now have recourse is precisely that of Pope John, who, once when he passed by here [the syna-

---

• From 1500 to our days:

We cite below only a few of the most consequential works from the vast number of writings attesting to the Jewish perfidy against the Church:

J.L. Vives, *De veritate Fidei Christianae*; P. du Plessis-Mornay, *Traité de la verité de la Religion Chrétienne*; P. Charron, *Les trois vérités contre tous les athées, idolâtres, juifs*; H. Grotius, *De veritate Religione Christianae*; Bossuet, *Discours sur l'histoire universelle*; J. Bartolocci, *Bibliotheca magna rabbinica*; P.-L. B. Drach, *Lettres d'un rabin converti aux Israélites ses frères*; J.M. Bauer, *Le judaïsme comme preuve du Christianisme*; P. Loewengard, *La splendeur catholique, du Judaïsme à l'Eglise* (cf. F. Vernet, *Juifs et Chrétiens*, col. 1751-1752).

d. Canon Law

The proscriptions established in past Canon Law about the Jews, which John Paul II also supposedly included in his "anathema," were summarized by Msgr. Kohn, an Austrian Bishop of the last century of Jewish origin and a professor of Canon Law:

1. Jews may neither have Catholic slaves nor employ Catholic maids for their houses or families. Catholics are forbidden to accept permanent paid employment in Jewish homes;

2. Catholic women are particularly forbidden from accepting employment as wet nurses in Jewish homes;

3. In case of illness, Catholics are forbidden recourse to the services of Jews or to use medicines prepared by Jewish hands;

4. Catholics are forbidden, under pain of excommunication, to live with Jews;

5. Jews should be barred from holding public posts that would give them authority over Catholics;

6. Catholics are forbidden to attend Jewish weddings and take part in their feasts;

7. Christians may not invite Jews for meals or accept invitations from them (cf. H. Delassus, *La conjuration antichrétienne*, vol. 3, pp. 1161-1162).

gogue] ... he ordered his car to be stopped in order to bless the throng of Jews who were leaving this very temple."[169]

Now then, that 22-year-old "tradition" of the Council and a single example of John XXIII hardly carry the weight to bring into question the 2,000-year-old tradition of Catholic teaching. Rather, the former's blatant opposition to the latter seems to signify a rupture with the Magisterium.

§ 108   In this case, John Paul II clearly appeared to break with a tradition of the Ordinary Papal Magisterium. Facing this patent contradiction, a faithful Catholic is obliged to ask: Who is right? The Church, who for serious reasons of a theological nature, was vigilant for 2,000 years against the malice of the synagogue? Or John Paul II, who, ignoring that wise rationale, went to the synagogue of Rome and, without even alluding to the ancient errors of the Jews, defended them and condemned the prior conduct and constant teaching of the Church on the matter?

C. Analysis of John Paul II's Allocution to the Jews

§ 109   To analyze the significance of the Pontiff's visit to the synagogue, let us look closely at the Allocution he delivered there. Here is the nucleus of the papal speech:

"Today's visit is intended to make a decisive contribution to the restructuring of good relations between our two communities, following the examples given by so many men and women from both parts who were and still are earnestly committed **to overcome the old prejudices** and allow for the ever fuller recognition of that 'bond' and 'common spiritual heritage' existing between Jews and Christians.

"This is the wish already expressed in paragraph n. 4 of the conciliar Declaration *Nostra aetate*,[170] to which I just re-

---

[169] John Paul II, Allocution in the synagogue of Rome, *L'Osservatore Romano*, April 14-15, 1986, p. 4 .

[170] John Paul II appears to refer mainly to the middle of chapter IV of *Nostra aetate*, which reads: "True, authorities of the Jews and those who followed their lead pressed for the death of Christ (cf. Jn 19:6), but what happened in His passion cannot be blamed upon all the Jews then living, without distinction, nor upon the Jews of today. Although the Church is the new people of God, the Jews should not be presented as repudiated or cursed by God, as if such views followed from the Holy Scripture. ... Indeed, the Church repudiates all persecutions against any man. Moreover, mindful of her common patrimony with the Jews, and motivated by the Gospel's spiritual love and by no political considerations,

ferred, about relations between the Church and non-Christian religions. **The decisive turnabout in relations between the Catholic Church and Judaism**, and with Jews individually, took place with this brief but incisive paragraph.

"We all are aware that three points are especially outstanding among the many riches of this n. 4 of *Nostra aetate*. I would like to emphasize them here before you, in these truly unique circumstances.

"*The first* is that **the Church of Christ discovers her 'link' with Judaism by 'sounding the depths of her own mystery.'**[171*] **The Hebrew religion is not 'extrinsic' to us, but is somehow 'intrinsic' to our religion. We have, therefore, relations with it that we do not have with any other religion. You are our beloved brothers and, in a certain way, one could say, our older brothers.**

"*The second point* stressed by the Council is that **no atavistic or collective guilt can be attributed to the Jews as a people for 'what was done in the Passion of Jesus'**[172*] **– neither indistinctively to the Jews of that time, nor to those who came later, nor to those of today. Therefore, the pretended theological justification of discriminatory or persecutory measures is inconsistent.** The Lord will judge each one – be he Jew or Christian – 'according to his own works' (cf. Rom. 2:6).

"*The third point* in the conciliar Declaration that I want to underscore is a consequence of the second: **It is not licit to say ... that the Jews are 'reprobates or accursed,' as this were taught in or could be deduced from Sacred Scriptures and the Old or New Testaments.** This was already stated in the same passage of *Nostra aetate* and also in the Dogmatic Constitution *Lumen gentium* (n. 6) ... Based on these convictions we support our present relations.

"**On the occasion of this visit to your synagogue, I want to reaffirm and proclaim their perennial value. This is, therefore, the meaning that should be attributed to my visit to you, the Jews of Rome.**"[173]

---

she deplores the hatred, persecutions, and displays of anti-Semitism directed against the Jews at any time and from any person" (NA, n. 4f-g).

[171*] See *Nostra aetate*, n. 4.

[172*] *Ibid.*

[173] John Paul II, Allocution in the Synagogue, p. 4.

Now let us analyze the fundamental statements of John Paul II, emphasized above in bold.

a. A 'Decisive Contribution' to 'Overcome the Old Prejudices'

§ 110

What did John Paul II mean by "old prejudices"? To better understand the underlying thinking of the Pontiff, we will begin by looking at various possible meanings of this expression.

a.a. Racial Prejudices?

§ 111

He certainly did not intend to liken the Church's anti-Jewish condemnation to the spurious Nazi theories of racial prejudice. The elevated religious motivation upon which the Church of Our Lord based her opposition to the followers of Annas and Caiaphas does not permit any analogy whatsoever with Nazi racism. Even those who were enthusiastic over the papal visit have discarded such an absurd hypothesis. For example, in an article in *La Civiltà Cattolica*, Fr. de Rosa says:

"This 'long period' of Christian anti-Semitism – based primarily on religious motives and not to be confused with modern anti-Semitism, which, having culminated in the 'holocaust,'[174] was caused by economic, nationalist and racist motives rather than religious ones, even if it may have taken advantage of the latter – ended with the pontificate of John XXIII and Vatican Council II." [175]

---

[174] The word "holocaust," or its Hebrew equivalent *Shoah*, is often used, above all by progressivists and the secular media, to designate the barbarous slaughter of Jews carried out by the Nazi regime during World War II. It became a characteristic talisman-word, employed to create a climate of compassion and sympathy for the Jews, inappropriately comparing them to the first martyrs of the Church. The impropriety of this usage lies in the fact that the latter were martyred on behalf of the one true Catholic Faith, whereas the Jews practiced a false religion. Further, the Nazi persecution waged against the Jews was of a racist character, whereas the one unleashed against the martyrs was clearly religious.

[175] G. de Rosa, "Ebrei e cristiani 'fratelli' nel 'fratello Gesù,' *La Civiltà Cattolica*, May 3,1986, p. 261.

a.b. Temperamental or Emotional Prejudices?

§ 112   Discarded the hypothesis that the "old prejudices" had a racial character, one could ask whether John Paul II was referring to some temperamental or emotional "prejudice" that could have existed in the Catholic Church against the Jews.

History has objectively recorded the facts that took place in the relationship between the Church and the synagogue. And even though such facts may displease the progressivist current, this does not change their essence. *Historia vero testis temporum, lux veritatis, vita memoriae, magistra vitae, nuntia vetustatis* [History is the witness of all times, the light of truth, the life of memory, the mistress of life and the messenger of antiquity].[176]

Analyzing the facts of History, we find more "old prejudices" of the Jews against Catholics rather than the other way around, as John Paul II affirms. Their constant hatred of the Church of Christ generated direct and indirect persecutions of Jews against Catholics. Let us set out some facts recorded by History of persecutions of both types.

Direct Persecutions of the Jews against Catholics

§ 113   The Jews never ceased to plot against the true Faith since the crime of Deicide. It was they who instigated the first persecution against the Church in Jerusalem with the arrest of St. Peter (Acts 12:3), the stoning to death of St. Stephen (Acts 7:54-58) and the beheading of St. James the Greater (Acts 12:1-2). They ordered the Apostles to be scourged (Acts 5:40) and instigated Saul's action against the disciples (Acts 8:3). After the conversion of St. Paul, they spread calumnies and stirred up revolts against him (Acts 13:50; 17:5). In the year 65, they took him out of Jerusalem to kill him. The Apostle of the Gentiles was saved by the pagan tribune Lysias, who, to deliver him from the hands of the infuriated Jews, ordered him flogged and sent him under a guard to Caesarea (Acts 24:7).

• St. Paul himself bears witness to this radical hatred directed against him when he wrote that the Jews "never ceased to combat the Church of Jesus Christ" (I Thes 2:14).

§ 114   • As soon as the nascent Church began to appear in Rome, the local Jews tried to drown her in the blood of the first Christians. Rome was burned in the year 64 AD during the reign

---

[176] Cicero, *De Oratore*. book 2, chap. 9:36.

of Nero. The mystery over whether it was Jews or pagans who gave the order for this destruction is debated even to this day. But those who profited from it were mainly the Jews who held sway over the Emperor.[177] The fire served as a pretext to set off the bloody persecutions of the pagan Emperors against the first Christians.[178 183]

§ 115   • After 70 AD, with the fall of Jerusalem to the troops of Vespasian and Titus, the writing of the rabbis became increasingly violent and hostile toward Christians.[179]

§ 116   • In the years 132-135, during the insurrection of the Jews of Jerusalem led by Simon Barcochba against the Romans, the Christians were brutally tormented by the followers of this false messiah.[180] Throughout the Empire, the synagogues became focal points of the persecution, as noted in the famous saying of Tertullian: "*Synagogae Judaeorum fontes persecutionum*"[181]

---

[177] Nero's favorite lover, Sabina Popea, was known to be sympathetic toward the Jews (cf. Flavius Josephus, Vita, 3, *Antiquitates judaicae*, 18-20; Tacitus, *Hist.*, I, 22, *apud* J. Zeiller, *Les premières persécutions. La législation impériale relative aux Chrétiens*, in Fliche-Martin, *Histoire de l'Eglise*, vol. 1, p. 290). The Jews who frequented Nero's palace, protected by Popea, are thought to have denounced the Christians as authors of the criminal fire by spreading the calumny that the minds of the Christians were filled with "ideas of heavenly vengeance, universal conflagration and destruction of the world" (cf. Jean Victor Duruy, *Histoire des Romains*, Paris: 1882, vol. 4, p. 507, *apud* J. Zeiller, *Les premières persécutions, ibid.*).

[178] In his *Commentary on the Holy Scriptures*, Cornelius a Lapide asserts: "The first persecution waged by the pagans [against the Christians] was provoked by the Jews and through the Jews, who stirred up the pagans against the Christians" (*Commentaria in Apocalypsim* 2:9).

[179] Cf. J. Klausner, *Jésus de Nazareth*, pp. 54-55, *apud* J. Lebreton, "Saint Jacques et Saint Jean," in Fliche-Martin, *Histoire de l'Eglise*, vol. 1, p. 243.

[180] In his first *Apologia* (1:31) St. Justin states: "Barcochba ordered that the Christians – and only the Christians – should undergo the most terrible tortures if they did not renounce Jesus Christ and blaspheme against Him" (31, 6, *apud* J. Zeiller, "La persécution sous les Flaviens et Antonins," in Fliche-Martin, *Histoire de l'Eglise*, vol. 1, p. 310).

[181] "The synagogue of the Jews is the source of the persecutions." Tertullian, *Adversus Gnosticos Scorpiace*, in PL 2, 166.

§ 117   • In the time of the Church of the Martyrs, the Jews were usually among those who incited the massacres of the Christians. According to the *Letter of the Church of Smyrna* (chapters XII and XIII), the Jews played an important role in bringing about the execution of St. Polycarp,[182] carried out on February 23, 155, the day of the "great Sabbath." When the Bishop-martyr was condemned to be burned, the rabble hurried to gather the wood for the fire, and, "as was their custom, the Jews were the ones who showed the greatest eagerness in this task."[183]

§ 118   • During the persecution of Decius in 250, St. Pionius and his companions Sabina and Asclepiades were sent before the judge in Smyrna on the anniversary of the martyrdom of St. Polycarp. A large number of Jews came to insult the Christians who refused to apostatize, and to demand their death, shouting, "These people have already lasted too long!"[184]

§ 119   • Pope St. Calixtus (217-222) was another illustrious victim of Jewish hatred in the first centuries of the Church. A former slave, St. Calixtus had made some unsuccessful business deals on behalf of his master and sought the help of his creditors, among whom some were Jews. The latter denounced him as a Christian to the pagan authority. The prefect had the Pontiff scourged and condemned him to forced labor in the mines of Sardinia.[185]

§ 120   • In his work *Contra Celsum* (6, 27), Origen authoritatively stated that in the early times of the Church, the Jews spread the calumnies that were so ominously fateful to the Christians. According to him, the Jews spread the rumor that Christians beheaded children and ate them in their nightly meetings in the catacombs.[186]

§ 121   • Julian the Apostate found his strongest allies in the Jews in his campaign against Our Lord Jesus Christ. St. Greg-

---

[182] Cf. J. Baltasar Pereira, *Epístolas dos Apóstolos e Apocalypse,* (Rio: Melhoramentos, 1937) . p. 638.

[183] Cf. *Martyrium S. Polycarpi,* XII, XIII, XVII, XVIII, *apud* F. Vernet, *Juifs et Chrétiens,* col. 1658.

[184] Cf. *Passio S. Pionii,* 3-4, 13-14, *apud ibid.,* col. 1658. See also Jacques Zeiller, "Les grandes persécutions du milieu du IIIᵉ siècle et la période de paix religieuse de 260 à 302," in Fliche-Martin, *Histoire de l'Eglise,* vol. 2, p. 149.

[185] Cf. J. Zeiller, "Le siège romain," *in ibid.,* vol. 2, p. 405

[186] Cf. F. Vernet, *Juifs et Chrétiens,* cols. 1658-1659.

ory Nazianzen affirmed that the Jews' centuries-old hatred for Christians was what motivated them to help the tyrant.[187]

§ 122   • Eusebius relates how Emperor Constantine the Great, in a letter about the celebration of Easter, recalled the implacable persecutions of the Jews against Christians. He advised: "Let there be nothing in common between us and the most inimical Jewish rabble."[188]

§ 123   • Jewish hatred was also present in the East. King Sapor's persecution of the Christians in Persia in the mid-fourth century was instigated by the Jews, "these perpetual enemies of Christians who are always found in stormy times, constant in their implacable hatred and always ready to make some calumnious accusation," according to the Acts of St. Simeon-bar-Sabae by the Patriarch of Seleutia, who died in 341.[189]

• At the beginning of the 5th century, the Jews in Alexandria unleashed an attack against Christians.[190]

§ 124   • In North Africa during the 5th and 6th centuries, Ethiopian Christians who had settled in Nedjran and Saphar were the victims of the anti-Catholic fury of the Jews. One symptomatic episode took place in the year 523 when Dhu-Nowas, chief of the Himarytes and Jewish by religion, stirred up the whole region and took Saphar, massacred the Catholic clergy and soldiers of the local garrison and transformed the church into a synagogue. After laying siege to Nedjran, he accepted the surrender of the inhabitants. Violating his promises, however, he ordered all the Christians to be slain.[191]

§ 125   • In the year 608, the Jews in Antioch took advantage of the invasion of Syria by the troops of Bonosius and attacked

---

[187] Cf. St. Gregory Nazianzen, *Oratio*, v. 3, *apud* H. Delassus, *La conjuration antichrétienne*, vol. 2, p. 683.

[188] Eusebius, *De Vita Constantini*, 3, 18, *apud* F. Vernet, *Juifs et Chrétiens*, cols. 1744, 1762.

[189] *Ibid.*, col. 1665.

[190] Cf. G. Bardy, "Atticus de Constantinople et Cyrille d'Alexandrie," in Fliche-Martin, *Histoire de l'Eglise*, vol. 4, p. 157.

[191] Cf. G. Bardy and L. Bréhier, "L'expansion chrétienne aux Ve. et VIe. siècles," *in ibid.*, pp. 526-527. See also Rohrbacher, *Histoire Universelle de l'Eglise Catholique*, vol. 5, pp. 24-26., which narrates the massacre of the Christians in Nedjran and transcribes the letter sent by Dhu Nowas (or Dunaan) to the Arab sheik Almondar boasting of having killed 280 Catholic priests and inviting him to do the same in his territories.

the Christians, killing a large number of them and burning their corpses. According to Graetz, they tortured the Patriarch St. Anastasius with sophisticated cruelty, dragging him through the streets of the city before murdering him.[192]

§ 126   • Around the middle of the 7th century, the Jews persuaded Caliph Omar, who ruled Jerusalem, to tear down all crosses in the city, especially the one on the Mount of Olives.[193]

§ 127   • On the Iberian Peninsula, the Jews were frequent collaborators with the Muslims in the conquest of Visigothic Spain.[194]

§ 128   • In 723 in Syria, an edict of Caliph Yezid ordered the destruction of all images "be they in temples, churches or houses." From a report of Monk John to the Second Council of Nicaea, Patriarch Nicephorus stated that it was a Jew from Tiberias who suggested Yezid take such measure, promising him a long reign should he do so.[195]

§ 129   • In the early 11th century, the Jews of Orleans, France, sent a letter to Sultan Hakem, who then ruled over the Holy Places, telling him that Christian armies were prepared to embark to re-conquer Jerusalem. This false story caused the Sultan to destroy the Church of the Holy Sepulcher and break the agreement allowing Catholic pilgrims to visit the Holy Land.[196]

News of this insidious Jewish intrigue and the consequent profanations in the Holy Land by the Moors understandably raised religious indignation throughout Europe. Even though there could well have been over-reactions, the first ones

---

[192] Cf. F. Vernet, *Juifs et Chrétiens*, col. 1665; L. Bréhier, "Les rapports entre Rome et Constantinople de l'avènement de Grégoire le Grand à la chute de Phocas," *in ibid.*, vol. 5, pp. 73-75.

[193] Cf. L. Bréhier, "L'Ekthesis, la fin du Règne et la succession d'Héraclius (638-641)," *in ibid.*, vol. 5, p. 141.

[194] Cf. R. Aigrain, "L'Espagne chrétienne," *in ibid.*, vol. 5, pp. 260, 266.

[195] Notwithstanding the "prophecy" assuring him a long reign, Caliph Yezid died one year after his edict was issued (cf. L. Bréhier, "La querelle des images jusqu'au Concile iconoclaste de 754," *in ibid.*, vol. 5, p. 446.

[196] Raul Glaber, a medieval chronicler, comments that "the Devil had decided to employ his favorite nation to infuse the poison of his wickedness against the servants of the true Religion" (*Historiae*, 3, 7). See also Adhemar de Chabannes, *Chronicon*, 3, 47-52, *apud* A. Dumas, "Le sentiment religieux et ses aberrations," *in ibid.*, vol. 7, p. 464.

to blame for excesses were the authors of the crime of profanation, the Muslims and the Jews, rather than those who sought only to vindicate the insults made against their Faith. To attribute that religious reaction to a temperamental or emotional outburst would be a gross and impious simplification.

Here we bring to an end this sampling of Jewish hatred against the Holy Church expressed through direct persecutions in the first 11 centuries of the Christian era.

§ 130   History also records many indirect persecutions instigated by Jews against Catholics. Next we will point out some of the more noteworthy.

Doctrinal Hostilities or Indirect Persecutions Waged by Jews against Catholics

In addition to combating the Holy Church directly, the Jews have infiltrated Catholic circles to distort faith in Jesus Christ and the Most Holy Trinity and thereby distort the Church. Bossuet attests to this in his commentary on the Apocalypse:

§ 131   "Since the beginning of Christianity, falsely converted Jews have mixed among the faithful striving to cultivate in their midst the hidden leaven of Judaism, principally by rejecting the mysteries of the Trinity and the Incarnation. Such were a certain Cerintho and Ebion, who denied the divinity of Jesus Christ and would not recognize but one person in God. ...

§ 132   "From time to time, these things [Jewish views] would emerge from hell, where they had been chained by the Gospel of St. John. Around the end of the second century (196), a sect called the Alogeans rose up.[197*] Its followers were known by this name because they did not admit the Divine Word [alogean comes from *a-logos,* no-word in Greek]. Out of hatred for the Word, announced by St. John, they rejected his Gospel and also his Apocalypse, in which Jesus Christ is also called the Word of God. ...

§ 133   "Another sect, which originated from this one, made so little of Jesus Christ as to consider Him less than Melchizedek.[198*] It repeated the Jewish theories that reduced the Trinity to mere names; the same was affirmed at this time by a certain Praxeas, against whom Tertullian wrote. Noetus also followed this error,

---

[197*] Epiphanius, *Haer.* 51.

[198*] *Ibid.*, 55, 57, 62.

which was later taken up by Sabellius, who made many disciples not only in Mesopotamia but also in Rome. ...

"Clearly these heresies were a remnant of this Jewish leaven ... and the Christians who adopted them were actually Pharisees and Jews, as St. Epiphanius and other Church Fathers called them.[199*]

§ 134

"But it became most obvious that these beliefs came from the Jews at the time of Paul of Samosata, Bishop of Antioch [260-268]. When Arthemon took up the heresy of Cerinth and Theodatus, which reduced Jesus Christ to a mere man, Paul adhered to it, along with Zenobia, Queen of Palmyra, who was linked to the Jewish religion.[200*] The Jews, therefore, were the authors of that impiety, and they incited this Queen to adopt it. ..

§ 135

"The consequences of this error for the Church were terrible, for it was adopted not only by Photinus, Bishop of Sirmium, but also by the Arians, the Nestorians and all the other sects that later attacked the Divinity or the Incarnation of the Son of God, since all were offshoots of this Jewish heresy.

"Therefore, with the spreading of these pharisaic doctrines, the Church suffered a long period of a type of persecution by the Jews."[201]

§ 136

There are many documents demonstrating that the two types of Jewish persecutions – a bloody one against Catholics and a bloodless one against the doctrine and customs of the Church – were carried out not only through the first thousand years of the Christian era, but have continued all the way to modern and contemporary times. The testimony of Bernard Lazare, a French Jewish journalist who lived at the end of the 19th century,[202] provides one example of this. Lazare showed the

---

[199*] *Ibid.*, 65-69.

[200*] Athanasius, *Ep. ad Solit. Theodor.*, 1. lib. II, *Haer. Fabul. in Paul Sam.*

[201] Jacques Bénigne Bossuet, *Oeuvres Complètes - Explication de l'Apocalypse* (Paris: Berche et Tralin, 1885), vol. 1, pp. 298-300.

[202] Bernard Lazare (1865-1903), a French writer and journalist, was born in Nimes and died in Paris. Adopting largely anarchist and class struggle views, he wrote for *Mercure de France, Journal, Figaro* and other publications. In 1894 he published *L'Antisémitisme, son histoire et ses causes* (*Anti-Semitism, Its History and Causes*); in it he described the Jewish role in the fostering of anti-Semitism. With the outbreak of the Dreyfus affair in 1894, he entered the fight

significant role played by his Jewish colleagues in the revolutionary process that started in the Middle Ages and has been steadily undermining the institution and doctrine of the Church and the work of Christian Civilization ever since.[203]

§ 137   Here is what Bernard Lazare affirms regarding the revolutionary role of the Jews in History:

"From the 10th to the 15th century, these 'Jewish' rationalists and philosophers have been collaborators in what could be called the general Revolution of mankind.

"Most of the Averroists were unbelievers or more or less assailed the Catholic Religion. They were the direct ancestors of the men of the Renaissance. It is owing to them that the spirit of doubt was elaborated. ... The Florentine Platonists, the Italian Aristotelians, the German Humanists all came from them. Thanks to them, too, Pomponazzo composed his treatises against the immortality of the soul, and Theism, which corresponded with the decadence of Catholicism, sprang up among the thinkers of the 16th century."[204]

§ 138   Lazare goes on to point out the role played by the Jews in the great rupture of religious unity in Christianity caused by the Pseudo-Reformation:

"The Reformation in Germany, as well as in England, was one of those movements when Christianity drank from Jewish sources. It was the Jewish spirit that triumphed with Protestantism. ... Exegesis and free examination are powerful destroyers, and it was the Jews who originated biblical exegesis, just as they were the first to criticize the forms and doctrines of Christianity."[205]

---

on behalf of Captain Dreyfus and became a major character in that famous case, which resulted in the demoralization of the Army and the monarchist circles of France. As a sign of its gratitude, the French Republic erected a statue in his honor (cf. H. Delassus, *La conjuration antichrétienne*, vol. 2, p. 684; entry Dreyfus, *Enciclopedia Universal Ilustrada*, Espasa-Calpe).

[203] For more on the revolutionary process in History, see Plinio Corrêa de Oliveira, *Revolution and Counter-Revolution*, (New Rochelle, NY: Foundation for a Christian Civilization, 1980), Part I, chap. 3.

[204] Bernard Lazare, *Anti-Semitism, Its History and Causes* (New York: The International Library Publishing Co., 1903; repr. London: Britons Publishing Co., 1967), pp. 128.

[205] *Ibid.*, pp. 132, 300.

§ *139*   Jewish influence was also felt in the French Revolution. Bernard Lazare points this out, giving the names of the chief collaborators and their functions:

"The Jewish spirit is essentially a revolutionary spirit; consciously or otherwise, the Jew is a revolutionist ... During the Revolution, the Jews did not remain inactive. Considering how few their numbers were in Paris, the position they occupied as district electors, officers of the legion and associate judges was important. ... One must wade through provincial archives to determine what part they played in affairs"[206]

§ *140*   Confirming Lazare's statements about the role of Jews in the French Revolution, a document titled "The Agony of the Roman World," published in the Hebrew journal *Haschophet* toward the end of 19th century, clearly asserts that the French Revolution was a work identifiable with Judaism:

"To no avail did the tiara [the Papacy] fight against the scepter of the Jewish Revolution of 1793; in vain would it [the tiara] seek to free itself from the iron grip of the Semitic colossus that clutches it; all of its efforts are useless. The danger is imminent, and Catholicism dies to the degree that Judaism penetrates the layers of society."[207]

In the same sense, the English review *The Mouth* in its October 1896 issue confirmed this view:

"The Jews do not even try to disguise the fact that, in their eternal hatred of Christianity and aided by the heads of Freemasonry, they were the authors of the [French] Revolution."[208]

§ *141*   Bernard Lazare further asserts that the Jews played an important role in the communist and socialist revolutionary upheavals of the 19th century:

"During the second revolutionary period, which started in 1830, they displayed even greater ardor than during the first. ... It is beyond a doubt that the Jews, through their wealth, their energy and their talents, supported and furthered the progress of the European revolution. ...

"As for their contribution to present-day Socialism, as is well known, it was and still is enormous."[209]

---

[206] *Ibid.*, pp. 298, 310.

[207] H. Delassus, *La conjuration antichrétienne*, vol. 2, p. 686.

[208] *Ibid.*

[209] *Ibid.*, pp. 310-312.

§ 142   Another fact should be added to the documents attesting to the persecutions stimulated by the Jews against Catholics: their doctrinal hostility and participation in the revolutionary process that has been destroying Christendom. The precepts of the *Talmud*, which, as we have seen,[210] manifest a great hatred of the Church and Catholics, aim to provide a religious foundation to the Israelites' loathing for Christianity. This hatred can be noted from the first days of the *Talmud* in the 2nd century, when its foundations were laid by Barchochbas, Akiba and Aquila, until today. Bernard Lazare notes:

"The *tanaim* [early 'teachers'] wanted to preserve the faithful [Jews] from Christian contamination; for this purpose the Gospels were likened to books on witchcraft, and Samuel Junior, by order of the patriarch Gamaliel, inserted in the daily prayers a curse against the Christians, the *Birkat Haminim*, which furnishes the foundation for the charge that the Jews curse Jesus thrice a day."[211]

So, even if other documents were lacking, these *Talmud* precepts would constitute the proof of the permanent hatred of the Jews for the Catholic Religion.

*

§ 143   Considering what has been presented thus far, we find that the hatred of the Jews against Catholics throughout History is so visceral and unrelenting that one would say it fulfills the revelation God made to Isaiah, saying: "All that this people speaketh, is a conspiracy" (Is 8:12). And: "They have conceived mischief (that is, hating their neighbor) and brought forth iniquity. They have broken the eggs of asps, and have woven the webs of spiders: he that shall eat of their eggs, shall die; and that which is brought out, shall be hatched into a basilisk ... the work of iniquity is in their hands. Their feet run to evil, and make haste to shed innocent blood" (Is 59:4-7).

*

§ 144   It seems quite clear to us that if there was ever an emotional "old prejudice" in the Church-Synagogue relationship, it was not on the part of Catholics, who suffered the effects of the

---

[210] See Note 138 of this Chapter

[211] B. Lazare, *Antisemitism, Its History and Causes,* p. 112.

Jewish conspiracy. Rather, it was held by the Jews, who took the initiative in the religious fight.[212] In passing, it should be noted

---

[212] Someone could object that the Inquisition persecuted the Jews and that the Church is *ipso facto* responsible for it. To this objection, we give this response:

a. The Tribunal of the Holy Inquisition, established to defend the integrity of the Faith, neither had jurisdiction over religious Jews nor did it prevent them from professing their false creed, so long as they did not propagate their errors among Catholics. The Tribunal dealt only with those who hypocritically converted to the Catholic Religion and entered the Church's fold or those who converted sincerely but later returned to their old errors (cf. Joseph de Maistre, *Cartas sobre a Inquisição Espanhola*, Niteroi: *Revista Leituras Católicas*, 1949, p. 27).

The Jews abused the freedom given to them by the Monarchs of the Iberian Peninsula by spreading their religious errors against the Catholic Faith and by their excessive number of false conversions. Because of such abuses, they became a serious danger not only to the Faith in the Kingdoms of Portugal and Spain, but also to the political stability of those States (cf. Ernest Lavisse and Alfred Rambaud, *Histoire Générale du IVe siécle à nos jours*, Paris: Armand Colin, 1984, vol. 4, p. 332; Juan Baptista Weiss, *História Universal,* vol. 8, p. 304).

Thus, in legitimate defense and in their capacity as temporal rulers, the Monarchs decreed that the Jews could either freely leave their territories at the expense of the State or remain as sincere and faithful Catholics or, at the least, they should stop spreading their false convictions. In the latter case, the Jews – and especially converted Jews – would be subject to the vigilance of the Inquisition insofar as matters of faith were concerned. It should be emphasized that such sanctions were adopted by the temporal power and not the spiritual power that belonged to the Church; therefore, they should not be attributed to her.

b. The tribunals of the Inquisition were mixed tribunals, composed of both churchmen and representatives of the temporal power. The churchmen judged crimes against the Faith and their sentences were restricted to the spiritual sphere. The representatives of the temporal power, in turn, delivered the sentences that, in accordance with the independent laws of each State, corresponded to those spiritual judgments of the Church. As a zealous defender of the autonomy and special rights of the spiritual and temporal powers, the Church did not take part in the execution of civil sentences, with the obvious exception of providing spiritual assistance to the condemned (cf. J. de Maistre, *Cartas sobre a Inquisição Espanhola*, pp. 17-18; Henri Hello, *A verdade sobre a Inquisição*, Petrópolis: Vozes, 1936, p. 11; E. Vacandard, entry Inquisition, in DTC, vol. 7, col. 2065).

Therefore, direct responsibility cannot be attributed to the Church for pronouncing and executing the civil sentences delivered by the Inquisition tribunals in the several countries where it existed. Nor can she be held accountable for possible injustices committed by the temporal arm of the Inquisition.

c. The temporal courts of medieval Europe habitually applied very rigorous punishments. The ethnic and cultural moral factors that contributed to that general climate are beyond the interest of this Note. The rigorous dispositions of the penal codes of that epoch are generally acknowledged by historians, even by those who are against the Inquisition (cf. Antonio Carlos Lea, *Em defesa dos cátaros, apud* W. Devivier, *Curso de Apologica Christã*, (São Paulo: Melhoramentos, 1924) p. 456. It was unavoidable, therefore, that in the inquisitorial process, representatives of the temporal power would execute the punishments according to the custom of that time. Nonetheless, "such rigors were not applied by the ordinary tribunals of the Church, i.e., the diocesan tribunals. In the tribunals of the Inquisition, however, given the gravity of the dangers, some punishments taken from the civil legislation were applied. Those punishments were eliminated or greatly attenuated as far as the dangers ceased to exist" (Devivier, *Curso de Apologica Christã,*).

Therefore, rigorous punishments were not characteristic of the medieval Inquisition, but of the temporal courts of that time. On the contrary the Inquisition mitigated or even abolished such cruel punishments as far as possible.

d. The Roman Inquisition, or The Holy Office, established by Pope Paul III in 1542, provides a characteristic example of the Holy Church's justice and equanimity in her judgments on matters of Faith. This was the only case where a Church tribunal had both temporal and spiritual functions. Directly under the jurisdiction of the Supreme Pontiff, the Roman Inquisition was known for its fairness and prudence in its exercise of temporal justice. It introduced several judicial reforms that favored the defendant, such as the provision of a defense attorney, the right to counsel and a notarized copy of the entire trial so that he might make a response.

Scholar John Tedeschi concluded his study on the Inquisition by recognizing that the Roman Inquisition was a model of legal justice and jurisprudence for modern Europe. He wrote: "It may not be an exaggeration to claim, in fact, that in several respects the Holy Office was a pioneer in judicial reform." (*The Prosecution of Heresy: Collected Studies on the Inquisition in Early Modern Italy.* Medieval and Renaissance Texts and Studies, n. 78, Binghampton, NY: 1991) pp. 7-9; see also "A outra face da Inquisição," *O Estado De S. Paulo*, March 16, 1986, Cultural Supplement, pp. 1-4).

The goodness of the Roman Inquisition under the papal aegis became proverbial. This is indirectly recognized by a testimony of the Great Jewish Sanhedrin, which we transcribed below (pp. 132ss). This is why one can borrow, without exaggeration, the words of Joseph de Maistre that Rome was the "paradise of the Jews" (*Cartas sobre a In-*

that before the theories of National Socialism came to light with their absurd pretensions of pagan origin, the conspiratory character of Judaism and its "prejudice" against the Church were widely known and generally acknowledged among Catholics. From a certain point of view, the Nazi and Fascist persecutions of the Jews became useful tools to save Judaism from those well-merited accusations.

The Goodness of the Church toward Persecuted Jews

§ 145   The Church never ceased to charitably invite the Jews to convert and to receive them with open arms when they so deserved it. She went even further than this – she always emphatically forbade the persecutions that often broke out among the Catholic people in reaction to the constant hatred of the synagogue against the Church.

§ 146   An impartial testimony of this position can be found in an official speech delivered at the Grand Sanhedrin in Paris on October 30, 1806 at the time of Napoleon. At that session, the Jews of France and Italy applauded the speech by rabbi Isaac Samuel Avigdor in which he acknowledged – with the endorsement of the Sanhedrin – the constant and unceasing benignity shown by the Church toward Jews. He began by calling to mind that the most celebrated Christian moralists prohibited persecutions, professed tolerance and preached fraternal charity. Some relevant excerpts of Avigdor's speech follow:

"St. Athanasius says, 'It is an execrable heresy to try to oblige by force, blows or imprisonment those who cannot be convinced through reason' (book 1). 'Nothing is more opposed to Religion,' says St. Justin Martyr, 'than coercion in matters of Faith' (book 5). St. Augustine asks, 'Shall we persecute those whom God tolerates?' In this regard, Lactance says, 'Forced

---

quisição Espanhola, p. 13), and apply to the gentle yoke of the Popes the popular German adage about those who lived under the temporal power of the Princes of the Church: *Unterm Krummstabe ist gut wohnen!* (How good it is to live under the crosier!) (see R. Aubenas, Hérétiques et sorciers, in Fliche-Martin, *Histoire de l'Eglise*, vol. 15, pp. 385-386).

Thus, the Church cannot be accused of injustices or persecutions of the Jews in the exercise of her temporal duties.

The objection, then, is erroneous in its premise – that the Inquisition persecuted the Jews – and in its consequence – that the Church would have done so as well.

religion is not Religion; it is necessary to persuade rather than force. Religion cannot be imposed' (book 3). St. Bernard says: 'Counsel, but do not force.' ...

"These sublime virtues of humanity and justice were often practiced by truly well-instructed Christians and, above all, by worthy ministers of this pure morality that calms passions and instills virtue.

"As a consequence of these sacred moral principles, at different times the Pontiffs protected and welcomed in their States persecuted Jews expelled from different parts of Europe, and churchmen from all the countries [of Christendom] often defended them in many States of that part of the world.

"Around the middle of the 7th century, St. Gregory defended and protected the Jews throughout the whole Christian world. In the 10th century the Bishops of Spain most energetically opposed the people who wanted to massacre them. Pontiff Alexander II wrote those Bishops a letter of congratulations for their prudent conduct on that occasion. In the 11th century, the Jews – very numerous in the Dioceses of Uzés and Clermont – were vigorously protected by the Bishops.

"In the 12th century, St. Bernard defended them from the furor of the Crusaders. Innocent II and Alexander III likewise protected them. In the 13th century, Gregory IX protected the Jews in England, France and Spain from great calamities that threatened them; he forbade, under penalty of excommunication, that they should be coerced to convert. ...

"Clement VI granted them asylum in Avignon. ... In the middle of the same century, the Bishop of Speyer prohibited persons who owed money to the Jews from refusing payment of their debts by resorting to the often used excuse of usury. The following century, Nicholas II wrote the Inquisition to proscribe forcing Jews to embrace Christianity. ...

"It would be easy to cite countless more examples of charitable actions toward the Israelites practiced by ecclesiastics well-instructed in the duties of man and their religion. ...

"The people of Israel ... have never had the means or occasion to manifest its recognition of so many benefits, a recognition made all the more agreeable inasmuch as it is owed to disinterested and highly respectable men.

"For the first time in 18 centuries, we find ourselves in this unique situation, where we can display the sentiments that imbue our hearts. This great and fortunate occasion, which we owe to our august and immortal Emperor, offers us a most opportune, excellent and glorious opportunity to express ... especially to the ecclesiastics, our full gratitude toward them and their predecessors.

"Thus, gentlemen, let us hasten to take advantage of this memorable occasion to pay the just tribute of recognition that we owe them. Let this room resound with the expression of our gratitude. Let us solemnly bear witness to our sincere recognition of the constant benefits they gave to the generations that preceded us."[213]

§ 147   The Jewish assembly applauded this speech, voted to accept it, and later inserted it in the proceedings of February 5, 1807. That assembly approved the following decree:

"The representatives of the Hebrew Synod in the Empire of France and the Kingdom of Italy present at the Hebrew Synod ... are filled with gratitude for the successive benefits received by the Israelites of different countries from the Christian clergy in the past centuries. We fully recognize the welcome that several Pontiffs and many other ecclesiastics have given at different times to the Israelites of diverse countries. ...

"It is here decreed that the expression of these sentiments be recorded in today's proceedings as a permanent and authentic testimony of the gratitude of the Israelites of this assembly for the benefits received by the generations that preceded them from churchmen of the various countries of Europe."[214]

This unique manifestation of gratitude on the part of the Grand Sanhedrin assembled in France stands as testimony to the benefits bestowed by the Church on Jews through the ages. Based on this decree and the material presented above on the persecutions instigated by the Jews against the Catholic Religion, we clearly conclude that the Holy Church never had a temperamental or emotional bias that could serve as foundation for John Paul II's assertion that her history includes "old prejudices" against the Jews.

---

[213] Isaac Samuel Avigdor, Speech in the Grand Sanhedrin, October 30, 1806, in "Procès-verbal des séances de l'assemblée des députés français professant la religion juive," p. 169-171., *apud* H. Delassus, *La conjuration antichrétienne*, vol. 3, pp. 1164-1167.

[214] Cf. H. Delassus, *La conjuration antichrétienne*, vol. 3, pp. 1167-1168.

a.c. 'Theological Prejudices'?

§ 148   In the absence, therefore, of an adequate historical foundation to uphold that the expression "old prejudices" used by John Paul II refers to racial or emotional prejudices against the Jews, one must ask whether the Pontiff was referring to doctrinal matters.

Was John Paul II referring to theological "prejudices"? To accept such a hypothesis, it would have to be asked if the very serious doctrinal questions that separate the Holy Church from the synagogue are "prejudices?" For example, would it be a "prejudice" to affirm the Divinity of Our Lord Jesus Christ? Or to profess the dogma of the Most Holy Trinity? Or perhaps to proclaim the articles of Faith that derive from that dogma?

These are questions that John Paul II did not answer. Instead, he left the minds of the faithful who followed the news of his visit to the synagogue of Rome floundering in perplexity, bewildered by a Pope who appeared to ignore such fundamental questions of our Faith in order to favor the Jewish religion.

b. 'A Decisive Turnabout in the Relationship of the Catholic Church with Judaism'

§ 149   *Svolta decisiva* was the Italian expression chosen by the Pontiff to describe the new relationship of the Catholic Church with Judaism. *Svolta* means a change of direction on a trodden road[215] A *svolta decisiva* is, therefore, a decisive turnabout.

According to John Paul II the Declaration *Nostra aetate* triggered a decisive turnabout in Church relations with Judaism, a turnabout to which, as seen, he wanted to offer a "decisive contribution" by doing away with "old prejudices." He could hardly have been more categorical in expressing a desire to abandon the previous doctrinal position of the Holy Church toward Judaism.

*

---

[215] Everton Florenzano, Dicionário Italiano-Portugues: *Svolta* - turn, turnaround, change, transformation; Nicola *Zingarelli, Il Nuovo Zingarelli - Vocabulario della Lingua Italiana*: *Svolta* - 1. action of turning oneself around, 3. figurative: important change: that discovery points to a *svolta* in the history of science.

c. "The Church of Christ Discovers Her Link with Judaism, Sounding the Depths of Her Own Mystery"

§ 150   Here John Paul II seems to confirm what was said about the use of "mystery"[216] as a theological *ersatz* for something one is hiding from the public. Those comments would thus apply as well to this part of the Allocution.

This statement by John Paul II is quite remarkable. We just listed the numerous Popes, Councils, Doctors and Saints who combated Judaism as a doctrinal evil. From the historical and doctrinal perspectives, it can be said that there is no greater and more continuous opposition between two religions than what exists between the Catholic Church and Judaism. If someone pretends to annul such an antagonism, he must employ strong arguments. It is the least we could expect. What argument does John Paul II use to terminate this bi-millenary antagonism?

None. Not even one. He merely appeals to a vague notion of "mystery." Catholics should change their attitude toward Jews because "the Church discovered her link with Judaism, sounding the depths of her own mystery." What does the mentioned "mystery" mean? No one can explain for sure.

Based on this enigma, without any further clarification, he goes on to assume the even more radical doctrinal consequences: Catholics should thrust aside their entire past and adhere to the new conciliar pro-Judaism position.

In practical terms, this use of "mystery" seems to be a way to shroud something that John Paul II does not want to reveal to the general public. What would it be? It would probably signify that the Conciliar Church and Judaism are becoming increasingly linked and closer to each other.

d. 'The Hebrew Religion Is Not Extrinsic to Us, but Is Somehow Intrinsic to Our Religion'

§ 151   This surprising declaration appear to confirm also what was said above about Judaism,[217] which, according to progressivist thinking, is the immutable matrix, whereas the Catholic Church is only a participation in this rich matrix.

---

[216] See § 95, Notes 150, 151 of this Chapter.

[217] See §§ 97, 98 of this Chapter.

e. 'You Are Our Beloved Brothers ... Our Older Brothers'

§ 152   Commenting on this statement of John Paul II, Fr. de Rosa notes in *La Civiltà Cattolica*:

"One could not express more forcefully the links that exist between Christians and Jews. In Christian terminology, 'brother' implies a community of faith. By calling Christians and Hebrews 'brothers,' the Pope makes a special reference to such community, even though the Jews do not believe, as Christians do, in Jesus Christ or the mystery of the Trinity."[218]

These few lines by the Jesuit commentator point to a contradiction made by John Paul II. The true meaning of the word "brother" is, as Fr. de Rosa rightfully observes, that of brother in the Faith. How is it possible, then, to have a communion of faith with those who deny its very foundations, such as the Holy Trinity and the divinity of Jesus Christ?

In addition to employing the expression "my dear Hebrew friends and brothers" in his greeting to the Jews at the synagogue,[219] John Paul II further calls the followers of Caiaphas "beloved brothers" and "older brothers." With these expressions, one sees that the Pontiff not only affirms a unity with them in the same religious profession, but also acts as if they have a "predilection" and "first-born rights" independent of the truths of the Catholic Faith.

How is it possible for the Jews to enjoy the same "predilection" of Catholics if, as Scripture clearly states, "without the Faith it is impossible to please God" (Heb 11:6)?

§ 153   John Paul II's mention of "older brothers" also seems to presume the "right of the first-born" that present-day Jews would have over Catholics.

Now then, the Jews' ancient and true right of the first-born, which was established in anticipation of the coming of Our Lord, presupposed the Faith. Without the latter, there would have been neither the promise nor the Old Covenant. This is what St. Paul states when he specifically addresses the Jews:

"Now faith is the substance of things to be hoped for, the evidence of things that appear not ... By faith Abel offered to God a sacrifice exceeding that of Cain. ... By faith Enoch was

---

[218] G. de Rosa, "Ebrei e cristiani 'fratelli' nel 'fratello Gesù,' p. 262.

[219] Cf. John Paul II, Allocution in the Synagogue of Rome, p. 4.

transported, that he should not see death. ... By faith Noah, having received an answer concerning those things that as yet were not seen, moved with fear, framed the ark for the saving of his house, by which he condemned the world; and was instituted heir of the justice, which is by faith.

"By faith he that is called Abraham obeyed to go out into a place which he was to receive for an inheritance; and he went out, not knowing whither he went. By faith he abode in the land. ... By faith also Sarah herself, being barren, received strength to conceive. ... By faith Abraham, when he was tried, offered Isaac. ... By faith also of things to come, Isaac blessed Jacob and Esau. By faith Jacob, dying, blessed each of the sons of Joseph. ...

"By faith [Moses] left Egypt. ... By faith he celebrated pasch. ... By faith the walls of Jericho fell. ... And what yet shall I say? For the time would fail me to tell of Gideon, Barak, Samson, Jephtah, David, Samuel and the prophets, who by faith conquered kingdoms, wrought justice, obtained promises, stopped the mouths of lions, quenched the violence of fire, escaped the edge of the sword, recovered strength from weakness, became valiant in battle, put to flight the armies of foreigners. ...

"And all these being approved [by God] by the testimony of faith, received not the promise [immediately], God providing some better thing for us, that they should not be perfected without us." (Heb 11, *passim*).

Further on the Apostle makes it clear that the faith of the ancient Patriarchs was the faith in Jesus Christ: "Remember your prelates who have spoken the word of God to you; whose faith follow, considering the end of their conversation, Jesus Christ [is always the same] yesterday and today; and the same for ever" (Heb 13:7-8).

§ 154 Faith was, therefore, the reason for the promise, and the promise referred to Christ. With Our Lord, the promise was fulfilled and the Old Covenant ended. Our Lord established the New Covenant, which replaced the old one: "Now in saying a new [covenant], he [God] has made the former old. And that which decayeth and groweth old, is near its end" (Heb 8:13).

Thus, both as the continuity of the Old Covenant and as the foundation of the New, faith in Our Lord Jesus Christ is the basis of any predilection and the only grounds for the right of the first-born.

Therefore, it makes no sense either to speak of the "predilection" of the Jews in our days or to attribute to them some religious "right of the first-born" over Catholics, completely ignoring the question of faith.

§ 155   This analysis of the Pontiff's words raises a question in the afflicted mind of a Catholic: Have the Jews changed and are they ready to accept the true Faith, or has John Paul II changed? Could he make such statements without abandoning the Catholic Faith?

f. 'No atavistic or collective guilt can be attributed to the Jews as a people for what was done in the Passion of Jesus; therefore, the pretended theological justification of discriminatory or persecutory measures is inconsistent'

§ 156   The first objectionable point that calls one's attention in this reasoning of the Pontiff is the inversion of the most elementary rules of logic. John Paul II assumes as a premise the conclusion, and his conclusion implies doing away with the normal premises of his reasoning.

Indeed, it is elementary in theological thinking that the obligatory premises are the data of Revelation coming from two sources, Sacred Scripture and Tradition. If John Paul II intended to exempt the Jews from the guilt of the crime of Deicide, he should have based himself on passages of Holy Scripture that would support his position. Or, in the absence of such foundation, he should have based himself on arguments provided by Tradition. Strangely enough, however, to buttress this unprecedented "absolution" of the Jews, the Pontiff fails to present any basis whatsoever from Revelation.

To make this extremely serious dogmatic judgment, he invokes only two points that do not constitute *per se* a solid basis for an argumentation: the notion of "mystery" he mentioned earlier[220] and the conciliar Declaration *Nostra aetate* (n. 4). The notion of "mystery" is unclear, as its very name indicates, and does not permit a conclusion of this gravity.

The text of *Nostra aetate* is likewise inadequate since it also fails to present data from Sacred Scripture or Tradition that justify the "absolution" of the Jews. Therefore, for all practical purposes, to cite the conciliar Declaration has the value of a petition of principle,[221] which is equivalent to say that it is devoid

---

[220] See §§ 92-95 of this Chapter.

[221] A petition of principle, or tautological argument, is a proposition that

of value.

Thus, John Paul II set a premise that should have been the conclusion of his argument.

§ 157   From this defective premise, he draws as conclusion the disconcerting affirmation that "the pretended theological justification of discriminatory or persecutory measures is inconsistent." What does he really mean by this conclusion? What is the "inconsistent" justification he mentions? Is he perchance referring to the excerpts from Sacred Scripture that clearly speak about the crime of Deicide as having been committed by the whole people and that thereby justify considering the Jews guilty?[222] If so, are we witnessing a revocation of the Holy Books? Would a Pope have the power to contradict Revelation?

Does he consider as "inconsistent theological justification" everything that the Popes, Councils, Fathers, Doctors and the Ordinary Magisterium of the Church have taught through the centuries about the guilt of the whole Jewish people for the crime of Deicide? If so, is he trying to revoke the centuries-old teaching of the Church? Again we ask: Does a Pope have such a power?

§ 158   Given the bizarre "probative" method used by the Pontiff, a serious analysis of his statement would lead one to conclude that John Paul II's speech was an unfortunate and arbitrary abuse of authority lacking any theological foundation. It should simply be accepted as an act by a Pope who justifies his position saying: "This is the way it is, *quia nominor leo...*"[223]

If this hypothesis is correct, such an act would be an authoritarian imposition of the inter-religious dialogue with Jews taken to the paroxysm of trying to invalidate the very foundations of the Catholic Faith. This is the inter-religious dialogue, however, that was first presented as an overflowing of the mercy of the Church. This conciliar mercy toward the Jews would thus

---

pretends to be an explanation or proof of something, but only repeats in identical or equivalent terms what was intended to be proved (e.g. *Nostra aetate* absolved the Jews of the crime of Deicide because it said it absolved them from that crime).

[222] See Note 140 of this Chapter.

[223] This is so "because I am the lion" refers to an Aesop's fable where the lion obliges the other animals to obey him simply because he is stronger than the others. In other words, "It's this way because that's the way I want it to be."

have led us to unjustly anathematize the whole past of the Catholic Church. From dialogue to anathema...[224] What a curious paradox!

g. 'It Is Not Licit to Say the Jews Are Reprobates or Accursed'

§ 159

Here the imperative nature of John Paul II's designs appears unequivocally. *Non licet...* Once again, he appears to be making a kind of anathema.

It would have been very useful for the Pontiff to have explained to Catholics how his statement harmonizes with what St. Paul says about the Jews: "But Israel, by following after the law of justice, is not come unto the law of justice. Why so? Because they sought it not by faith, but as if it were possible of works. For they stumbled at the stumbling stone, as it is written: Behold I lay in Sion a stumbling stone and a rock of scandal" (Rom 9:31-33).

§ 160

In contradiction with John Paul II's "anathema," the Apostle goes on to explain why Israel was rejected:

"That which Israel sought he has not obtained; but their election (by God) has obtained it; and the rest have been blinded (by their malice), as it is written: God has given them the spirit of insensibility; eyes that they should not see; and ears that they should not hear, until this present day. And David said: Let their table be made a snare, and a trap, and a stumbling block, and a recompense unto them. Let their eyes be darkened, that they may not see; and their backs bowed down always (under the weight of the law)" (Rom. 11:7-10).

St. Paul is also clear when he speaks about the Jews who left the Church after having converted:

"For if we sin willfully after having the knowledge of the truth, there is now left no sacrifice for sins, but a certain dreadful expectation of judgment, and the rage of a fire which shall consume the adversaries (of God). A man making void the law of Moses (by becoming an idol-worshiper) dies without any

---

[224] The book by Roger Garaudy, *From Anathema to Dialogue*, was considered a milestone in the dialogue between the Vatican and Communism. Garaudy, a known French Communist writer, praised conciliar Vatican policy for leaving out the condemnations in order to open up to the modern world – as well as to Communism. Now the reverse side of the coin of that conciliar policy is showing its draconian face.

mercy under two or three witnesses; how much more do you think he deserves worse punishments, who has trodden under foot the Son of God, and has esteemed the blood of the testament unclean, by which he was sanctified, and has offered an affront to the Spirit of grace?

"For we know him who has said: Vengeance belongs to me, and I will repay. And again: The Lord shall judge his people. It is a fearful thing to fall into the hands of the living God." (Heb 10:26-31)

This excerpt from the Epistle to the Hebrews also opposes John Paul II's desire to exempt the Jews from God's curse:

"For it is impossible for those who were once illuminated, who have tasted also the heavenly gift, and who were made partakers of the Holy Ghost, who have moreover tasted the good word of God, and the powers of the world to come, and [afterward] who are fallen away; [it is impossible for them] to be renewed again to penance, crucifying again to themselves the Son of God, and making a mockery of him. For the earth that drinks in the rain which comes often upon it, and brings forth herbs for those who till it, receive blessings from God. But that which brings forth thorns and briars, is reprobate, and very near unto a curse, whose end is to be burnt." (Heb 6:4-8)

The "anathema" of John Paul II clashes with these and many other passages of Revelation.

*

The Pontiff closes the core of his Allocution by emphasizing the points we have just analyzed and asserting that his "anathema" against the previous teaching of the Church has a perennial character:

"On the occasion of this visit to your synagogue, I want to reaffirm and proclaim their perennial value [of the *Nostra aetate* and its consequences]. This is, therefore, the meaning that should be attributed to my visit to you, the Jews of Rome."[225]

*

---

[225] Cf. John Paul II, Allocution in the Synagogue of Rome, p. 4.

D. In Response to John Paul II's Concessions, the Jews Reaffirm their False Convictions

§ 161

However bewildering these words of John Paul II are for Catholics, they nevertheless express only a part of the reality, the Pontiff's apparent desire to abandon the 2,000-year-old position of the Catholic Church regarding the errors of the Jewish religion. The other facet of the reality is the ceremony – the hymns and psalms – of the rabbis who received John Paul II, as well as the speeches by the Jewish representatives. Let us now analyze these symbolic acts.

a. Passages from Scripture, Hymns and Psalms Sung & Read by the Jews[226]

§ 162

Since this is the first time in the History of the Church that a Pope visited a synagogue, the ceremonies made by both sides are particularly symbolic. This is especially so if we bear in mind that the Hebrew people by nature are prone to express their thoughts and feelings much more through metaphors and symbols than by discursive and systematic expositions.

Further, since the greatest clash between religious convictions that ever occurred is the struggle between the Faith of Our Lord Jesus Christ and the false faith of the Jews, it seems indispensable that one who wants to know Jewish dispositions toward the Catholic Church should analyze the Jewish ceremonies during John Paul II's visit to the synagogue of Rome.[227]

---

[226] Of the seven Jewish ceremonies that took place during the visit of John Paul II to the synagogue of Rome, only five will be analyzed here. No commentary will be made on Psalms 118 (117 in the *Vulgate*) and 150 (151 in the *Vulgate*), whose texts have no special allusion to Jewish thinking or the symbolism of John Paul II's visit.

Since no precise listing of the psalms used in that Jewish ceremony could be found in the Catholic sources reporting the visit – *L'Osservatore Romano* (April 14-15, 1986, p. 5), *La Civiltà Cattolica* (n. 3261, p. 273), *La Documentation Catholique* (n. 1917, p. 433) – I requested information directly from the synagogue of Rome. Its office provided me with a copy of the Italian-Hebrew bilingual booklet the Jews used on that day. I quote, therefore, straight from this booklet. The cited texts are my translations from its Italian original.

[227] a. **Criterium of analysis**: We do not intend here to univocally presume the symbolic meaning of the ceremonies performed by the Jews on that papal visit as a doctrinal statement. As in any ceremony, the Jewish psalms and chants read and sung there primarily reflect

          After the Pope was seated in the place of greatest prominence in the synagogue on equal footing with Elio Toaff, the chief rabbi of the Roman Jews, another rabbi began to recite a passage from Genesis (15:1-7) alluding to God's promise to Abraham:

"After these facts the word of the Lord was directed to Abraham in a vision, in these terms: 'Do not be afraid, Abraham, I am your shield; the reward you will receive will be very large.'

"And Abraham said: 'Lord God, what will You give to me? I am alone; the inheritor of my house is Eliasar from Damascus.' He added: 'You did not give me a descendant, my domestic servant will be my heir.'

"The Lord answered him immediately: 'Your heir will not be him, but one who will come from your body.' He led him outside and said: 'Look at the sky and count the stars, if you can.' And added: 'As numerous as they will be your descendents.'

"He had faith in the Lord who increased his merit. Thus the Lord said to him: 'I am the Lord who took you from Ur-Casdim to give you this land.'"[228]

This excerpt clearly manifests that the present-day Jews see themselves as heirs to the promise made to Abraham. Now then, as St. Paul taught in passages inspired by the Holy Ghost,[229]

---

the state of mind of those who planned and carried out the program. For an observer, a sense of propriety suffices to detect their state of mind toward Catholics, who were represented by John Paul II. This allows him to assess the successive affronts made by the Jews against Catholics on that occasion, as well as the reaffirmation of their errors. Therefore, the analysis made here of the doctrinal meaning underlying the symbolism of the ceremony is not intended to go beyond this criterion of common sense.

b. **Possibility of conversion**: Someone could object that this Work fails to contemplate the possibility that John Paul II went to the synagogue as part of a clever maneuver to convert the Jews. The response is simple. Since the end does not justify the means, it is not possible for any Catholic – above all a Pope – to give the impression that he is abandoning the Faith in order to achieve a hypothetical conversion of the Israelites. In addition, John Paul II did not make the least mention that the Jews should renounce their false faith, nor did the Jews show the least propensity to do this. Therefore, whether in the moral or practical sphere, the objection lacks any foundation.

[228] *In ocassione della visita del Pontefice Giovanni Paolo II*, Communità Israelitica di Roma: Templo Maggiore, 1986, p. 4.

[229] Heb 3, 6, 7, 8, 9, 11; Rom 2:25-29; 3:27-30, especially the excerpt:

the promise made to the Patriarch is fulfilled with Our Lord Jesus Christ, and His spiritual offspring is the Holy Church. Hence, insofar as they obstinately continued to affirm that the promise of Faith is carnal rather than spiritual, and is based on the law of Moses rather than on grace,[230] the Jews reaffirmed in that ceremony the error of denying Our Lord, the apex of the Old Covenant and the founder of the New.

§ 164   Rabbi della Rocca immediately went on to read the text of Micheas (4:1-5) ending with this passage, which the Jews apply to themselves:

"For every one of all peoples will walk in the name of his god; but we will walk in the name of the Lord our God forever and ever" (Mich. 4:5).

Reciting this excerpt in the presence of John Paul II, the visible head of the Catholic Church, is to strongly insinuate that Catholics – a "people" different from the Jews – do not worship the true God while the Jews do. Again, the intention to insult Jesus Christ and the dogma of the Trinity – whose Persons for the Jews are false gods – is present, and also the intention to reaffirm their ancient errors.

§ 165   What did John Paul II do after this insult and the speeches that will be analyzed below? He recited Psalm 133 (132 of the *Vulgate*), exalting the joy of brothers living together in unity.

§ 166   Responding to this anodyne joy of John Paul II, the chief rabbi reads Psalm 124 (123 of the *Vulgate*), which reveals Jewish resentments: Catholics are implicitly viewed as enemies of God, the unjust and bestial persecutors of the Israelites, who are the true faithful protected by the Lord. The text reads:

"For not through the law was the promise to Abraham, or to his seed, that he should be heir of the world; but through the justice of faith. For if they who are of the law be heirs, faith is made void, the promise is made of no effect" (Rom 4:13-14).

Further on, in another passage, St. Paul says: "For all are not (true) Israelites (heirs to the promises) that are of Israel. ... That is to say, not they that are the children of the flesh are the children of God; but they that are the children of the promise" (Rom 9:6-8). Many other passages could be cited that affirm the same.

[230] These falsities were brilliantly refuted long ago by Catholic apologists. Among others, see Tertullian, *For the Conversion of the Jews*, translated by John Collorafi and Atila Guimarães (Los Angeles: TIA, 2007) Chaps. I, III, IV, VI, XIV.

"If the Lord were not for us, let Israel now say; if the Lord were not for us, when men rose up against us, probably they would have swallowed us up alive. When their fury was enkindled against us, then the waters [of calamity] would have drowned us; a torrent would have passed over us; the impetuous waters would have passed over us.

"Blessed be the Lord, who has not given us to be a prey to their teeth. Our persons have been delivered as a bird out of the snare of the fowlers. The snare is broken, and we are delivered. Our help is in the name of the Lord, who made heaven and earth."[231]

Such allusions to alleged Catholic persecutions of the Jews are not only insulting, but also unfounded, as was clearly demonstrated earlier. [232]

§ 167   After this violent metaphoric allusion made while reading Psalm 124, implicitly blaming Catholics for the persecutions they suffered, all the Jews present – about 1,500 – stood up to sing the hymn *Ani Ma'amin* (I believe), their equivalent of a profession of faith.[233]

The honor of Holy Church was gravely humiliated. Faith in Jesus Christ was implicitly denied by a Vicar of Christ, who went to a synagogue to assist at a profession of "faith" by those who are heirs to the Deicide and whose inexorable design is to destroy our Holy Mother Church.

§ 168   After chanting the *Ani Ma'amin* – which the Jews are said to have sung as they were led to Nazi labor camps[234] – those present observed one minute of silence for the victims of Auschwitz. The timing of this act cast an even more unfavorable light on the alleged persecutions by Catholics. Indeed, it would seem that the organizers of the ceremony were trying to blame the Holy Church for the Nazi butchery or at least to liken the persecutions waged by the German Third Reich to those allegedly carried out by Catholics. Here again, one notes a desire to offend the Church.

---

[231] Comunità Israelitica di Roma, *In ocassione della visita del Pontefice Giovanni Paolo II*, p. 6

[232] See §§ 113-142 of this Chapter.

[233] Cf. Carlo de Lucia, "La visita del Papa alla Sinagoga, 'Care amici e fratelli ebrei e cristiani...'", *L'Osservatore Romano*, April 14-15, 1986, p. 5.

[234] *Ibid.*

§ 169
Next on the program was the singing of Psalm 16 (15 of the *Vulgate*),[235] which reads:

"Their sorrows were multiplied, those who follow strange gods. I will not share the blood of their offerings, nor will I pronounce their names with my lips" (Ps. 16:4).

Since the Jews deny the divinity of Our Lord Jesus Christ and the Holy Trinity, such affirmations by rabbis and Jews were certainly intended to refer to Catholics – "those who follow strange gods."

After this affront, the refrain was recited: "Nor will I pronounce their names with my lips." This phrase clearly excludes any possibility that the names of Jesus Christ and the Holy Trinity would be recognized by the Jews and any possibility of their conversion. Incidentally, throughout the entire ceremony, the Jews avoided the least mention of Our Lord's name.

§ 170
They continued reciting the Psalm, alluding to the false notion that the inheritance of the present-day Jews is the true inheritance of God:

"The Lord is the portion of my inheritance and of my cup; you will restore my inheritance to me" (Ps 16:5).

The Psalm ends with a text that, applied to the errors of the synagogue, signifies that the latter follows the true ways of the Lord, leading to eternal happiness. This is an indirect way to intone victory over the Church, the sole means to life eternal. It reads:

"You have made known to me the ways of (immortal) life; you shall fill me with joy in your presence; at your right hand are pleasures forevermore" (Ps 16:11).

Thus, in this last Psalm chanted during John Paul II's visit to the synagogue of Rome, one can see the clear intention of offending Catholics, the "followers of false gods," and a reaffirmation of the old Jewish errors.

As the chanting of Psalm 16 (15 of the *Vulgate*) drew to an end, John Paul II and the chief rabbi embraced each other again and then left for a private meeting. The media organs covering the event did not report what was said or done at that encounter.

---

[235] The synagogue's booklet was missing Psalm 16; we are quoting it from the chronicle of the event by Carlo de Lucia, in *L'Osservatore Romano*, April 14-15, 1986, p. 5.

§ 171   During the ceremony, John Paul II received a copy of the *Torah*, a sacred book of the Jews and a *menorah*, a seven-branch candelabrum.

The ceremony ended, according to the booklet distributed in the synagogue, with the text of another profession of "faith" that the Jews chanted together. I believe it was a simplified formula of the longer profession of "faith," the above-mentioned *Ani Ma'amin*, that had already been sung.

Here are the words of the canticle, as recorded in the Jewish booklet, intoned by the Hebrew choir as John Paul II exited the synagogue:

"I believe with perfect faith in the coming of the messiah. And even if he takes a long time coming, I will wait every day until he comes."

Again, another blatant offense against Our Lord Jesus Christ. By chanting this at the end of the ceremony, the Jews categorically denied that Christ is God and the Messiah, reaffirming the old errors of their religion. If they thus affront the Word Incarnate, what scorn do they have for the Pope, the Vicar of Christ?

Outside the building of the synagogue, John Paul II embraced the chief rabbi for a third time.

*

§ 172   Reviewing this ceremony, one finds the following consequences:

- The implicit reaffirmation by the Jews of their doctrinal errors, namely, the negation of the divinity of Jesus Christ, the Most Holy Trinity, the Catholic Faith, grace, and so on.

- The symbolic reaffirmation that they are the only true followers of God.

- The manifestation of numerous, thinly-veiled insults artfully made against the Holy Church and Catholics: that they follow false gods, nurture a torrential furor against Jews, are beasts that tear apart Jews with their teeth as their prey, were accomplices in the Nazi persecutions, and so on.

Finally, as an aggravating factor, it should be noted that, according to habitual Vatican procedure, this ceremony was prepared beforehand and agreed upon by the pertinent organs of the Holy See. That is, the Vatican – and probably also the Pope – knew beforehand that these offenses would be made and approved them.

b. The Speeches of the Rabbis

§ 173   The opening address to John Paul II by the representative of the Hebrew community of Rome, rabbi Giacomo Saban, also had an arrogant tone with veiled slights and offenses. The following points should be noted:

In passing, he pejoratively called the Christian era the "vulgar era": "Soon after the end of the first millennium of the Vulgar Era ... a son of this community in Rome ... wrote the *l'Arukh*, the first compendium of norms of the Hebrews in the Diaspora."[236]

He claimed that Vatican II drew the Catholic Church closer "to the faith of Israel," although he refused to call the Catholic Faith by its name, referring to it as "the faith of the world":

"***Nostra aetate***, one of the Council documents, the one that pertains most closely to us, **introduces a different relationship between the faith of Israel and that of the world which surrounds us**, restoring to us not only what was denied to us through the centuries, but also the dignity that we had the right to see recognized."[237]

§ 174   He made recognition of the State of Israel by the Holy See a condition for taking the next step in the "fraternal dialogue" proposed by *Nostra aetate*:

"I believe I should express the hope to see the end of some reticence toward the State of Israel. The land of Israel, emotionally and spiritually, has a central place in the heart of every Jew, and a change of attitude in its regard would please not only those present here, but the whole Judaic world. ... This would be, therefore, a further step in the 'fraternal dialogue' of which *Nostra aetate* speaks. ... I do not hesitate to believe this will be done."[238]

---

[236] Cf. Giacomo Saban, Greeting by the President of the Israelite Community of Rome, *L'Osservatore Romano,* April 14-15, 1986, p. 5.

[237] *Ibid.*

[238] *Ibid.*

As is known, for the Jews the State of Israel represents a messianic aspiration linked to the long-awaited dominion of Israel over the whole world.[239] Thus, the rabbis' request that the Holy See recognize Israel must be viewed in light of the Jews' religious conviction of world hegemony.

§ 175   In a later speech by chief rabbi Elio Toaff, the following reaffirmations of the false Jewish faith and more insults to the Holy Church and the Catholic Faith should be pointed out:

He called the Church's 2,000-year policy toward the Jewish errors an "inadmissible teaching of scorn":

"We find ourselves, therefore, **facing a true and authentic turnabout in the policy of the Church**, which is now looking at Jews with sentiments of esteem and respect, **abandoning its teaching of scorn,** whose inadmissibility Jules Isaac ... called to the attention of Pope John."[240]

§ 176   He affirmed the unshakable "fidelity" of the Jewish people to their false faith throughout History, which supposedly would make them the last surviving people of Antiquity. It is noteworthy that this self-eulogy of Judaism as a religion, expressed immediately after the insolent criticism of the conduct of the Holy Church toward Jews, transcribed above, clearly implies that the Jewish "martyrs" were victims of the Church's "teaching of scorn." He stated:

"In the historic moment in which we are living, my thoughts turn with admiration, recognition and sorrow to the infinite number of Jewish martyrs, who serenely faced death for the sanctification of the Name of God. **To them is due the merit that our faith never wavered and fidelity to the Lord and to His Law never diminished through the centuries. Through their merit the Jewish people still lives, the only one of all the peoples of Antiquity."[241]**

He proposed spreading the Jewish errors as a way to achieve the irenic and ecumenical yearnings of John Paul II:

---

[239] Cf. H. Delassus, *La conjuration antichrétienne*, vol. 3, pp. 1233-1248.

[240] Cf. Elio Toaff, Greeting by the Chief Rabbi of the Israelite Community of Rome, *apud L'Osservatore Romano,* April 14-15, 1986, p. 5.

[241] *Ibid.*

"**We propose to disseminate Israel's idea of moral and spiritual monotheism in order to unite men and the world in love.**"[242]

§ 177   He also made veiled mention of the Gnostic-Jewish doctrine of the Eternal Feminine:[243]

"At the same time we reaffirm the universal paternity of God over all men, drawing our inspiration from the prophets who taught that **this filial love unites all living beings in the maternal bosom of the infinite, as in its natural womb.**"[244]

§ 178   He insisted that the State of Israel be recognized, thus proclaiming the religious-messianic-hegemonic role that the Jews attribute to it:

"**The return of the Hebrew people to their land must be recognized as a good and irrevocable victory for the world, for this is a prelude ... to that era of universal fraternity to which we all aspire** and to that redeeming peace whose firm promise is found in the Bible. **The recognition of this irreplaceable role of Israel in the plan of final redemption promised by God cannot be denied.**"[245]

Thus did the speeches of the rabbis constitute a categorical reaffirmation of the Jewish errors, their false hopes and strong offenses against the Holy Church.

E. Conclusion of this Analysis

§ 179   The conclusion to the analysis of this visit, in our view, is clear and painful. John Paul II went to the synagogue of Rome for these purposes:

- To try to annul the foundation in Revelation for the crime of Deicide;

- To condemn the wise 2,000-year-old conduct of the Holy Church in relation to the Jews;

---

[242] *Ibid.*

[243] This doctrine, which also is understood as a basis of progressivist thinking, will be analyzed in Vol. VIII of this Collection, *Fumus Satanae*.

[244] Cf. Elio Toaff, Greeting by the Chief Rabbi, *L'Osservatore Romano*, April 14-15, 1986, p. 5.

[245] *Ibid.*

- To praise their false faith and "anathematize" whoever should criticize or censure the followers of Caiaphas from the religious standpoint.

In contrast, the rabbis, explicitly in their speeches and symbolically in their recitation of psalms and passages from the Bible, made this arrogant retribution:

- They insistently reaffirmed their false faith;
- They condemned the historic attitude of the Church;
- They insulted the honor of the Church and of Catholics;
- They proclaimed the need for Jewish hegemony over the world;
- They demanded the Holy See recognize their State, to which they attributed a messianic destiny.

This is what took place during the visit of John Paul II to the synagogue of Rome. *Qui habet aurem, audiat...*[246]

*

§ 180   In this Chapter I, we could go on to analyze offenses against the Catholic Religion represented by eulogies made by Catholic ecclesiastics and theologians of Islam, Buddhism, Hinduism and Atheism. However, the pages dedicated to the first Items – Protestantism, the Eastern Schism and Judaism – far exceeded the space allotted to this part. For this reason, the Author finds himself obliged to include a bibliographical appendix at the end of this Chapter so that the Reader can find other direct or indirect eulogies of the enemies of the Church.

*   *   *

---

[246] He that has an ear, let him hear (Apoc 2:7).

Bibliographical Appendix to Chapter I

Below are some works that contain other offenses against the Catholic Religion that could be included in this Chapter. The titles are distributed by the eulogies of the Conciliar Prelates and theologians toward different religions.

Protestantism:

Yves Congar, *La crisi nella chiesa e Mons. Lefèbvre* (Brescia: Queriniana, 1976), p. 48; *Jean Puyo interroge le Pére Congar* (Paris: Centurion, 1975), pp. 49, 63, 151; *Un peuple messianique*, (Paris: Cerf. 1975), p. 88; *La parole et le souffle*, (Paris: Desclée, 1984), pp. 57, 115; Jean Danielou, "Problema do diálogo," in V.A., *Cinco problemas que desafiam a Igreja hoje*, (São Paulo: Herder, 1970) pp. 133-134; Avery Dulles, "Ecumenismo: problemi e possibilità per il futuro," in V.A., *Verso la Chiesa del terzo millennio* (Brescia: Queriniana, 1979), pp. 118-119; Roger Etchegaray, "Una nuova speranza per la vecchia Europa," *L'Osservatore Romano*, November 10, 1983, p. 5; M. von Galli, "Matrimonio mixto," in V.A., *La reforma que llega de Roma* (Barcelona: Plaza-Janes, 1970), p. 172; Leo Alting von Geusau, "La Chiesa, `scandalo' del mondo," in V.A., *La fine della Chiesa come società perfetta* (Verona: Mondadori,1968), p. 156; John Paul II, Speech at the Ecumenical Council of Churches, *L'Osservatore Romano*, June 14, 1984, pp. 1, 5; Speech to the Leaders of the British Christian Churches, *L'Osservatore Romano*, April 30, 1983, p. 1; Walter Kasper, "L'Insegnamento dei Concilii Laterano IV e Tridentino," *L'Osservatore Romano*, October 8, 1983, p. 9; Hans Küng, "Vaticano III: Problemi e prospettive per il futuro," in V.A., *Verso la Chiesa del terzo millennio* (Brescia: Queriniana, 1979), p. 76; *Veracidade - O futuro da Igreja* (São Paulo: Herder, 1969), p. 130; "La riforma liturgica del Concilio Vaticano II e la riunione con i cristiani separati," in V.A., *I grandi temi del Concilio* (Rome: Paoline, 1965), pp. 108-110; *O que deve permanecer na Igreja* (Petrópolis: Vozes, 1976), p. 14; *Vida eterna?*, p. 230; "Ecumenismo concreto fra comunità svedesi," *L'Osservatore Romano*, November 29, 1984, p. 5; "Eclesiologia, antropologia e teologia nel pensiero e nell'opera di Lutero," *L'Osservatore Romano*, December 17, 1983, p. 7; Gérard Philips, *La Chiesa e il suo mistero* (Milan: Jaca, 1975), p. 560; Karl Rahner, "La Immaculada Concepción," in *Escritos de Teología*, vol. 1, p. 230; Edward Schillebeeckx, *Le mariage*, p. 345; "Igreja ou igrejas?" in V.A., *Cinco problemas que desafiam a Igreja hoje*, p. 29; *Cristo, sacramento dell'incontro con Dio* (Rome: Paoline, 1970), p. 273; Joseph E. Vercruysse, "Per una valutazione obiettiva dell'opera di Martin Lutero," *L'Osservatore Romano*, November 10, 1983, p. 2; Johannes Willebrands, Statement to RAI-1 TV Network, *L'Osservatore Romano*, November 7-8, 1983, p. 4.

Eastern Schism:

Antonio Acerbi, *Due Ecclesiologie* (Bologna: Dehoniane, 1975), p. 67; Yves Congar, *Jean Puyo interroge le Pére Congar*, p. 51; *La parole et le souffle*, p. 20; "Paul VI und der Ökumenismus," *L'Osservatore Romano*, (German ed.), September 23, 1977, p. 4; P. Duprey, "Ein ganz aussergewöhnliches ökumenisches Ereignis," *Der Christliche Osten*, n. 31, 1976, pp. 41-43, *apud* W. Siebel, *Katholisch oder Konziliar*, p. 422; Leo Alting von Geusau, "La Chiesa, 'scandalo' del mondo," in V.A., *La fine della Chiesa como società perfetta*, p. 156; John Paul II, Message to Dimitrios I, ecumenical patriarch of Constantinople, *L'Osservatore Romano*, June 14, 1984, p. 3; Speech at the Orthodox Center of Chambèsy, *L'Osservatore Romano*, June 12, 1984; Speech to the Secretariat for the Union of Christians, *L'Osservatore Romano*, November 17, 1984, p. 5; Hans Küng, *Veracidade - O futuro da Igreja*, pp. 130, 140; "Vaticano III: problemi e prospettive per il futuro," in V. A., *Verso la Chiesa del terzo millennio*, p. 103; Paul VI, General audience of August 2, 1967, in *Insegnamenti di Paolo VI*, vol. 5, pp. 410-413; Paul VI, Allocution after the Trip to Turkey, in *L'Osservatore Romano*, 8-3-1967, apud P. Delhaye, *Fe y pluralismo teologico en el Magisterio del ultimo decenio*, p. 164; Edward Yarnold, "La pluralité des formulations de la doctrine," *La Documentation Catholique*, November 2, 1984, pp. 868-869.

Judaism:

Hans Urs von Balthasar, "Dieu a parlé un langage d'homme," in *Parole de Dieu et Liturgie* (Paris: Cerf, 1958), p. 85; *La gloire et la croix – Les aspects esthétiques de la Révélation – II Styles: de Jean de la Croix* à Peguy (Paris: Aubier & Montaigne, 1972), pp. 291-293; G. Baum, "L'Olocausto e la teologia politica," *Concilium* 1984/5, pp. 68-69; Yves Congar, *Chrétiens en dialogue* (Paris: Cerf, 1964), pp. 530, 534; *Église catholique et France moderne* (Paris: Hachette, 1978), p. 145; R. Etchegaray, Riconciliazione con gli ebrei, *L'Osservatore Romano*, October 5, 1983, Supplement, p. III; Roger Etchegaray, Talk in the Synod of 1983, *L'Osservatore Romano*, 10-5-1983, Synod 83 Supplement, n. 4, p. III; Tommaso Federici, "Religione e religioni oggi," in V.A., *Incontro tra la religion*, (Verona: Mondatori, 1969), p. 29; Mario von Galli, "Cristianos y judíos," in V.A., *La reforma que llega de Roma* (Barcelona: Plaza & Janes, 1970), pp. 186-188; Boaventura Kloppenburg, *A eclesiologia do Vaticano II* (Petrópolis: Vozes, 1971), p. 42; Hans Küng and Pinchas Lapide, *Gesù segno di contradizione* (Brescia: Queriniana, 1980), pp. 13, 16; Hans Küng, *Veracidade - O futuro da Igreja*, pp. 121-122; *A Igreja*, (Lisbon: Moraes, 1969), vol. 1, pp. 192-203; John Paul II to the representatives of the French Jewish community on May 31, 1980, in *Insegnamenti di Giovanni Paolo II*, 1980, vol. III/1, pp. 1560-1561; C. MacLeod, "A Bíblia, o judaísmo e as relações judeu-cristãs," *Concilium* 1976/2, pp. 71-73, 76-78; Johann Baptist Metz, "Al conspetto degli eboci - La teologia cristiana dopo Auschwitz," *Concilium* 1984/5, pp. 50-52; *Mas allá de la religión burguesa*, pp. 25-29; G. Pattaro, *Riflessioni sulla teologia post-conciliare* (Rome: A.V.E., 1970), p. 109; Cornelius Rijk, "As relações judeu-cristãs e o uso dos livros sagrados de outras religiões no culto cristão," *Concilium*

1976/2, pp. 92, 96; "Gesù annuncia il Regno," in V.A., *Il Regno di Dio che vienne* (Turin: Elle Di Ci, 1977), pp. 250-251.

Islam:

Michael Fitzgerald, "Liturgia cristã e textos islamíticos," *Concilium* 1976/2, pp. 66, 70; John Paul II to the representatives of the Muslim community in France, May 31, 1980, *Insegnamenti di Giovanni Paolo II*, 1980, vol. III/1, pp. 1558-1559; John Paul II to Muslim youths in the stadium of Casablanca, *Secretariatus pro non Christianis Bulletin*, 1985, XX/3-60, p. 242; Hans Küng, *Veracidade - O futuro da Igreja*, pp. 122-123; Nerbert Lohfink, *Profetas ontem e hoje*, p. 86; Y. Moubarac, "L'Islam - Les questions que le Catholicisme se pose à propos de l'Islam," in V.A., *Bilan de la Théologie du XXe. siècle*, (Tournai-Paris: Casterman, 1970), vol. 1, pp. 379-380; D. Power and H. Schmidt, Editorial, *Concilium* 1976/2, pp. 3-4.

Buddhism:

Paul Cheng, "La devozione popolare," *L'Osservatore Romano*, October 5, 1983, Supplement, p. I; P. Cheng, Talk at the Synod, *L'Osservatore Romano*, Synod Supplement, 10-5-1983, p. 1; R. Corless, "Perspectiva cristã sobre a libertação budista," *Concilium* 1978/6, pp. 86, 92-94; E. Cornélis, "Le Bouddhisme," in V.A., *Bilan de la Théologie du XXe. siécle*, vol. 1, pp. 353-355; D. Dubarle, "Espiritualidade budista e o sentido cristão de Deus," *Concilium* 1978/6, pp. 74-76, 78; H. Dumoulin, "Liberação no budismo," *Concilium* 1978/6, pp. 30-32; H. Enomiya and Lassalle, "Diálogo budista-cristão no Japão hoje" *Concilium* 1978/6, p. 125; A. Fernando, "Revelação cristã e iluminação budista," Concilium 1976/2, pp. 43-45, 47-49, 53-55; John Paul II, Allocution to the Leaders of the Main Religions in the Chapel of the Nunciature in Seoul, *L'Osservatore Romano*, May 6, 1984, Supplement, p. XV; Homily in the Mass for Peace in the World in Bangkok, May 10, 1984, *L'Osservatore Romano*, 5-11-1984, Supplement, p. XXVIII; Hans Küng, *Vida Eterna?* (Madrid: Cristiandad, 1983), pp. 10-12; Henri de Lubac, *La rencontre du Bouddhisme et de l'Occident* (Paris: Aubier-Montaigne, 1968), pp. 210-211; Interview in *Il Messagero*, February 2, 1983, p. 3; "L'Accademia S. Bonaventura per il dialogo con il Buddismo," *L'Osservatore Romano*, February 24, 1984, p. 6; A. Pieris, "Buddismo: sfida ai cristiani," *Concilium* 1986/1, pp. 94-96; Edward Schillebeeckx, "Igreja Cristã e outras religiões," in V.A., *Cinco problemas que desafiam a Igreja hoje*, p. 23; P. J. Schoonenberg, "Interpretação ou compreensão do homen Jesus Cristo," in V.A., *Cinco problemas que desafiam a Igreja hoje*, p. 82; G. F. Svidercoschi, "Saggezza e fede," *L'Osservatore Romano*, May 11,1984, p. 3; Hans Waldenfels, "Palavra e silêncio no budismo," *Concilium* 1976/2, pp. 37, 41-42; J. W. Walgrave, "Relazioni sacro-storiche tra la Chiesa e i culti non cristiani," in V.A., *I grandi temi del Concilio*, (Rome: Paoline, 1965), pp. 941-943; Marcello Zago, "O diálogo entre cristãos e budistas no sudeste asiático," *Concilium* 1978/6, pp. 114-115.

Hinduism:

A. Camps, "Nouveau dialogue avec l'hindouisme en Inde," *Concilium* 181, 1983, p. 121; M. Dhavamony, "Culto cristão e escrituras sagradas do hinduísmo," *Concilium* 1976/2, pp. 12, 16-17; T. Matus, "La ricerca di Dio nell'induismo," *Concilium* 1976/2, pp. 18-23; John Paul II, Speech to the authorities of New Delhi, February, 1, 1986, *L'Osservatore Romano*, February 12, 1986, Supplement, pp. II; Speech in homage to Mahatma Gandhi in the city of Raj Ghat, February 1, 1986, *L'Osservatore Romano*, February 12, 1986, Supplement, p. III; Speech to the representatives of various religions, February 2, 1986, *L'Osservatore Romano*, February 12, 1986, Supplement, pp. IX- X; Simon Ignatius Pimenta, "Autentica inculturazione," *L'Osservatore Romano*, October 5, 1983, Supplement, p. III, Talk at the Synod of Bishops, *L'Osservatore Romano*, Synod 1983 Supplement, p. III; R. de Smet, "La Théologie en Inde," in V.A., *Bilan de la Théologie du XXe. siécle*, vol. 1, pp. 365, 367-369; J. W. Walgrave, "Relazioni sacro-storiche tra la Chiesa e i culti non cristiani," in V.A., *I grandi temi del Concilio*, pp. 937-939.

Atheism:

M.-D. Chenu, *Jacques Duquesne interroge le Père Chenu*, p. 66; "O comunismo é uma idéia cristã 'enlouquecida'?" in V.A., *Os maiores teólogos respondem*, pp. 158-159; Y. Congar, *La parole et le souffle*, p. 114; *Église catholique et France moderne*, pp. 16, 256; *Un peuple messianique*, p. 119; "Theology's Tasks After Vatican II," in V.A., *Theology of Renewal*, vol. 1, p. 51; "Dialogue entre les Pères Congar et Girardi," *I.C.I.*, n. 351, January, 1, 1970, pp. 24, 25, 28, 32; Diez-Alegria, *Cristianismo sem Cristo?* (Caxias do Sul: Paulinas, 1970), p. 136; H. Küng, *Veracidade - O futuro da Igreja*, pp. 86-87; Luis Maldonado, *La nueva secularidad* (Barcelona, Nueva Terra, 1968), p. 98; E. Schillebeeckx, "La théologie," in V.A., *Les catholiques hollandais*, p. 13; P. J. Schoonenberg, "Interpretação ou compreensão do homen Jesus Cristo," in V.A., *Cinco problemas que desafiam a Igreja hoje*, pp. 82-83; Bernard Sesboué, *O Evangelho na Igreja*, (São Paulo: Paulinas, 1977), p. 16.

* * *

Chapter II

OFFENSES AGAINST GOD MADE BY CONCILIAR AND POST-CONCILIAR HEADS

§ 1

In Chapter I, we saw some of the shocking consequences of the spirit of the Council. It has caused John Paul II and Benedict XVI, highly placed Vatican dignitaries as well as important theologians to make dithyrambic eulogies of heretics, schismatics and Jews. Now, it seems appropriate for the Reader to turn his eyes on another type of offense: those made against God. Thus, he can better know the *animus injuriandi* of the progressivist current.

An injury against God is one of the gravest sins that can be committed. Such sin touches the deepest essence of the concept of Religion, by which man lovingly recognizes God as the omnipotent Creator and binds himself to Him (religion comes from the Latin verb *relego, relegere*, i.e., to retake the abandoned road). This sin is a direct offense against the first two Commandments of the Decalogue that order us to love God above all things and not to take His holy name in vain. These constitute the foundation of the Law and the Old Testament and are confirmed and fortified by the New Testament with the First Great Commandment: "Thou shalt love the Lord thy God with thy whole heart, and with thy whole soul, and with thy whole mind" (Mt 22:37).

§ 2

It is one thing for someone to commit an isolated sin; it is something altogether different when a series of offenses are systematically made following a defined plan[1] and established method and are based on a philosophical structure. In this case, the gravity of each offense is greatly increased, since it becomes the expression of an opposite doctrine. For this reason, through the centuries Holy Mother Church slowly refined a whole symptomatology to characterize the heretic, even when he does not reveal his thinking.[2]

---

[1] On the explicit plan of the progressivists, see the Table of Content in Vol. IV, *Animus Delendi I* & Vol. V, *Animus Delendi II* of this Collection.

[2] Cf. A. V. Xavier da Silveira, "Não só a heresia pode ser condenada pela autoridade eclesiástica," *Catolicismo*, November 1967; "Atos, gestos, atitudes e omissões podem caracterizar o herege," *Catoli-*

Further, should this series of offenses be not just the actions of an individual but the expression of a whole current in the bosom of the Church, one can conclude that the gravity of the action has reached its very apex.

It is to know this grave sequence of offenses against the Divine Creator made by conciliar leaders that we invite the Reader.

1. God Is an Idol, the Opium of the People; He Should Die

§ 3

The first shocking text that distorts the notion of God is by Cardinal Leo Jozef Suenens, one of the four Moderators who directed the Council and doubtlessly one of the most influential Prelates at Vatican II.[3] Here he criticizes God as the Church has always presented Him:

"Men and Christians ... have made an idol of God, a caricature of God. Before condemning atheism, we must know what [image of] God it wanted to destroy. Let us stop a moment and examine some current images of God that were still very common a while ago:

"To many, God seemed a creator who had set the world in motion at its origin, rather than the creator who is always present yesterday and today.

"Many conceived the divinity in a fixed, static, abstract vision immersed in a context that largely followed the Hellenist model. Once in a while, God would intervene in this world, as if by miracle.

---

cismo, December 1967. On the main characteristics of those under suspicion of heresy, see in this Volume, Chapter I, Note 2.

[3] Suenens' strong influence on the direction taken at Vatican II is found in the Pastoral Constitution *Gaudium et spes,* which caused a "charismatic shock" that established the "decisive line of the Council," in the words of Fr. Chenu. That Constitution originated from a speech by Suenens in the Conciliar Hall on December 4, 1962 (cf. M.-D. Chenu, "The History of Salvation and the Historicity of Man in the Renewal of Theology," in V.A., *Theology of Renewal*, vol. 1, p. 155).

In his chronicle on the Council, Fr. Antoine Wenger comments on that speech of Suenens, noting that, with it, "Cardinal Suenens established a new program for the Council" (Cf. *Vatican II - Chronique de la deuxième session*, Paris: Centurion, 1963-1966, p. 242). The title of the Dogmatic Constitution on the Church, *Lumen gentium*, was also taken from one of the Cardinal's interventions (Cf. Gérard Philips, *La Chiesa e il suo mistero*, Milan: Jaca Books, 1982, p. 19).

"God was considered not as the first cause in relation to the secondary causes immanent in the world, but as the principal cause in relation to the instrumental causes. God gives rain and fertility; God makes it rain on the good and the bad. 'It is better to confide in God than in horses and cars...' Along these same lines, God interferes in the world. This gave rise to a series of insoluble problems (liberty-grace, the science of God-liberty).

"This God, who is found at the origin of the world, as the architect and engineer in an attitude of repose, as the one who explains and covers for the ignorance of man and his incapacity, is the same God who at present guarantees the established order, the *status quo*, who shields authority with the divine right and protects the strong against revolutions, who counsels the poor to be patient and impedes social reform, this God is the opium of the people.

"We can analyze diverse caricatures of God. To cite only one, let us consider the caricature of God of providence who 'providentially' spared us from a calamity, but permitted the same calamity to fall on someone else. This is a type of 'rubbish' providence. ...

"It is truly understandable that this God should die so that the world can live, and also so that God can live. God is not dead: He changed places (moved). In this sense, once the work of critique is finished, one can speak of 'God after the death of God.'" [4]

§ 4   Echoing these offenses are those proffered by Fr. Bernard Sesboüé, S.J., then a member of the International Theological Commission. Commenting on the traditional conception of God, he says:

"It has often been said that contemporary atheism is fed by the deformed images of God presented by Christians. ... There is the God who is the simple mechanic of the world, the God whose arbitrary and omnipotent paternity takes pleasure in a childish destruction of man, the God who cruelly punishes those who fall by weakness or by wickedness, the God who is the policeman of the social order, the God who allows no place for liberty and is satisfied by the homage

---

[4] Leo Jozef Suenens, "Cristianismo sem Deus?" in V.A., *Cristianismo sem Cristo?* (Paulinas: Caxias do Sul, 1970), pp. 63-66.

of slaves, etc. **Undoubtedly these are caricatures**, but certainly these characteristics obscure the revelation of the God of Jesus Christ, who liberates and saves.[5]

§ 5   Fr. Chenu also rebels against the notion of a transcendental God and calls Him "a false God" and "an idol":

"This Christian [simpleton] is ... tempted to resolve the duality of body-spirit and of time-eternity by an escape to the beyond, to the world of sacrality and transcendence. **Today we are trying to achieve unification** in an opposite way: **by placing the eternal into the temporal, the spiritual into the corporal, by bringing God back to the profane.** ...

"In the same way, **we insist on immanence, on anthropology.** It is a way of rediscovering the theology of the Incarnation, that is, a regime where God is on earth. **It is only in earthly events that I perceive the presence of God, his economy and his providence. Otherwise I transform him into a false god, an idol, a place of escape and, as the Marxists say, of alienation.**"[6]

§ 6   In his turn, the most influential conciliar theologian of the German world, Karl Rahner,[7] writes:

"What is understood by the word 'God' is extremely vague; in fact, what many understand by this word is false and constitutes the abiding cause of atheism."[8]

§ 7   Since atheists do not believe in the transcendence of God and eternal life, but instead expect the realization of a future utopia on this earth, the progressivists changed the meaning of the word "God" and the concept of divinity to be in accord with the atheists. Although they continue to use the word "God," they no

---

[5] Bernard Sesboüé, *O Evangelho na Igreja* (São Paulo: Paulinas, 1977), p. 177.

[6] *Jacques Duquesne interroge le Pére Chenu – Une théologie en liberté* (Paris: Centurion, 1975), pp. 79-80.

[7] On the influence of Rahner on Vatican II and the warm support he received from Paul VI, see Vol. II, *Animus Injuriandi I*, Introduction, Note 14 k,o,t; Chap. III, Note 42.Theologian and author Battista Mondim confirms: "Rahner contributed decisively to make of Vatican II the council of the dialogue between the Church and the world" (*Os grandes teólogs do século vinte*, São Paulo: Paulinas, 1979, vol. 1, p.95).

[8] Karl Rahner, "Qual é il messaggio cristiano? Necessità di una nuova formulazione," in V.A., *L'Avvenire della Chiesa* (Brescia: Queriniana, 1970), p. 110.

longer apply it to the transcendent God,[9] but rather to the uto-pian future that the communists desire. As they say, the "God of the Above" was absorbed by the "God of the Ahead."[10]

Thus, they apparently continue to believe, since they re-fer to "God," but, in fact, they have essentially adopted the athe-ist and communist position of believing exclusively in an earthly future. It is a ruse to deceive the faithful. By using the word "God," they appease Catholics; but by their real understanding of the concept, they follow the atheists.

§ 8   The texts cited above already contained this double meaning of God. The use of this new notion of God becomes clearer, however, in the next passage by Cardinal de Lubac. He concludes by agreeing that atheism can play "a providential role" in a "new blossoming of the faith." De Lubac affirms:

"If, as has been written, 'modern atheism is no longer an arrival point but a point of departure,' if 'this is the situation where we find ourselves and on whose basis we must think and act,' then it is permitted to hope that this new march will be a march toward God. **God is never behind**, among the dregs. Whatever direction our steps may lead us, behold He is ahead of us, behold He calls us, and if we have truly progressed, we will find Him augmented. Thus, **we can also endure, without faltering, the temporary night into which we are plunged by 'eclipses of God' and even conceive, without fear, the pos-**

---

[9] On the difference between the true Catholic concept of the transcen-dence of the Absolute in relation to the contingent, that is, of the Cre-ator in relation to the creature, and the false progressivist concept of transcendence, which considers only the insufficient transcendence of the genre in relation to the species, see Vol. VII, *Destructio Dei*, Chap. IV.2; Vol. IX, *Creatio*, Chap. V.

[10] Along these lines, Fr. Pierre Teilhard de Chardin writes: "The time had now come when I could see one thing, that, from the depths of the cosmic future and the heights of heaven, it was still God, it was *always the same God*, who was calling me. It was a God of the Ahead who had suddenly appeared athwart the traditional God of the Above. ... For the basic truth is: If we say 'God of the Above' + 'God of the Ahead,' what does this new equation, fundamental to all Religion in the future, give us if not an ultimate God whose dimensions are 'Theocosmic,' that is, 'Christic'?" (*Le coeur de la matière*, Paris: Seuil, 1976, pp. 65, 67).

On the absorption of the "God of the Above" by the "God of the Ahead," see Vol. VII, *Destructio Dei*, Chap. IV.2.C; in Vol. X, *Peccatum, Re-demptio*, Chap. VIII, 2.F, will address the evolution in God himself.

sible providential role of an atheism where a new blossoming of the faith is being prepared."[11]

§ 9   Addressing the concept of God and his relationship with atheists, Msgr. Sartori, then president of the Association of Italian Theologians, insinuates that Catholics will remain the "rich men of the Gospel" as long as they do not renounce the gifts of God, whereas the atheists are the "poor" whom we should help. Although he admits the existence of God, Sartori seems to conceive a God different from Church teaching when he insists that each man must renounce his gifts from God and his own individuality so that only the "gift of others" lives in him. These words by the theologian draw our attention:

"Ecumenism is teaching the churches that the greatest happiness lies in discovering that we are empty and, therefore, we need to receive, to fill ourselves with the gift of others, which begins by esteeming the gifts of others.

"I am thinking even of the statements of some atheists: In an interview, citing and playing with a phrase by Dietrich Bonhoeffer, Geno Pampaloni maintained, '**It is necessary for the faithful to live as if God did not exist so they can be in harmony with those who do not believe.** What I say to my atheist friends is that we, on the contrary, should live as if God did exist.'

"In an interview with J. Guitton, French scientist J. Rostand said: '**You faithful can stop thinking about God** because you already have him; we atheists do not have him. I at least am always thinking about him.' **Perhaps the poor of God, the poor in faith, also are included among the biblical 'poor' in whose midst God is present and the Spirit is working**. We, on the contrary, live like rich men, satiated; the gifts of God are our riches. ...

"The capacity to esteem and value what comes from outside one's own initiative – this is a theme for reflection for one in authority. **It requests from the one who has the mission to live for others and in others, the divestment and emptying of himself**, instead of pretending that the law, and even the gifts belonging to others, should spring from oneself." [12]

---

[11] Henri de Lubac, *Athéisme et sens de l'homme* (Paris: Cerf, 1968), p. 89.

[12] Luigi Sartori, "Lo Spirito é effuso su tutti," in V.A., *Lo Spirito Santo pegno e primizia del Regno - Atti della XIX Sessione di formazione ecumenica organizzata dal Segretariato Attività Ecumeniche (SAE)*

§ 10

In this Item 1 we have seen either frontal offenses against God by the denial of Catholic doctrine, or affirmations that the very concept of God has changed to harmonize with the teaching of atheists and Marxists. Among those making such offenses are some of the most important theologians of the Conciliar Church.

2. God Has Demonic Traits; Hell Is His Proper Domain

§ 11

Innumerable progressivists believe that the internal relationship of the Three Persons of the Trinity is not one of perfect harmony and happiness, as the Church has always taught. They imagine an opposition between the Eternal Father and the Son that supposedly is reflected in Creation. The Father represents the law, justice, the separation between good and evil; consequently, he rewards the good and chastises the evil. The Son, on the contrary, is characterized by a sentimental love for the wicked; he is willing to pardon them at any cost and draw them close to himself, thus defying the designs of the Eternal Father.[13]

This type of Hegelian conflict between the two Divine Persons and its projection in Creation is supposedly resolved by the synthesis that surmounts them both: the Holy Spirit. The principal purpose of this "Spirit" is to be a symbiosis between truth and error, good and evil, light and darkness.

The Eternal Father emphasizes the supremacy of the good; the Son is turned principally toward the wicked; the Spirit blends and brings them together.

This view, profoundly opposed to Catholic doctrine, presents God the Father as draconian and cruel since he practices "discrimination" between good and evil. The era inaugurated by the Son would be more "amiable" since it began to abolish the prejudices of the Father. The era of the Spirit is, for progressivists, the ideal one, because it would reach a synthesis, or, simply said, the opposite of what the Father represents.

This syncretistic theory, which will be dealt with in more detail later in this Collection,[14] is nurtured by a romanticist climate that favors the wicked and a prejudice against the clear affirmation of truth and the supremacy of good over evil.

(Turin: Elle Di Ci, 1982), pp.115-116.

[13] Besides this Item 2 (§§ 11-14), see Chap. III, §§ 12-20 of this Volume; see also Vol. II, *Animus Injuriandi I*, Chap. I, §§ 5-14; 17-21; Vol. VIII, *Fumus Satanae*, Chap. VI.

[14] See Vol. VIII, *Fumus Satanae*, Chaps. V, VI.

Consistent with this thinking, we present in this Item offenses progressivists make against God the Father, deeming His transcendence and justice "demonic characteristics." Further, hell and the lost world are considered His suitable domain.

§ 12   Fr. Hans Urs von Balthasar, one of the main spokesmen for Progressivism, claims that for God not to be "demonic," the Holy Spirit must diminish himself to the level of the wicked so that – without requiring their conversion – the Spirit can assume them, or draw them into himself, and prevail.

In the texts below, von Balthasar also contends that because the God of Justice asks man to suffer for His greater glory, He would have demonic characteristics as well as Marcionite, Tertullianist, Calvinist and Jansenist leanings.

Let us explain in our own words the first part of his text, which is somewhat obscure.[15] Von Balthasar affirms that the Spirit of God dwells in the interior of man. Thence he infers that there would be no essential difference between divine love and human love. The former would supposedly assume the latter. He further declares that the difference between man and the absolute (God) has been overcome and all that remains are the Trinitarian differences. Finally, he supposes that God in the whole world and even in Hell, abolishes, through an infusion of divine love, the differences between Himself and Creation. All differences are assumed by Him and become Trinitarian differences.

He continues: "**This process appears**, first, **in the creating work of the Father, which – despite all its possible and real decadence, its tragic aspect and demonic character – is not only claimed beforehand by the heart of the Creator, but is raised up and assumed by him. If this were not the case, God the Creator would have to admit demonic characteristics** – either an extreme indifference or a submission to fatality. **A God who, from the height of his intangible happiness,**

---

[15] "In Christian life, man is neither conquered by God ... nor brought before the Absolute in his tragic difference ... For the Spirit of God is interiorized in him and brings man's differences into the difference of the intra-divine love, and thus completes, conserves and overcomes them. God reveals the abysmal depth of this difference and the mortal seriousness of his love, by raising up the tragic and apocalyptical differences between God and the World, between God and Hell, to the very heart of his own difference, which encompasses everything" (H. U. von Balthasar, *De l'Integration – Aspects d'une théologie de l'Historie,* Bruges: Desclée de Brouwer, 1970, p. 83).

would allow his creatures to suffer and use those sufferings for his own glorification, would not have a relationship with his creatures that should be imitated. ...

"Finally, one sees this process ... in the redeeming work of the Holy Spirit who triumphs over the difference of guilt that exists in sinners, but not by the superiority of a God who judges everything as if he were holding the destiny of man in his hands. **If he overcomes it, it is through an infinite effort by the Spirit who penetrates the hopeless rigidity and torpor of a finite and corroded conscience so that, taking that guilt as the starting point, he opens it to infinite love.** ...

"**These are possibilities that can be understood neither from the Christian standpoint nor by the draconian laws of a Marcionist Yahweh ... nor by the infernal decrees ... of a Tertullianist, Calvinist, Jansenist God.** They can only be understood by a doctrine of the Holy Spirit whose love precedes these later tragic contradictions. It is at this precise point that the doctrine of the Church is inserted."[16]

§ 13   The same Hegelian conception of a dispute between the Father and the Son appears in the text below, which pretends that the Word Incarnate brought light to the world of darkness that was the domain of the Eternal Father. Von Balthasar writes:

"If the Son sets out to look for his enemy and brings him the love he does not have, it is because he sees God behind his enemy, God the Father who created that man, making him in his image and likeness. ...

"That is to say, **the Son comes as a Light to the darkness of the world, which does not receive or understand him, and goes to the alien, the stranger. Doing this, the Son places himself in the domain of the Father, because that lost world is the sacred creation of the Father. Hell is also the domain of the Father; he is the God-Judge, the guardian of his own sacred order of the world.** Entering these domains, the Son places himself at the service of the Father, who wants to deliver him over for the sake of the world and who sends him out for the work of Redemption. ...

"And if it is true that everything was created by the Father in the Son, then the Father permitted this darkness and distancing from sinners only because he foresaw the future coming

---

[16] H. U. von Balthasar, *De l'Integration*, pp. 83-84

of his Son. **It was the Father's plan that everything that had been alienated be embraced by the love of the Son**, which will never be withdrawn. But, **in order to follow the most profound will of the Father, the Son deliberately had to take a step toward the darkness, toward the world of hatred and perdition. In Christian love**, as it was originally, **the love of one's enemies is the principle of all heavenly love**."[17]

§ 14   A similar offense against God can be found in the writings of Fr. Luis Maldonado, liturgist and professor at the University of Salamanca. Maldonado endorses the criticisms of atheists, finding them, however, insufficient. In the following excerpt, the Spanish theologian calls traditional Faith in God "theism":

"[Luther's] theology of the cross rightly ends with this image [of 'God as the foundation and the apex of society's temporal power and morals]. For **this theist God is the one who judges and condemns the God of Jesus Christ in Jesus Christ: he is, therefore, judged and condemned by him. The God of theism, constructed with ingredients of Aristotelian philosophy and Stoicism, is the God who cannot suffer, who is impassible, immobile, immutable**. His image was formed through the logical process of analogy and induction from effect to cause.

"Modern thinking criticizes this God for three fundamental and closely-related reasons: *First*, because **such a God was a fraud to cover up social injustice and the self-deceptions of the individual; with his sacral aura he thus 'sanctioned' and legitimized' the unjust or distorted foundations of those structural mechanisms**, both collective and individual;

"*Second*, because **this conception imagines God at the expense of man (God is powerful, man is weak, etc.), it projects on the divine image the models and attributes of the Egyptian Pharaohs, Persian Kings and Roman Emperors. This notion of God is the summit and root of the strongest and most powerful of this world; it forgets other deep-seated attributes of Jewish tradition – frailty, love, fidelity, the nomadic spirit**;

"*Third*, **since this God is the ultimate cause of everything, he is responsible for the suffering of innocents; he is, therefore, a monstrous being. A God who cannot suffer cannot love. He is a narcissist, a cold, frozen and dead being**.

---

[17] H. U. von Balthasar, *El problema de Dios en el hombre actual* (Madrid: Guadarrama, 1960), pp. 292-293.

"With this approach, which follows the Aristotelian method based on analogical-causal reasoning, atheism situates itself on the same plane as theism. Its results, however, are different and opposed. **Instead of a god, it discovers the devil. But its criticism [of God] is not sufficiently radical because it has been conditioned too strongly by the adversary.** It allows itself to be led to his terrain." [18]

§ 15

The assertions of these theologians are offenses against God for two reasons:

- *First*, because He is transcendent and not an immanent being as they imagine;
- *Second*, because they pretend a supposed opposition that exists between God the Father and God the Son.

3. The Dogma of the Trinity Is Unacceptable to Today's Man; It Leads to a False Interpretation of God

§ 16

The honor due the Catholic Faith is acutely attacked when an important dogma such as the Holy Trinity is denied as obsolete. Understood as such, we include this denial among the offenses in this Volume III and not as a mere denial of the Faith, where it could be included more properly as one of the fruits of the Council.

§ 17

The German Jesuit Karl Rahner, viewed as one of the greatest theologians of the conciliar era, denies the dogma of the Most Holy Trinity by affirming that the concept of one God in three Persons "has failed" and needs to be reworked:

"Departing from the basic Augustinian-Western conception, an a-trinitarian treatise '*de Deo uno*' logically appears before the treatise on the Trinity. For this reason, **the theology of the Trinity ... gives the impression that it can only say things that are absolutely formal about the divine persons** ... and that it refers only to a Trinity absolutely closed in on itself ... not open to the outside. ...

"What is certain is that in a 'psychological' Augustinian theology of the Trinity, the content is filled with the formal concepts of *processio, communicatio essentiae divinae, relatio* ... **It must be admitted that following this method we do not go very far.** ... **One starts with the** inter-mundane **philosophical**

---

[18] Luis Maldonado, *La violencia de lo sagrado* (Salamanca: Sígueme, 1974), p. 266.

concept of knowledge and love; from this a concept of word [the Son] and the 'appetitive force' of love [the Holy Spirit] develops, and, at the end of the speculative application of these concepts to the Trinity, we must confess that the application has failed." [19]

§ 18   Rahner goes on to say the Trinity means little or nothing in the life of a Catholic:

"**The clear cognizance of faith in the incarnation does not prove that the Trinity means anything in the normal piety of a Christian.** Thus **one can say that** in theology ... without more ado, **the *Pater Noster* is directed in the same way – originally and without distinction – to the Holy Trinity,** to the three divine persons; **and that the sacrifice of the Mass is likewise offered to the three persons.**"[20]

§ 19   For Rahner the concept of the Trinity is "secondary," just a pedagogical synthesis of the "salvific experience":

"The God of the Old Covenant – the *Théos* pure and simple – is already known and professed in the historic-salvific experience of Revelation. About this already known God, who has already agreed to have a relationship with man, one learns in the accounts of the New Testament that he sends us his Son and the Spirit of the Son. **One must avoid the confusion that it is the triune God who acts as an actual partner in the Old Testament. The concepts of 'triune God' and 'Trinity' are legitimate, but secondary; they synthesize the salvific experience and concrete revelation in a 'short formula.'**"[21]

§ 20   In the text below, we see Rahner combating the notion of Person in the Trinity. For him, each one of the Persons would be only a way of being – he uses the expression "a distinct way of subsistence" – of the same Person, which can be known by man when he carefully contemplates the divine communication he receives interiorly. Rahner concludes by saying that today it is no longer licit for a Catholic to say that he believes in the Three Persons, a conclusion highly injurious to the Faith. Rahner writes:

---

[19] Karl Rahner, "O Deus trino, fundamento transcendente da História da Salvação," in V.A., *Mysterium Salutis*, vol. II/I, pp. 290-291.

[20] K. Rahner, "Algumas observações sobre o tratado dogmático 'De Trinitate,'" in *O dogma repensado* (São Paulo: Paulinas, 1970), p. 221.

[21] K. Rahner, "O Deus trino, fundamento transcendente da História da Salvação," p. 317.

"How can the concept of 'person' be correctly explained and interpreted? ... The self-communication of the one God takes place in three different modalities of occurrence, in which the one same God is concretely given to us. ... God is the concrete God in each of these modalities, which are naturally connected in a relative way to one another but are not coincident.

"Translating this to affirm the 'immanent' Trinity,[22] we can say that **the one God subsists in three distinct ways of subsistence. 'Distinct way of subsistence,' then, would be the concept, not referring to the person, which designates the different subsistent, but to the** *personalitas*, **which causes the concrete reality of God, which in each case occurs in a different way, to be what occurs precisely** *in that way*, **since that occurring-in-that-way must always be considered as belonging to God in himself. Then, the particular person (in God) would be God as existing and occurring in that determined and distinct way of subsistence.**

"**The expression 'distinct way of subsistence'** requires further explanation. **We judge it better, less dangerous** and closer to the theological language of the Church **than the word proposed by Karl Barth: 'ways of being.'**...

"Obviously, with this expression 'distinct way of subsistence' there is also the risk of the *individuum vagum* that we mentioned above in regard to 'person': The concrete becomes absolute and an abstract concept ... But **if in our affirmations of faith and theology we are not satisfied with saying Father, Son, Spirit and a single God, which today is certainly no longer possible or licit, then this risk becomes inevitable**.

"Nonetheless, the expressions 'distinct way of subsistence' and 'God in three distinct ways of subsistence' have some advantages over the concept of person: **'Three persons' of itself does not express anything about the unity of these three persons; it is necessary to add this unity from outside to the "three persons'.** The word 'way,' however, at least opens the possibility that the same God, as triply distinct, is concretely 'tri-personal' and, inversely, the 'tri-personality' simultaneously expresses the unity of the same God." [23]

---

[22] Rahner habitually distinguishes between the "immanent Trinity" - which he considers to be the internal life of God - and the "economic Trinity" - how the God operates on men and History. This topic will be addressed in Vol VII, *Destructio Dei*, Chap III.1.

[23] K. Rahner, "O Deus trino, fundamento transcendente da História da Salvação," pp. 348-350.

Trying to justify this surprising change in the most fundamental dogma of the Catholic Faith, Rahner proposes the relativization of the dogma by changing the meaning of "person." He believes that professing faith in the Three Persons of the Trinity forcibly leads minds to a "false and heretical" position with regard to God. In the same work, he writes:

"More problematic ... is the concept of 'person.'[24] ... Its history up until its utilization in the Trinitarian dogma shows that neither its meaning nor its aptitude to express that dogma are absolutely evident. Further, the concept of 'person' also had its ulterior history after it was admitted into doctrinal thinking and Church dogma. The word acquired certain meanings with which the concept should not be linked in dogmatic language. For example, **someone today who hears the expression 'three persons' almost forcibly links it ... to the idea of three distinct centers of consciousness and action, which leads to a false and heretical interpretation of the dogma.**[25]

---

[24] The classical conception of person – an individual substance of a rational nature – was defined by Boethius in the 5th century and later adopted by the Scholastics. In Vol. VII, *Destructio Dei*, Chap.IV.3, we will study in detail how Progressivism, based on modern philosophies, tries to change the traditional notion of person.

[25] This "anathema" by Rahner clashes frontally with the dogma of the Most Holy Trinity, which is based on Scripture, Tradition and the Church Magisterium. Thus, the Jesuit theologian offends against both the dogma and its foundations, namely:

A. Sacred Scripture

a. The Old Testament

In the Old Testament, the notion of God opens out into three distinct Persons only in light of the revelation of the New Testament, where the complete and explicit revelation of the mystery of the Holy Trinity is found. Within these limits we found the following passages that refer to the Trinity: Gen 1:2; 26; 3:22; 5:7; Wis 9:1-2; 17; Is 9:6; 11:2-3; Dan 7:13-14; Ps 144:29-30; 2 Kgs 23:2; Ez 11:19; 36:26).

b. The New Testament

In the New Testament the passages referring to the three Persons of the Holy Trinity are:

• The Annunciation narration: "The Angel Gabriel was sent from **God [the Father]** into a city of Galilee, called Nazareth, to a Virgin espoused to a man whose name was Joseph, of the House of David; and the Virgin's name was Mary. ... And the Angel answering, said to her: **The Holy Ghost** shall come upon you, and the power of the Most

High shall overshadow you. And therefore also the Holy which shall be born of you shall be called the **Son of God**" (Lk 1:26-35).

• At the theophany in the baptism of Our Lord in the River Jordan: "And Jesus being baptized, forthwith came out of the water; and behold, the heavens were opened to Him: and he saw the **Spirit of God** descending as a dove, and coming upon Him. And behold a voice from heaven saying: This is **My beloved Son**, in whom **I [the Father]** am well pleased" (Mt 3:16-17).

• When Our Lord sent the Apostles to convert the nations: "Go out, therefore, and teach all nations; baptizing them in the name of the **Father**, and of the **Son**, and of the **Holy Ghost**" (Mt 28:19).

• St. John the Evangelist, who speaks most often of the Holy Trinity, writes: "And **I [the Son]** will ask the **Father**, and He shall give you another **Paraclete** ... The **Paraclete, the Holy Ghost** whom the **Father** will send in my name, He will teach you all things" (Jn 14:16, 26). And later: "But when the **Paraclete** comes, whom **I [the Son]** will send you from the **Father, the Spirit of truth, who proceeds from the Father**, He shall give testimony of Me" (15:26). See also 1 Pet 1:12; 1 Cor 6:21; 12:4-6; 2 Cor 1:21-22; Gal 4:6.

B. Tradition

There are abundant testimonies pertaining to the Holy Trinity in the rites of the early Church, her symbols of Faith and her doxologies, the confessions of her Martyrs and the writings of her Doctors and apologists. The texts below are almost exclusively from the pre-Nicene period, when the Trinitarian doctrine took its definitive form.

a. The *baptismal rite* consisted of a triple ablution with the express invocation of the three Divine Persons. The Didaché says: "Baptize with living water in the name of the Father, and of the Son, and of the Holy Ghost" (VII, 1-3). And Tertullian: "Not once, but three times do we wash ourselves, on pronouncing the name of each one of the Persons" (*Adversus Praxeam*, 26, in PL 2, 190). St. Basil adds that the Church practiced this rite of triple ablution not based on Scripture, but from apostolic tradition (cf. *De Spiritu Sancto*, 27, 66, in PG 32, 187).

b. The *Symbols* contain the profession of Faith in the Trinity. The Symbol of the Apostles of the 2nd century, for example, attests to belief in "one God, the Father Almighty, the Creator of heaven and earth, the sea and all things therein; and in Jesus Christ, the Son of God, who became man for our salvation, and in the Holy Ghost, who announces through the prophets the decrees of God" (St. Irenaeus, *Contra haereses*, book I, chap. 10, 1, in PG 7, 549).

c. Since the times of the Apostles, Christians glorified the Triune God with diverse *doxologies*, such as the words pronounced by St. Polycarp in the fire during his martyrdom: "Lord God Almighty, Father of Jesus Christ, Thy beloved and blessed Son ... Glory to Thee and to Him and to the Holy Ghost, now and forever. Amen" (Martyr, S. Polic., n. 14, ed. Funk).

d. Examples of *confessions of the Martyrs* would include those of St. Evodius, who said: "I confess that Christ is God with the Father and the Holy Ghost" (*apud* Ruinart, *Acta Martyrum*, ed. Verona, p. 65, n. 6). St. Euplius of Catania, before his martyrdom, declared: "I adore the Father, the Son and the Holy Ghost. I adore the Holy Trinity, outside of which there is no God. I sacrifice and immolate myself to the Father, the Son and the Holy Ghost" (*apud ibid.*, p. 362). Similar confessions are found in the acts of many other martyrs.

e. In the *writings of the Fathers* we find, among innumerable others, the work of Pope St. Dionysius, who refutes the Trinitarian heresies and expounds the true doctrine: "The separation of the admirable Divine Unity into three divinities cannot be tolerated, nor should the dignity and supreme grandeur of God be diminished with the word *made* or *created*; but it is necessary to believe in God the Father Almighty, and in Jesus Christ His Son, and the Holy Ghost. In this way the Divine Trinity will be preserved integrally, as well as the Holy Unity or monarchy" (*Epist. ad Dionys. Alex. apud* St. Athanasius, PG 25, 462-463).

St. Athanasius mentioned the many Fathers who defended this doctrine when he apostrophized the Arians: "You new Jews, how many Fathers can you claim who approve your affirmations? Not even one who is serious and prudent" (*De decretis Niceae Synodi*, 27, in PG 25, 465). St. Augustine added: "All the authors I have read who wrote before me about the Trinity who is God, in expounding the books of the Old and the New Testaments, taught in accordance with the Scriptures that the Father, the Son and the Holy Ghost are inseparably equal in one and the same substance or divine unity, and, therefore, are not three Gods but only one" (*De Trinitate*, I, 7, in PL 52, 824).

C. The Church Magisterium

Among the many documents that were written after the 3rd century, we cite only three:

a. The Symbol *Quicumque*, known as the Symbol of St. Athanasius, affirms: "For there is one Person of the Father, another of the Son, and another of the Holy Ghost. ... The Father is not made, nor created, nor begotten by anyone. The Son is not made, nor created, but begotten by the Father alone. The Holy Ghost is not made, nor created, nor generated, but proceeds from the Father and the Son" (D 39).

b. The Decree against the Jacobites, from the Bull *Cantate Domino* of February 4, 1441, issued by the Council of Florence, solemnly states: "The sacrosanct Roman Church, founded by the word of Our Lord and Savior, firmly believes, professes and preaches one true God, omnipotent, immutable and eternal, Father, Son and Holy Ghost; one in essence, three in persons; the unbegotten Father, the Son begotten of the Father, and the Holy Ghost proceeding from the Father and the Son; that the Father is not the Son or the Holy Ghost; that the Son is not the Father or the Holy Ghost; that the Holy Ghost is not the Father

"Undoubtedly, theology can theoretically protect its concept of person from such changes in meaning by stabilizing it with a 'definition.' But **the Church is not actually the mistress and sovereign guide of this history of concepts. For this reason**, in principle, **it is not impossible that the word will evolve historically in such a way that**, despite the right, which in thesis is given to the Magisterium to 'regulate language in a communitarian way' ... **it will become impossible** with the passing of time **to apply this word to the kerygma**[26] **without the risk of a tri-theist error.**

---

or the Son; but the Father alone is Father, the Son alone is Son, the Holy Ghost alone is Holy Ghost.

"The Father alone begot the Son of His own substance; the Son alone was begotten of the Father alone; the Holy Ghost alone proceeds at the same time from the Father and the Son. These three Persons are only one God, and not three Gods, because the three have one substance, one nature, one divinity, one immensity and one eternity" (D 703).

c. The Preface of the Most Holy Trinity said at the Masses of the 24 Sundays after Pentecost is a concise profession of the Faith in the dogma of the Holy Trinity. It reads:

"It is truly meet and just, right and for our salvation, that we should at all times, and in all places, give thanks unto Thee, O holy Lord, Father almighty, everlasting God; Who, together with Thy only-begotten Son, and the Holy Ghost, are one God, one Lord: not in the oneness of a single Person, but in the Trinity of one substance. For what we believe by Thy revelation of Thy glory, the same do we believe of Thy Son, the same of the Holy Ghost, without difference or separation. So that in confessing the true and everlasting Godhead, distinction in persons, unity in essence, and equality in majesty may be adored. Which the Angels and Archangels, the Cherubim also and Seraphim do praise: who cease not daily to cry out, with one voice saying: Holy, Holy Holy..." (*apud* Leonard Goffiné, *Manual do Christão*, Rio: Colégio da Immaculada Conceição, 1940, p. 58).

[26] Rahner explains what he understands by the word *kerygma* (from the Greek = announcement, message):

"In the modern usage of this New Testament term, the word *kerygma* designates the word proclaimed, in the name of God and of the Church, as the word of God and of Christ himself - who makes what is said effectively present in the lives of the hearers, be it the community of the faithful or individuals (to convince or edify). ... *Kerygma* is the first foundation and the norm for dogma and theology, finding its proper and full realization in the word of faith spoken to each one individually in the sacrament, as a manifestation of the divine salvation that takes place by means of its own manifestation" (K. Rahner and H. Vorgrimler, *Petit Dictionnaire de théologie catholique*, Paris: Seuil, 1970, p. 251).

"Even at present when the Ecclesiastical Magisterium ... maintains this concept of person for a communitarian profession with a fixed terminology, **it is not forbidden to theology – and it may even have the duty – to examine whether the word 'person' in each concrete case is really irreplaceable. ... It may happen that theology will summarize this same explanation in a word other than 'person' and that** its correct meaning, applicable here, **will perhaps be better and simpler to understand and, consequently, kerygmatically more advantageous than the word 'person.'**" [27]

§ 22   Following Rahner's line of thinking, Fr. Leonardo Boff offers a "suggestion" to change the name of the Trinity. He proposes that it no longer be called only the Father, Son and Holy Spirit but also the "Mother, Daughter and Holy Spirit." The Reader can gauge for himself the offense this represents against the Catholic Religion. Boff affirms:

"The Most Holy Trinity consists ... in moments of God's one single self-communication, moments of the unfathomable mystery manifested as Light (knowledge) and self-communicated as a gift (love), without losing its character of incomprehensible and impenetrable mystery. Now, **if this is what is *thought* when we profess our faith in a triune God, then we can express it equally well using feminine terminology, Mother, Daughter and Holy Spirit,** as long as we intend to profess the same reality as is expressed in the other form, the traditional masculine tradition, and we intend to restate the faith of the Fathers." [28]

§ 23   To make such an astonishing statement, this leader of Liberation Theology bases himself on a statement by John Paul I.[29] In fact, during his brief pontificate of 33 days, John Paul I found time to allude to this strange doctrine. In his *Angelus* message of September 10, 1978, he said:

"We also, who are here, have the same sentiments: We are the objects of undying love on the part of God. We know He has eyes always open on us, even when it seems to be dark. **He is Father; even more, He is Mother.** He does not want to hurt

---

[27] K. Rahner, "O Deus trino, fundamento transcendente da História da Salvação," p. 316.

[28] Leonardo Boff, *O rosto materno de Deus* (Petrópolis: Vozes, 1979), pp. 102-103.

[29] *Ibid.*, pp. 6, 101.

us. He only wants to do good to us, to all of us. **If children are sick, they have additional claim to be loved by their mother. And we too, if by chance we are sick with badness, on the wrong track, we have one more claim that entitles us to be loved by the Lord.**"[30]

§ 24   Boff's interpretation of the words of John Paul I does not seem to be arbitrary, since then-Cardinal Joseph Ratzinger viewed them in the same way. Indeed, he affirms this in his book *The Ratzinger Report*:

"Nevertheless, it seems that even a Catholic can maintain (indeed, a Pope has recently recalled it) that **God is beyond the categories of His creation. Hence He is Father as well as Mother.**"[31]

*

We close this Chapter II with the belief we have provided the Reader with sufficient elements to gauge the *animus injuriandi* of progressivist theologians regarding the honor owed to God. Consequently, he can also know an important facet of the spirit of the Council

*   *   *

---

[30] Cf. John Paul I, "Na oração, a esperança de paz," *L'Osservatore Romano*, September 17, 1978, p. 1.

[31] J. Ratzinger, *Rapporto sulla Fede* (Rome: Paoline, 1985), p. 97.

Chapter III

MORE OFFENSES AGAINST OUR LORD
JESUS CHRIST

1. Christ, Founder of a 'Church of the Condemned'

§ 1

In Volume II of this Collection,[1] we saw the esteem of Fr. Hans Urs von Balthasar, mentor of John Paul II and Benedict XVI,[2] for the person of Judas Iscariot. We also saw how progressivist leaders think the Holy Church has in her very essence traces of both sanctity and sin. According to them, she is a *casta meretrix*.[3] We also analyzed the gravity of the offenses made against God the Father and Our Lord.[4] In this Volume, therefore, we will not return to those topics, even though they would fit well in the present Chapter, as well as the previous one.

§ 2

Here we will examine a notion that complements the ones found above in the writings of von Balthasar, one that opens the way for a new type of offense. It is the concept of the "Church of the Condemned."

§ 3

Expressing progressivist thinking, von Balthasar has a strange conception of the Church – an entity made up of three parts: the official Church (the Petrine Church), the Church of Love (the Johannine Church) and the Church of the Condemned (the Church of Judas).[5]

---

[1] Cf. Vol. II, *Animus Injuriandi I*, Chap. I, §§.3-4.

[2] The Reader who has studied the previous Volumes of this Collection is already aware of the importance the Vatican gives to the thinking of von Balthasar. We only call to mind the solemn audience where John Paul II, in the presence of 16 Cardinals and numerous Archbishops, Bishops and Church dignitaries, awarded the Swiss-German theologian the Pope Paul VI International Prize (Cf. Vol. II, *Animus Injuriandi I*, Chap. I, Notes 1, 4, 5, 6.

[3] *Ibid.*, Appendix I, §§ 29-31, 65-91, 104-116.

[4] *Ibid.*, Chap. I, §§ 5-14, 17-21.

[5] Here we clarify that the designation "Church of Judas" is our own. In his writings, von Balthasar only speaks about the "community of the condemned" (see excerpt on § 6, see also § 21). Nevertheless, since the author considers Judas as "the synthesis of the non-general [the marginalized], as abandoned as the Crucified himself" (see excerpt

§ 4   Contrary to what one would expect, the Petrine Church is the least important of the three. She is a Church made up of sinners, of men who did not fulfill their respective vocations. For this reason, she has an obliterated vision of Christ and His mission. The Petrine Church, as a whole, would have been absent from the Passion. Von Balthasar explains:

"From the way in which the Church has imaged herself in the story of the Passion, it becomes patent that she recognizes that here there can be no immediate 'imitation of Christ.' Although Peter's betrayal and the flight of the other disciples may well be subject to a prophetic imperative (Mt 26:31-33) and were predicted by the Lord himself (Jn 16:32), this does not prevent the disciples from being exposed in their infidelity, cowardice and inconstancy and from being pilloried before the world. ...

"All that Peter undertakes in the context of the Passion turns out to be wrong: his request that the Lord should not suffer, which makes him like 'Satan, whose thoughts are not those of God but of man' and approximates him to Judas (Mt 16:23; cf. Lk 22:31); his affirmation that he will not betray, even if all the others do so – he will be the principal one who denies (Mt 26:34 and parallels); in his zeal in defending the Master from attackers he draws the profane sword, but he was admonished that by doing so he would perish by it (Jn 18:11; Mt 26:52), whereas Jesus, by healing Malchus, takes up a position against him. ...

"The only way left for Peter to be there is to step aside and weep bitterly – more for himself than for the Lord. The others fled in haste, and the young man of the Gospel of Mark, who leaves his own piece of clothing in order to escape (Mk 14:52) constitutes the symbolic and paradoxical antitype to Jesus being stripped of his garments – what the latter obediently allows to befall him is for the young man an involuntary deprivation."[6]

§ 5   But the Johannine Church or Church of Love was present at the Passion. For this reason, von Balthasar proclaims it to be superior to the Petrine Church. The Johannine Church is composed principally of Mary, St. John and the Holy Women. Von Balthasar writes:

---

on § 19 of this Chapter), we believe that calling the "community of the condemned" the "Church of Judas" is consistent with his thinking.

[6] H. U. von Balthasar, "Mysterium Paschale," in V.A., *Mysterium Salutis*, vol. III/6, pp. 77-78.

"Behind the official Church of males, there appears 'at a distance' the Church of women who 'followed him and ministered to him; there were 'several others', says Mark, in addition to the three he names (15:41). They will be present at the burial and will be the first witnesses of Easter. They stayed there, 'watching,' contemplative, not openly pitying themselves or ascribing to themselves an active role for their tears. ...

"In the face of all this, the Johannine account brings a mysterious clarification: the presence of a Church of love at the foot of the Cross (in contrast to the absent official Church), represented above all by the *Mater Dolorosa* and by the 'disciple whom Jesus loved' to whom he entrusts His Mother: a nucleus of the Church ... which later ... introduced itself into the Petrine Church, to 'remain,' despite everything, as an obscure remnant, without a decisive role for Peter."[7]

§ 6   However, more preferred than the Church of Love, which passively participated in the sufferings of Christ, supposedly was the mysterious 'Church of the condemned,' which actively participated with Him in the sufferings of the Passion. Von Balthasar maintains:

"The only active participant is an outsider, on whom the Cross is imposed (Lk 23:26), along with **the two 'malefactors' with whom Jesus is crucified and who form a new community of the condemned. It is they who now are more preferred than the elect.**"[8]

§ 7   What does von Balthasar really mean by this surprising statement that there is a "community of the condemned" superior to the official Church and more preferred by Our Lord than "the elect," that is, Mary Most Holy, St. John and the Holy Women?

To answer this question, we must distinguish in the "community of the condemned" *first*, who was good – the good thief, St. Dismas, and *second*, who was bad. Then it becomes easier to judge the comparison proposed by von Balthasar.

§ 8   1. Let the Reader suppose that von Balthasar is referring only to the relationship between Jesus and the good thief.

Through an action of Our Lord's mercy, the good thief converted. This action culminated when the Lamb of God, from

---

[7] *Ibid.*, p. 78.

[8] *Ibid.*

the height of the Cross, heard the supplication of Dismas and promised him Heaven: "Amen I say to you, this day you shall be with me in paradise" (Lk 23:43). It is profoundly moving that Our Lord made the first canonization in the History of the Church on the gallows of the Cross.

Such mercy, however, does not mean that St. Dismas was superior to Our Lady because he was physically crucified and she was not. The whole doctrine of Mary as Co-Redeemer is based on the precise opposite thinking. Our Lady morally suffered all the pains of her Divine Son, and her soul was pierced by a sword (cf. Lk 2:35).

For 2,000 years, the Church – in her doctrine and her piety – has taught that the greatest consolation of Our Lord during his Passion came from His Most Holy Mother. The physical suffering of the good thief cannot be compared to the incommensurable moral suffering of Mary.

§ 9   The *cause of suffering* cannot be compared: Mary's suffering was caused by her conformity with the voluntary immolation of her Son; Dismas' suffering was the punishment for his crimes.

The *moral value of the one who suffered* cannot be compared: Mary was innocent and consented to the holocaust of the undefiled Lamb; Dismas was guilty.

The *aim of the suffering* was likewise different: Mary's aim, like that of the God-Man's, was the Redemption of mankind; that of Dismas was to expiate his own sins and earn his personal salvation.

Finally, the *nature of the sufferings* cannot be compared: the suffering of Mary was primarily moral, and physical only as a consequence; the suffering of Dismas was primarily physical, and moral only as a consequence.

Thus, nothing permits one to suppose that the suffering of the good thief in union with Jesus was greater than the suffering of the "elect," that is, of Mary Most Holy, St. John and the Holy Women.§ 7

§ 10   Equally groundless, we note in passing, is the distinction made between the "three churches" and the comparison between the "Church of love" and the "official Church." At the time of the Passion, the official Church was not yet headed by St. Peter. The Supreme Pontiff of the Church was Jesus Christ Himself, as St. Paul states various times in his Epistle to the Hebrews.[9] Thus, the holocaust of the Lamb of God is *par excellence* an action of the official Church performed by the High Priest – Jesus Christ – with a Bishop as acolyte – St. John – and assisted by the faithful – Our Lady, the Holy Women and even the presence of a catechumen, St. Dismas.

For these reasons, one sees that the romantic distinctions of von Balthasar, who imagines separations between the "three Churches," are baseless. Those distinctions have only two practical objectives: to try to disparage the "official Church" and to exalt the "Church of the condemned."

§ 11

2. Up until now we supposed that the theologian is referring only to the relationship between Jesus and Dismas. This supposition, however, does not correspond to the thinking of von Balthasar. He clearly includes the bad thief in this privileged "community of the condemned" when he says:

"The only active participant is an outsider, on whom the Cross is imposed (Lk 23:26), along with **the two 'malefactors' with whom Jesus is crucified and who form a new community of the condemned. It is they who now are more preferred than the elect**." [10]

In this "community of the condemned," the bad thief supposedly plays a role as well. From Catholic tradition, we know that the bad thief condemned himself; therefore, von Balthasar's pretension is very strange indeed. How could it be possible for the Immaculate Lamb to form a "community" with him? Such perplexity increases upon seeing, as will be shown further on, that Judas himself was also part of this "community."

Von Balthasar's thinking becomes clearer when he places Judas – united with the bad thief – into the "community of the condemned," distinct from the two other mentioned communities, the community of saints (the "Church of love") and that of sinners (the "Petrine Church").

In his work, *Le Coeur du Monde*, the theologian imagines a desperate Judas Iscariot talking to Jesus on Holy Saturday:

"There is a communion of saints, and there is also a communion of sinners. Perhaps they are the same thing ... Only one ardent pathway of guilt and repentance serves them all. And

---

[9] Cf. Heb 2:17; 3:1; 4:14; 5:5-10; 7:20-28; 8:1-7; 9:11-14.

[10] H. U. von Balthasar, *Mysterium Paschale*, p. 78.

amid this dark stream of good and bad suffering, the redeeming drops of your blood also flow, O Lord. You will save them.

"But I have been expelled from this community of sinners. ... The others, as men formed by a divine pedagogy, say: 'It would be good that you humbled me, for by this means I learned to know your justice and mercy.' I have long since gone past this pedagogy; in me sin no longer has any improving aspect. ... To the one on your right, you have promised Paradise. I heartily concede it to him. He has earned it. He did not know what he was doing. Be happy together in your celestial garden! As for me, do not torture yourself over me. **I will always be the one on your left.** And stop torturing me with your torture."[11]

§ 12   One sees that Dismas represents the light face of the "Church of the condemned," whereas its dark face is represented by the bad thief Gesdras and Judas. Thus, the "condemned-light," like Dismas, would be saved, whereas the "condemned-darkness," those who "remained on the left side" with the bad thief and Judas Iscariot, are plunged into Hell.

But how is it possible, the Reader may ask, for Christ to unite Himself also with the damned "represented by the left arm of the Cross?" According to von Balthasar, there is an explanation for this.

§ 13   Christ, for their sake, supposedly became a reprobate, a despairing soul. He would have been cursed by God the Father and, for this reason, all the ignominy and infamy of both earth and Hell were concentrated in Him. His descent into Hell was neither to free the just who were in Limbo awaiting the Resurrection, as the Church teaches, nor to be adored by the reprobates and devils to their great chagrin, as taught by the Church Doctors.[12] Rather, His descent into Hell was supposedly due to His Father's condemnation and His own co-naturality with the reprobates.

---

[11] H. U. von Balthasar, *Le Coeur du Monde*, pp. 159-161.

[12] St. Robert Bellarmine defends the thesis that Our Lord descended into all infernal places, including the Hell of the devils and the reprobates, where He willed to make patent His triumph and be adored by the vanquished. To support this thesis, he cites St. Ambrose, St. Gregory of Nyssa, Eusebius Emissenus and St. Cyril of Jerusalem (*De Christo capite totius Ecclesiae*, book 4, chap.16, in *Opera Ommia*, Palermo/Naples/Paris: Pedone, 1872, vol. 1, p. 286). For more details, see Vol. II, *Animus Injuriandi I*, Chap I, Note 14.

In Hell were all the accursed, all the traitors, all the men-darkness who passed through History. Christ, out of love for the condemned in Hell, would have sunk lower, in the eyes of God the Father, than all of the damned. He would have fallen into the deepest abyss of Hell, which von Balthasar calls "the heart of the world." And since, in the eyes of the Father, He is the greatest and most despised of reprobates, He would have attracted all of the condemned, gathered them around Him, formed only one body with them and redeemed them.

The rising process in Christ's Resurrection would have started, therefore, in the deepest recess of Hell, and it would have gathered together those who were most similar to Him: the condemned. This would have been the principal victory of Christ, His greatest glory.[13]

§ 14   To von Balthasar, however, Christ does not represent only the community of the men-darkness. He also represents, in a contrary sense, the community of the men-light, the saints.

Thus, for von Balthasar, Heaven and Hell, the saints and the damned would unite in Christ in a "sublime" and mysterious amalgam. For this reason, the crucifixion of Christ between two condemned thieves – one ready to accompany Him to Heaven and the other ready to be cast, also with Him, into Hell – is supposedly the appropriate symbol of that "reality."

The following excerpts from works by von Balthasar affirm what we have just summarized.

In the first work, Jesus Christ is considered the "accursed one," the one rejected by God the Father:

"Just as a man who undergoes death and burial is mute, no longer communicating or transmitting anything, so it is with this Man Jesus, who was the Word, the revelation and the mediation of God: **He dies, and what was a manifestation of God in his life breaks off**. This rupture is not simply the natural rupture of a man dying according to the Old Testament, who descends into the grave and returns to the dust from whence he came.

"His death is the plunging down of the 'Accursed' One (Gal 3:13) far away from God, of the One who is 'sin' personified (2 Cor 5:21), who, falling where he is 'thrown'

---

[13] Von Balthasar's most famous work, *The Glory of the Lord* (*Herrlichkeit*) – profusely quoted in Vol. II of this Collection – develops the theme of this supposed sado-masochist "triumph." See also Vol. IV, *Animus Delendi I*, Chap. II, § 11, Notes 15, 17.

(Apoc 20:14), experiences 'self-immolation' (Apoc 19:3); 'the city of nothing that became a ruin' (Is 25:10): 'Terror, and the pit, and the snare! He who flees at the sound of the terror shall fall into the pit; and he who climbs out of the pit shall be caught in the snare' (Is 24:17-18; Jer 48:43-44). Here the idea of the second death dies: **He who is rejected and cursed by God at his definitive 'judgment' (Jn 12:31) sinks down to the place where his destiny lies.**"[14]

§ 15   Further in the same work, von Balthasar claims that Christ was cursed and delivered by His Father to His death on the Cross:

"That God 'delivers' His Son is part of the most unheard-of affirmations in the New Testament. We must understand the expression 'delivery' in its full meaning, without diluting it to a mere 'mission' or 'gift.' Here is accomplished what Abraham was spared from doing with his son Isaac: **Christ was deliberately given over by the Father to His destiny of death. God delivered Him to the forces of perdition**, whether these be called 'man' or 'death' ... **'God made Christ to be sin'** (2 Cor 5:21). **Christ is the accursed of God.**"[15]

This notion of Christ betrayed by His Father appears in another of his books. In it, this abyss into which Christ was plunged is called "heart of the world."[16] In von Balthasar's imag-

---

[14] H. U. von Balthasar, "Mysterium Paschale," pp. 31-32.

[15] *Ibid.*, p. 74.

[16] To understand von Balthasar's use of the expression "heart of the world," one should consider the observations we made in Vol. II, *Animus Injuriandi I* , Chap. I, Note 35. For the convenience of the Reader, we repeat them here:

A Reader unaccustomed to reading progressivist authors, and particularly von Balthasar, will understandably have some difficulty following the texts of this Item about the Heart of Christ. Indeed, the author indiscriminately applies different meanings to this expression, which can confuse the reader. To prevent such an effect in our Reader – and primarily to clarify the offenses made by von Balthasar – we present the principal meanings used by the author for the expression Heart of Christ:

A. Heart of Christ = heart of the world. According to several progressivist theologians, the ensemble of the universe is an "incarnation" of the Word. Hence the existence of a Cosmic Christ, who, in one way or another, encompasses both the spiritual and material aspects of the universe. The heart of this Comic Christ, then, is a center from which energies emanate in a latent state and into which already "spiritual-

ination, it is Jesus who now speaks:

"Celebrate, o my heart, the immensities of the heart of the world! Although the triune ocean of eternal life cascades from above into that little shell, so too billowing up from below and clashing against him is the opposing ocean of all countries and centuries, the gloomy tide of the world, **the black foam of sin, treachery and cowardice, defiance and pride, anguish and infamy.**

"**Everything surges up, assaults, plunges and crowds into the heart of the world. The two oceans clash against each other into that shell like fire and water, and the eternal struggle between heaven and hell is decided on that narrow**

---

ized" energies converge after being liberated from the life cycle. Some, like Teilhard de Chardin (cf. *Le Milieu Divin; Le Coeur de la Matière*), imagine this center as the concentration of an energetic atmosphere or as a *pneuma* that hovers over creation. Others, like Karl Rahner (cf. *Die Theologie der Thode*), imagine that this energized center is found inside the Earth and the souls of the deceased go there. Von Balthasar appears to favor this latter view, as he insinuates that Hell is the natural habitat of the Heart of Christ.

B. Heart of Christ = divine heart. This would be the love of the Divine Persons, therefore, the Holy Spirit. Such love is paradoxically reflected in the betrayal of one of the Persons by another (the Father betrays the Son). The Heart of Christ would also be the love of the Word Incarnate for mankind upon the realization of the Redemption. As such, it would be a point that surpasses good and evil, truth and error, friends and foes, Heaven and Hell. For von Balthasar, these differences were overcome by the love of Christ, symbolized by His Heart.

C. Heart of Christ = human heart. Two applications stem from this:

a. Applied directly to Our Lord, it would be His Sacred Heart which, pierced by the lance, gave birth to the Church just as the rib taken from Adam gave birth to Eve.

b. Applied directly to man and indirectly to Our Lord, the expression Heart of Christ takes in the unruly passions of human love. Thus, it would be inconstant like the human affections of fallen nature. Such a Heart would be irrational, given over to the excesses of the senses, abandoned to the passions and, finally, moved by carnal attraction.

In every meaning he adopts – one not necessarily connected to another – von Balthasar adds literary hyperboles and poetic-theological effusions. This undoubtedly makes his exposition somewhat obscure and convoluted.

Nevertheless, we hope these explanations will help the Reader comprehend the grave improprieties and offenses against Our Lord.

battlefield. A thousand times it was on the brink of succumbing under the assault, but he remained steady, resisted and was victorious. **In one stroke it swallows the whole goblet of heaven and hell; and along with the deepest misery it savors the most sublime bliss.** ...

"**The little heart will not burst** as it resists the double onslaught, the double storm of love and hate, the double lightning bolt of judgment and of grace. **It will not burst even when the Father, veiled, joins his betrayers and forsakes Him, leaving Him alone in the midst of the world, tossed about by the most frigid darkness of hell, ablaze with its flames, laughed at by every grimace of sin, filled with unimaginable anguish, buried alive, indescribably perplexed.**" [17]

§ 16   And yet, according to von Balthasar, this Christ betrayed by the Father, [18] wanted to hand himself over in order to redeem those in Hell. Thus, Christ supposedly affirmed:

"Understand what it means to give oneself. ... This is how I decided to give myself; to deliver myself by my own hands. **Give myself to whom?** It matters little. **To sin, to the world,** to all of you, **to the devil,** to the Church, to the kingdom of heaven, to the Father. I decided to be the abandoned one *par excellence*. **The corpse over which vultures gather**. The one consumed. The one eaten. The one swallowed. The one buried under the rubble. The one drained to the last drop. The ball in the match. **The one exploited. The one squeezed to the very dregs, the one crushed into infinite particles. The one dissolved. The one volatilized into the air. The one liquefied into the ocean. The one dissolved into the totality**. Such was the plan. **Such was the will of the Father. And by fulfilling it through obedience** ... **I have filled the world from heaven to hell.**" [19]

§ 17   Von Balthasar pretends that this descent of Christ into Hell and His uniting with the enemies of God was the only way for the Redemption to be achieved. For the theologian, the Re-

---

[17] H. U. von Balthasar, *Le Coeur du Monde*, pp. 49-50.

[18] On von Balthasar's defense of God the Father's supposed betrayal of Christ, see Vol. II, *Animus Injuriandi I*, Chap. I, §§ 5-14. See also his work *La Gloire et la Croix – Péguy* for passages that support this apologia (Paris: Aubier-Montaigne, 1972, pp. 362-364).

[19] H. U. von Balthasar, *Le Coeur du Monde*, pp. 194-195.

demption is the overcoming of the problem of good and evil.[20] He considers this dichotomy between good and evil a fragmenting of the human being before God. Indeed, he affirms:

"The death that enters the world 'through sin' (Rom 5:2) tears apart the being of man as God envisaged it. Neither philosophy nor religion can restore to its plentitude this fragment of earthly life, slipping away as it goes toward death. Neither of them can find beyond death this missing part. ... The shattered image can only be restored by God, by the mediation of the 'second celestial Adam.' And **the center of this restorative action is necessarily the exact place of the rupture: death, Hades, perdition far from God.** ...

---

[20] Given the somewhat hermetic nature of the following text, three objections could be raised to our thesis: 1. Von Balthasar does not actually speak of the Redemption *per se*; 2. He does not speak specifically of the problem of good and evil; 3. He does not mention conquering these two. Hence our commentary is without foundation. To these objections, we present the following clarifications:

1. Von Balthasar considers that Christ ("the second celestial Adam") effects the "restorative action" between life and death (cf. § 1 of the quoted text). Later, he states that God, "so as to raise and save" the human being, "binds together the fractured extremities of the idea of man" (cf. § 2). Therefore, he does refer to the redeeming action of Christ.

2. When he addresses the subject of death, von Balthasar refers to its cause as sin and evil. After referring nominally only to life and death (cf. § 1), he says that "sinful and mortal man" "lost himself in death," without "finding God" (cf. § 2), which is to say that he condemned himself. This becomes even clearer when he affirms that death is an "abyss of grief, indigence and darkness" (cf. § 2), or when he cumulatively refers to "death, Hades and perdition far from God" (cf. § 1).

3. The author indicates the way that leads "to plenitude" for the human being who is fragmented by life and death (cf. § 1). Such plenitude would be restored by the "identity between the Crucified and the Risen One" (cf. § 2). For its part, the identity of Christ would be expressed by "the experience of the human condition beginning from within" (cf. § 2), the experience of "every dimension of the cosmic being," including "even the abyss of Hell," which would give him the "criteria to judge man" (cf. § 3). Therefore, the identity of Christ is to be simultaneously the judge and the criminal, to be simultaneously good and evil (cf. § 3). In other words, He overcomes the distinction between good and evil. This is how the plenitude of life is restored.

Therefore, our commentary is based upon von Balthasar's thinking, even though the author does not explicitly state his conclusions.

"If God wished to 'experience' the human condition starting 'from within,' so as to raise it from inside and thus save it, he should stress principally that point where sinful and mortal man finds himself 'at wit's end' – where man lost himself in death without, for all that, finding God. This is the point where man plunged into an abyss of grief, indigence and darkness, into the 'pit' from which he cannot escape through his own powers. God has perforce to place the emphasis on this experience of being 'at one's wit's end,' in order to bind together the fractured extremities of the idea of man. And this is what we actually find in the identity between the Crucified and the Risen One.

"It is only when God himself has lived out this ultimate experience of this world, a world which, through human freedom, has the possibility of withdrawing obedience to God and so of losing Him, that He will no longer be merely a God who judges His creatures from the above and from outside. But, thanks to His intimate experience of the world, as the Incarnate One who knows from experience every dimension of the cosmic being **(even in the abyss of Hell), God now takes on the criteria to judge man.'"[21]

§ 18   The theologian returns to the idea that Christ must experience the pain of loss. He writes:

"By His solidarity with the dead ones, **Christ has spared them the integral experience of death (as *poena damni*), ... but the Savior took upon himself representatively all of that experience.** It is precisely thus that **He shows himself as the only one who, by going beyond the common experience of death, gauged the depths of the abyss.** Departing retrospectively from here, **one can reject ... as incomplete a 'theology of death' that limits Jesus' solidarity with sinners to the mere act or decision to deliver the existence concentrated at the moment of death.**"[22]

In Volume II, we saw how von Balthasar pretended that Christ died screaming like a madman and a reprobate,[23] which confirms our interpretation of the text above.

The idea of abandonment and a supposed despair experienced by Christ are once again stressed by this acclaimed theologian:

---

[21] H. U. von Balthasar, *Mysterium Paschale*, pp. 6-8.

[22] *Ibid.*, p. 114.

[23] Cf. Vol. II, *Animus Injuriandi I*, Chap. I, §§ 17, 18.

"**The cry of abandonment** – which in Mark is the only word from the Cross ... as relativized as the 'fourth word' ... In the theological context, it is a 'trenchant' word, like the Johannine word *taraché*: a word that directs us to the culmination of Jesus on the Cross, and **by no means constitutes the beginning of the recitation of a psalm that ends with the glorification of the suffering individual and demands to be interpreted in that context.**"[24]

§ 19   To von Balthasar, this imaginary despair of Christ would be similar to the despair of Judas. The sacrifice of the Man-light would then be similar to the sacrifice of the man-darkness. One despised for being innocent, is raised to the height of the Cross; the other, despised for being guilty, hangs himself from the height of the fig tree. One irrigates the earth with the blood He shed; the other fertilizes it with the excrement of his scattered entrails...

For one who studies this macabre symbolism by von Balthasar, it is difficult not to conclude that the theologian believes the suicide of Judas Iscariot played a role of co-redemption. He states:

"**Judas who betrays is the Old Covenant that closes up on itself and does not want to move forward; but he is also the New Covenant that draws together its indignity in this figure, one of the Twelve. ... He is as abandoned as the Crucified One himself; he has no way out** (Mt 27:1-9), **just like Jesus suspended between heaven and earth; and instead of shedding his blood, he scatters his entrails.**"[25]

§ 20   Christ dies and descends into Hell. Here the Redemption begins, according to von Balthasar. The damned supposedly came under the "spell" of the Heart of the Man-God, who was cast into Hell because of them. And, as the enigmatic text of the theologian suggests, from Hell Jesus begins to form his mystical body.[26] He states:

"**In death, in Hell, His [Christ's] heart,** bearing a new fruit, **will have to dissolve** and – now almost wholly destroyed, almost completely melted into a shapeless sea – **He will give**

---

[24] H. U. von Balthasar, "Mysterium Paschale," p. 84.

[25] H. U. von Balthasar, *De l'Integration*, p. 331.

[26] On the absurdity and incoherence of such an assertion, see the exposition of the authentic Church teaching on this topic in Vol. II, *Animus Injuriandi I*, Chap. I, §§ 8-9, Notes 17, 18.

himself to them [the reprobates in Hell] as the love potion which will finally bewitch their all-too-reluctant hearts.

"The Heart of the World must first create his own world for himself. The Head of the World must form his own body for himself."[27]

§ 21   Is it possible that the "mystical body" – whose Head would be Christ Himself – would also include the reprobates in Hell? Such a notion is shocking. Nonetheless, that is what can be understood from the excerpt above. In Volume II, we analyzed other conceptions of this "mystical body of Christ,"[28] whose main fundament is found in the following text by von Balthasar:

"Father ... refuse me not the right of confessing You even in the terrors of Hell and even in the very form of sin, so that You also may be glorified through Me in these, My members [that is, the damned] and branches. For henceforth we – they and I – are one indistinguishable unity. ... Even Your enemies here [in Hell] – My friends – belong to You. And I do not place myself as a protective wall before them to shield them from Your wrath. Rather **I take them into My hand like the celebrant takes his paten, and I raise them up to You; they belong to You because they belong to Me, and all that is Mine is Yours."**[29]

§ 22   The victory and glory of von Balthasar's Christ begins with his assimilation of Hell into himself:

"I now am in everything in all, and this is why the death that annihilated Me is My victory. My descent, **My vertiginous collapse, My going under (under myself) into the lower regions, into everything that was foreign and contrary to God, down into the underworld: This was the ascent of this world into Me, into God. My victory."**[30]

§ 23   The Resurrection supposedly started with the rescue of those condemned to Hell. This same thesis is confirmed in another work:

"'He died for all, so that all those who live might live no longer for themselves but for Him who for their sake died and was raised' (2 Cor 5:14). **The descent [of the One alone] into**

---

[27] H. U. von Balthasar, *Le Coeur du Monde*, pp. 62-63.

[28] Cf. Vol. II, *Animus Injuriandi I*, Chap. I, §§ 8-9, Notes 17, 18.

[29] H. U. von Balthasar, *Le Coeur du Monde*, pp. 87-88.

[30] *Ibid.*, pp. 195-196.

the abyss becomes the ascent of all from the same depths, and the condition for this dialectical change-about consists, on the one hand, in the 'for all' of the descent, ... and on the other, in the prototypical Resurrection with which this passage deals. For if Christ had remained immersed at the bottom of the abyss, then 'all' would not have been raised." [31]

§ 24   From the moment that Christ died, according to von Balthasar, the struggle between Heaven and Hell, love and hatred disappeared. The opposing elements all blended together in Him:

"There is no more struggle between love and hate, between life and death. The two parts became equal, and love's emptying out has become the emptiness of Hell. One penetrated the other perfectly."[32]

Thus, everything – even sin – was assumed by the heart of Christ:

"How I thank You, Lord, for resolving the painful wildness of the world only by dissolving it into the blessed wildness of Your love, and for melting everything raging and conflicting in us in the crucible of Your creator's might. And to do this in such a way that everything that is shimmers in us in an ambiguous and fascinating way, shines in You in perfect harmony thanks to Your redemption. ... **Everything, even sin, is material for Your building.** Through Your expiation, You take each thing to yourself and, without destroying its being, You confer upon it a new being. **You change mud into jewels, sensual love into virginity, and on the despairing You bestow a future."**[33]

§ 25   In summary, the "community of the condemned," symbolized by the link between Jesus and the thieves at His right and left on the Cross – would include, according to von Balthasar, the Savior and the damned in Hell. In this blasphemous theory, Christ would be the head of the condemned, the head of this "mystical body" of the wicked.[34]

---

[31] H. U. von Balthasar, "Mysterium Paschale," pp. 33-34.

[32] H. U. von Balthasar, *Le Coeur du Monde*, p. 162.

[33] *Ibid.*, p. 233.

[34] The logical consequence of this vile invention by von Balthasar would be the identification of Our Lord Jesus Christ with the Antichrist, who is head of the mystical body of the wicked, according to the teaching of St. Thomas Aquinas (*Super Epistolas Pauli*, 2 ad Cor. VI:15 , lect. 3, 236, Rome: Marietti, 1953, p. 494).

§ 26   We close the exposition of this surprising progressivist notion of Redemption by returning to the initial thought about the "three churches." Through the symbolism of the Cross, one can better understand the ideal being defended by the progressivists regarding the Church. She, as Christ, should always be crucified in the synthesis of the Hegelian conflict between the two opposed poles.[35]

On one side is the "church of the condemned," whose "members-darkness" are symbolized by the unrepentant thief Gesdras and, on the other side, we find its "members-light" represented by the good thief Dismas. That is, like Christ, the Church would be always condemned, at times taking on the moral posture of the thief who converts and, at other times, that of the thief who revolts and is condemned to Hell. This supposedly is the "redemption" carried out by the Church.

In their turn, the members who accept this miserable laceration and passively receive all the offenses made against her, conforming themselves to the attacks launched to destroy her – these would be the members of the "church of love," symbolized by Mary, John and the Holy Women at the foot of the Cross.

The others, members of the "official church" who do not understand the "sublimity" of what is taking place between these two "churches," are the mediocre and pusillanimous ones, the members of the "sinning church" symbolized by St. Peter.

§ 27   If someone who wanted to destroy the Catholic Faith and the Church was searching for a theological explanation for this purpose, he hardly could find a more convenient thesis than the one just expounded. It is founded on these excerpts by Fr. Hans Urs von Balthasar, a theologian highly esteemed and promoted by both John Paul II and Benedict XVI.

We did not call the Reader's attention to the offenses made against Our Lord, because this particular Item is turned toward exposing not just simple offenses, but audacious and grave blasphemies that clash with the most elementary Catholic sense.

---

[35] "The Church and Christians cannot ... situate themselves within the *Mysterium Paschale*. Their place is neither in front of nor behind the cross, but on both its sides: without ever settling on one vantage point or another, they look from one, then another, as ceaselessly directed. And yet this back-and-forth game by no means lacks a support, because the Unique One is the identity of Cross and Resurrection" (H. U. von Balthasar, *Mysterium Paschale*, p. 188).

2. Christ Supposedly Prefers Prostitutes & the Lawless

Following the logical sequence of what was explained, progressivists claim that Our Lord would prefer public sinners and the scandalous to the good faithful who keep the Commandments of the Catholic Religion.

§ 28   The first text offensive to Our Lord and Religion is again from Hans Urs von Balthasar, who imagines Christ complaining about those who try to follow the Law of God:

"You seek after holiness, which is a sign that you do not have it. The saint ... does not strive after it. Unwittingly, unconcerned, paying no heed to himself, he falls down before his brothers to wash their tired feet. Forgetting his own hunger for God, he seats them at the table and serves them."[36]

A little further he continues:

"The wise men of this world proclaim: Blessed is he who possesses an asbestos chamber where neither the water nor the fire of life can assail him. **Blessed is he who disciplines and restrains his passions** so that they form an insurmountable rampart around his citadel against the tempests of fate.

"But I say to you: Blessed is he who exposes himself to an existence never brought under self-mastery ... but rather abandons himself to my ever-transcending grace. ... Not blessed are the proud and prudent of this world, but rather the oppressed and harassed who daily must face my enigmas and cannot solve them. ...

"This is why I have invited to my banquet the poor, the beggars, the crippled and the lame **and all those who have withdrawn to the furthest margin of the good society: the vagabonds and the tramps, the ragged and the miserable. These are my cherished, respected guests; to move among them for me is a pleasure. I cultivate familiar relations with bohemians and prostitutes**, because they will enter the Kingdom of Heaven before you. ...

"What do I care for your piety, the adequacy of your 'spiritual life'? Compassion is what I want, not sacrifice."[37]

§ 29   Fr. Hans Küng upholds much the same thesis:

"To the great scandal of the pious, He [Our Lord] identifies himself with all the 'poor devils': the heretics and

---

[36] H. U. von Balthasar, *Le Coeur du Monde*, p. 192.

[37] *Ibid.*, pp. 198-199.

the schismatics (the Samaritans), the morally depraved (the whores and adulteresses), the politically compromised (the tax collectors and collaborators) ... and the general rabble who neither know nor practice the law."[38]

§ 30   Fr. Luis Maldonado, professor at the University of Salamanca, takes a more philosophical approach, asserting that it is not only Jesus, but also God and the Church who prefer the sinners to the saints. He writes:

"For a long time up until now, theology followed the Aristotelian-Platonic principle that 'the equal is known by another equal" – that is, God is known by the divine footsteps He left in His creation (through the analogy between God and His creatures). ...

"But, how is God known in Jesus when Jesus eats with sinners, lives with the lawless, forgives the godless and dies from the torture of the cross, reserved for those cursed by God? Here God is not found in one who is like Him, but rather in one who is contrary and opposite. He is found, through Jesus, in the places where the divine footstep is wiped out, where there is only darkness, scum, abandonment, marginality, the absence of law.

"Therefore, the principle of analogy does not suffice. It is necessary to employ the dialectical principle, intuited on the practical level by another Greek, Hippocrates (*contraria contrariis curantur* – the opposite is cured by the opposite) and expanded by Schelling ('every being is revealed only in his opposite; love in hatred, unity in division').

"The Christian God can be known and found in His non-identity. The Christian community cannot be a copy of society or its upper crust. Its place and its affection are in the anti-society: that is, among the poor and marginalized. This would be the translation of the theology of the cross into ecclesiology."[39]

§ 31   Another social consequence of this warped view point, is drawn by Fr. Gonzalez Ruiz, a leader of the Christians for Socialism movement. He states:

---

[38] Hans Küng, "Qual é il messaggio cristiano?," in V.A., *L'Avvenire della Chiesa*, p. 117; cf. *O que deve permanecer na Igreja* (Petrópolis: Vozes, 1976), p.35.

[39] L. Maldonado, *La violencia de lo sagrado*, p. 263.

"Christ is present among us as a subverter of the public order, of the established order or, rather, of the institutionalized disorder. In fact, Pilate condemned Jesus before the law as a disturber of the Roman peace in the Middle East, although personally he considered Him without fault. **Today also we would like to diminish this presence of Christ** that speaks too directly to us, giving a dynamic meaning to our human reality, history and evolution.

"We would like to reduce it to something hieratic, sacred and static. The modern man is confused about religion today because he has had enough of these static gods, gods manipulated to benefit the dominant class and to keep mankind from revolting, especially the exploited and oppressed. Thus, **we understand the distress of our old Christian world when persons like bishops and priests, in the name of Christ, use shocking words such as 'revolution'"**[40]

Who is this Christ akin with heretics, schismatics, prostitutes and every kind of religious and social outcast? Certainly He fails to represent the divine majestic visage of the Incarnate Word. How can one not see the depiction of this revolutionary Messiah as an offense against Our Lord Jesus Christ?

3. Christ Described as an Androgynous Being, a Model for Homosexuals

§ 32   As Vatican II opened the Church windows to let in new winds,[41] many extravagant theories began to gush into Catholic circles. They called themselves "theologies" and demanded a place at the discussion table of "theological pluralism." Such is the case of "liberation theology" in Latin America and "feminist theology" and "homosexual theology" in North America.

Such "theologies" are understood as "signs of the times"[42]

---

[40] J.M. Gonzalez Ruiz, "Cristianismo: Mensagem de libertação," in V.A., *Cristianismo sem Cristo?*, pp. 87-88.

[41] According to Henri Fesquet, John XXIII pointed to a window and spoke of the need for the Council to open the windows and "let some fresh air in the Church" (*Le Journal du Concile*, Forcalquier: Robert Morel, 1966, p. 44).

[42] The expression signs of the times (Mt 16:4) – which has become so fashionable in progressivist language – was used by John XXIII in the Encyclical *Pacem in terris*. The Pontiff also used the expression in the Bull *Humanae salutis* to summon the Council when he spoke about

and are taken seriously by innumerable Prelates in the Church, even in the highest echelon of the Hierarchy.

Given the support that such "theologies" receive and the direction in which they are taking the Church, it behooves us to examine at times in this Collection what they are saying and teaching.

As the Reader may have noted, the expositions in both this and the previous Volumes are based on authors who are highly regarded by the official Church cupola. As a general rule, we cite lesser known or more controversial authors only to confirm what the principal theologians have asserted.

In this Item 3 we will open an exception to this method in order to lift the tip of a veil that seems to reveal the future direction doctrine will take in the Conciliar Church. Thus, in a certain way, we will give the Reader elements to know yet another aspect of the spirit of the Council. Parallel to this, we will continue to point out the grave offenses made, which are *grosso modo* tolerated by the current leadership[43]

*

§ 33   American Fr. John McNeill, a Jesuit theologian and psychotherapist who studied at Louvain University and founded the homosexual movement Dignity, wrote a book presenting a theological defense of homosexuality. It is well known that this vice

---

the need to discern the "signs of the times": "We seem to glimpse, amidst so much darkness, more than a few signs that give solid hope of better times for the Church and humanity" (B. Kloppenburg, *Concílio Vaticano II*, Petrópolis: Vozes, 1966, vol. 1, p. 84).

The expression inspired the first part of the text of the Pastoral Constitution *Gaudium et spes*, which describes the situation of the modern world (cf. Charles Moeller, *L'élaboration du schema XIII - L'Eglise dans le monde de ce temps*, Tournai: Castermann, 1968, p. 89).

The conciliar document affirmed that discernment of the "signs of the times" was essential for the Church to fulfill her mission: "The Church has always had the duty of scrutinizing the signs of the times and of interpreting them in the light of the Gospel. ... Thus she can respond to the perennial questions which men ask about this life and the life to come, and about the relationship of the one to the other." (GS, n. 4)

[43] In Volume IV, *Animus Delendi I*, Chap III, §§ 2-12, we will study the progressivist strategy whereby the moderates and the *arditi* work together to achieve the same goal.

constitutes a grave social and religious problem in the United States[44] because of the large number of those addicted to this vice and the growing strength of their organizations. McNeill's work – *The Church and the Homosexual* – was controversial even before its publication. Nonetheless, it was launched, boasting an *imprimi potest* from the Provincial of the Company of Jesus in New York and with the permission of the Order's Superior General, then Fr. Pedro Arrupe.[45]

---

[44] A well-documented overview demonstrating how widespread this vice has become in the U.S. is found in the book by Fr. Enrique T. Rueda, *The Homosexual Network - Private Lives & Public Policy* (Old Greenwich: The Devin Adair Co., 1982), pp. 342-370; see also Richard Cowden-Guido, *John Paul II and the Battle for Vatican II* (Manassas: Trinity Communications, 1986), pp. 146-157. For a documented account of the homosexual and pedophile crisis in the U.S. clergy that came to public knowledge in 2002-2003, see my book *Vatican II, Homosexuality and Pedophilia*, (Los Angeles: TIA, 2004), chap. V.

[45] a. **The McNeill affair:**

McNeill narrates: "After various delays a final revised copy of the manuscript was sent to Rome in 1975. A reply was finally received in October. **Fr. Arrupe turned over authority to give the *imprimi potest* (permission to publish) to the Provincial of the New York Province of the Society of Jesus**. He stated that he did not object to publication, as long as certain suggestions and guidelines were accepted and followed" (John McNeill, *The Church and the Homosexual*, Boston: Beacon Press, 1993, Appendix 3, pp. 220-221).

Shortly after this permission was granted, the Congregation for the Doctrine of the Faith (CDF) issued the document "Declaration on Certain Questions of Sexual Ethics," which affirmed there could never be a pastoral justification of homosexual activity. McNeill replied to the CDF document in his upcoming book and re-submitted it to his superiors. On January 28, 1976, he received an answer from the Provincial Superior, Fr. Eamon Taylor, saying: "**In my opinion, the adjustments you have made in your manuscript in accordance with the agreements reached in our conversation of November 10 are responsive to the recommendation of Fr. General's letter of September 19, and ... as a result, I am pleased to grant the *imprimi potest*, as of this date**" (*ibid.*, p. 221).

The adjustments suggested by Fr. Arrupe and mentioned by Fr. Taylor must have been very superficial since McNeill went on to write: "I hasten to ensure my readers that at no point have I been asked to change or in any way alter my insights or convictions in order to receive official permission to publish" (*ibid.*, p. 222).

In November 1986 the news came that Fr. John McNeill had been expelled from the Company of Jesus because of his preaching in favor of homosexuality (cf. *The Washington Post*, November 8, 1986, pp. A1, A9; *Jornal do Brasil*, November 9, 1986).

On that occasion, the public was informed that in 1977 the Vatican had revoked approval for the book *The Church and the Homosexual* on the initiative of Cardinal Franjo Seper, then Prefect of the CDF (cf. *Jornal do Brasil, ibid.*; *The Washington Post, ibid.*). The latter had also ordered McNeill to be silent about homosexuality or sexual ethics. After nine years of this order, the Superior General of the Society of Jesus, then Fr. Peter Hans Kolvenbach, told Fr. McNeill either to stop his preaching on homosexuality and his religious assistance to the "gay" movement or to leave the ranks of the Society of Jesus. McNeill chose to leave the Jesuit Order rather than give up his ideas and ministry (cf. *ibid*).

The silence imposed on McNeill had little practical result, since it was unknown to the public. Further, McNeill's book – including the pages showing the approval of the New York Provincial and the consent of Fr. Arrupe – continued to be sold in large numbers in English and translated into other languages. The homosexual movement he founded, Dignity, also continued to grow and expand.

The punishment separating McNeill from the Society of Jesus is undoubtedly a moral and disciplinary sanction. But from another standpoint, it is a political maneuver of the Order to disengage itself officially from McNeill's ideas. Thenceforth the priest could continue his work and speak the way he pleased without compromising the Society of Jesus. There was no reported threat of the Holy See to consider him a heretic, excommunicate him or laicize him; no practical measure was taken to hinder his freedom outside the Order.

Instead, there was the surprising benevolence of the Jesuit Provincial of New York, Fr. David Tolan, who called the priest "an extraordinarily good man" who "tried to stay within the letter of the law laid down for him" (cf. *ibid.*). Fr. Tolan added that McNeill remains a priest and, to regularize his situation, he only needs to find a Bishop who will accept him in his Diocese. Therefore, in practical terms, one can say that McNeill was set free to continue his preaching without compromising the Jesuit Order.

The Society of Jesus adopted a similar political procedure, *servatis servandis*, towards Fr. Urs von Balthasar, who in 1950 was also released from Jesuit obedience so that he could better dedicate himself to the founding of a secular institute committed to the cultural transformation of society. That institute, *Johannes Gesellschaft* [the Society of St. John], was seen at the time as a bold, pioneer initiative, but today it is regarded as a model for the Church of the future... (This was told to the Author of this Volume by the well-informed Fr. Barnabas Ahern, a member of the International Theological Commission, in an interview

§ 34   Although he does not directly call Our Lord a homosexual, Fr. McNeill presents Him as a model for homosexuals. His words follow:

"These reflections bring us to Jung's final, surprising observation concerning the positive aspects of male homosexuality. This has to do with the particular gift the homosexual community has received which renders it able of contributing in a special way to the spiritual development of humanity. [Jung says:] 'He [the homosexual] is endowed with a wealth of religious feelings, which help him to bring the *ecclesia spiritualis*

---

in Rome on March 6, 1983).

Von Balthasar confirmed this interpretation of his break with the Order, saying, "The rupture I had foreseen took place when – to obey a formal command of St. Ignatius – I had to abandon the Society of Jesus, my spiritual homeland, so I could develop his idea in the world" ("Von Balthasar: La mi opera è abbozata più che terminate," *L'Osservatore Romano,* June 24, 1984, p. 4).

Is this not what happened with McNeill and his homosexual ministry? It seems to us that what he was affirming then was admitted by most of the progressivist milieu in the following decades. This is why his book continues to reveal the direction in which the winds are blowing in the Conciliar Church.

b. **The Hunthausen affair:**

In October 1986, the media in the U.S. and other countries published with fanfare the news of the "Hunthausen affair," where the Vatican "condemned" Archbishop Raymond G. Hunthausen of Seattle. One of the various points falling under the "condemnation" was the Archbishop's support of homosexuality (cf. Joseph Berger, "Vatican Reveals Why It Punished Archbishop," *The New York Times, apud Jornal do Brasil,* October 29,1986).

In June 1987 news came of Archbishop Hunthausen's rehabilitation by the Holy See (cf. *Vida Nueva,* Madrid, June 13, 1987). A commission composed of Cardinal Joseph Bernardin, Cardinal John O'Connor and Archbishop John Quinn recommended that the Vatican restore Hunthausen's full pastoral authority, withdraw the Auxiliary Bishop appointed to supervise his action and to take over many of his activities, and appoint a new Coadjutor Bishop to assist the Archbishop of Seattle. The proposals were accepted by the Holy See and Hunthausen's full authority was restored. Hunthausen stoutly maintained that his Archdiocese remained fundamentally the same and that he never had to alter the general direction of his ministry or compromise his progressivist stances (cf. Thomas Bokenkotter, *A Concise History of the Catholic Church,* New York: Doubleday, 2004, p. 447)

into reality, and a spiritual receptivity that makes him receptive
to revelation.'

"The components of that particular gift have already
been recognized. For we have already noted that the homosexual
community enjoys a special freedom that potentially could allow it to escape a hyperactive, aggressive, closed attitude and
allow it to be passive and receptive; attitudes that are essential to
prayer and to reception of revelation. It is not by chance that in
those cultures where the 'macho' image reigns, religious prayer
and worship are considered activities only fit for women. The
homosexual male can free himself from a need of violence and
dedicate himself to the quest of peace. He can have a special
sensitivity to the value of the person. ...

"He can dedicate himself to a life of service to his fellow
humans. Further, we have seen that the homosexual community,
if it were granted freedom to be itself and exercise its talents,
could contribute to the liberation of all humanity to a fuller understanding of personhood.

"There is an ideal identity image of what it means to be
a full human person proffered to us by God in the New Testament: That image is given us in the person of Jesus Christ. **Each
one of the special qualities Jung attributes to the homosexual
community is usually considered a striking characteristic of
Christ** – the qualities that distinguished him from the ordinary
man. ...

"**The point I am trying to make here is**, obviously, **not
that Christ was a homosexual - any more than He was a heterosexual in the usual significance that the cultural context
gives to this designation** – but, rather, that He was an extraordinarily full human person and an extraordinarily free human
person."[46]

By affirming that Our Lord was neither a homosexual
nor a heterosexual in the typical sense of the word, the Jesuit
priest suggests that Our Lord could have been a sexless or bi-
sexual person.

§ 35   This insinuation of an androgynous Christ by the American Jesuit of "homosexual theology" is effectively affirmed by
the Brazilian Franciscan Leonardo Boff of "liberation theology,"

---

[46] J. McNeill, *The Church and the Homosexual*, pp. 146-147.

whose theses were supported by Cardinals Aloisio Lorscheider and Evaristo Arns along with 20 other Brazilian Bishops.[47] This is what Boff has to say:

"On the one hand, the historical feminine provides a route to the feminine in God.[48] On the other, it signifies the creature made in the likeness of that feminine in God. Hence, the feminine has an eternal dimension. In one historic concretization, this proposition is absolutely correct and true – in Jesus Christ, a male human being hypostatically assumed by the Second Person of the Most Holy Trinity.

"The modern understanding that every human being is at once *animus* and *anima*, masculine and feminine in different proportions, clarifies the issue for us. **Jesus is masculine and feminine. He lived the masculine fully, since He was male. However, He perfectly integrated the feminine dimension also. Everything in Jesus, including the feminine, was hypostatically assumed by the Eternal Word. Therefore, in Jesus the feminine belongs to God and is divinized and ...** *this* **feminine of Jesus is God.**"[49]

§ 36

American scholar Rosemary Radford Ruether, a pioneer of "feminist theology," speaks out even more clearly on this topic. She unhesitatingly affirms the model of an androgynous Christ, basing her novel teaching on Gnostic documents. She writes:

"We can find an alternative view in the mystical tradition that preserves the gnostic concept of a Christ who unites man and woman. In fact, in the second *Letter of Clement* we read: '**The same Lord, asked by someone when His kingdom would come, said: 'When the two are one, the external as well as the internal, both man and woman, neither man nor woman (12:2)'.**

"Here Christ is the reintegrated androgynous person,

---

[47] As was widely reported at the time, in September 1985 these two Prelates went to Rome to personally defend Friar Boff against the grave accusations made by the Congregation for the Doctrine of the Faith. For more on Friar Boff's "condemnation," see Vol. V, *Animus Delendi II*, Introduction, Note 9 p.

[48] This Collection will make a more detailed study of the notion of the feminine in God in Vol. VIII, *Fumus Satanae*, Chap. I; see also Vol. VI, *Inveniet Fidem?*, Chap. V, §§ 147-161, Note 126.

[49] L. Boff, *O rosto materno de Deus*, p. 102.

from the original unitarian creation: in Him the separation between man and woman is overcome. Women also can participate in this single nature of Christ, but only on the condition that they reject sexual desires and do not have children. According to the *Gospel of the Egyptians*, Jesus declared: 'I came to destroy the works of the woman'; whereas the *Gospel of Thomas* legitimizes the inclusion of the woman in the redemption of Christ, making Jesus say: 'Look, I will guide her to make her male so that she too may become a living spirit resembling you males. For every female who makes herself male will enter the Kingdom of Heaven.' The mystical tradition and the androgynous gnostic tradition are clearly andro-centric."[50]

§ 37

Von Balthasar also concurs with this progressivist thesis and affronts Christ:

"In the purely sexual sense, there is neither man nor woman in Christ, but, on the other hand, it is in Christ himself and in His Church that the sexual finds its highest and most authentic meaning. The gratuitous and unreserved gift of Christ causes such reciprocity of the masculine and feminine that the woman delivering herself to the man loses any aspect of inferiority. This is because Christ, who delivers and abases himself even to the Cross, realizes His mission to constitute a radiant and spotless Church, which has the dignity of His own body."[51]

Further, he continues: **"The Son realizes in himself the archetype of both the feminine and the masculine ... in an interpretation that excludes the supremacy of one sex over the other**."[52]

From the documents presented in this Item 3, we see that this androgynous Christ promoted by Progressivism leads toward the ideal of a feminine Christ. Besides revealing the disturbing direction Progressivism is taking, these statements represent a grave offense against the purity of Our Lord Jesus Christ.

*

---

[50] Rosemary Radford Ruether, "Cristologia e femminismo," in V.A., *La sfida del femminismo alla teologia* (Brescia: Queriniana, 1980), p. 130.

[51] H. U. von Balthasar, "Sobre la dignidad de la mujer," *Communio*, October-November 1982, p. 9.

[52] *Ibid.*, p. 10.

4. Christ: a Madman and a Clown;
His Divinity, an Unacceptable Myth

In this Item we assembled various different offenses against Our Lord Jesus Christ. Some lack the most elementary respect for the Divine Word Incarnate; others consider His Divinity a myth.

A. Christ as Don Quixote - St. Peter as Sancho Panza

§ 38   In view of the increasing importance the Conciliar Church is giving to the Swiss theologian Hans Urs von Balthasar, we call the Reader's attention to a few more of his texts:

He transcribes an excerpt by Rudolf Kassner comparing Our Lord to Don Quixote and St. Peter to Sancho Panza. His endorsement to that insult is clear when he calls the crucifixion of the Prince of Apostles a "grotesque" scene. He writes:

"The figure of Peter as such is impossible. ... A fisherman of Galilee is transplanted to the center of the Empire and inherits the Empire that kills him. It kills him not as it killed his Master and Lord, whom he denied, but the other way around - upside down, his feet in the air. In this way he amends for his treason. **It is so sublime it cannot but also be grotesque!**

"'**Like Sancho Panza and Don Quixote, Simon Peter and Christ form a pair. Simon Peter is at the service of his Lord**. This means that every complication of a psychological order is eliminated. **Have you ever seen a sheep dog with his master?** It is alert, watching for his smallest gesture, anxiously awaiting the next order from a look from his face. **This is how Simon Peter was. ...**'[53*]'"[54]

In another work where von Balthasar analyzes the so-called "anthropological reduction" – all of theology should be reduced to the human dimension – of the modern era, he seems to legitimate various offenses made by other authors. Among such affronts, we single out the description of Christ as the "fool and the clown":

"Next to Kierkegaard, a few other witnesses emerge: **Léon Bloy, who rejects ... both the pharisaical objectivism**

[53*] Rudolf Kassner, "Simon Petrus," *Neue Schweizer Rundschau*, N.F. 15, 1947-1948, pp. 717, 727.

[54] H. U. von Balthasar, *El complejo antirromano - Integración del papado en la Iglesia universal* (Madrid: BAC, 1981), pp. 366-367.

of a complacent orthodoxy and the pharisaical subjectivism of sanctity (Huysmans, etc.) and who also addressed the paradox of the Cross; Dostoevsky in *The Insulted and the Injured, The Idiot* and *The Brothers Karamazov*, and **Georges Rouault, who tried repeatedly to emphasize the fool and clown in the figure of Jesus, 'all covered with blood and wounds.'** Behold the end of the anthropological reduction even in its most serious, dialogical and existential forms."[55]

Our Lord Jesus Christ supposedly was like the mad slapstick hero Don Quixote of Cervantes or a clownish figure like the drawings of Rouault. ... These offenses are approved by von Balthasar, one of the mentors of John Paul II and Benedict XVI.

B. The Incarnation of Christ: An Unacceptable Myth, Impossible to Demonstrate

§ 39

Fr. Karl Rahner tries to justify the "feeling of today's man" who supposedly considers the divinity of Our Lord "a myth." He writes:

"The feeling of today's man is that many pronouncements of theology deserve the name of myth and can no longer be believed seriously. Obviously this impression is false. But there are real reasons for it that cannot be attributed subjectively to pride and ignorance, or objectively to the mysterious nature of the truths and realities of the Faith. It is enough to think how theological formulas must sound today to the ears of an average man and the meaning he is almost forcibly led to give them.

"Let us look coldly at the spiritual situation as it is in our days: **a modern man without a Christian education**[56] **hears the statement, 'Jesus is God made man.' He will immedi-**

---

[55] H. U. von Balthasar, *Solo l'amore é credibile* (Turin: Borla, 1965), p. 50.

[56] "Christian education" here shoud be understood under the light of Rahner's theory of the "anonymous Christian" (see Vol. V, *Animus Delendi II*, Part II, Chap. III, §§ 9-16). This "Christian education" refers to an interior experience of an immanentist nature that allegedly reveals to each person who Christ is. This interior "revelation" spills over to others through the person's "testimony." Without this personal experience, theological arguments based on reason have no value; the same can be said for the teaching of the New Testament and the Church proving that Our Lord is God in human flesh.

ately reject this statement because, for him, it is reduced to a myth, which *a priori* should not be taken seriously into consideration or discussed. This is what we do, by the way, when we hear that the Dalai Lama considers himself a reincarnation of Buddha."[57]

§ 40

Fr. Piet Schoonenberg, S.J., confirms this passage by Rahner and adds further insult to the injury. Together with Fr. Edward Schillebeeckx, Schoonenberg authored the controversial *Dutch Catechism* that won a great prestige for him among the Bishops of the Netherlands. He affirms:

"It is impossible ... to prove theoretically in a clear and convincing way that Jesus is greater than Buddha. ... The truth of Jesus Christ must be made evident to the world through the testimony of our faith and our love."[58]

§ 41

English theologian Fr. Nicholas Lash, Professor of Divinity in the University of Cambridge from 1978 to 1999, asserts that Our Lord Jesus Christ is not, in fact, God. He is "divine" only in the relative sense that every man loved by God becomes in some way "divine." This is tantamount to denying the divinity of Christ or to concurring it is a myth. Lash asserts:

"How can we understand the notion of 'divine filiation'?[59] Jesus was, like all of us, a product of nature and history. As such, He was destructible and He was, in fact, destroyed. None of us, however, is merely a 'product.' We are not merely produced; we also are, in different ways and with the most varied degrees of efficiency, treated with tenderness. ...

"To declare that Jesus is the Son of God is, as I see it, to state that He was not only produced but loved in an efficacious, indestructible and 'absolute' way. If we consider that

---

[57] K. Rahner, "Théologie et anthropologie," in V.A., *Théologie d'aujourd'hui et de demain* (Paris: Cerf, 1967, p. 114).

[58] Piet J. Schoonenberg, untitled, in V.A., *Cinco problemas que defiam a Igreja hoje* (São Paulo: Herder, 1970), p. 78.

[59] In this excerpt, Fr. Lash tries to nullify the Catholic Dogma that Jesus Christ is hypostatically united to the Word, the Second Person of the Trinity, and, therefore, is the Son of God the Father. Lash pretends that the divinity of Jesus Christ does not come from the hypostatic union, but from being generated by God with love. Then, since everyone is loved by God, Jesus Christ would be son of God only in this relative way.

the 'production of love'... is a divine attribute, we are thereby declaring our conviction, derived from reflection about His destiny, that to be produced with love, to be effectively loved with a love that transcends destruction in mortality, is an aspect of what means and will mean to be a human being."[60]

§ 42   A similar affront to the divinity of the Word Incarnate comes from the pen of Fr. Jon Sobrino, an exponent of "liberation theology." According to him, the divine filiation of Our Lord is only analogical and metaphoric, that is to say, a myth. He writes:

"The formulation 'Son' – a human word and for this reason never completely able to describe Jesus – reflects the obedience and fidelity of Jesus to the Father in His earthly life. It depicts the theological experience of a crucified people: confidence in liberation, obedience at the service of liberation, fidelity in this service even to its final consequences. What is implicit in the metaphor of 'Son' comes from the reality of being 'brother' of Jesus.

"The formulations of faith in Christ are important, but secondary with regard to what one really believes. In Latin America He is called the Liberator. Theologians can and should profoundly analyze these formulations to show their equivalence with those in the New Testament and the Magisterium. But the important thing is the carrying out of this faith. As Karl Rahner recently said, 'If Jesus in fact make so decisive an impression on a person that he understands the value of unconditionally giving himself – in life and in death – to this Christ and decides to believe in the God of Jesus,'[61*] then this person really and fully believes in Jesus as the Son of God."[62]

§ 43   The leading Dutch scholar Fr. Bas van Iersel says essentially the same:

"Jesus is undoubtedly called 'God' (Jn 1:18; 20:21; 1 Jn 5:20). I only ask: Is this really so evident? If the use of the word 'God' signifies equality between Father and Son, certainly other passages speak about inequality with the same emphasis (for example in 5:26 and 17:3). When, after the resurrection,

---

[60] Nicholas Lash, "Filho de Deus: Reflexões sobre uma metáfora," *Concilium*, 1982/3, pp. 23-25.

[61*] K. Rahner, *Qué debemos creer todavia?* (Santander, 1980), p. 106.

[62] Jon Sobrino, "A fé de um povo oprimido no Filho de Deus," *Concilium,* 1982/3, pp. 42-43.

Jesus says: 'I ascend to My Father and to your Father, to My God and your God' (20:17), does not John place the resurrected Son of God on the same level as us who are men and before God?

"And in chap. 14:28, Jesus says outright: 'The Father is greater than I.' Does this deny to Jesus, the Son of God, the attribute 'God'? By no means. But **the ambiguity it presents obviously brings to mind that one who calls Jesus God is speaking likewise in metaphors, and perhaps even more so than when one calls Him the lamb, the way, the life, the wine and bread.** ...

"With the New Testament as starting point, I once again carefully read the Chalcedonian definition of faith. ... My honest reaction was and still is one of astonishment and surprise. **The language used there is far from expressing all that interrelates with experience and life.** The abstract terms (divinity, humanity, rational soul, equal in essence, indistinguishable, person, hypostatic union) clearly show that they were trying to find a kind of philosophical exactitude and univocality. Perhaps that was a benefit. I fear, however, that perhaps it was also a great loss.

"**This language makes it impossible to understand the expression 'Jesus is the Son of God,' even as a metaphor.** This is, I believe, irrefutable. And even if the Fathers of Chalcedon only wanted to say **that Jesus is at the same time true God and true man, it nonetheless is very problematic. For that expression insinuates that the two conditions have the same linguistic status. This makes us forget that the name 'God' can be used only in a tautological or metaphoric way.**"[63]

For these theologians the dogmas of Faith that Our Lord is God and the Incarnation of the Word of God are considered myths that cannot be taken seriously and metaphors impossible to demonstrate. These are clearly offenses against the honor of one of the most fundamental dogmas of our Holy Faith.

*

---

[63] Bas van Iersel, "Filho de Deus no Novo Testamento," *Concilium*, 1982/3, pp. 65-68.

We close Chapter III having seen an impressive array of texts that affront and insult Our Lord Jesus Christ. This ensemble presents a good reflection of the progressivist *animus injuriandi* that is tolerated, to say the least, by today's Vatican in the name of the spirit of the Council. As such, it is an expressive example of it.

*   *   *

Chapter IV

OFFENSES AGAINST THE CATHOLIC FAITH

§ 1   The progressivists believe that the object of the Catholic Faith should no longer be an ensemble of immutable truths. Instead, they depart from the relativist premise that there is neither absolute truth nor precise formulae to express it. For them, the Faith is historical and existential.

They pretend that the formulae of the Faith can vary according to different times and historical situations. They claim that even the truths revealed in Sacred Scripture and Tradition, fixed in clear and definitive expressions such as the Creed and the dogmas of the Faith, are nothing but uncertain, oscillating approximations conditioned by historical circumstances. So, the Faith and its formulations are changeable. This change should always follow the customs and ideas of man in each epoch. Accordingly, the Faith today should adapt to the thinking of modern man, that is, to modern philosophy.

In another Volume of this Collection we will demonstrate that this is how the progressivists conceive the Faith.[1] In this Chapter our aim is to call attention only to the insults to the honor of the Catholic Religion.

In the following Items we will provide the Reader with texts from theologians who, by criticizing the immutability of the Faith and casting doubt on the authenticity of the sources of Revelation, directly or indirectly offend the Catholic Religion.

1. The Catholic Faith: an Oppressive Burden, a Weak Flickering Flame

§ 2   Cardinal Joseph Ratzinger, today Pope Benedict XVI, whom many see as a conservative leader in the Church, has hitherto failed to make any public statement recanting his previous theological works of a markedly progressivist character. In fact, before occupying the post as Prefect of the Congregation for the Doctrine of the Faith, Joseph Ratzinger was a well-known representative of Progressivism.

---

[1] Vol. VI, *Inveniet Fidei?, passim*

At the Council's start, he was "one heart and one mind" with Karl Rahner.[2] As secretary to Cardinal Josef Frings, Archbishop of Cologne, Fr. Ratzinger played an important role in preparing the speech the Prelate gave in the Conciliar Hall attacking the Holy Office.[3] Fr. Ratzinger was also a close colleague of Hans Küng as a fellow professor at the University of Tübingen (1966 to 1969),[4] and the latter acknowledged his help with an amiable mention in the preface of Küng's important work, *The Church*.[5] In 1964 Fr. Ratzinger participated in the founding of the magazine *Concilium*, a bastion of post-conciliar Progressivism.[6] In 1972, along with von Balthasar and others, he was one of the founders of the magazine *Communio*,[7] a supposedly "moderate" progressivist alternative to *Concilium*.

§ 3 If these initiatives were not enough to attest that he adhered to Progressivism, we could mention this significant landmark: Before the Council, Ratzinger's own writings were under suspicion of heresy by the very Congregation he later headed.[8]

As we have said, until today Ratzinger – as priest, Bishop, Cardinal and Pope – has made no public retraction of his past

---

[2] The expression is Rahner's, quoted in *30 Giorni* (Portuguese edition), August-September 1984, p. 54.

[3] In his intervention during the 63rd General Assembly of the Council, Cardinal Josef Frings severely lambasted the Holy Office, asserting that "its course of action in many cases does not correspond to the mentality of our time, is harmful to the Church and a cause of scandal to non-Catholics" (*apud* B. Kloppenburg, *Concílio Vaticano II*, Second Session, vol. 3, p. 253). Commenting on this attack, Cardinal Henri de Lubac called it a "radical" criticism of the Holy Office, recalling that the aged and nearly-blind Cardinal-Archbishop of Cologne often turned to his secretary, Fr. Joseph Ratzinger, to write his speeches. De Lubac adds, "It is not an exaggeration to say that the old Holy Office ... was destroyed on that day by Ratzinger in union with his Archbishop, Cardinal Seper ... started the renewal. **Ratzinger, who has not changed,** continues it" (Henri de Lubac, *Entretien autour de Vatican II*, Paris: Cerf, 1985, p. 123; cf. *30 Giorni*, July 1985).

[4] Cf. *Folha de S. Paulo*, May 19, 1985.

[5] "I cordially thank my colleague in dogmatic theology, Prof. Joseph Ratzinger, who directs the Institute of Ecumenical Studies with me, for his precious help" (H. Küng, *A Igreja*, vol. 1, p. 8).

[6] Cf. *Folha De S. Paulo*, May 19, 1985.

[7] *Ibid.*

[8] Cf. ICI, May 15, 1969, p. 9.

writings. On the contrary, in his book-interview, *The Ratzinger Report*, he affirms that he has not changed his past position.[9]

For this reason, texts by Joseph Ratzinger prior to his being named to the Roman Curia and his election to the Papacy will be presented by this Work as expressions of Progressivism. Should the Benedict XVI really want to appear conservative in the eyes of Catholics, he must shoulder the burden of explaining the contradiction of his past thinking with some of his later positions, since *contraria simul esse non possunt*.[10]

§ 4

Writing about the Faith in today's world, Fr. Ratzinger says that it has become inconvenient and "an oppressive burden." He insults the Catholic Religion by affirming:

"Does the dogma of the Triune God really express the faith of the Bible, or is it not rather the product of the Greek mind eager to satisfy its speculative curiosity? ... What does it exactly mean: God is One and Triune? Does this topic still matters to us today? **Let us not consider all the theological sentences in the ancient Church that bother us today, but take only one example** from the circle of medieval dogmas ... **the doctrine of transubstantiation. ...**

"As it is, the subtle content of this definition **can be represented by the average man only in a rough way; its meaning seems increasingly unacceptable, especially since there is the additional difficulty that the medieval concept of substance has long since become inaccessible to us. ...**

---

[9] In the book-interview *Rapporto sulla fede,* published in English as *The Ratzinger Report,* journalist Vittorio Messori poses questions to Cardinal Ratzinger. Alluding to Ratzinger's participation in the management and staff of the progressivist magazine *Concilium,* Messori asks: "What significance does this collaboration have for the man who was to become Prefect of the former Holy Office? Was it a false step? A sin of youth? And what happened in the interim? A change in your thinking? A 'repentance'? ... The reply was prompt and serious: '**It is not I who have changed**, but the others.'" (pp. 14-15).

Further on, Messori adds that Cardinal Ratzinger maintained his previous thinking when he took on the post of Prefect of the Congregation for the Doctrine of the Faith: "When I asked Ratzinger whether it had been hard for him to change from the condition of theologian (formerly watched by Rome...) to that of one who inspects the work of theologians, he did not hesitate to answer: 'I would never have accepted this service to the Church if my task were primarily one of inspecting'" (p. 17). See also Note 3 of this Chapter.

[10] "Opposite positions cannot be held at the same time."

"Thus, it seems to me, **we have reached the heart of the uneasiness that we, present day men, feel when we consider the clash between faith and knowledge. ... What really troubles us in the Christian faith is,** to a large extent, **the burdensome excess of definitions that have accumulated in the course of History, and now present themselves to man demanding the assent of faith.** The difficulty lies precisely here: we can see that there is always an extraordinary sympathetic resonance aroused when an author seems to penetrate the multitude of definitions in a transparent way and resolve them all in the unity of a simple assent of faith. **When we hear that this book or that lecture has produced a liberating effect, it becomes evident that there are men today who feel the form of faith today as a burden. ...**

"Paradoxical as it may seem, the days in which we live are characterized by a great yearning for faith. It is evident that the world of planned economy, of research, of exact calculation and experiment, is not enough. In the final analysis, **people want to be liberated from this just as much as from the old-fashioned faith, which, by its contradiction with modern knowledge, has become such an oppressive burden to them.**"[11]

§ 5   Fr. Ratzinger goes on to say that today the Faith finds itself in "a vacuum," so outdated that it can find no resonance in the thinking of the modern man, even if the latter wanted it. By saying that Faith is no longer supported by philosophy, Ratzinger reveals his opposition to Scholasticism, which was the foundation of Catholic thinking, and his adherence to the notion of a philosophy that evolves with History. He writes:

"There are multiple reasons for the dilemma in which the Christian faith finds itself today. One of the most important is that **the faith has been abandoned by philosophy and, therefore, suddenly finds itself in a vacuum.** In the early Church and in the Middle Ages, philosophy offered man an image of the world where faith was logically situated and accessible to man. At the beginning of the modern era [however] philosophy created a sphere separate from the exact sciences – from which God was excluded – and the realm of faith. ...

"Beginning with Immanuel Kant, the rupture of the unity of philosophical thought has become increasingly evident. **The reliable certainty that man can find his way, by solid intel-**

---

[11] J. Ratzinger, *Fé e futuro* (Petrópolis: Vozes, 1971), pp. 16-17.

lectual argument, beyond the realm of physics, to the essence of things and their foundation, has disappeared almost completely. ...

"As [modern] metaphysics progresses, that unity of the past regresses. There is no longer only one philosophy, but many philosophies. Thus, the human mind does not accept only one philosophy as basic, but rather one opinion, a well-founded opinion, to be compared to other opinions that are considered equally well-founded. Therefore, the faith no longer finds a place in human thinking where it can anchor itself with total security; and if it tries to do so, the effort will be almost in vain." [12]

§ 6   In another work Ratzinger makes a similar assertion in an equally offensive manner:

"The gravest scandal of the Christian faith is its lack of historic sense. It did not change the world; at least, so it appears. ... Hence, **the central word of Christianity, the message of the redemption, is empty. It remains an empty word. But if the faith produces nothing, then one can only say that it is an empty theory, unable to be either confirmed or denied, and, therefore, a theory without importance.**[13]

§ 7   Cardinal Henri de Lubac, one of the most expressive leaders of the progressivist thinking that was victorious at the Council, considers faith to always be a "weak, flickering flame." He states:

"Faith is always and in each of us a 'weak flame' that flickers, and the spectacle contemporary atheism offers us, either in its tranquil triumph or in the pressure it exerts on us, can make it more difficult for many to keep this weak flame alive."[14]

§ 8   As for this pressure of atheism, a Catholic should not try to combat its influence, according to de Lubac. He should always accept it rather than be on guard against atheists. This contradiction, he affirms, is something difficult but good: "This difficulty itself is wholesome."[15]

---

[12] *Ibid.*, pp. 41-42.

[13] Joseph Ratzinger, "Questioni preliminary ad una teologia della redenzione," in V.A., *Redenzione ed emancipazione*, (Brescia: Queriniana, 1975), p. 178.

[14] Henri de Lubac, *Athéisme et sens de l'homme*, pp. 78-79.

[15] *Ibid.* p. 79.

§ 9   To Cardinal de Lubac, faith is totally subjective. This can be inferred from the somewhat obscure text below, which claims that Catholics should not have a strong, firm and objective faith that allows us to judge the wicked, since such an intent would be "sacrilegious." The ideal would be to have the constantly vacillating faith he just defended. Speaking about the faithful, he writes:

"The firmness of his faith, if it is authentic, will always be the opposite of a haughty rigidity. What is more, **looking beyond objective truths, the faithful will not pretend to know, ultimately, who believes or does not believe.** He respects the deepest secret of each one. **He knows that only God sees the depth of each heart and this dividing line that is always oscillating between true faith, which is acquiescence, and real disbelief, which is refusal. He does not have the sacrilegious intent ... to fathom the abyss of God."**[16]

§ 10   Addressing the crisis of the Church, Fr. Mervyn Fernando, O.M.I., a known scholar on Buddhism, offends the honor due the Catholic Faith by calling it "a heavy load of indigestible doctrines." Fernando comments:

"If the Church had been more Buddhist in her catechesis, that is, if she would have promoted and encouraged the faithful to see and experience for themselves the Way, the Truth and the Life instead of insisting on an a-critical acceptance of doctrines based only on her authority, perhaps the crisis would not have occurred. To make things worse, **the faithful were obliged to bear the heavy load of indigestible doctrines under the pretext of faith**. The important distinction between faith in Jesus Christ and theology or doctrinal formulae of Denzinger, Manuals and Catechisms was disregarded."[17]

Therefore, the Catholic Faith with her marvelous ensemble of dogmas, a most worthy reflection on this earth of Divine Wisdom, would be, according to some theologians, nothing but an onerous burden, an anguishing weight, and a heavy load of indigestible doctrines. According to others, our Faith of old would be a weak flickering flame, an empty theory, and a falsification. Clearly, such statements are grave offenses against the honor due the Faith.

---

[16] *Ibid.*

[17] Mervyn Fernando, "Desafio budista ao Cristianismo," *Concilium*, 1978/6, p. 101.

2. Faith in Sacred Scripture Is Contested; Other Affronts

§ 11   For Benedict XVI, then Fr. Joseph Ratzinger, the miracles of the Old Testament should no longer be the object of belief for Catholics; instead, they are obstacles to their Faith. He affirms:

"Who of us has the energy or the patience today to endure to the end the experience [of Pascal, who experienced the 'God made man, the God who is near us, who speaks, acts, loves and becomes angry'], so often contradicted by appearance? For **all the stories of miracles in the Old Testament are still there, not so much as a sign of faith for us today but rather as an obstacle to it**, expressing a cosmology that regards the universe as ruled by all kinds of spirits, not in accordance with fixed laws, but by caprice, so that miracles seem every bit as normal as they are alien in a world ruled by rational principles."[18]

§ 12   Further on, Fr. Ratzinger goes so far as to say that St. Paul's interpretation of the Old Testament is no longer acceptable:

"But was he correct objectively? **It is evident that the Pauline interpretation of the Old Testament follows a method that is no longer accepted as valid and, as a consequence, to modern philologists or historians his interpretation is almost wholly unacceptable.**"[19]

§ 13   Joseph Ratzinger's attachment to Protestant and Modernist tendencies[20] becomes even more patent when he employs

---

[18] J. Ratzinger, *Fé e futuro*, p. 14.

[19] Ibid., p. 30.

[20] Such tendencies were condemned by the Council of Trent and the Encyclical *Pascendi,* see Chap. I, Notes 28, 39 of this Volume.

If the present Pope continues to hold these same opinions, it would be difficult not to conclude he incurs the rigorous condemnation of the Council of Trent, especially since he continues to interpret Scriptures following the modernist historical method.

The declaration of the Council of Trent reads: "In order to restrain insolent spirits, it [the Council] decrees that no one, relying on his own skill, shall – in matters of faith and of morals pertaining to the structure of Christian doctrine – distorting the Sacred Scripture as he pleases, presume to interpret the same Holy Scripture contrary to that sense which Holy Mother Church, to whom it falls to judge the true sense and interpretation of the Holy Scriptures – has held and does hold, or to interpret Scriptures contrary to the unanimous consent of the Fathers, even if such interpretations were never intended to be ever published.

the historical method to cast doubt on the God of Moses, the God of the Old Testament. In effect, Ratzinger considers the whole Bible a non-objective ensemble of stories that reflected the culture and thinking of that time. He uses the method of asking offensive questions and answering them affirmatively in an implicit way. He writes:

"The Bible, venerated by faith as the word of God, has its human character disclosed to us by historical-critical scholarship. Its literary forms are a product of the world that generated it, and its manner of thought, even in respect to genuinely religious topics, has been influenced by the world in which it arose. **Can we still believe in the God who called out to Moses from the burning bush, who smote the first-born sons of Egypt or who led His people in war against the Canaanites? A God who struck down Uzzah dead because he dared to touch the Ark of the Covenant?**

"For us, is all of this not just the ancient East, interesting and even significant perhaps as a phase in human consciousness, but only a phase in human consciousness, not the expression of the divine word?" [21]

§ 14   Questioning the divine authority of Sacred Scripture appears also in an excerpt by Benedict XVI's old colleague, Fr. Hans Küng. His denial of faith in Scriptures is so peremptory and offensive that it needs no comment. He states:

"Life after death may not be merely asserted. **In fact, it would be disastrous if theologians ... were to think that they could resolve so grave a question by simply relying on God's 'revelation,' God's 'word,' God's 'Scripture.' As if simple recourse to 'it is written' ... were itself evidence of factual truth, as if arguments of authority alone could put an end to critical discussion. ...**

"How can I be so certain that God's 'revelation,' to which I appeal, **does not perhaps rest on an unfounded assumption? That God's 'word' is not perhaps merely our theological superstructure, our projection, in brief, a human illusion: at any rate, a word produced by human beings?**

Let those who oppose this be denounced by their Ordinaries, and be punished according to the penalties established by law" ("Decree concerning the Edition and the Use of the Sacred Books," *Documentos Pontifícios*, n. 95, Petrópolis: Vozes, 1959, p. 6).

[21] J. Ratzinger, *Fé e futuro*, p. 13.

That this 'Scripture' is not just the expression of our projections and our illusions, purely human words about human desires and longings?

"From all this it follows that theology cannot avoid the demand for *verification of belief in eternity.* **If faith demanded that reason be renounced and a *sacrificium intellectus* were required, then in principle this faith would be unbelievable, unintelligible, even more, inhuman.**"[22]

§ 15   After denying the whole of the Sacred Scripture, Küng goes on to deny its parts. He claims that references to the resurrection of the dead at the end of the world are an "illusory speculation." He then denies the objectivity of the book of Daniel, which deals with that topic. He asserts:

"Does not this whole fantastic apocalyptical literature [that is, 'the tangled knot of rough speculations about the end of man and the world'] **discredit from the beginning any serious belief in a resurrection [of the dead]? Is belief in a resurrection not merely an illusory speculation in apocalyptic guise, born out of human oppression and human misery? Can we not say that this is a classic historical paradigm of Feuerbach's theory of projection theory and Freud's theory of illusion?**

"Initially, it must be admitted without more ado that the content of the Book of Daniel raises more questions than it answers. Questions arise not only regarding the predictions it makes, but also their fulfillment. ... Likewise it is well known that the course of history prophesied in the Book of Daniel in the four empires scheme (Babylonian, Median, Persian and Greek empires) has been discredited by history, so that that schema, even in its later ecclesiastical variant (the Babylonian, Median-Persian, Greek and Roman empires) was definitively abandoned in modern times.[23] ...

---

[22] H. Küng, *Vida eterna?* (Madrid: Cristiandad, 1983), pp. 129-130.

[23] This completely unfounded "historic" affirmation of the conciliar expert is particularly disconcerting. It was Daniel who, more than five centuries earlier, prophesized with detailed precision the dates of the Incarnation and Passion of Our Lord Jesus Christ, as well as the destruction of Jerusalem (Dan 9:24-27). His prophecy of the "70 Weeks," one of the most famous in the whole Old Testament, is brilliantly corroborated by History.

Tertullian, who was debating with the Jews of his time, demonstrates irrevocably how this prophecy of Daniel was fulfilled:

"It is necessary now for us to examine the predicted times for the Nativity of Christ, for His Passion, and for the dispersion of the city of Jerusalem, that is, its devastation. Indeed, Daniel said that both the Holy City and the Holy Place would be scattered by the leader to come, and that the Temple would be destroyed unto its foundation.

"Let us thus look for the times when Jesus Christ our ruler should appear. We find them recorded in Daniel. After having computed those times, we shall prove that He has come, not only according to the times prescribed, but also according to the signs that followed His coming and by the works He did.

"We prove these things by the consequences that followed His coming, as the prophecy declared, so that we may believe that all these things were both foreseen and fulfilled. Thus, regarding Him, Daniel predicted in what way, when, and for what reason He would liberate the nations; and Daniel also showed why, after the Passion of Christ, this city had to be destroyed.

"He says: *In the first year under Darius, the son of Assuerus of the race of the Medes, who reigned over the kingdom of the Chaldeans, I Daniel understood in the books the number of the years [that should be accomplished until the desolation of Jerusalem]. And while I was still speaking in my prayer, behold, Gabriel, whom I had seen in a vision at the beginning, flying, touched me almost at the time of the evening sacrifice. And he instructed me, and spoke to me, and said: O Daniel, I am now come forth to give you understanding. From the beginning of your prayers this order was issued: and I am come to announce it to you, because you are a man of desires: therefore, do you ponder on these words, and understand this vision.*

"*Only 70 weeks remain upon your people, and upon the Holy City, until the prevarication be completed, the sin brought to an end, injustice vanquished, and eternal justice come into sight; so that the vision and prophecy are fulfilled, and the Holy of the Holies anointed.*

"*And you shall know, and see, and understand, that from the issue of the order to restore and rebuild Jerusalem, unto Christ the king, there shall be 7 ½ weeks, and 62 ½ weeks: and it shall convert, and shall be built unto joy and entrenchment, and the times shall be renewed. And after these 62 weeks, the anointed shall be slain, and [the people that shall deny him] shall not be his. And he shall destroy the city and the sanctuary together with the leader who is coming, and they shall be broken as in a cataclysm; until the end of a war, they shall break even unto [their total] destruction. And he shall confirm the testament in many.*

"*In 1 ½ weeks my sacrifice and libation shall be taken away, and there shall be in the sanctuary the execration of devastation, and even until the end of time, consummation shall be over this devastation* (in the Vulgate, Dan 9: 1-2, 20-27).

"Let us note, therefore, the limits fixed by the Prophet and how he precisely predicts that 70 weeks would be coming, in which they would build by length and breadth [the Holy City] and the times would be renewed, if they would receive Him. But God, foreseeing what would happen – that they would not only refuse Him but would actually persecute Him and deliver Him to death – summarized this and said that in 62 weeks He would be born and He would be anointed the Holy of Holies, but after 7 ½ weeks passed, He would have to suffer, and the city would be destroyed after 1 ½ weeks – when the 7 ½ weeks would be completed. Indeed, he says: *and the city and the sanctuary he shall destroy together by the chief who is coming, and they shall be broken as in a cataclysm, and he shall destroy the pinnacle [of the Temple] to its fundaments.*

"How, therefore, do we show that Christ came within the 62 ½ weeks?

"We will count from the first year of Darius, as this was the time when Daniel received this vision. For he says, *understand and keep perfectly these words of which I make you the witness.* Hence we must begin to count from the first year of Darius, when Daniel received this vision. Let us see, therefore, how the years are fulfilled up to the coming of Jesus Christ.

"For Darius reigned 19 years; Artaxerxes reigned 40 years; then King Ochus, who is also known as Cyrus, reigned for 24 years; Argus for one year; another Darius, who was also named Melas, for 22 years; Alexander the Macedonian for 12 years.

"Then, after Alexander, who reigned over both the Medes and the Persians whom he had conquered and who established his kingdom in Alexandria, that city which he named after himself; Soter reigned there in Alexandria for 35 years; to whom succeeds Philadelphus, who reigned for 39 years; who was succeeded by Evergetes for 25 years; then Philopater for 17 years; after him, Epiphanes for 24 years; then another Evergetes for 39 years; Soter for 38 years; Ptolemy for 38 years; Cleopatra for 20 years and 6 months; yet again, Cleopatra reigned together with Augustus for 13 years; after Cleopatra, Augustus reigned for another 43 years. All the years of the empire of Augustus numbered 56.

"We see then that in the 41st year of the empire of Augustus, who reigned after the death of Cleopatra, Jesus Christ was born. And the same Augustus lived for 15 years after the birth of Christ. So, up to day of the birth of Christ 41 years [of Augustus] passed.

"Thus, the 437 years and 6 months were completed. The 62 ½ weeks were fulfilled, completing 437 years and 6 months, up to the day of Christ's birth, the epoch when the eternal righteousness was manifested, and the Holy of Holies, that is, Christ, was anointed, and vision and prophecy were sealed, and sins were forgiven, which by faith in Christ's name were remitted to all who believe in Him.

"But what does it mean to say that vision and prophecy have been sealed? All the Prophets announced that Jesus Christ should come and suffer. So, given that His coming fulfilled the prophecy, the Prophet said that vision and prophecy were sealed. Because by fulfilling all that the Prophets previously announced of Him, Jesus Christ is the seal of all the Prophets. Indeed, after His coming and His passion, there is no longer vision or prophet announcing a future advent of Christ.

"If this is not so, let the Jews show us some books of prophets after Christ, or visible miracles worked by Angels such as those the Patriarchs used to see until Jesus Christ, whose advent sealed vision and prophecy. And rightly does the Evangelist say, *The law and the prophets were until John the Baptist* (Mt 11:13). For when Christ was baptized, that is, when He sanctified the waters in His baptism, the plenitude of the previous spiritual graces became concentrated in Jesus Christ, closing all visions and prophecies, which by His coming were fulfilled. This is why Daniel accurately said that His advent seals vision and prophecy.

"After having shown that the number of years and the time of 62 ½ weeks had passed, and that Christ came, that is, He was born, let us see how the other 7 ½ weeks, that were separated from the previous weeks, were fulfilled.

"Augustus still lived 15 years after the birth of Christ. He was succeeded by Tiberius Caesar, who ruled the empire for 22 years, 7 months, and 20 days. In the 15th year of his rule, Christ suffered His passion, being about 30 years of age. Afterward, Tiberius Caius Caesar, also called Caligula, reigned for 3 years, 8 months, and 13 days; Nero, for 9 years, 9 months, and 13 days; Galba reigned for 7 months and 6 days; Otho reigned for 3 months and 5 days; Vitellius reigned for 8 months and 10 days; Vespasian, in the first year of his empire overcame the Jews in war; and there were completed 52 years and 6 months; for he reigned for 9 years. So, on the day of their defeat, the Jews fulfilled the 70 weeks predicted by Daniel.

"When these years were fulfilled, and the Jews defeated, the libations and sacrifices ceased there [in Jerusalem], and thenceforth could no longer be celebrated in that place. For all the anointing was destroyed in that place after the passion of Christ. Indeed, it had been predicted that the anointing would be destroyed in that place, as it was also prophesied in the Psalms: *They have destroyed my hands and my feet* (Ps 21: 17).

"This suffering and destruction [of the city] was completed at the end of the 70 weeks [as a consequence of the crucifixion], during the reign of Tiberius, under the consulate of Rubellius Geminus and Fufius Geminus, in the month of March, at the time of the Passover, on the eighth day of the Calends of April, on the first day of unleavened bread on

"How, then, can one find a theological basis for the hope of resurrection in such a dubious book?"[24]

§ 16

Karl Rahner also addressed the resurrection of the dead in the Book of Daniel. Although more moderate than Küng, he likewise interprets the Scriptures in a relative way, employing a kind of free-examination on this topic. He considers the truths about the resurrection of the dead to be nothing more than "images" that cannot be reconciled among themselves. He writes:

"On this question it is very important to bear in mind that **the different parts of Scripture, as they reveal the events at the consummation of the world and the concomitant resurrection of the dead, paint figures that cannot be brought together in one homogeneous picture. ... The use of cosmic images** (the conflagration of the world, the stars falling to the earth, etc.) **clearly shows such disparity and such abandon, liberty and variability that one cannot think that their original authors were unaware of this. ...**

"**It is completely superfluous to try to harmonically balance on a single plane all of these imaginative elements. ...**

---

which Moses commanded the Jews to slay a lamb in the evening. Accordingly, the whole synagogue of the children of Israel did immolate Him, saying to Pilate, who desired to release Him: *His blood be upon us, and upon our children* (Mt 27: 25) and, *If you release this man, you are no friend of Caesar* (Jn 19: 12), so that all things that had been written of Him might be fulfilled. (Cf. Tertullian, *Adversus Judaeos*, in PL 2, cols. 651-656; *For the Conversion of the Jews*, trans. by John Collorafi and Atila S. Guimarães, Los Angeles: TIA, 2007, Chap. VIII, pp. 37-42).

Also, contrary to what Küng claims, the prophecy of the Four Kingdoms – the Chaldean, Persian, Greek and Roman (Dan 2:29-45) – began to be fulfilled during the lifetime of the prophet Daniel, who saw the Chaldeans destroyed by the Persians. His prophecy continued to be accurately fulfilled until the German barbarians took over the Roman Empire, which he also had symbolically predicted (Cf. Cornelius a Lapide, *Commentaria in Danielem Prophetam*, chap. 2, pp. 21-23).

In addition to these impressive historic confirmations, the authority of the Book of Daniel was proclaimed by a declaration of the Council of Trent (session IV). Its authenticity is also affirmed in argumentations of St. Augustine, St. Athanasius, St. Cyprian, St. John Chrysostom, St. Gregory and many other Fathers, as shown by Cornelius a Lapide (*Prolegomena in Danielem Prophetam*, pp. 3-5).

[24] H. Küng, *Vida eterna?*, pp. 154-156.

It is not possible in this case also to distinguish clearly between the matter and the form."[25]

§ 17   As he talks about the Resurrection of Our Lord, von Balthasar employs the same tactics as Rahner to relativize the Scriptures as a source of Revelation. The author calls the narratives of the Resurrection "images" whose central truth cannot be known. He also claims that the testimonies of the Resurrection have no value since they were subjective. Von Balthasar affirms:

"It was not easy to preach the Resurrection of Jesus to the pagans, who were unfamiliar with the biblical categories. **The analogies drawn by Paul** from the world of nature in 1 Corinthians 15:35-41 **are not very illuminating.** This is why he soon starts referring once again to Jewish and apocalyptic images. ...

"**This extensive collection of images used for the Resurrection – and here there is nothing but images, for 'Resurrection' and 'restoration to life' are images too – leads us to the conclusion that this mystery, in its uniqueness, cannot be reconstituted from any known point.** The images gather around an inaccessible center, which alone has the magnetic force capable of arranging around itself this garland of images. **And if these images cannot be combined to form an objective unity, no more do the subjective experiences of the witnesses come together ... to constitute only one meaning of their testimony.**"[26]

The author later returns to the same critique of the Gospel narratives: "**The Resurrection accounts of the Gospels are partially irreconcilable, considered either in their continuity or in their opposition.**"[27]

§ 18   Von Balthasar also questions the objectivity of the Gospels in their accounts of the empty tomb of Our Lord after His Resurrection. The irreverence he shows toward the revealed text makes it clear that he does not really believe in the supernatural character of the Gospel, but considers it only a historical and subjective testimony. He writes:

"There are marked differences of opinion as to whether the ancient Pauline Resurrection formula mentioning the burial

---

[25] Karl Rahner, *Resurrección de la carne* (Taurus/Madrid: Escritos de Teología, 1963), vol.2, pp. 216-217.

[26] H. U. von Balthasar, *Mysterium Paschale*, pp. 136-137.

[27] *Ibid.*, p. 190.

implies an empty tomb, and, supposing that it does, **whether the empty tomb should be credited to the account of the Jewish-apocalyptical intellectual environment,** which could only conceive a resurrection of the dead in the material mode of a corpse coming back to life. Whereas, on the one hand, **one almost can doubt the historicity of the empty tomb** ... on the other hand, it is certain that this aspect was later developed in an apologetic way, and this could hardly be avoided since the sign [the empty tomb] ... would soon be interpreted apologetically by the enemies of Christians."[28]

In a footnote citing a book by Protestant theologian H. V. Campenhausen, von Balthasar adds another affront: **"This tendency is manifested in Matthew, whose narration of Pilate's request that guards be placed at the tomb (27:62-66; 28:4-11,15) is fraught with internal contradictions. ... The narration can be considered as exaggerated as the apocryphal gospels."**[29]

§ 19   Von Balthasar finishes by relativizing the dogma of the Resurrection once again. He considers that the account of the empty Sepulcher is still an open question. He says: "Given the conclusion of Mark [about the empty tomb], we cannot come to any decision."[30]

Further on, von Balthasar discusses in more detail this "conclusion of Mark." He asks whether Holy Church had not adulterated the ending of the Gospel of St. Mark for her own convenience. It is an extremely offensive hypothesis... He writes:

"The problem of the conclusion of Mark places us before a sheer option. The abrupt breaking off of the Gospel is extremely surprising indeed. 'Either the original conclusion has been suppressed, or it was never there, or it has been lost accidentally.' (H. Grass). ... **Was the narration eliminated because in it was an obstacle to the announcement of the early Church? Something that could not or appeared not to harmonize with other traditions that she wanted to impose? ... Here we have an open field for endless speculation."**[31]

§ 20   In his book *Jesus of Nazareth*, Pope Benedict XVI concurs with similar progressivist criticisms when he approvingly

---

[28] *Ibid.*, pp. 168-169.

[29] *Ibid.*, p.169.

[30] *Ibid.*

[31] *Ibid.*, p. 165.

mentions them. Here he addresses St, Luke's witness that after the Resurrection, Our Lord had a physical body similar to ours. Benedict XVI attributes "exaggerations" and "contradictions" to this affirmation, clear insults to the Sacred Books. He states:

"Most exegetes take a view that Luke is exaggerating here in his apologetic zeal, that a statement of this kind seems to draw Jesus back into the empirical physicality that had been transcended by the Resurrection. Thus Luke ends up contradicting his own narrative, in which Jesus appears suddenly in the midst of the disciples in a physicality that is no longer subject to the laws of space and time.

"I think it is helpful here to consider the other three passages in which the risen Jesus is presented participating in a meal."[32]

§ 21   Following this same modernist method of interpreting the Sacred Scripture, von Balthasar calls into question the supernatural character of the Gospel, claiming that St. Luke's account of the Ascension was no more than a "forced reaction" to the historical need of the times:

"Luke's passage on the Ascension is no more than a forced reaction to the growing 'materialization' of the reports on the New Testament apparitions [of the resurrected Jesus]."[33]

§ 22   Benedict XVI also opposes the Gospel passage on the Ascension. First he ridicules it, and then he gives an interpretation of the presence of the risen Christ quite similar to those of Teilhard de Chardin. Throughout his whole book, Benedict XVI always uses the word "ascension" between quotes, giving the striking impression he considers it to be a legend. He comments:

"The departing Jesus does not make His way to some distant star. He enters into communion of power and life with the living God, in God's dominion over space. ... Now He is no longer in one particular place in the world as He had been

---

[32] Benedict XVI, *Jesus of Nazareth - Holy Week: from the Entrance into Jerusalem to the Resurrection* (San Francisco: Ignatius Press, 2011), p. 269

[33] H. U. von Balthasar, *Mysterium Paschale*, p. 150

before the 'Ascension': now, through His power over space, He is present and accessible to all - throughout history and in every space."[34]

§ 23   For the Reader it may be useful to know these other details of the Pope's Teilhardian interpretation of the Resurrection:

"We could regard the Resurrection as something akin to a radical 'evolutionary leap,' in which a new dimension of life emerges, a new dimension of human existence. ... This is what is meant by **those passages of St. Paul**'s prison letters (cf. Col 1:12-23 and Eph 1: 3-23) that **speak of the cosmic body of Christ, indicating thereby that Christ transformed body is also the place where men enter into communion with God** and with one another and thus are able to live definitively in the fullness of indestructible life."[35]

§ 24   Karl Rahner, praised by Paul VI for his collaboration at the Council,[36] goes further than the other authors cited in this Item, drawing the final consequences from the "historical method." According to him, the words of Our Lord narrated in the Holy Gospels should not be understood as revelation since they only express the thinking of those who wrote them.

They are nothing more than the "theology of the community" of that time. Rahner affirms:

"Today's Catholic exegesis and biblical theology ask which words of Jesus, in their literal expression, can be considered original words of the historical Jesus, and which – in their intent, importance, presentation, conceptualization, etc. – already came from the 'theology of the community.'

"This is not simply equivalent to saying that, from the historical point of view, every word of Jesus, considered in itself, must already be an original occurrence of revelation ... As stated, **not every word of the historical Jesus can be identified with the concept of an original revelation**."[37]

§ 25   Another known theologian who played a large role at Vatican II is the Dominican Edward Schillebeeckx. In his writ-

---

[34] Benedict XVI, *Jesus of Nazareth,* pp. 283-284.

[35] *Ibid.*, p. 274.

[36] Cf. A. Wenger, *Vatican II - Chronique de la deuxiéme session,* p. 254; G. Mondin, *Os grandes teólogos do século vinte,* vol. 1, p. 98.

[37] K. Rahner, *Teologia e Bíblia,* (São Paulo: Paulinas, 1972), pp. 93-94.

ings we find the same relativist spirit that characterizes Progressivism. As a consequence, he denies the rational and historical value of the Gospel to prove the divinity of Our Lord Jesus Christ. In an offense similar to the others we have seen, he affirms that the Gospel does not prove the Catholic Religion is better than the others:

"This faith **[the Christian Faith] affirms that Jesus is a revelation of God** and that He is the manifestation of all religiosity so that every other interpretation of the faith is either false or a partial interpretation. ... **But this same faith also affirms that this cannot be proven rationally. We profess it as men who believe; we do not affirm it as men who think rationally. From a purely rational standpoint, if we were to place all the other religious books alongside the Gospel, it would be impossible to conclude that the latter better represents religion and that, therefore, I must deliver myself to Christ. ...**

"**The Christian faith is linked to the apostolic interpretation of the man Jesus**, an interpretation made by men who knew Him intimately and who, departing from this knowledge, arrived at a specific interpretation. **Does this interpretation really correspond to the true Jesus? It is impossible to say more than what historical probability permits.**"[38]

§ 26   In this Item we have already seen some of the most expressive conciliar theologians who consider the Gospel a "myth": Rahner, Ratzinger, Schillebeeckx, Küng and von Balthasar, considered the "prophet" of Vatican II.[39] In this group we also find Fr. Leonardo Boff, one of the stars of Liberation Theology. It is curious to note that, with regard to the denial of Faith in the Gospels, Ratzinger and Boff are in accordance.

§ 27   In the text below, Boff defends the feminist position on women's emancipation. He describes the cultural ambience of those times to conclude that one must disregard the "mythological" passages of the New Testament, since they preach the submission of women to men:

---

[38] E. Schillebeeckx, Untitled, in V.A., *Cinco problemas que desafiam a Igreja hoje*, pp. 19-20.

[39] It was Cardinal H. de Lubac who called Hans Urs von Balthasar a prophet of the Council, since, according to the French scholar, in his many writings the Swiss theologian anticipated the main themes addressed at Vatican II (cf. *Paradoxe et mystére de l'Eglise*, p. 181). De Lubac's quote can be found in Vol. II, *Animus Injuriandi I*, Chap. I, § 4.

"Later Christianity failed to maintain the innovative breach inaugurated by Jesus Christ. True, women initially played an important role in the Christian community's proclamation and practice of the faith. ...

"Despite this novelty – facilitated by the fact that discrimination against women in the Roman Empire was much less than in Judaism – the New Testament reflects the attitude toward women of the prevailing cultural ambience. For example, despite the understanding and tenderness that he asks for women, **Peter accepts the prevailing ideology that they are 'the weaker sex'** (1 Pt 3:7) and demands their submission to their husbands (1 Pet 3:1; Tim 2:5; 1 Cor 14:34; Eph 5:22-24; Col 3:18).

"In 1 Timothy the author states forcefully: 'I do not permit a woman to act as a teacher, or in any way to have authority over a man; she must be silent. For Adam was created first, Eve afterward; moreover, it was not Adam who was deceived but the woman. It was she who was led astray and fell into sin.' (2:12-15). ...

"This is the kind of argument that was endlessly repeated in ecclesiastical circles, even to very recent times. Admittedly **mythological texts are used in their literal sense to legitimate a situation of men's domination of women.**"[40]

In this Item 2 we have presented examples of different types of offenses against the respect due the Sacred Books. Among them: the miracles of the Old Testament are unacceptable; Faith in Scriptures is senseless, non-human; the Holy Books themselves are a theological super-structure and only transmit the illusions and longings of the times; the Bible narratives are confused, imaginary and mythological, its accounts are subjective and contradictory. Further, it should not be said that the Sacred Scripture is better than the books of any other religion.

The Reader thus has another group of offenses to help him compose a general picture of the *animus injuriandi* that characterizes the spirit of the Council.

*

---

[40] L. Boff, *O rosto materno de Deus*, pp. 79-80.

3. Offenses against the Dogma of Original Sin [41]

§ 28   In addition to the grave consequences pointed out in the previous Item related to the relativization of the truths contained in Sacred Scripture, the progressivists, like the modernists before them, want to take a step forward. They desire to legitimize the doctrine of universal evolution.

To achieve this legitimization, they always stumbled on a seemingly insurmountable obstacle in the first chapters of Genesis. The Holy Ghost, through the pen of Moses, narrates the creation of man by a direct action of God upon the "slime of the earth" (Gen. 2:7); afterward, He created woman from "the rib which he took from Adam" (Gen. 2:22). This clear account makes it impossible to claim that man evolved from an animal.

Likewise, the description in Genesis of Adam and Eve (cf. Gen 4:5) as the origin of all mankind directly precludes polygenism, both in its creationist version – different human couples were created by God separately in different places – as well as in its evolutionist version – different races evolved independently from separate species of apes.

§ 29   The biblical description of original sin as a moral transgression committed by our first parents (cf. Gen 3:1-3) and of the chastisements that fell on them (cf. Gen 3:14-20) confirms that the human state was originally perfect (cf. Gen 1:26-31); that the guilt of sin came from Adam and Eve alone; and that from the moment man lost the original state of innocence, from the natural standpoint, man only decayed – rather than "evolved" as progressivists pretend.

§ 30   Already at the time of St. Pius X, the modernists were trying to relativize the first chapters of Genesis. Perceiving their intentions, the Holy Pontiff, through the Biblical Commission, issued a severe condemnation against them, forbidding that those chapters be given any interpretation except for the literal one.[42]

---

[41] Why are the offenses against original sin included in this Chapter IV and not in Chapter V? Since the offenses against the teaching on original sin also imply a denial of the truths contained in Genesis, we decided it was more appropriate to expound them here, after the insults to Sacred Scripture.

[42] Faced with the growing modernist tendency to allow an "historic interpretation" of the first chapters of Genesis, the Biblical Commission under the pontificate of St. Pius X issued the following condemnation on June 30, 1909 in the form of questions and answers:

"Concerning the historical character of the first three chapters of Genesis

"**Question 1**: Do the various exegetical systems, which have been designed and defended under the guise of science to exclude the literal historic meaning of the first three chapters of Genesis, rest on solid foundations?

"**Answer** - No.

"**Question 2**: Notwithstanding the historical nature and form of Genesis, the special connection of the first three chapters with one another and with the following chapters, the multiple testimonies of the Scriptures both in the Old and the New Testaments, the almost unanimous opinion of the Fathers and the traditional interpretation - also transmitted by the people of Israel - always held by the Church, is it permitted to teach that the aforesaid three chapters of Genesis do not contain accounts of events that really occurred and that, therefore, do not correspond to objective reality and historical truth, but are fables derived from the mythologies and cosmogonies of ancient peoples – after being purged of any polytheist error - and accommodated by the sacred author to the monotheistic theory; or they are allegories and symbols without any foundation in objective reality, proposed to inculcate religious and philosophical truths under the form of history; or finally, they are legends, in part historical and in part fictitious, freely composed for the instruction and edification of souls?

"**Answer** – No, to both parts of the question.

"**Question 3**: May the literal historical sense in particular be called in doubt when dealing with facts narrated in the same chapters which touch the foundations of the Christian religion: such as, among others, the creation of all things by God in the beginning of time; the special creation of man; the formation of the first woman from the first man; the unity of the human race; the original felicity of our first parents in the state of justice, integrity and immortality; the command given by God to man to test his obedience; the transgression of the divine command at the instigation of the devil under the form of a serpent; the degradation of our first parents from that primeval of innocence, and the promise of a future Redeemer?

"**Answer** - No." (DS 3512-3514) ...

This clear and peremptory statement oriented the teaching of the Magisterium for several decades. However, on January 16, 1948 a letter from the Secretariat of the Biblical Commission addressed to Cardinal Emmanuel Suhard, Archbishop of Paris, came to light (cf. DS 3862-3864). Although we will not analyze here the intentions behind such letter, it was utilized by the progressivists to try to circumvent the decisions of St. Pius X. Indeed, they alleged that the new letter introduced the possibility of a "scientific" reinterpretation of the literary style of the first chapters of Genesis, stating: "It is necessary ... to closely

In spite of the heavy curtain of silence that has fallen over this condemnation, it maintains until today its full vigor and validity.

With the progressivist avalanche that fell upon the Church at the Council and after it, the tendency to deny the literal interpretation of the first chapters of Genesis, especially the dogma of original sin, began to show itself openly. Through the writings of progressivist leaders, the attack against the traditional dogma became increasingly bold, as we will see in the texts below.

§ 31   Fr. Edward Yarnold, S.J.,[43] professor of theology at Oxford University, clashes frontally with the warning of St. Pius X. Further, he insults the honor of Catholic doctrine by stating that the account of the original sin is "irrelevant" and a "myth." His conceit and *animus injuriandi* are apparent in his final statement, which scorns St. Paul's teaching, which confirms the literal interpretation of Genesis. In his work *The Theology of Original Sin*, Yarnold writes:

"The traditional interpretation of the doctrine of the fall and original sin ... is open to many objections. **To the modern**

---

examine the literary procedures of the ancient peoples of the East, their psychology, their ways of expressing themselves and their particular notion of historic truth" (DS 3864). Progressivists were thus able to claim that this letter relativized the concept of historical truth and paved the way for the historical method of interpreting the Scriptures. Their liberalizing efforts were cut short very soon, however, when Pius XII issued the Encyclical *Humani generis* of August 12, 1950. In it, he affirmed: "One should particularly deplore a certain excessively free interpretation of the historical books of the Old Testament. Those who favor this system, in order to defend their cause, wrongly refer to the Letter which was sent not long ago to the Archbishop of Paris by the Pontifical Commission on Biblical Studies (January 16, 1948: AAS, vol. 40, n. 38, pp. 45-48)."

After summarizing the letter's contents, Pius XII reaffirmed the infallible nature of the truths contained in the first chapters of Genesis: "If, however, the ancient sacred writers have taken anything from popular narrations ... it must not be forgotten that they did so with the help of divine inspiration, which protected them from any error whatsoever in selecting and evaluating those documents. Therefore, by no means can anything of the popular narrations inserted in the Sacred Scripture be considered on a par with myths or other such things" (*ibid.*, nn. 38, 39).

Thus, the precepts of St. Pius X remain valid.

[43] Fr. E. Yarnold was recommended to the Author of this Volume by the well-known conciliar chronicler Fr. Giovanni Caprile, S.J. in an interview at the *Civiltà Cattolica* office in Rome on February 3, 1983.

mind perhaps the most damning objection is simply that this doctrine is completely irrelevant. I cannot believe, the common man thinks, that what Adam did can make any difference in my life.

"**The first step towards the rehabilitation of the doctrine on original sin is to realize that the account of the fall** in the third chapter of Genesis **must not be taken in its literal sense as history or science. It is a theological account in the form of a 'myth'** meant to explain how sin and evil in the world came into being, not from God but as a result of man's free choice and the decision of his ancestors. ...

"**The inerrancy of the Bible** means that the message proclaimed in that passage is true; but it **does not imply that the terms in which this message is couched are the only possible terms or that they have a validity** *per se*. ... **It is possible that a biblical author did not distinguish in his own mind between message and conjecture. But the conjecture is *not* the message.**

"**Accordingly, we need not have scruples about considering ourselves more informed than St. Paul in this respect; whatever he may have thought about the story of the fall in Genesis, respect for the Bible does not oblige us to believe in its literal truth.**"[44]

§ 32   After returning to the offense that the Church teaching is only a "myth," Yarnold introduces the idea that original sin was not the sin of Adam and Even, but the ensemble of sins of our ancestors:

"**The stories written about the fall by the Yahwist [Moses] are for the most part myths that he has adapted to show that man's own sin is responsible for the various evils of human life**: death, suffering, divisions, women's inferior status and the universal tendency to evil. This doctrine implies the solidarity of the human race; **it is not the individual's own sins that bring these evils upon him, but the sins of his ancestors.**"[45]

§ 33   Yarnold tries to make his argument acceptable by adopting a modernist concept of myth:

---

[44] Edward Yarnold, *Teologia del peccato originale* (Catania: Paoline, 1971), pp. 107-110.

[45] *Ibid.*, p. 53.

"The account of the fall in Genesis is not meant to be a literal reporting of an historical event. It is rather what is called a myth in the technical terminology of anthropology. The use of this word does not imply that the story is simply a fictitious legend; on the contrary, it means that a truth is too deep for straightforward expression and, therefore, is formulated in symbolic terms, hence the expressions used are typical of a story."[46]

§ 34   Fr. Yarnold draws some consequences from this "symbolic character" of Genesis when he interprets the state of innocence as an aptitude to make sex without complications:

"Nudity caused him [Adam] no shame (2:25). This last point should perhaps be interpreted not precisely as a proof of sexual innocence, but rather as the ability to make straightforward and uncomplicated relationships with others." [47]

§ 35   Further on the same theologian expounds and defends at length the progressivist doctrine on original sin, which would not have been an individual act, but a collective act: the rejection of a new stage of evolution that had been presented to mankind. Original sin is the "sin of the world." Hence his conclusion that monogenism[48] and the fall are "irrelevant myths." He writes:

"In the last few years many Catholic theologians have felt free to construct a bold reinterpretation of the doctrine [on the original Fall]. Among them are A. Hulsbosch, P. Schoonenberg, A. Dubarle, P. de Rosa and the authors of the *New Dutch Catechism*. Naturally each writes with his individual nuances, but it is possible to state a common position without doing any injustice to any one of them. Protestant theologians such as C. H. Dodd speak in similar terms.

"The doctrine of the fall, they would agree, is not about man's origins but about his present condition and his future. Man is unperfected: He is capable of evolving to a more advanced state, which includes a development in his social respon-

---

[46] *Ibid.*, p. 47.

[47] *Ibid.*, p. 46.

[48] Monogenism is the belief that the whole human race descended from a single pair, which is the traditional teaching of the Catholic Church. It is distinguished from polygenism, the theory that states that the species sprang from more than one pair.

sibilities. **Man is also imperfect: Collectively or individually, he has not reached the stage of evolution that it was in his power to reach; in other words, man sinned.** ...

"**Every individual sins personally,** and so fails to fulfill his moral potentialities; **to that extent he checks and deflects the process of evolution and deviates its progress.** But we are not simply individuals. Our progress is conditioned by the choices of others. ... Moreover, no man is an island. We are not individuals who by chance have relations with others; our relations with others constitute what we are. We find ourselves in a selfish, divided society, and inevitably we ourselves become selfish and out of harmony with our fellow creatures. ...

"**Original sin, therefore, is our attachment to a society that prevents us from loving God and our neighbor as we ought.** But however divided we may be from our society by our selfishness, we are united with it in this way: **We freely yield to society's pressure and contribute to it ourselves.** ... The world's sinfulness is more than the sum of each individual's personal sins. ... **The sin of the world is a collective will in which I am a partner, a pressure by the group on the individual, which I share and to which I contribute.**

"**Naturally, if one adopts this interpretation [of original sin and actual sin], it is not necessary to defend monogenism with all its difficulties. Just as the fall is a myth, so also descent from Adam is a myth. One need not even argue that monogenism is false; it is simply irrelevant.**"[49]

§ 36   Other well known authors – in addition to Yarnold and the theologians he mentions – are of a similar opinion. The text below comes from two recognized Jesuit professors of Gregorian University, Fr. Maurizio Flick and Fr. Zoltán Alszeghy, whose works are used as textbooks in innumerable institutions of higher learning in the Church.

§ 37   In the conclusion of their co-authored work on original sin, Flick and Alszeghy deny there was ever a paradisiacal state of innocence prior to sin and call for doing away with the expression original sin. They insult the honor due Catholic doctrine by stating that the revealed history of the origin of man (etiology) is "completely meaningless." They write:

---

[49] *Ibid.*, pp. 110-113.

"While admitting that the condition of humanity was changed by the original fault, **we do not think there was *a state preceding sin* in which the human phenomenon would have been different than it is today.** In our view, the change caused by the fault is sufficiently explained by the loss of a virtuality which would have guided humankind – progressively but more swiftly – to the development of its capacities and the satisfaction of its needs.

"Therefore, **in our view, the *'state of original justice'* should be explained neither as a superior stage of humankind that was lost by a later decadence (it is difficult to insert the term 'earthly paradise' into the image of an evolving world), nor as a simple transposition of eschatological perfection to the beginning of human history** (in fact, **in this second case**, sin would not cause any change in the human condition and the **revealed etiology would be totally meaningless**). ...

"**The question is often asked whether it is convenient today to keep the term *original sin* introduced by Augustine. ... We think it advisable at times to replace the *originated original sin* in catechesis and preaching with other expressions,** such as 'belonging to the kingdom of sin and death, alienation from God, the incapacity to orient one's existence toward God,' etc., which express the fundamental malice of the human heart, introduced by man and healed only by Christ.

"**One could also substitute *originating original sin* with terms less connected to the accounts of paradisiacal history; for example, one could speak of the sin of humanity and the sin of man**, expressions that opportunely set aside the questions left unresolved by revelation."[50]

§ 38   These authors consider it "anachronistic" to insist on a common inheritance of man that comes from original sin. They assert:

"It is understandable that in the past, when the family and tribe had a strong social influence, one would tend to express solidarity with the wreckage of the human genre by basing it on a biological relationship of all men with Adam, the first sinner and common father of all. In our times, other forms of solidarity are more accepted than genetic descent. For this reason, **it seems anachronistic to insist upon the importance of the common**

---

[50] Maurizio Flick and Zoltan Alszeghy, *Il peccato originale* (Brescia: Queriniana, 1974), pp. 372-373.

ancestry of the first sinner, as if this alone would explain the transmission of original sin to all men."[51]

§ 39   Msgr. Philippe Delhaye, secretary of the International Theological Commission for 15 years and a professor at Louvain University, is considered a "moderate." He believes the word sin, in the expression "original sin," has only an analogical meaning. He writes:

"To understand sin, one must reconstruct the context of the Covenant. However, personal sin also has another essential aspect [the position taken *pro* or *contra* God]. This is so essential that **every other use of the word sin has to be analogical, such as in the case of 'original sin,' the 'structures of sin,' and 'sin of the world.'**"[52]

Now then, if the word sin has an analogical sense, what should we think about the concept of sin that constitutes one of the foundations of Morals? To what degree should Catholic Morals also be considered analogical? Does not this position of Delhaye relativize Morals and insult the honor of Catholic doctrine?

§ 40   Addressing a different topic, Von Balthasar notes in passing that the narration in Genesis is only a "legend":

"Here we also look at the origin of language; the second account of creation necessarily implies its divine origin because Adam was alone and without a woman. Nevertheless, **it would be reading too much into the legend** to deduce only from this the objective priority of the order of grace."[53]

§ 41   Fr. Joseph Fuchs is a German Jesuit who taught at Rome's Gregorian University for almost 30 years and a specialist in Moral Theology. During an interview with the Author of these lines, he affirmed the same progressivist thinking about original sin. Further, he insulted the honor of Catholic doctrine by calling the account in Genesis a mere "story," a "legend" Fuchs states:

---

[51] *Ibid.*, p. 324.

[52] Philippe Delhaye, "Senso del peccato e risponsabilità personale," in J. Tomko (ed.), *Peccato e riconciliazione* (Rome: Paoline, 1983), p. 54.

[53] H. U. von Balthasar, "O acesso à realidade de Deus," in V.A., *Mysterium Salutis*, vol. II/1, p. 30.

"The understanding of original sin depends upon the epoch. There is something that we could call original sin. What is it? This is difficult to ascertain. But that something which can be called original sin exists, this is accepted. However, the name, the way it is described – Adam in paradise, etc. – these are etiological stories.

"The Greek word *aition, aitios* denotes a story [a myth to explain the origins of something], a kind of legend. It is meant to explain a reality even if what happened did not actually occur that way. Nonetheless, by telling this story one is able to explain man in his initial state."[54]

§ 42   During an analysis of the spousal relationship of the Church to Christ, Hans Urs von Balthasar also refers to the paradise account as a "legend":

"The possibility of this simultaneity [that the Church would be both the body and the spouse of Christ] is inscribed in the paradise legend where woman takes her rise from man (Eph 5:30-33) in an indissoluble reciprocity (I Cor 11: 7-12), so much so that Christ too, from whom the Church originates, was 'born of a woman' (Gal 4:4)."[55]

§ 43   Fr. Joseph Ratzinger, today Benedict XVI, seems to support the same conception of evolution and to deny these fundamental texts of Scriptures when he raises the following questions:

"In the very next chapter [of the Bible] new problems emerge with the story of the fall. How can one bring this into harmony with the knowledge that, on the evidence of natural science, man starts not from above, but from below; that he does not fall, but slowly rises, even now having only just accomplished the metamorphosis from animal to human being? And what of paradise? Long before man existed, pain and death were in the world. ...

"And another thing: the first man was scarcely self-conscious ... He was far from possessing the full endowment of reason, which the old doctrine of paradise attributes to him."[56]

---

[54] Joseph Fuchs, interview with the Author, Rome, February 4, 1983.

[55] H. U. von Balthasar, *Mysterium paschale*, pp. 88-92.

[56] J. Ratzinger, *Fé e futuro*, p. 11.

§ 44

In addition to these well known "moderate" theologians, it seems convenient to cite one *ardito* to show how the thinking of the Conciliar "moderates" and *arditi* is fundamentally the same on various important points. Thus, the *ardito* Leonardo Boff shares the same conception of original sin as the "moderates" cited above, among them Fr. Ratzinger. In his book, *The Maternal Face of God*, Boff offers this definition of original sin:

"By original sin we mean that original situation that generates the incapacity for love, the closing up of man in himself. ... **This perversion of the root of human life lies *ultimately* in the inhuman dimensions of human life, the dimensions of personal and social injustice, the historical wickedness of the forms of human sociability – in short, in our situation of original sin. We are all born into the sin of the world**, and we perversely collaborate with our tragic destiny."

In this Item 3, the Reader saw innumerable offenses against the honor and respect due the dogma of original sin. With this he can also determine progressivist thinking on the topic, which is something completely different from the perennial Catholic doctrine expressed in the teachings of the Pontifical Biblical Commission of St. Pius X.

*

Regarding the honor due our Holy Catholic Faith, this Chapter IV presented an ensemble of offenses against it that indubitably reflects the *animus injuriandi* of the spirit of the Council.

*   *   *

Chapter V

INSULTS TO THE DOGMAS OF THE FAITH
AND THE LAST FOUR THINGS

§ 1
    The progressivist presuppositions the Reader needs to follow this Chapter well are basically the same as those laid out in the previous one: They show how historicity is meant to relativize the immutable truths of the Catholic Faith and the divine character of Sacred Scripture. Progressivists also use another tactic to combat dogma and the Four Last Things – Death, Judgment, Heaven and Hell. Based on historical mutability and evolution, they claim that also the Faith – and all its dogmas – should adapt to the needs of present-day man.

    Thus, adaptation to the world and to modern man, advocated by Vatican Council II as a "pastoral" initiative and originally turned toward institutional, liturgical and social questions, flows into the doctrinal sphere, clearly assailing the immutable and perennial nature of our Holy Faith.[1]

    Primum in intentione, ultimum in executione – the first objective one has in mind is realized only at the end of the process of execution. Applied here, one would say that Vatican II's "pastoral" policy only achieves its final goal when it goes against the dogma of the Catholic Church and changes it to adapt it to present-day man... Throughout the length of this Collection, the Reader can verify this process at work.

1. Dogmas: Obstacles, Awkward Labels that Must Change

§ 2
    The first testimony offensive to Catholic dogma comes from a text by Fr. Joseph Ratzinger, already analyzed from another standpoint in this Volume. According to him, dogmas are "obstacles" for the present-day man:

    "The list of difficulties that seem to make faith and knowledge irreconcilable continues as we cross the threshold of the New Testament and step onto the road of Church history. ... **Does the dogma of the Triune God really express the faith of the Bible, or is it not rather the product of the Greek mind eager to satisfy its speculative curiosity? ... What does it ex-**

---

[1] Cf. Vol. I, *In the Murky Waters of Vatican II*, Chap. IX, §§ 57-84.

actly mean: God is One and Triune? Does this topic still matters to us today? Let us not consider in the ancient Church
all the theological sentences that today bother us, but take
only one example from the circle of medieval dogmas ... the
doctrine of transubstantiation. ...

"As it is, the subtle content of this definition can be represented by the average man only in a rough way; **its meaning
seems increasingly unacceptable, especially since there is the
additional difficulty that the medieval concept of substance
has long since become inaccessible to us.**"[2]

§ 3   In another work Fr. Ratzinger calls the language of Catholic dogma "second class language":

**"The language of the dogma does not stand of itself;
it is, in a certain way, a second class language.** It refers to
the language of the Bible and the language of preaching, which
must make the word of the Bible fully valid to face the questions
of man."[3]

§ 4   Cardinal Leo Scheffczyk, professor of Dogmatics in
Munich and consultant for the Congregation for the Doctrine of
the Faith for many years, maintains that the supernatural truths
we know from Revelation and the perennial Magisterium of
the Church are no different from natural truths. He concludes
against infallibility in the truths of the Faith – dogma – which
for him are "exaggerated labels" that tend by their nature to discredit natural truth. Scheffczyk writes:

**"It is evident that the truth that emerges from affir-
mations of the faith does not act or affirm itself in a manner
different from other truths.** We agree that we should not lose
sight of the difference between the *content* of natural propositions and that of the pronouncements of Revelation. But **as far
as the concept of truth is concerned, this is irrelevant because, in this regard, the only thing that matters is to know
whether that affirmation corresponds to the reality**.

**"Thus, one can say that the formulae of the faith,
from the formal aspect of truth, are not really different from
other affirmations** and that their persuasive force comes solely
from the objective value of the judgment expressed.

---

[2] J. Ratzinger, *Fé e futuro*, pp. 15-16.

[3] J. Ratzinger, "Sobre la cuestión de la validez permanente de las
formulas dogmaticas," in *ITC*, "*El Pluralismo teologico*" (Madrid: BAC,
1976), p. 67.

"Thus one sees ... that **the actual truth that comes to the limelight in propositions of faith is not in fact different from the one that continuously comes to the fore in human affirmations in general.** This is to say that **the truth of the faith, in its claim to be true, in no way is an exception emanating from natural conditions** ... by which man would be convinced of something other than the truth itself. **To label this truth as 'infallible' is to efface its natural context and make it an exaggeration that could discredit the truth itself, because then its pretension to impose itself would seek the endorsement of an exterior authority**" [4]

§ 5

Responding to questions in an interview, Cardinal Congar describes belief in original sin, the existence of the Devil and the real presence in the Eucharist as a "disastrous thing-ism":

"*Question* – Shouldn't it be **feared that** if theology fails to come up with new expressions of revealed datum, **we will see simplistic beliefs** – quite different from true tradition [sic!] – reappear among the Christian people about **original sin, Satan and the real presence in the Eucharist?**

"*Answer* – **Clearly it is possible to return to this awkward 'thing-ism' that did not respect the mystery of the revealed truths and ended in visualizations absolutely contrary to the faith.**"[5]

§ 6

Hans Küng is equally peremptory in attacking the definitive formulae of dogmas and the Creed, calling them "stiff" and "petrified" because they do not change with historical circumstances:

"**Neither the dogmas nor the written symbols of faith are stiff, petrified formulae, stripped of the historicity that animates everything that is human. They also are products of a given historical situation, and we must constantly strive to free them from the shell in which their own historic time has encased them, and reinsert them into a more encompassing historic perspective** to better understand them. ...

"**In particular we must wrench the dogmas and the written symbols of faith ... from the boundaries, biases and**

---

[4] Leo Scheffczyk, "A verdade enunciada em proposições e o 'permanecer na verdade,'" in Karl Rahner (ed.), *O problema da infalibilidade* (São Paulo, Loyola, 1976), p. 157.

[5] *Jean Puyo interroge le Père Congar*, p. 225.

polemical character imposed on them by their times and ... interpret them in a more balanced, adequate and better way."[6]

In Volume II of this Collection, *Animus Injuriandi I*, we presented various offenses against different Marian dogmas, which were called obsolete, fictitious and excrescences.[7] The Reader can easily transpose to this Item that whole ensemble of offenses to have a fuller picture of the spirit of the Council with regard to dogmas.

2. Heaven, Hell and Purgatory - Childish Notions that Should Go

§ 7   To better assess the lack of respect that progressivists profess for the Last Four Things, we will offer a brief explanation of their strategy and doctrine, comparing them with the traditional Catholic Magisterium. This explanation should help the Reader follow the various testimonies cited in this Item 2.

The Church has always taught that every man has a particular future after he dies. He will be judged according to his merits and sins and, depending on God's verdict, will go to Purgatory, Heaven or Hell. This irrevocable sentence – as far as Heaven and Hell are concerned – will not change after the Last Judgment and the resurrection of the bodies; it remains the same for all eternity. The punishment of those in Purgatory is transitory. To teach us about this final future of man, the Church dedicated the treatise on the Last Four Things, the *Novissimis*, part of her Dogmatics.

§ 8   In an indirect attack on the *Novissimi*, progressivists have replaced the Latin expression *de Novissimis* with its Greek equivalent, eschatology (from *eschata,* the final things), also legitimate and capable of expressing the same reality.[8] In progressivist parlance, however, eschatology has connotations that differ from the perennial Magisterium, particularly in regard to the dogmas on Heaven, Hell, Judgment and the resurrection of the body, as professed by Catholics in the Creed.

§ 9   Indeed, departing from the theory of a universal evolution of the whole human race, progressivists call eschatology

---

[6] H. Küng, *A Igreja*, vol. 2, p. 51.

[7] Cf. Vol. II, *Animus Injuriandi I*, Chap. III, §§ 23-26a.

[8] Cf. K. Rahner and H. Vorgrimler, *Petit dictionnaire de théologie catholique* (Paris: Seuil, 1970), p. 161.

the last phase of this evolution, the *Christogenesis* in which man supposedly will overcome death and become divinized.[9] The model of this divinized man is none other than the God-Man: Christ in his resurrected state. Thus, the Resurrection would be the first milestone of a new phase of mankind, and its final stage will be marked by the second coming of Christ, when the whole human race supposedly will rise to the divine sphere.

§ 10   The period between the Resurrection and Christ's second coming would be the space of time it takes mankind to evolve to the divine. The world, therefore, is continuously moving toward this end in a variable, gradual way, like water is transformed into vapor as it boils. Since now mankind is evolving toward that final divine phase, progressivists say that eschatology is inchoatively present in our times.[10]

§ 11   The collective character of this transformation is essential in the progressivist notion of man's evolution to the divine. For it, what counts is the ensemble of mankind rather than the individual salvation of a soul. All the "saved" or "condemned" individuals are no more than drops of liquid that evaporated and condensed somewhere in the cosmos, waiting together to be re-

---

[9] *Christogenesis* – a term accepted by countless progressivist theologians, including Benedict XVI – would be the final phase of the universal process of evolution, which Teilhard de Chardin calls *Cosmogenesis*. According to Fr. Teilhard de Chardin, *Cosmogenesis* is divided into three stages: *Biogenesis*, followed by *Anthropogenesis* (or *Noogenesis*) and finally *Christogenesis*.
Here is how he explains the process: "Established as the Prime Mover of the evolving movement of complexity-consciousness, the cosmic Christ becomes cosmically possible. And at the same time, *ipso facto* he acquires and develops in complete plenitude, a veritable *omnipresence of transformation*. For each one of us, every energy and everything that happens is 'superanimated' by his influence and his magnetic power. To sum up, *Cosmogenesis* reveals itself, along the line of its main axis, first as *Biogenesis*, and later as *Noogenesis*, and finally culminates in the *Christogenesis*" ("Le Christique," in *Le Coeur de la Matiére*, p. 109).

[10] Karl Rahner confirms this notion about our times: "The end times have already begun, even should this final stage last for many centuries. The final stage of the whole history of salvation is already occurring as a participation [of man] in the resurrection of Christ. ... We see, therefore, that the full redemption [of mankind] is reached 'already now'" ("Sobre el sentido del dogma de la Asunción," *Escritos de teologia*, vol. 1, pp. 249-250).

united with the ensemble of mankind in its final step of divinization. These individual souls would be like drops of wine that
had already evaporated and then cooled again in a condenser
coil, transformed into a cognac, awaiting the rest of the wine to
be distilled.

§ 12   Therefore, Heaven and Hell are nothing more than
primitive and simplistic names to designate the different cosmic
spheres where individual souls await that collective integration,
the Last Judgment, also just another simplistic expression.

§ 13   Once the eschatological era is reached – which is the final
phase of *Cosmogenesis* – we will see "a new heaven and a new
earth." According to Progressivism, mankind, already immersed
in the divine, will enter a new evolutionary cycle. Less has been
said by the progressivists about this new stage of man. As a point
of reference, they say that man will be divinized, although this
does not appear to be the final state in the evolutionary process.

§ 14   Such eschatology has been present in an inchoative way
since the Resurrection of Christ and will develop until it reaches
its plenitude: the divinization of man, or heaven. For this reason,
progressivists also use the concepts of Heaven, Hell and Purgatory to describe the interior steps of "divinization" that each man
– or each group of men – reaches on this earth. Hence, for them
the concepts of Heaven and Hell are primarily the interior psychological stages of each individual, and also of mankind. This
is why they say, for example, that a situation of oppression or
"alienation" of a man or society is Hell; that their emancipation
or "liberation" is Heaven, and so on.

This framework of the progressivist thinking is presented
to help the Reader accompany the background of the texts that
follow, which offend against Catholic dogma on the *Novissimi*.[11]

A. Evolution and Eschatology, Concepts at Variance with Catholic Doctrine

§ 15   Yves Congar presents a summary of the factors that most
influenced the modern changes in the Church regarding the Four
Last Things. He cites five causes, placed in order of importance,
the first being evolution, followed by eschatology. He comments:

---

[11] This summary of progressivist doctrine is as incomplete as it is brief.
An overview of this doctrine will be given in greater detail in Vol. VII,
Destructio Dei, Chap. III, 3, of this Collection, with the different presen-
tations offered by the most important progressivist thinkers.

"This situation [created by traditional catechesis regarding the Four Last Things] is profoundly changed today, so that we are facing a new presentation of salvation. Without intending to make a complete analysis, we can discern the following factors for this change.

"a. A living presence of the 'others' in the consciousness: **A new sense of the world's dimensions regarding** not only its socio-cultural and demographic spaces, but also **its historical-evolutionary duration. We have passed from the idea of the world starting 5,119 years before the birth of Jesus ... to a Teilhardian vision of an immense** *Cosmogenesis* **and** *Anthropogenesis*. If man appeared more than two million years ago, what happened to those millions of beings who came before Abraham and Jesus? What will happen to the hundreds of millions today who have no possibility of knowing the God of Jesus Christ and being touched by the universal Church as sacrament of salvation? **The axiom 'no salvation outside the Church' obviously must receive a new explanation, and, in fact, it has.** ...

"b. Biblical and patristic studies ... have made it possible to rediscover the eschatological meaning. **It is no longer just a matter of the 'final end' of each individual ... but of the trans-historical aim that God wanted for the whole of history: which places in Christianity a value of absolute hope for this world. This value was missing in the classic type of 'religion.'"**[12]

§ 16   Stressing this overview, Congar defines salvation as something that differs from traditional teaching and thus insults Catholic dogma:

"Christ is Savior forever and everyday. It does not suffice only to say that He was. **Saying this [in the past] would be to envisage salvation as a kind of material treasure already acquired, capital deposited in a safe to which only priests ('the Church') had the keys.** Jesus saves throughout all of History, and His salvation, His redemption, will continue until the end. This is why the Scripture speaks of salvation either in the future or in the present as something we are approaching and being prepared for here on earth. The 'new creation' is an ongoing process. Christian life is a walking toward a future that is already present."[13]

---

[12] Yves Congar, *Un peuple messianique* (Paris: Cerf, 1975), pp. 149-150.

[13] *Ibid.*, p. 125.

These texts confirm that the Four Last Things are seen by progressivists as part of the general evolution of the universe as stated in the introduction of this Item 2.

B. The Four Last Things: Result of a Physicist' Inquiry and a Sickly Treatise

§ 17   Fr. Congar considers the *Novissimi* to be the fruit of an erroneous "physicist" mentality:

"From the 15th century on, ecclesiology generally lacked the sense of eschatology. Without eschatology having a voice, **the 'final ends' were seen less as the objective and realization of the global order than as an accumulation of 'things' that are found somewhere behind the curtain of death and can be studied in the same way as earthly 'things.' One asks, *Quid sit ignis purgatorius?* [What is the purifying fire?] and *Utrum visio Dei sit per speciem?*[14]** [Is the vision of God reached through abstract concepts?] **the same way that we raise questions in physics about the nature of fire or in metaphysics about knowledge through concepts. In short, a kind of physics of the final ends.**"[15]

§ 18   A similar criticism is found in the words of von Balthasar:

"There is no longer a question of situating the eschatological 'places' (Heaven, Hell, Purgatory, Limbo) in the interior of this universe - since this theological cosmos, whose upper and lower borders touch the divine and the demonic, was transformed into a physical cosmos. Also set aside was ... the 'end of the world' (of the planet Earth) as an event dependent on theology. It was necessary, therefore, to transpose the 'final ends' of man, his history and the cosmos, to an entirely new dimension that above all is a dimension of revelation and faith.

---

[14] Although *species* in Latin can be translated simply as sense of sight or gaze, in Thomist language *species* is man's intellectual notion of something. Thus, *species* is not the thing itself but an abstract concept formed in the mind of the observer. It is by considering this concept that man comprehends, and it is by making use of it that he transmits his knowledge to others. Hence St. Thomas asks if in in Heaven the comprehension of God will continue to operate through the *speciem.*

[15] Y. Congar, in *Revue des Sciences Philosophiques et Theologiques*, 1949, p. 463, *apud* H. U. von Balthasar, "Eschatologie," in V.A, *Questions théologiques d'aujourd'hui* (Paris: Desclée de Brouwer, 1965), vol. 2, p. 276.

"This had a twofold consequence: **these *escatha* [final things] became in an entirely new way 'non-figurative'[16] to the mind** (because the whole system of the world, every man on earth who is born, lives and dies, from now on sees himself in a dimension manifested to the world solely by the revelation of God), and precisely because of this all theology became linked to the *escatha* and escathologized. In reality, **since then the final things have been the world, man and history to the degree that they are touched by this decisive, transubstantiating act of God.** ...

"**No longer do we integrate the 'final things' into a cosmos (understood in its old theological meaning); we link the cosmos to divine action.**"[17]

§ 19   Fr. Chenu[18] affirms that the teaching of the Church has produced a "sickly treatise on the Four Last Things":

"**For the last four centuries**, generations of theologians have assembled manuals that treat sacred history like a preliminary study, leaving exegetes as an 'auxiliary' discipline ... and **when they finally reached eschatology, the result was a sickly treatise on the Four Last Things.** During this period, we were fully 'scholastic' in the pejorative sense of the word."[19]

Therefore, for Cardinal Congar and Frs. von Balthasar and Chenu – three of the most significant representatives of conciliar theology – the Four Last Things supposedly expressed a natural physicist mentality and a sickly doctrine. Undoubtedly, offensive expressions in themselves...

*

---

[16] For von Balthasar the traditional teaching of the Church on Heaven, Hell and Purgatory as physical places is "figurative," that is, imagery influenced by a "physicist" type of research.

[17] H. U. von Balthasar, "Eschatologie," in V.A., *Questions théologiques d'aujourd'hui*, vol. 2, pp. 275-276.

[18] About the influence of Fr. Chenu's thinking on conciliar documents and notably on Paul VI's Encyclical *Populorum progressio*, see Vol. II, *Animus Injuriandi I*, Introduction, Note 14 m.

[19] M.-D. Chenu, "The History of Salvation and the Historicity of Man in the Renewal of Theology," in V.A., *Theology of Renewal*, vol. 1, pp. 165-166.

C. The Dogma of Heaven: Result of the Church's Failure to Manage the World

§ 20 Written in the pedantic language that often characterizes Rahner's works, the text below questions the existence of Heaven. It is unnecessary to say that the existence of Heaven is a truth professed by every Catholic in the Creed as a dogma upheld by all the Popes, Saints and Doctors of the Church.[20]

Rahner also claims that it is absurd to ask where Heaven is to be found. He affirms in passing that glorified bodies are non-physical and sustains that this new cosmic state will be achieved at the end of the evolutionary process. Rahner states:

"But if we think that the interior finiteness of our own physical spatiality is not a presupposition, but an interior moment of non-glorified matter and the result of its history, then it will not be impossible for us to think ... that this spatiality and heaven's 'nature of space' are two heterogeneous and incommensurable unities. This means that, on the one hand, **it is absurd to ask *a priori* where heaven is if by 'where' we understand a point of our physical spatiality**; on the other hand, it is possible to uphold with great 'realism' the corporeality of glorified persons, along with their own spatiality and localization.

---

[20] On the perennial teaching of the Church on Heaven, see:

St. Hilary of Poitiers, *Tractatus in Psalmos*, 120, n. 16, in PL 9, 660, ed. Hartel; St. Cyril of Jerusalem, *Catechesis*, III, *De baptismo*, n. 5, in PG 33, 433; Aphraates, *Dem.*, 22, *De morte et novissimis temporibus*, 12, in Graffin, *Patrologia Syriaca* (Paris, 1894), pp. 1014-1015.; St. Basil, *Homilia I in Hexaemeron*, n. 5, in PG 29, 13; St. Bede, *Hexaemeron*, 1.I, c.I, in PL 91, 14; Bandini, *Sententiarum*, 1.II, dist. II, in PL 192, 1031; Bandinelli, in Gietl, *Die Sentenzen Rolands* (Freiburg im Breisgau, 1891), pp. 88, 104; Alexandre de Halès, *Universae theologiae summa*, part. II, q. 19, m. III, a.2, Cologne, 1622, p. 63; St. Bonaventure, *In IV Sententiarum*, 1.II, dist. II, part. II, a.1, q.1, *Opera* (Quaracchi, 1889), vol. 2, p. 71; St. Albert the Great cites St. Augustine, St. Beda and Walafrid Strabon, *Summa theologiae*, part. I, tr. 18, q. 73I, m.II, a.1, ad 3 (Paris, 1894), p. 727; *Compendium theol. verit.*, 1.II, c.IV, *in ibid.*, vol. 34, p. 43; St. Thomas Aquinas, *Summa theologiae*, I^a., q. 41, a.4; Richard of Middletown, *Super IV Sententiarum*, 1.II dist. II, a.3, q.I (Brescia, 1591), vol. 2, p. 43; Duns Scotus, *In IV Sententiarum.*, 1.II, dist. 14, q.I (Antwerp, 1620), vol. 2, p. 191; Durand de Saint-Pourçain, *In IV Sententiarum*, 1.II, q.1, n. 3 (Lyon, 1569), p. 112; Biel, *In IV Sententiarum.*, 1.II, dist. 14 (Brescia, 1574), p. 91; Suarez, *De opere sex dierum*, 1.I, c.IV (Paris, 1856), pp. 21-27, *apud* P. Bernard, entry "Ciel," in DTC, cols. 2484, 2487, 2489, 2491, 2504-2505.

"In the physical cosmic system of our experience we have no reason to envy celestial individuals. But today, as physics teaches us more than ever to think in terms of visualization, we find it less difficult than before to take the existence of heaven seriously – in a non-visual way. When the history of the cosmos and the world of spirits will reach its full consummation, everything will be transformed. Then, the new world that will come can be called either the new heaven or the new earth."[21]

§ 21   In this context, Rahner goes on to state that to imagine souls in Heaven enjoying a happiness only of the spirit until the resurrection of the dead is to "betray man's reality." The offense against the honor due Catholic dogma becomes clear in the text:

"**Whoever discards the earthly world, banishing the 'finished' man from this earth in a spiritualist way ... to transfer him to a blessed state of (supposed) pure spirit, restricts and betrays the true reality of man, son of this earth.**"[22]

§ 22   Following this same line of thinking is the Dominican Christian Duquoc, professor of Dogmatics at Lyon's Faculty of Theology. His Christology influenced certain "liberation theologians." He claims that the reason the Church considers Heaven separate from the Earth is because of her failure to manage the world. In addition to denying faith in the dogma of Heaven, this is a lack of respect for the Church and her doctrine. Duquoc states:

"The promise of Jesus cannot be deprived of all its earthly resonance. Jewish Messianism at the time of the New Testament ... was based on a temporal interpretation of the promise. ... Israel's finest teachers imagined that the peace of God to be proclaimed by the Messiah would benefit all men. The election of the people of Israel would serve to prepare a future in which all nations would benefit. Christians did not abandon this belief.

"Far from eradicating it, the paschal happening reinforced it. ... Millenarianism is a good testimony to the intensity of the first Christian hope. ... In my opinion, **it was political reasons that destroyed all the credibility of a paradise established on earth**, of an era that would escape the time of need and misery, when everything would finally be permitted in innocence and in fraternity. ...

---

[21] K. Rahner, "La resurreción de la carne," in *Escritos de Teología* (Madrid: Taurus, 1963), vol. 2, p. 222.

[22] *Ibid.*

"The separation between 'paradise' and earth ... is a consequence of the failure of the Christian Empire and Christendom, which did not know how to manage our world. Thanks to the failure of this management, which did not know how to establish the dreamed-of fraternity and abundance in liberty, heaven was banished** and only a moral type of relationship with the earth was conferred to it. **It became the object of an individual reward** and was no longer anticipated in time.

"The radical separation between history and *escathon* (heaven) and the opposite way people now think of the beyond theoretically express the incapacity of the Church to practically accomplish what she preaches** and to incarnate what she promises to be: the anticipation of the Kingdom."[23]

§ 23

Later, Duquoc, drawing closer to the language of Marx and his followers, makes this statement:

"'Heaven' is something that accuses time, renders futile any attempt to overcome it, and favors resignation and exploitation."[24]

§ 24

For his part, the Benedictine Aelred Cody, professor at Rome's Pontifical Biblical Institute, also insults Religion by writing that the notion of Heaven is a fruit of the influence of Stoicism. There is nothing new in Cody's thinking, however; he merely draws consequences from the concepts put forward by the conciliar theologians mentioned above. He writes:

"In Christianity the concept of Heaven as a 'place' of enjoyment of eschatological goods became widespread. ... However, in texts like these [in the New Testament] ... Heaven is not a material, spatial Heaven situated above the earth and forming a part of the created universe. It is, instead, the antithesis of a created and visible heaven and earth, and the symbolic expression of a transcendent form of existence characterized by divine glory.

"The setting of this exaggerated concept of Heaven was sought in various ambits of Antiquity. Obviously, it included a certain dosage of dualism ... a kind of Platonic dualism characteristic of the Hellenist world. ... It seems that

---

[23] Christian Duquoc, "Um paraíso na terra?" *Concilium* 1979/3, (Petrópolis: Vozes), pp. 89-92.

[24] *Ibid.*, p. 94.

the originally stoic ideal of the bodily liberation influenced cultured Jews as well as early Christian thinkers."[25]

§ 25   Prof. Robert Favre, a layman, aligns himself with progressivist theologians by describing hope for Heaven as a profound "narcissism." In an article published in *Concilium*, the professor at the University of Lyons says:

"The pleasure of feeling oneself to be immortal, **the contentment of the just man who awaits his reward and believes he merits it, the hope of a soul immersed in suffering and longing for the eternal encounter, the plea of a creature overwhelmed by his imperfection and finiteness: All these feelings reveal** - however worthy the expression that can clothe them may be - **the profoundly narcissist nature of the 'old man' who still has not converted."**[26]

Favre adds: "**One must consider suspicious everything that transforms Heaven into a refuge, everything that enhances it either as a compensation or a trade-off for our earthly abode.** The criticisms of Voltaire, Diderot and Holbach, even before those of Marx and Nietzsche, vigorously attack this exaltation of Heaven presented as our one and only 'homeland,' the adversary of this earth."[27]

§ 26   Fr. Jan Kerkhofs, S.J., professor emeritus of Pastoral Theology at the Catholic University of Louvain, explains how secularization has undermined faith in Heaven and Hell, which he offensively brands as "naïveté":

"There were times when theologians with fertile imagination made detailed descriptions of Heaven, conceived as 'a new heaven and a new earth,' reposing on a celestial dome that covered the flat disk of the earth. Above all this was the throne of God. Heaven was divided into a complex hierarchy of spheres inhabited by venerables, blesseds, saints and a whole gamut of angels, cherubim, powers, etc., culminating with Mary, the final gate to the supreme heaven of the Most Holy Trinity. To this Heaven – above – corresponded a Hell – below – with a hierarchy ... of zones of punishment that corresponded to the different degrees of human malice, and at the very bottom of all was the chief of the bad angels, Lucifer. ...

---

[25] Aelred Cody, "O Novo Testamento," *Concilium* 1979/3, pp. 39-40.

[26] Robert Favre, "Variações sobre o tema do céu no século das luzes," *Concilium* 1979/3, p. 60.

[27] *Ibid.*, p. 57.

"This classic notion of 'Heaven' (and 'Hell') became less pronounced toward the end of the 20th century. Although it is almost impossible to verify scientifically how much the faith of the people has changed on this matter ... **the naïveté of our forefathers' belief in Heaven has clearly disappeared, partly because of the process of secularization, whose spirit of doubt that infiltrates everything also infiltrated here,** and partly because the new symbols of the 'heavenly reality' have still not been accepted."[28]

§ 27   Kerkhofs believes that the symbols of the heavenly reality that he just mentioned should be found in the private and inter-personal experiences of individuals and groups:

"People seek experiences of eternity and happiness in their own lives or in their interpersonal relations. Some find the path in love or the more profound dimensions of fraternity ... or in different ways of satisfying the conscience or a new attention to experiences of the Spirit (in charismatic movements and many religious groups)."[29]

Finally, Stephen Happel, professor of Systematic Theology at St. Meinrad School of Theology (Indiana, U.S.) and later the dean of the School of Theology and Religious Studies at the Catholic University of America, although paying tribute to a hermetic language, professes a radical materialism by not admitting Church teaching on the soul. His text is rife with offenses against the honor of Catholic doctrine on Heaven, which he claims is nothing more than "pictorial" elements typical of a "classicist culture" interested in preserving a certain cosmology. Happel writes:

"If Christian representations of eschatology are to be given any weight in determining a material future, **one must 'de-spiritualize' human experience in time. A good part of the Christian discourse on Heaven,** notwithstanding the graphic details in popular preaching, **has tended to the notion of the personal immortality of the spiritual soul. ...**

"What was useful in a classicist culture as a way to **preserve the meaning of the spirit as conscience, to explain personal permanence and to maintain a certain cosmology, can no longer respond to the strong sense we have today of**

---

[28] Jan Kerkhops, "Diversas representações do céu," *Concilium* 1979/3, pp. 6-7.

[29] *Ibid.*, p. 14.

the physical character of subjectivity. **With the aim of preserving the meaning of the personal 'spirit,' one postpones the incarnate character**[30] **of this finite life to the 'end of time.'**...

"Much too rapidly did human temporality separate the spirit – as the 'true' being – from matter. But **if one wants to seriously consider the pictorial elements of Christian eschatology, then, it is essential to have an anthropology that treats human temporality as spatial.**[31] **Every human effort, from the smallest perception to the highest abstract conceptualization, is something material**. The human consciousness of time is 'incarnate.'... This temporality also cannot be separated from the physical world."[32]

Paying tribute to materialism, the texts of this Letter C deny the existence of Heaven and show an offensive irreverence toward the honor due the Church Triumphant.

D. Preaching on Hell is Called Egoistic, Bourgeois, Capitalist & Sadistic

After attacking the Last Four Things in general and Heaven in particular, progressivists continue their insults by denying Hell.

§ 28   The Reader will recall the strange defense of Judas' treason[33] and the enigmatic "Church of the Condemned" supposedly founded by Christ.[34] The thinking underlying those offenses virtually denies the existence of Hell, or at least supposes it to be empty after the death of Christ. For, as we have seen, the souls of the damned are supposedly those who identified more fully with Christ and followed Him more immediately to Heaven.

§ 29   We now take another step along the same route. The background thinking of the next group of offenses is that the

---

[30] 'Incarnate' in progressivist parlance here means "vested in concrete and present forms."

[31] "Spatial," to the author, means that which refers to contemporary time and space.

[32] Stephen Happel, "As estruturas de nossa convivência (mit sein) utópica," *Concilium* 1979/3, p. 100.

[33] Cf. Vol. II, *Animus Injuriandi I*, Chap. I, §§ 11-16.

[34] In this Volume III, Chap. III, §§ 1-27.

Church must deny the existence of Hell[35] and forbid preaching and teaching on it.

---

[35] Quite different from this progressivist notion is the doctrine of the Catholic Church about Hell as a place for the punishment of devils and reprobates.

a. The Church Magisterium

• The Athanasian Creed: "And those who have done good shall go into life everlasting, and those who have done evil into everlasting fire" (D 40).

• The Council of Arles (473), where the priest Lucidius submits to the sentence of the assembled Bishops: "Your correction is for the common good, and your sentence is a good medicine. Hence, I avail myself of this supreme remedy: In order to purify myself, I accuse myself of my past errors by means of a salutary confession. Thus, in accordance with the recent sentences proclaimed by the Council [of Arles], I condemn with you the opinion (DS 330) ... that says that fire and Hell do not exist (DS 338). ...

"I also declare that the eternal fire and flames were prepared for mortal sins, because those who persist to the end in their human malice merit that divine punishment, and it falls justly on those who do not believe these things with all their hearts" (DS 342).

• Pelagius I, in the letter *Humani generis* (557) to King Childebert: "I confess that ... by virtue of a most just judgment, [Jesus Christ] will deliver to the pains of the eternal and inextinguishable fire, so they may burn eternally, the evildoers who remain of their own will as 'vessels of wrath fitted for destruction' (Rom 9:22), and who either did not know the ways of the Lord or, having known them, fell away seduced by various prevarications," (DS 443)

• Innocent III, in the letter *Maiores Ecclesiae causas* (1201) to Archbishop Imbert of Arles: "The punishment for original sin is the loss of the beatific vision, but the punishment for actual sin is the torment of the eternal fire" (DS 780).

• IV Ecumenical Council of the Lateran: "We firmly believe ... that all men, both the reprobates and the predestined, shall rise with their own bodies which they now have, so that the reprobates may receive eternal punishment with the Devil and the predestined may receive everlasting glory with Jesus Christ, according to whether their works were good or evil" (D 429).

• Innocent IV, letter *Sub catholicae professione* to the Bishop of Tusculus (1254): "If someone, however, dies impenitent in mortal sin, he certainly will be tormented forever by the flames of the eternal Gehenna" (DS 839).

• Council of Florence, bull *Laetentur coeli* (1439): "We hereby declare ... that the souls of those who die in mortal sin ... go immediately to Hell" (D 693).

§ 30   Commenting on excerpts of Péguy and approving them,[36] von Balthasar insults Religion, calling it "egoistic and bourgeois" in its teaching on condemning souls to Hell:

"The Church is the people of humanity and is in complete solidarity with humanity in its totality. ... With this, the central problem of Péguy is exposed, which explains his whole life and work: the problem of the eternal perdition of a member of humanity; damnation, Hell. ... Joan[37] and Péguy do not understand how charity could be understood as different from solidarity. ... **A religion that resigned itself to watching so many of its brothers be eternally lost and that does not miss them eternally is fundamentally egoistic from the standpoint of**

---

b. Foundation in Sacred Scripture

The basis for the existence of Hell as a concrete place is found in the Sacred Scripture, which leave no shadow of doubt that *scheol* is a place (cf. Nm 16:31; Job 10:21-22; Ps 48:18; 54:16; 62:10, etc.). Now then, if *scheol* is a place, consequently so also is Gehenna, since it is situated at the bottom of *scheol* (Cf. Ez 32:30; Is 5:14; 14:15; 24:21-22, Ps 48:15).

In the New Testament it suffices to mention Mt 5:27-30; 10:28; 13:42, 49-50; 25:41, 46; Lk 8:31; 16:19-31; Ph 2:10; II Pet 4; Apoc 9:11; 19:20; 20:1-3, among other passages.

For the sake of brevity, we omit here texts that refer to the material fire of Hell.

c. Teaching of the Fathers & Doctors

Traditional teaching is unanimous on the punishment of the eternal fires of Hell. Suarez says that this is a truth of "the Catholic Faith" (*De angelis*, 1.VIII, c.16, n. 2, p. 1054). In the same sense see St. Augustine, *Retractationes* II, 24; St. John Chrysostom, *Homiliae*, 49-50, *Ad populum*; St. Cyril of Alexandria, *In Isaiam*, 1.I, c.5; St. Gregory the Great, *Dialogorum libri quatuor*, 1.IV, c. 43; St. Robert Bellarmine, *De Christo*, 1.IV, c. 8-9, *De purgatorio*, 1.II, c.6 (cf. M. Richard, entry "Enfer", in DTC, col. 101).

[36] Von Balthasar's endorsement of Péguy's thinking can be noted throughout his work *La Gloire et la Croix - Péguy*, especially on pages 277-279, where he says "**Charles Péguy can be considered the best representative of a theological aesthetics** because he establishes in the Catholic field exactly the same polemical turning point against the 'spirit of system' that Kierkegaard made against Hegelianism. ... For Péguy, in its depth, aesthetics is the same as ethics by virtue of God's incarnation in Christ."

[37] Von Balthasar reference to Péguy's work about St. Joan of Arc.

salvation and, for this reason, is already at heart bourgeois and capitalist."[38]

§ 31   Further on, the author transcribes a text of Péguy manifesting his solidarity with all reprobates, after admitting their condemnation would be a "perverse imagination":

"**'We are in solidarity with the eternal reprobates. We do not allow that men be treated inhumanely. ... This is the profound movement that inspires us... We do not acknowledge that there is even one exception. ... An eternity of living death is a perverse, inside-out invention.'**[39*]"[40]

§ 32   Von Balthasar upholds the progressivist opinion that Hell is only an interior psychological state:

"A new and uninterrupted charismatic interpretation runs through the centuries of the Church. It constitutes the New Testament reflection of the experience of divine abandonment and of what the Doctor of the Church St. John of the Cross experienced and described as the 'dark night.' That experience has often been considered, both before John and after him, as an experience of condemnation and Hell.

"Above all it **would be useful to recall that, for a whole Christian line of tradition, Hell was understood primarily as an interior state (and not as a 'place' or as 'exterior torment')**; and that, as a consequence, in 'Hell' a particular experience of time reigns, that of a *tempus informe*: a stopping in a time that flows. ... **In modern times 'Hell' has been considered more and more as a state of one enclosed in himself and not liberated by God, until he is transformed into an existential element of the present life.**"[41]

§ 33   In one of his works Hans Küng calls the Church's traditional preaching about Hell "sadistic fantasies." He goes so far as to imply that such teaching was influenced by "sex complexes." Küng writes:

"The problem of 'Hell' must not be quietly dismissed even if only because **the *fear of Hell* ... has done incalculable**

---

[38] H. U. von Balthasar, *La Gloire et la Croix - Péguy*, p. 283.

[39*] A. Péguy, pp. 192-193.

[40] H.U. von Balthasar, *La Gloire et la Croix - Péguy*, pp. 315-316.

[41] H.U. von Balthasar, *Mysterium Paschale*, p. 51.

harm through the centuries. **Whoever has read a sampling of the many sermons on Hell from the time of the Fathers onward, those, for instance, of John Chrysostom or of Augustine ... can understand how such barbarous and at times sadistic fantasies of the damned and all kinds of absurd torments in Hell were able to take shape in the minds of the Christian people and even in Christian art. ...**

"It cannot be silenced: What are involved here are sex and guilt complexes, sin and confession mechanisms as well as the Church's power over souls, which found no better way to secure them than by the fear of eternal condemnation."[42]

§ 34   Küng continues his offenses by adopting the thinking of certain Catholic authors. Because of its preaching on Hell, Catholicism was "perverted" into the "bloodiest and most murderous religion that ever existed." He states:

"What the Catholic theologians Thomas and Gertrud Sartory have written in their book *There Is No Fire Burning in Hell* – the most comprehensive modern presentation of the theological problem of hell – sounds harsh but merits consideration: ... **'Christianity is the bloodiest and most murderous religion that ever existed.** Christians today must live with this reality, this is the past that they have to 'surpass.' **And the real cause of this perversion of the Christian spirit is belief in Hell.'"**[43]

Thus, in this letter D that closes here, we have seen not only grave offenses against Religion but have already caught glimpses of blasphemy, such as that statement of von Balthasar, "We are in solidarity with the eternal reprobates."

*

---

[42] H. Küng, *Vida Eterna?,* pp. 219-220.

[43] *Ibid.,* pp. 220-221.

E. Purgatory as a Place Should Be Changed to Interior Purification

§ 35

As an illustration of the general thinking of progressivists, Küng attacks the dogma of Purgatory as a place[44] and imagines it instead as the encounter of man with God. He writes:

---

[44] Some texts of the Papal Magisterium about the existence of Purgatory that reflect the perennial thinking of the Church:

• Benedict XII, Instruction *Iam dudum* (1341) condemning the errors of the Armenians: "Likewise, the Armenians commonly maintain that in the other world there is no Purgatory of souls because, as they affirm, if a Christian confesses his sins, they are forgiven as well as the penalties pertaining to them. Accordingly, the Armenians do not pray for the dead to have their sins forgiven in the next life, but pray in general for all the dead, as they do for Mary Most Holy and for the Apostles" (DS 1010).

• Council of Florence, Bull *Laetentur coeli* (1439): "We define that those who died in the grace of God, before they have made satisfaction (for their sins) by the worthy fruits of penance ... their souls are purified after death with the punishments of Purgatory; and that the prayers of the living faithful are efficacious to release them from these punishments" (D 693).

• Leo X, Bull *Exsurge Domine* (1520), against Luther's errors, condemned the proposition: "One cannot prove through the Sacred Scripture that Purgatory is in the canon" (DS 1487).

• The Council of Trent, Decree *De Purgatorio* (1563): "Whereas the Catholic Church, instructed by the Holy Ghost, based on the Sacred Letters and on the ancient Tradition of the Fathers, has taught in the sacred Councils, and recently also in this Ecumenical Council, that there is a Purgatory, and that the souls there detained are helped by the prayers of the faithful" (DS 1820).

• Decree *De Justificatione*: "If anyone says that, after receiving the grace of justification, the guilt and the debt of eternal punishment of every repentant sinner are blotted out in such a way that there remains no debt of temporal punishment for him to pay in this world, or in the next in Purgatory, before the doors of the kingdom of Heaven can be opened to him; let him be anathema" (DS 1580).

• Pius IV, Bull *Iniunctum nobis* (1564): "I, (name), believe and profess with a firm faith each and every item which is contained in the Creed that the Holy Roman Church professes, to wit: (DS 1862) ... I firmly hold that there is a Purgatory, and that the souls therein detained are helped by the prayers of the faithful" (DS 1867).

• St. Pius X, Letter *Ex quo* (1910): "With the greatest imprudence doubt is raised as to whether the sacred dogmas on Purgatory and the Immaculate Conception were acknowledged by the holy men in the early centuries" (DS 3554).

"As we have seen, to die ... must be understood not in the Platonic or Aristotelian-Thomist sense, as a separation of body and soul, but as an act of consummation that mercifully judges, purifies, enlightens and saves. In this way, **through the work of God, man becomes wholly and entirely man, that is to say, he is 'saved'. Man's** *purgatory is God himself* in the wrath of His grace: **Purification is the encounter with God in the sense that it judges man and cleanses him,** and also liberates and enlightens him, saves and perfects him.

"Consequently, Catholic theologian Gisbert Greshake is correct when he says: 'From this standpoint we can understand what was pointed out earlier, that **God himself – the encounter with Him – is purgatory.** From this we can deduce that **it is not necessary for us to resort to a special place or still less to a special time or special event to understand purgatory. Still less do we need to concoct awkward ideas about the 'poor souls.'** Instead, we can understand what the Church teaches and has taught from the earliest times as the moment of the encounter with God in death. This is how many recent theologians see it, and **also how the Dutch Catechism and the Common [Ecumenical] Catechism interpret it.**

"**For that reason, we should avoid the expression** *purgatory* **as much as possible**, especially the German expression *Fegefeuer* [purifying fire], **and speak instead of purification and cleansing applied to the moment of the encounter with God. What should be particularly clear is that purgatory is not** – as popular piety so often presents it – **a 'demi-hell' that God has created to punish the person who is not entirely bad, but also not entirely good. Purgatory is not a demi-hell, but the moment of the encounter with God,** that is, the encounter of the unfinished man, still immature in his love, with the holy, infinite, loving God; an encounter that is profoundly humiliating, painful and therefore purifying.'[45*]"[46]

§ 36 In another book, Küng explains what he understands as Purgatory. It is difficult to avoid the impression that the author, in addition to denying the Faith, delves into Pantheism. He explains:

"***Purgatory, purification*: We should neither imagine it as a place or a time of purification, nor as an intermedi-**

[45*] Gisbert Greshake, *Stärker als der Tod, Zukunft, Tod, Auferstehung Himmel-Hölle, Fegefeuer,* (Mainz: Topos-Taschenbucher, 1976), p. 92.

[46] H. Küng, *Vida eterna*, pp. 234-235.

ate realm or interim phase after death. ... **For man dies as a whole with body and soul, as a psycho-somatic unity**. ... But this death does not mean a total annihilation ('total death' as *annihilatio* and, at best, a permanence in the 'memory' of God or of men). **The essential thing is that when he dies, man does not enter into nothingness, but into God, and so into that eternity of his divine 'now,' which makes irrelevant for the one who dies the temporal distance of this world between personal death and the Final Judgment.**"[47]

§ 37   Fr. Maldonado considers Catholic teaching on Purgatory semi-pagan and "almost mythical":

"In the clash of the two different mentalities, the pagan mentality of the people that tenaciously survived and resisted death, and the ecclesiastical mentality, **the clerics had no other solution but to make concessions and accords.** In fact, they had to give increasing importance to the liturgy of the dead. **They accepted this almost mythical way of understanding that intermediary time between death and judgment as a purgatory. Purgatory was like a province re-conquered by the pre-Christian conceptions of death.**"[48]

§ 38   In passing, let us note that offenses against Catholic teaching on the particular and final judgment also are not missing. For example, Cardinal Giacomo Biffi, Archbishop of Bologna, considers the notions of these two judgments as "childish" and "mechanical." He calls the distinction between them "rough and imperfect." A journalist reports an interview with Biffi:

"According to Biffi, '**the theological formulation of two judgments (the universal and the private) separated chronologically is in itself rough and imperfect in its conception.**' It was useful to protect those two truths of faith – the universal judgment and the immediate verdict after death. '**But these truths can also survive in a less childish and mechanical conception.** It suffices to recall that a temporal succession does not exist beyond [our] time. **When a man dies, he finds himself at the end of human history** as he is judged, in a judg-

---

[47] H. Küng, *Vida eterna?* pp. 230-233.

[48] Luis Maldonado, *Génesis del Catolicismo popular* (Madrid: Ed. Cristiandad, 1979), pp. 154-155.

ment that is simultaneously private and universal, as Revelation shows us."[49]

These texts on Purgatory and Judgment reveal the tip of the iceberg of the new conciliar doctrine. They also permit one to view new aspects of the *animus injuriandi* that characterize the spirit of the Council.

*

As we have seen throughout the various Items of Chapter V, many leading theologians of Progressivism who inspired Vatican II negate the dogmas and the Four Last Things and insult the honor due these truths of Faith.

*   *   *

---

[49] Giacom Biffi, "Por uma escatologia renovada," in *La Scuola Cattolica*, 1968, *apud* Gianni Valente, "Um teatro vazio," *30 Dias*, February 1994, pp. 57-58.

Chapter VI

AFFRONTS TO THE SACRAMENTS

§ 1   In principle to make a thorough study of the Sacraments it would be necessary to explain what the progressivists understand by grace. However, since this concept requires many other doctrinal considerations, we decided it would be more orderly to undertake such a study elsewhere in this Collection, when we will study the destruction of Dogmatics[1] as one of the fruits of the Council. In this Chapter we will present only those excerpts on the Sacraments that more directly insult the honor due the dogma and the truths of the Faith.

§ 2   Since progressivists imagine the Church as leaven for the unification of mankind – Church as sacrament of the world[2] – along the path toward an evolutionary transformation, some of them oppose the traditional notion of sacrament that principally seeks the personal sanctification of each Catholic. They have a special revulsion for the teaching that sacraments should be dispensed through fixed formulae and become supernatural realities at the moment that the sacramental formula is pronounced in accordance with an established ritual. Progressivists consider this to be a kind of "magical act."

     This insult, with its characteristically Protestant stench, is found in writings of conciliar and post-conciliar theologians.

*

     In this Chapter we have ordered the affronts from the universal to the specific, citing first the offenses against the Catholic Religion in its Sacraments in general, and then the insults against each Sacrament in particular.

§ 3   The first text, by Fr. Edward Schillebeeckx, stresses the natural aspect of the sacraments as a "symbolic" help for man so he can better support his life. This is what he calls the "anthropological aspect" of the sacraments, placing their tonic note more on the invocation of men rather than on the action of grace.

---

[1] Cf. Vol. X, *Peccatum, Redemptio*, Chaps. VIII, IX.

[2] Cf. Vol. XI, *Ecclesia*, Chap. I, §§ 179-186.

Already present in this text is the term "magic," which he applies with increasing emphasis to the traditional notion of sacrament according to the Church Magisterium. He also questions whether the sacraments must be seven in number. Schillebeeckx writes:

"The fact that the sacraments are seven is based on the very nature of the Church. Certainly anthropological factors play a part in fixing this number. Birth, adolescence, the daily need for nourishment, moral disorders, matrimony, illness and death, the awareness of the *tremendum*, or the majesty of God before whom one does not dare present himself without the intercession of an earthly mediator (a priest).

"For the religious nature of man all these are the fundamental elements of life through which man feels that something superior and important is happening to him. These are vital and fundamental problems that make man spontaneously feel that life and its most important moments are not in his control. **He instinctively seeks to surround such moments with sacred symbols that would invoke a higher Principle of life which will take pity on him and assure him a happy outcome to such crises**.

"In the past **these symbols may have been understood as a kind of magic** or in a religious way. But in those fundamental moments of life, mankind instinctively feels the misery of its condition and its need for redemption. ... Unquestionably here is a religious anthropological basis – nuanced in its multiple forms – for the ritual confession of man's sense of impotency and the ritual invocation of a higher Power of life. **This in part justifies the existence of seven sacraments, though it is absolutely not an *a priori* proof that there should be seven, neither more nor less**."[3]

§ 4   In the same work, Schillebeeckx refers to the obedience of those who follow the formulae and rites of the Sacraments as "magic." We call the Reader's attention to the theologian's suggestions that the sacramental rite is only a "symbol" rather than the efficient cause of grace. He states:

"From the whole of this exposition it becomes clear that **a sacramental physicism, with the scruples and anguish this generates, is not present in the sacraments, but rather a sym-**

---

[3] E. Schillebeeckx, *Cristo sacramento dell'incontro con Dio*, pp. 250-251.

bolic religious act of the Church. .... And precisely because this is an act of the Church, about which the faithful person lacks the competence to decide on his own, he must follow the ritual of the Church in all the prescribed details. **But any conception of extreme rigorism or magic, where an involuntarily mispronounced word supposedly annuls the value of the ritual, is completely contrary to this!**"[4]

§ 5   Further on the author emphasizes the "religious commitment" of the person who receives the sacrament as being an essential part of it, tendentiously omitting what the Church teaches about *ex opere operato*. According to this traditional teaching, for the sacraments to be validly administered and received, the intention is all that is needed, not faith, not holiness, not even the state of grace.[5] But, according to Schillebeeckx, when a person does not have this "commitment," the sacrament is nothing but an "untruthful sign." He affirms:

"The sense and purpose of every sacramental action is oriented precisely to bring about the encounter with Christ. **Since an encounter must involve both parties, the religious commitment of the recipient, or the 'one who encounters,' belongs to the essence of the complete sacrament**, as a personal encounter with the living God. **If, by the mediation of the sacrament, this personal life – the true inter-subjectivity characteristic of personal encounter with Christ and with God – does not take place, then the symbolic sacramental act is an untruthful sign**, at least for the one who receives it: For he contradicts by his interior disposition what he professed in the sacramental and through it."[6]

---

[4] *Ibid.*, pp. 182-183.

[5] According to Catholic doctrine, the ministration of the sacraments produces grace *ex opere operato* (by the fact of being administrated), that is, the sacrament is operated as long as the minister and the recipient have the intention to do what the Church does and observe the conditions and formulae established by her. For its validity, no account is taken of the degree of virtue of either the one who administers it or the one who receives it. However, if the person ministers it or receives it in a holy way, he adds moral merit to it, without changing the essence of the sacrament. These accessory good dispositions are part of the *ex opere operantis* (by the way it is administered and received). Cf. A. Goupil, *Les sacraments*, vol 1, pp. 26-28; see also in our Collection Vol. X, *Peccatum, Redemptio*, Chap. IX.

[6] E. Schillebeeckx, *Cristo sacramento dell'incontro*, pp. 187-188.

§ 6   In developing his thesis about the sacramentality of the Church based on the nuptial love (the so-called "agape") that the Christ-Sacrament[77] has for her, Schillebeeckx continues with his affronts, calling the traditional concept of the sacraments "physicist" and "magic" and insisting they are not supernatural realities, but mere symbols. He adds that they are valid only as an ensemble, but not each sacrament in particular:

"We have thus entered progressively into the essence of the Church's sacrament. But **only the ensemble constitutes a definition of the sacrament – *signum efficax gratiae*, the efficient sign of grace – that provides to this sacrament only a pale, albeit not inaccurate, sketch. We are far away from physicism and magic. We have only one and the same objective manifestation, expressed by veiled symbolic sacramental acts**: It is the mystery of the sanctifying cult of Christ in his Church and, through her, the expression of the *agape*, or benevolent love of God in Christ Jesus, and of the nuptial love of His Church, of the believer who frees himself from his own *ego* and moves toward a reality that transcends himself."[8]

§ 7   In another book, Schillebeeckx considers *ex opere operato*, the doctrine whereby the Sacraments work their beneficial action as they are administered, as a "thing-ification":

"**The personal vocation, the direct appeal of the living God, which is human existence, is very frequently compromised by a thing-ification of religious life. It is specifically in the doctrine on the sacraments that this state of mind led to considering the sacramental life almost exclusively as a cause and effect process.** Hence one concluded that in the sacraments we receive grace above all *passively.* In the synthesis that follows, we present the Church's sacrament from the standpoint of *inter-subjectivity* or the *existential person-to-person encounter.*"[9]

§ 8   Interpreting the sacramentality of the Church, Cardinal Yves Congar also warns against the "ritualistic danger" of exaggerating the role of the sacraments. Congar states:

---

[7] The Christ Sacrament is another progressivist expression similar to the Cosmic Christ mentioned in Chap. V, Note 9 of this Volume.

[8] *Ibid.*, pp. 314-315.

[9] E. Schillebeeckx, "Les sacraments, organes de la rencontre de Dieu," in V.A., *Catholiques et Protestantes* (Paris: Seuil, 1963), p. 231.

"According to Tradition, such is the meaning of sacramentality in the Church. **Certainly a danger existed – and exists – of sacralizing [the sacraments] in a ritualistic way and, in the final analysis, an almost magical way. This would be a deformation and, therefore, a betrayal of God's gifts.**"[10]

*

The progressivist charges against the sacraments in general have also been made against each sacrament in particular. Next we will point out documents pertaining to specific sacraments that both confirm what we explained on the progressivist concept of the sacraments and insult the Catholic Faith.

§ 9   Referring to the Eucharist, von Balthasar writes about a strange nuptial conception of the Church and, by extension, of the sacraments. The theologian considers the relations between Christ and the Church as analogous to the sexual relations between a man who seduces and a woman of frivolous life.[11] Here he returns to his erotic analogies that imagine the Church as a woman made pregnant by the semen of Christ, which would be the Eucharist.

§ 10   In the two excerpts below, one should note that von Balthasar envisions the "eucharistic seed" as human semen in the biological process of reproduction. Let the Reader judge for himself the author's shameless insult he makes to the Catholic Faith:

"**The mystery of the Eucharist** likewise **is** based on the primacy of Christ's virginal renunciation **in order to descend once again to the plane of carnal fecundity and there, by His donated flesh and blood, to make the fruits multiply a hundredfold**, in incalculable proportions. **One should not fear to say that this limited extension of the natural function of man's fecundity becomes universal in the eucharistic Lord, in the ensemble of His corporality. The flesh offered in the sacrifice on the cross is the seed of new life through all the ages of the feminine-Church and, through her, of the historic cosmos.** In this Teilhard de Chardin is right.

"And since **the spouse who always receives anew this eucharistic seed** is also always the visible Church who, in her visible members – in fact or at least in spirit – is virginal, **something of that generating force of the new Adam in the new**

---

[10] Y. Congar, *Un peuple messianique*, p. 53.

[11] Cf. Vol. II, *Animus Injuriandi I*, Chap. IV, §§ 26-30.

Eve also passes through the history of the Church and the world."[12]

Von Balthasar again compares the Eucharist to the semen that brings life – the Holy Spirit – to the Church:

"The Church is born from 'semen,' which is the body and blood of Christ, who delivered himself to death to give life to the world. But the 'life' that makes Him living [in the Church] is His 'Spirit,' which must be, as He showed himself, a divine-human Spirit: **the Spirit that above the cross is expelled along with the water and the blood** and was consigned to the Father is inseparable from the Holy Spirit which the Resurrected Christ communicates to His Church. After the Ascension the same Spirit ... is sent to the Church as united to the Father and the Son in the Trinity."[13]

§ 11   In another work von Balthasar continues to use the metaphor of sexual relations between man and woman to explain the Holy Eucharist, thus corroborating his previous offense. In the text below, the affront is presented in a more veiled manner; the meaning becomes evident only in the final phase:

"Because here also [in the Church], here above all, is where **Christ would like to have a human relationship with men. It was here that He invented the miracle of His Eucharist: He is in you and you are in Him. An eternal nuptials**

---

[12] H. U. von Balthasar, *De l'Intégration*, p. 312.

• It may seem contradictory to the Reader that the text compares a virgin to a spouse who engages in sexual relations with her husband – in this case, the Church with Christ. Such bewilderment is understandable, for in fact the two concepts exclude one another. However, in progressivist thinking, the idea of virginity, as well as chastity, does not exclude sexual relations. Rather, virginity reflects a supposedly more advanced evolutionary phase of carnal love where man and woman would be harmonized in a "spiritual love." According to this interpretation, chastity or virginity would also be able to relate to the Cosmic Christ in terms of a "carnal" relationship. The final "love relation" of humanity and its integration into the Cosmic Christ would have the sexual relationships as its primary model, whether inside or outside wedlock, as long as the act is inspired by 'love' (cf. Teilhard de Chardin, "L'Evolution de la Chasteté," in *Les Directions de l'Avenir*, Paris: Seuil, 1973, pp. 82-87).

[13] H.U. von Balthasar, "Chi è la Chiesa?," In *Sponsa Verbi*, Brescia: Morcelliana, 1969, p. 185.

between you and Him, compared with which the union of man and wife is but a poor and brief rough draft. Under this veil of bread and wine He desires to dwell among us in a living way to partake in man's joys and sorrows. ...

"**And once a year, or perhaps even twelve times, we condescend to please Him, We permit Him to realize the work of His love in us [!]. We 'practice'**[14] **(laurels to the inventor of this word!). Or, rather, we allow Him to practice on us.**" [15]

These are some excerpts that show the Reader a new conception of the Eucharist, gravely offensive, that has been promoted by von Balthasar, a theologian considered to be the main mentor of John Paul II and Benedict XVI and who today is lauded even in conservative circles of the Church.

*

§ 12   Regarding the sacrament of Holy Orders, we cite only one text of the conciliar *perito* Msgr. Ferdinand Klostermann. He was honored with the title of Chaplain of the Pope and named advisor to the Commission for the Apostolate of the Laity. Klostermann draws the final consequences of the communitarian character of the sacraments, raising the possibility that a Bishop could be consecrated even by a community of the faithful. He also casts doubts on the indelible character of the ordination of priests and the Sacrament of Holy Orders itself, seeing in it something "pagan, mythical and magical."

---

[14] For von Balthasar, "to practice" is synonymous with engaging in love relations whose matrix is the sexual act. Therefore, for him, in the Holy Eucharist there is a sexual-mystical relationship between Christ and the faithful. Hence his euphoria about the verb "to practice," which can be understood clearly by those who know the whole of his thinking. But he avoids saying this directly in order not to scandalize the ingenuous.

It is astonishing and repugnant that Fr. von Balthasar imagines himself in the position of "spouse" in relation to this cosmic entity, which supposedly "practices" in him, that is, realizes in him his psychosexual pleasure...

More texts on this erotic conception of Eucharist can be found in Vol. VI, *Inveniet Fidem?*, Chap. V.6.D.E.

[15] H. U. von Balthasar, *Le Coeur du Monde* (Paris: Desclée de Brouwer), 1956, pp. 136-137.

In our opinion this text demonstrates his desire to offend and his intention to deny the nature of this sacrament. Klostermann states:

"According to New Testament writings, the members of the college of twelve were expressly ordained for life by the Lord himself. ... According to the pastoral letters to Timothy, by the imposition of hands a charisma was conferred on them ... for the service of the community. ... From the text alone, however, it is not clear whether this charisma was given for the whole life or only for the duration of the service, for the actual exercise of that function.

"This question stands out particularly because of the doctrine on the sacramental character of ordination, the so-called *character indelebilis*. ... **It seems worthwhile to consider whether or not the essence of this 'character' has at times been interpreted in an overly fixist and static way, thus contributing to make the ordained person, especially in the eyes of the people, a consecrated person in the pagan sense, a mythical and magical minister. For this reason, we should ask whether this interpretation can and should be replaced with another that is more dynamic and existential. ...**

"From this dynamic perspective, the reflections of Hans Küng ... referring to the possibility of opening other ways in pastoral service and for the apostolic succession of pastors seem much more possible. ...

"One question remains to be asked: Can any ordination for the directive service be considered sacramental – even without the imposition of hands, as Karl Rahner proposes – with regard to the choice and acceptance of the primatial power of the Pope? Could the Church change the sign, the imposition of hands and other sacramental signs? **Could a group of priests, or even a community, consecrate a Bishop in cases of extreme necessity where they had no possibility of communication with the outside?**"[16]

Here the Reader has a brief sketch of where the Sacrament of Orders is heading in the Conciliar Church: to be transformed into a sacrament conferred by the community. The traditional concept of this Sacrament, as conferred by the Bishop

---

[16] Ferdinand Klostermann, "Principi per una riforma di struttura della Chiesa," in V.A., *La fine della Chiesa come società perfetta* (Verona: Mondadori, 1968), pp. 272-273.

under the mandate of the Pope, is considered to be something pagan, mythical and magical.

§ 13   The progressivists also apply this new communitarian concept of sacrament to Baptism. Borrowing from the Protestants, they pretend that to be baptized the person must consciously manifest his faith and only then does he enter the Church. This is what we find in the text below by Hans Küng, which also makes serious offenses against the sacrament of Baptism:

"**Baptism** is not a mute sign, but a meaningful word; it **is not a magical-sacral action, but a proclaiming action that requires faith.** ...

"**Of itself, Baptism is useless**. Baptism supposes *metanoia* [from the Greek: change, transformation], Baptism supposes faith. It is true that faith by itself does not provide a foundation for Baptism: Baptism is more than a simple confession of faith. ... On the other hand, **Baptism is not the simple foundation of faith: faith is not merely the natural result or automatic fruit of Baptism. ...** *Faith*, **inasmuch as it is an act of total commitment of a person and a fully confident reception of grace, is a** *condition* **of Baptism.**"[17]

§ 14   Fr. Huizing, professor of Canon Law at the University of Nijmegen, adheres to the same presuppositions of Fr. Küng. In the text below, he considers the traditional Catholic rite of Baptism as following an "egotistic and sterile notion" of Sacraments:

"In the present day historical situation of the Church in the world – after **a long tradition that presented an egotistic and sterile notion of the sacraments understood as an automatic and formal redemption instead of a commitment to the mission of Christians in the world – the practice of the Baptism of children, although legitimate, must be seriously reconsidered. At least, we should not impose on parents the obligation of baptizing their children.**"[18]

From this the Reader sees that a Protestant notion of Baptism was assumed by several of the Catholic theologians who played important roles either at the Council or after it.

*

---

[17] H. Küng, *A Igreja*, vol. 1, pp. 298-299.

[18] Peter Huizing, "Vatican III: Una costituzione sulla Chiesa," in V.A., *Verso la Chiesa del terzo millenio* (Brescia: Queriniana, 1973), p. 169.

§ 15   Regarding the Sacrament of Penance, Schillebeeckx categorically requires the penitent to make an exterior act of "insertion in the Church" in order to obtain the grace of forgiveness of sins. Without this public manifestation, the sacrament would be nothing more than a "magical automatic device." He writes:

> **"If a confession ... is not also at the same time a personal prayer that integrates the penitent into the sacramental visibility of the Church and so brings him into contact with Christ's heavenly act of salvation ... this confession cannot give the grace of forgiveness. Hence it is quite evident that the sacrament is not a sort of magical automatic device."**[19]

§ 16   In a co-authored work under the responsibility of Cardinal Joseph Tomko, Fr. Alfredo Marranzini, S.J., professor of dogmatic theology at the Pontifical Faculty of Southern Italy, and frequent collaborator to *L'Osservatore Romano*, says something similar, although with certain cautions proper to the "official line" of the Vatican. He also discourages frequent confessions because it become "a habit and loses its value":

> "The confessional dialogue certainly was a privileged method for one school of sanctification and the fight against sin. However, **the fact that so much attention was concentrated on telling one's sins, and less on conversion with all its personal and communitarian demands, has perhaps contributed to the present state of crisis. Frequent confession of venial sins,** if not lived in all its dimensions, **becomes a habit and loses its value. Therefore, the falsely spread thinking that it is 'enough' to confess grave sins because absolution 'does it all' in an almost mechanical sense is harmful. Confession,** which for some was no longer an expression of an authentic way of conversion, **deteriorated into an almost magical ritual devoid of all meaning as well as human content."**[20]

§ 17   Bishop Noël Kokora-Tekry of Gagnoa on the Ivory Coast considers the traditional notion of the sacrament of penance "distressing." To change this situation, he suggests giving a festive air to Confession. These are the words of the African Prelate during a Vatican Synod of Bishops:

---

[19] E. Schillebeeckx, *Cristo, Sacramento dell'incontro con Dio* (Rome: Paoline, 1970), pp. 193-194.

[20] Alfredo Marranzini, "Identità, sviluppo dogmatico e variazioni sul sacramento della riconciliazione," in J. Tomko, *Peccato e riconciliazione*, p. 145.

"Today's rituals for the celebration of the Sacrament of Penance make it a sacrament-chastisement that one receives to avoid Hell. **In face of this behavior of servile fear, it is urgent to promote a new catechesis stressing above all the merciful love of God,** the richness's of his gift of forgiveness **and the meaning of communitarian feast, of reconciliation with Christ. For this we desire more concrete and relevant forms for the celebration of Reconciliation that make it a feast, a feast for the whole community.** ...

"This would serve to liberate this sacrament from its distressing aspect and give it a festive sense, the joyful return of the prodigal son – as every sinner is – to his family **with music playing in an atmosphere of a common feast."**[21]

One can see, therefore, that the Sacrament of Penance is not excluded from the complete reversal Progressivism is making in Catholic doctrine. Like the other Sacraments, its traditional rite is considered "magical" and "automatic." Clearly we are facing a new theology that entails countless offenses against the Sacraments.

*

These are some insults to the honor due the Sacraments found in works by important progressivist authors. They are undoubtedly adequate to express the *animus injuriandi* of Progressivism and the spirit of the Council.

*   *   *

---

[21] Noël Kokora-Tekry, "La riconziliazione è una festa," *L'Osservatore Romano*, October 6, 1983, Supplement Synod, p. IV.

Chapter VII

OFFENSES AGAINST CATHOLIC MORALS

§ 1   Regarding Morals, Progressivism opposes the perennial teaching of the Church as well. Their leaders advocate that the concepts of natural and supernatural be reformulated[1] based on the evolutionary concept of the world[2] and the immanence of what they call the Cosmic Christ in all created beings. According to this thinking, the presence of a divine energy – "grace"[3] – supposedly reveals to every man's conscience the best moral position he should take.

§ 2   This premise gave rise in *aggiornati* Catholic circles to what is called Situation Ethics, which replaced objective, abstract and universal moral norms with predominantly subjective, "existential" and concrete norms. The latter are conditioned by the thinking of each individual or the thinking of the "community" in a given historic situation. Moral relativism was thus installed in a sector of the Church.

§ 3   Pius XII condemned Situation Ethics in its most radical expression, and especially its absurd consequence of abolishing objective moral norms.[4] Even though his condemnation

---

[1] Cf. Vol. X, *Peccatum, Redemptio*, Chaps. VIII.2.A.

[2] See Chap. V, §§ 7-14 of this Volume.

[3] Cf. Vol. X, *Peccatum, Redemptio,* Chap. VIII.

[4] Pius XII spoke against Situation Ethics in his Radiomessage of March 23, 1952 and Allocutions of April 18 and November 13, 1952. The Pontiff's censure is summarized in the Instruction published on February 2, 1956 by the Supreme Congregation of the Holy Office. It reads:

"Against the moral doctrine and its application transmitted by the Church, there began to spread in many regions, even among Catholics, the ethical system generally presented under the name 'Situation Ethics,' which they say does not depend on the principles of objective ethics ... but follows its same lines and is subordinated to it.

"The authors who defend this system affirm that the decisive and final rule of action does not belong to an objective order determined by natural law, which makes one know that rule of action with certainty. Rather, it is a certain inner judgment and interior personal light within

was strong and timely, it left one small linguistic loophole, through which the progressivists, albeit with difficulty, managed to smuggle in their ideas.[5] With their characteristic shrewd-

---

each individual that makes him know what he should do at the moment he faces a concrete situation. Thus, according to them, this final decision of man is not, as objective ethics teaches ... the application of the objective law to a particular case, taking into consideration the particular circumstances of the situation and weighing them in accordance with prudence. ...

"According to these authors, the traditional concept of 'human nature' does not suffice; one must have recourse to an 'existential' concept of human nature that, regarding many things, does not have objective absolute value, but only a relative value and, therefore, can change. ... The traditional concept of 'natural law' only has this relative value. For, according to their opinion and doctrine, many things presented as absolute postulates of natural law are based on existential concepts and, consequently, are relative and mutable and can always be adapted to any situation.

"They say and teach that once men admit and apply these principles, they would supposedly be preserved or liberated from many otherwise insoluble ethical conflicts. They could do this by judging what to do in each particular situation by following their personal interior light that comes from intuition, each one according to his conscience and not primarily by following objective laws.

"Many points of this system of 'Situation Ethics' are contrary to the truth and the judgment of sound norms of reason, They reveal symptoms of Relativism and Modernism and seriously conflict with the Catholic Doctrine taught throughout the centuries. Further, many of its propositions are similar to various systems of non-Catholic ethics.

"Taking these things into consideration, in order to avert the danger of the 'New Morals' of which the Supreme Pontiff Pius XII spoke in the Allocutions of March 23 and April 18, 1952, and in order to protect the purity and soundness of Catholic Doctrine, this Supreme and Sacred Congregation of the Holy Office hereby forbids this teaching on 'Situation Ethics,' under any name it may assume, to be introduced and approved in universities, seminaries and houses of formation for religious [men and women] and its dissemination or defense in books, dissertations, meetings, lectures ... or any other means" (AAS, 48, 1956, pp. 144-145).

[5] Referring to condemnations like this, which are excellent but not totally impermeable to subtle adverse infiltrations, Fr. Chenu noted that such texts always leave the door open for the progressivists to maneuver: "Evidently, in all these texts [including the Encyclical *Humani generis*] there was, as always, a proviso, a footnote, a small paragraph leaving an opening that allowed the work to go ahead. Fr. de Lubac

ness, they carefully studied the condemnation and noticed that the main attack was aimed at doing away with objective moral norms. To circumvent this condemnation, they reformulated their theory, although keeping the same foundations and drawing the same consequences.

§ 4

According to this reformulation, they accepted "objective moral norms." However, when one analyzes what they describe as "objective moral norms," it is clear that they are just making a play of words. The "objective norm" they admit is, as they say, the "universal entity" of the human being.[6] In other words, it is the *pleroma*[7] where they imagine a pan-Christic inte-

---

took advantage of this loophole to write *Méditation sur l'Eglise*, a very beautiful book" (*Jacques Duquesne interroge le Pére Chenu*, p. 131).

[6] Such reformulation of the concept of "objective norm" gave rise to what Fr. Schillebeeckx calls "moderate situationism," defended among others by Rahner and Fuchs. Schillebeeckx explains:

"Multiple attempts have been made by some Catholics to integrate into Catholic morals the nucleus of truth that finds its expression in Situation Ethics, although there have been only few attempts at a synthesis (Steinbückel and Schuler; articles by J. Fuchs, K. Rahner and G. de Brie). This current characteristically affirms the existence of a 'universal human nature' upon which a 'generally valid natural law' is based. The 'universal entity' of the human being and the actual individuality of each person are in full agreement [with each other]. ...

"This *moderate situationism* aims both to guarantee the absolute validity of general norms and to defend the situational moments of our existence where no absolute norms can be applied. For this reason, God reveals his will in two ways: in general orientations through His laws (natural law and the revelation of salvation), whose interpretation is entrusted to the doctrinal authority of the Church. But since these orientations are not sufficient, God also shows His will through the interior work of grace; this grace is interiorly directed to the interpretation of the practical situation in life as an appeal to man" (E. Schilleebeckx, "L'Etica della situazione," in V.A., *I grandi temi del Concilio*, pp. 895-896).

[7] *Pleroma* (from the Greek = plenitude, fullness) is a term increasingly used by progressivists. Although it has a legitimate and orthodox meaning (cf. Col 1:15-20; 2:9), progressivists in general, and Teilhard de Chardin specifically, use it to refer to the spiritual reality supposedly formed by the absorption – in a para-human sphere – of the ensemble of energies that emanate from the global evolutionary process. These energies would include the souls of groups, individuals, or other forms of life less noble than the human.

gration of all men will take place.[8]

Therefore, the use of the expression "objective moral norm" does not imply a true return to Catholic Morals and the abandonment of Situation Ethics. It is only a semantic adaptation to escape Pius XII's condemnation and enable progressivists to continue disseminating the same ideas. Using this tactic, the same principles continue to be defended under different names: existential morals, anthropological morals, new morals, and so on.

§ 5   So, for the partisans of Progressivism the perennial concepts of good and evil have changed. Good is no longer what brings man closer to the likeness of God on this earth and leads him to eternal salvation through the practice of the Commandments. Instead, it is everything that causes all men – independent of individual merit or guilt – to unite in a de-individualizing and egalitarian way, seeking the realization of the final messianic *pleroma*.[9] In contrast, for them evil is all that represents a rejection of this universal integration. This refusal – individualization – is called "egoism."[10]

The final *pleroma* supposedly will be the stage where every individual will be absorbed in one universal spirit. This is, according to the Teilhardian conception, the phase that immediately precedes the divinization of humanity.

[8] Vol. X, *Peccatum, Redemptio*, Chaps VIII.2.E; IX.2.

[9] *Ibid.*

[10] This progressivist concept, which seeks to equate a legitimate self interest with a morally evil egoism, is false and fallacious. For it is a legitimate first principle that every being should turn to himself in an upright way: *omnis ens appetit suum esse*. If man did not do so, he would not have conditions to develop himself or to seek the Absolute that fulfills him. This elementary principle of Philosophy is ratified by Revelation in the words of the Divine Master summarizing the New Commandment: 'You shall love the Lord your God with your whole heart. ... **You shall love your neighbor as yourself**' (Mt 22:37-39). Therefore, the love of one's neighbor presupposes the righteous love of oneself, which in turn evidently presupposes a just individualization, in accordance with Boethius' celebrated definition of person: '*rationalis naturae individua substantia*' (*De duabus naturis*, III).

This doctrine is confirmed, for example, in the Bull *Auctorem fidei*, in which Pius VI, condemning the errors of the Jansenist Synod of Pistoia (1786), affirms: "Whereas the doctrine of Pistoia does not recognize, between the dominant cupidity [of fallen human nature] and victorious charity, the existence of intermediary sentiments that spring

From this stems a new visualization of individual morals and social morals.

§ 6   Regarding **individual morals**, many progressivists consider as good only that which is turned toward the realization of the other – that which "fulfills the human person." For them, the "fulfillment of the person" takes place only when the person no longer thinks in terms of 'I,' but solely in terms of 'you.' Thus, the moral action of an individual supposedly is good only when each person no longer seeks his own good.

Furthermore, they suppose that the bad inclinations caused by original sin are not present in the human passions, and that the unruly passions themselves become good to the degree they cease being "egoistic." Thus, even the body's sexual instinct, and the corresponding sensuality in the soul, are considered good when it is used for the "fulfillment" of the other.

As a consequence, in matrimonial morals the end of marriage no longer is to perpetuate the species and the education of the offspring, but rather "love": the fusion of the spouses in a sensual love where, by renouncing each one's individuality, the couple supposedly "fulfills" the initial donation of the "I" to the "you," thus integrating them into the universal Christic-evolutionary flux.[11]

§ 7   Regarding **social morals**, for similar reasons of integration, good supposedly is everything that favors collectivization;

---

from nature and are laudable as such; those which remained, along with the love of beatitude and an inclination to the good, as vestiges and remnants of God *remanserunt velut extrema lineamenta et reliquiae imaginis Dei* (St. Augustine, *De spiritu et littera*, c. 28). **Thus they pretend that, between the divine love that leads us to the kingdom of God and the illicit human love that is condemned, there were not a licit human love that should not be censured**. This doctrine is false and has already been condemned" (n. 24, *apud* A. Gaudel, "Péché Original," in DTC, vol. 12, col. 549).

To suppose that every act of turning toward oneself is morally evil, as progressivists imagine, entails the self-immolation of the individual personality, and lead us shortly to self-destructive Pantheism or to sado-masochism. This concept of "egoism" will be dealt with again in this Collection in Volume VII.

[11] On the progressivist concept of person, see Vol. VII, *Destructio Dei*, Chap. IV.3.C. John Paul II's personalist concept of Original Sin and Redemption can be found in Vol. VIII, *Fumus Satanae*, Chap. V.4 and Vol. X, *Peccatum – Redemptio*, Chap. III.3.A.

evil is all that maintains individualism. Hence, in political and socio-economic matters, we find the religiously motivated attack by progressivists against private property, which is the base of the natural social order, founded on two Commandments of God's Law (the 7th and the 10th) and on the teaching of the Papal Magisterium.[12] Notwithstanding, progressivists consider private property a "structure of sin."[13]

Therefore, one sees that progressivist morals, although using the same terminology as Catholic Morals – good, evil, egoism, sin, etc. – is in fact conceived in a manner totally contrary to the teaching of our Holy Religion.

We will now present some texts that both confirm this overview and are offensive to Catholic Morals.

1. Catholic Morals: Deformed, Hypocritical, Scrupulous & Indolent

§ 8

Speaking about Situation Ethics, Fr. Edward Schillebeeckx distinguishes three currents: the *first* originated from French Existentialism, primarily Sartre, Simone de Beauvoir and Jeanson, and is characterized by radicalism and atheism; the *second* follows German Protestantism, based on Geisebach, Brunner and Thielicke, and is characterized by belief in God and the denial of the Church's role in guiding the "conscience." Schillebeeckx also includes in this "theist" current the Existentialism of Karl Jaspers and Gabriel Marcel.

The *third current* is the Catholic one, in which Schillebeeckx includes those who "made multiple attempts to integrate the nucleus of truth that finds its expression in Situation Ethics into Catholic Morals,' such as Steinbückel and Schuler, and also Joseph Fuchs, Karl Rahner and G. de Brie.[14]

---

[12] Among other pontifical documents, see: Pius IX: Encyclical *Qui pluribus* of November 9, 1846; Leo XIII: Encyclical *Quod apostolici muneris* of December 28, 1878; Encyclical *Humanum genus* of April 20, 1884; Encyclical *Rerum novarum* of May 15, 1891; St. Pius X: Motu proprio *Fin dalla prima* of December 18, 1903; Pius XI: Encyclical *Quadragesimo anno* of May 15, 1931; Encyclical *Divini Redemptoris* of March 19, 1937; Pius XII: Speech to the 9th Conference of the International Union of Catholic Associations of May 7, 1949.

[13] On the attacks of John Paul II, official Church organs and Prelates against the "structures of sin" identified as the structures of the Western society, see Vol. V, *Animus Delendi II*, Part I, Chap. V, §§ 73-86.

[14] Cf. E. Schillebeeckx, "L'etica della situazione," in V.A., *I grandi temi del Concilio*, pp. 891-893.

§ 9   Schillebeeckx explains the position of Catholic moralists, like himself, who are partisans of a Situation Ethics that tries to avoid the condemnations of Pius XII by using the expression "objective norm." We emphasize in bold the insults to Catholic Morals:

"The Situation Ethics of believing men seeks to find precisely what is the will of God for each one of them, here and now. 'It is in man's conscience that God invites us to make a moral decision about what God is asking, which is found *objectively formulated* in the *situation*.'"[15*]

"The 'new' of Situation Ethics lies in the fact that it discerns the objective norm of conscience not in abstract norms that would apply equally for all men, but rather in *practical* norms. That is to say, the concrete situation in which an individual is engaged *personally* and *one time alone*, is for him the objective norm that should regulate his conduct, and this situation is the revelation of the will of God for him. **Therefore, the Situation Ethics of believers views the orientation of conduct by abstract norms as a deformation of the moral conscience, as being hypocritical, rigid, scrupulous and indolent and, finally, a reckless judgment of one's neighbor.**"[16]

§ 10   Fr. Karl Rahner gives an example of this alleged "deformation of the moral conscience":

"We may think ... that **compared to her reaction to the problems of society, the economy and international relations, the Church has shown in the 20th century an extraordinarily intense reaction against the danger of errors in relatively secondary problems (such as sexual morals).** The Catholic capitalist of South America, blinded by his misguided conscience, in practice must have felt less distressed and disturbed than the Catholic husband facing the problem of birth control."[17]

§ 11   Speculating on the Church of the future, Fr. Bernhard Häring, a well known German moralist, declares:

[15*] J. Fuchs, "Morale théologique et morale de situation," *Nouvelle Revue Théologique*, 1954, p. 1085.

[16] E. Schillebeeckx, "L'etica della situazione," p. 890.

[17] K. Rahner, "Differenza tra morale teoretica e reale," in V.A., *La salvezza nella Chiesa*, (Rome-Brescia: Herder-Morcelliana, 1968), p. 142.

"Based on statistics on abuses and the reaction to prohibitive norms, **Christian morals must stop being falsified and rendered fruitless.**"[18]

§ 12   Fr. Benjamin Forcano, professor of Moral Theology at Salamanca, the Claretian Theological Institute, the Institute of Saint Pius X and the Pontifical University, is unsparing in his criticism of traditional Catholic Morals, which is denigrates as "old" and "sterile":

"Let us now go on to other **causes that more directly affect moral theology** itself from the standpoint of how it is taught and the structuring of its content:

"a. A non-stimulating teaching: **The teaching of morals used to give the impression that it was old, abstract, without strength, conventional, foreign to the vocabulary and concerns of modern life**. It taught much moderation and self-control and set boundaries of what was allowed and forbidden, but it did not stimulate persons to grand and noble things. It was not a morals of conquest. ...

"d. A teaching separated from dogma: **This teaching was unable to achieve its true objective of transforming man's life into Christ by imitating His life. This was because it sought to impose a 'rule' of life, moral imperatives not based on the contents of Christian doctrine, that is, on dogma. On the other hand, the actual teaching of dogma was one separated from life and, therefore, sterile**. It was taken for granted that Christians knew this dogma and did not question it. In this way, the purpose of theology was reduced mainly to expounding controversial points with preciseness, refuting heresies and preserving orthodoxy. The departure point for the moralist was the doctrine on grace, which constitutes Christian life. That is to say, to live in the state of grace, one must avoid sin. So, logically the moralist focused his attention on sin.

"It was, then, more a matter of imposing a faith than proposing one. In parallel, it was to preserve the customs demanded by this faith. A faith that one possessed by the mere fact of having been baptized soon after birth. **The ideal was to conserve the faith and some customs: A static ideal, necessarily accompanied by preserving measures.**"[19]

---

[18] Bernhard Häring, "La speranza di Haering: ... e il Papa renuncerà al privilegio di nominare i vescovi," *Adista*, May 7-12, 1990, p. 9.

[19] B. Forcano, *Caminos nuevos de la moral* (Valencia: EDICEP, 1973), pp. 26-27.

§ 13   Further on, Forcano accuses traditional morals of being "childish, hypocritical and puritanical":

"a. Childishness: **A morals that tends excessively toward defining Christian duties easily becomes overprotective, underestimates the potential of the human person, his responsibilities and conscience, and helps to propagate conformist attitudes, thus strangling personal initiative, boldness and creativity. It shapes a passive and childish mentality.**

"b. **Façades, appearances, hypocrisy:** The emphasis is placed on achieving a purely exterior and material conformity with that what is prescribed by the law. **By striving primarily for this exterior fulfillment of the mandate, one can easily slide into pretense, dissimulation, impure interior intentions.** ...

"d. **Puritanism: This is the reaction of those who are scandalized by the recent changes, who oppose all renewal,** who believe that past times were better, **who remain faithful to their pious practices and customs as if this were fidelity to doctrine and moral principles.**

"**This reaction is often irrational,** the result of a simple maneuver of the instinct of self-preservation. **It comes from individuals who lack personality, with somewhat childish attitudes (passivity, excessive dependency, mechanical habits,** etc.).

"**This reaction can give way to haughty and despotic attitudes if this instinctive repudiation of everything new is joined by a scorn for others ... and an arrogant conviction of one's own integrity, purity and truth.**"[20]

§ 14   Fr. Antonio Hortelano, professor of Moral Theology at Rome's Alphonsian Academy and at the Pontifical Lateran University, served as an adviser for the elaboration of the new *Code of Canon Law*. Presenting an overall view of the present crisis in traditional moral theology, he endorses a series of criticisms made about both its methodology and its contents. Offenses against Catholic Morals are present throughout his comment:

"1. Critique of the methodology of traditional morals: Traditional morals was criticized first *for having lost contact with the sources of revelation.* Indeed, until very recently and even now, many persons thought that the contents of Christian morals differed little from that of non-Christian morals, including atheism. ... **The questions and solutions that we find in**

---

[20] *Ibid.*, pp. 32-33.

traditional morals are almost always drawn from a humanist philosophy accepted by most men of good will. ...

"Christ and Christianity adopted man and, with him, all of his authentically human values, but they are situated beyond man and transcend him. If this dimension of Christian morals has been often forgotten, it is because, from the methodological standpoint, **traditional morals gradually separated itself from the sources of revelation**. ...

"Secondly, **traditional morals is criticized from the methodological standpoint *for having become excessively juridical*. ... This 'concubinage' of morals with law, as B. Häring humorously puts it, caused much harm to morals.** ... The fact that most Catholic moralists were celibate priests removed from real life is what caused Christian morals to present this aspect of appearing detached from reality, for which it has often been criticized. **Until recently, indeed, morals spoke a language unintelligible to the man in the street, totally removed from his vital concerns**.

"2. Criticism of the content of traditional morals: First, traditional morals was criticized for being a morals founded more on *fear* than on love, not only clashing with the most recent pedagogical studies but even with the Gospel, which appears to give primacy to love in Christian behavior. **We have often transformed God into a policeman, a judge or an executioner** ...

"**Nietzsche was right when he said that traditional Christian morals turned men into beasts of burden** – the dromedary complex – instead of lions, fearless defenders of liberty. **A Christian often feels morals as a heavy, unbearable burden that he has to carry on his back without any illusion, solely out of fear of a God who, for the least oversight, could condemn us to eternal death in Hell. This fear created in many a profound feeling of anxiety that often degenerated into obsessive scruples-related neuroses.**

"Another criticism made about the contents of traditional morals is that it is *more negative than positive*. Instead of opening before man's fascinated eyes an inebriating task that can shake mankind's inertia to explore new frontiers, traditional morals often limited itself to presenting us a catalog of sins: Do not steal, do not kill, do not do this or that. With this, **traditional morals became a veritable moral pathology**.

"For instance, it is disheartening to leaf through the table of contents of manuals on sexual morals published some years ago: 'Sins according to nature, sins against nature, sins of thought, action and desire, sins committed alone, sins committed with a person of the opposite sex or of the same sex, sins with cadavers and possible sin with the Devil,' etc. Reading these lists, instead of feeling stimulated to love – and to love in a beautiful and fascinating way – our spirit becomes discouraged, and we can even reach the point of thinking that perhaps those who believe that love is ugly and filthy are right."[21]

§ 15   Fr. Eduardo López Azpitarte, S.J., professor if Moral Theology at the Faculty of Theology of Granada, Spain, makes strong criticisms of the Church's traditional morals and applauds the demise of a past he characterizes as a time of "cheap moralism":

> **"Today we have to laugh, and rightfully so, when we look at the many statements and attitudes found even in the [moral theology] manuals of the last years.** ... Such positions mirrored the ambience and cultural climate in which the Church found herself. ...

> "In practice oriented to the confessional, Christian morals was concerned above all with the clarity and exactness of its norms. It was concerned to know what was commanded by the authority of God or the Church in order to confront it with our own behavior. **A list of formulae like these, to which man subjects himself with childish docility, is as opposed as possible to a person's dignity and autonomy.** ...

> "**An autonomous and free morals**, as the Christian one has to be, **must not accept ethical imperatives simply because they were commanded. ... The epoch of a cheap moralism is over**, and it no longer suffices to say that this or that is bad or sinful, even if we hold up the holy will of God to support the obligatory nature of our statements. ... **If we apply what was said here to the field of sexuality, it supposes the disappearance of a series of taboos that still have not been eliminated entirely.**"[22]

These offenses against the honor due Catholic Morals are so many – traditional Morals supposedly is distorted, hypo-

---

[21] Antonio Hortelano, *Problemas Actuales de Moral* (Salamanca: Ediciones Sigueme, 1981), vol. 1, pp. 42-46.

[22] Eduardo López Azpitarte, *Sexualidad y matrimonio hoy - Reflexiones para una fundamentación ética* (Santander: Sal Terrae, 1980), pp. 10-11; 24-25.

critical, scrupulous, indolent, outdated, childish, etc – that we conclude only by stressing that the ensemble analyzed in this Item 1 reflects well one more aspect of the *animus injuriandi* characteristic of the spirit of the Council.

2. Traditional Church Morals on Sex: a Morbid Dualism

§ 16   The principles of the New Morals are focused on the "fulfillment" of man and no longer on the glory of God. Thus, they ignore the bad inclinations caused by original sin and take a generally lax attitude toward the sexual passions – which before the Church always considered the ones that were the most virulent and corrupted by original sin.[23] This approach had to generate, by the espansive force of the sexual instinct, a preeminence of the role of sex in the New Morals.

§ 17   An example of the exaggerated role attributed to sex, when existentialist principles are adopted, is found in the official document of the Canadian Conference of Catholic Bishops of April 6, 1984. Note the insult to Catholic Morals in the statement that "a false dualism has contaminated Christian tradition for a long time."[24] The Bishops affirm:

---

[23] St. Thomas Aquinas teaches that all of faculties of man were corrupted by original sin, but those related to procreation – the concupiscible, the reproductive and the sense of touch – were not only corrupted but also infected:

"St. Augustine says that the infection of original sin is most apparent in the movement of the members of the genital organs, which are not subject to reason. Now, these are the organs that, through the union of the two sexes, serve for reproduction, wherein there is the delight of touch, which is the major stimulus for concupiscence. Therefore, the infection of original sin is found mainly in these three faculties: the reproductive, the concupiscible and the sense of touch.

"We call infectious the corruption that by its nature can be transmitted from one person to another; hence leprosy, murrain and the like are called infectious. Now, the corruption of original sin is transmitted by the act of generation, as stated above. Therefore, the powers that concur in this act are chiefly infected. Now, when ordered toward generation, this [sexual] act is at the service of the reproductive faculty, and it includes delight of the touch, which is the most powerful object of concupiscible appetite. Consequently, while all the parts of the soul are corrupted by original sin, these three [the reproductive, the concupiscible and the sense of touch] are said to be especially so" (*Summa Theologiae*, I.II, q. 83, a. 4).

[24] Regarding the human body and especially its reproductive function, the consequences of original sin have always been the object of

"**Every human being is profoundly influenced by his sexuality**. However, the effect of this influence is largely determined by the way that each one of us responds to this precious gift. **The multiform reality of sexuality can be the decisive force for existential and enduring relationships.** At the same time, it can be the occasion for a shameful and degrading exploitation of other persons, especially women.

"Sometimes sexuality is considered a simple biological function like eating and drinking. Biology undoubtedly plays its role in it. Nevertheless, **sexuality is something very important: that is, it is a social reality that puts us in touch and eventually in communication with other persons. ...**

"**Sexuality includes the physical desire of the other person** even if it cannot be reduced solely to the instinct. However, **sexual pleasure, which in itself is the joy of living and a pleasurable welcoming of the gift of life,** can also bring evil and violence. ... **The pleasure can mean many things. It can signify the affirmation of the other person, man or woman, in his dignity,** but it can also suggest a denial of his personality. ...

"Finally, **against a false dualism that has contaminated Christian tradition for a long time, we cannot forget that 'we are our body'** (cf. 1 Cor 6:12-20). **Therefore, we would be committing a grave error if we thought we could use our body or that of others as a simple means without at the same time involving our own personality or that of others. ... Sexual activity in all its forms is something that belongs to our person and touches the deepest part of our personality. ...**

"**Sexual language expresses and determines the totality of our being.** In its ambivalent potentiality of openness or separation, **sexuality is at the center of human interaction and communion, without which we cannot exist either in childhood or as men and women.** True sexuality is an experience of creative growth. This experience is found above all in the procreation of a new life, which can become the privileged mo-

---

utmost vigilance in Catholic Morals. This approach gives primacy to the soul, which is less contaminated than the body. For progressivists, this is a "false dualism;" the body must be liberated from this primacy of the soul. The faculties of the body, especially sexuality, should be given preeminence over the faculties of the soul.

In a text quoted further on in this Chapter (see § 24), Fr. Antonio Hortelano identifies pathological dualism as "any distinction between good and evil, light and darkness ".

ment to transform diversity into communion and by this means humanize history."[25]

§ 18   It is difficult to imagine a conception of life that emphasizes sex more than this one advocated by the Canadian Bishops. This apologia does not presuppose the legitimacy of the sexual act practiced **only** within matrimony. This is evident from the purpose of the document, which is to provide orientation to resolve the problem of prostitution. Therefore, according to the Canadian Bishops, as long as there is a sincere desire to fulfill the dignity of the partner of the opposite sex, free love is legitimized. Anyone who carefully analyzes such a document is led to this perplexing conclusion.

§ 19   We find this progressivist thinking everywhere in the Conciliar Church. It is an underlying cause for the constant insults made against traditional Catholic Morals, described as archaic, dualistic, Manichaean, etc. At the same time, Sigmund Freud and other anti-Catholic psychoanalysts are promoted.

§ 20   Confirmation of this is found in an article by Gianfrancesco Zuanazzi, professor of the Institute of Studies on Marriage and the Family of the Pontifical Lateran University in a book directed by Cardinal Jozef Tomko, then Secretary of the World Synod of Bishops. Along with insults to Catholic Morals – called "an archaic pre-morals of taboos and prohibitions" – Zuanazzi believes we can learn something from Freud's teaching, comparing it to that of the great Catholic masters of the spiritual life. He affirms:

"These disciples [of Freud][26] coherently follow the road opened by their master and propose a morals founded on the laws of psychology and health. They condemn not only the moral constraints rooted in the punitive threat of a rigid and oppressive super-ego,[27] but also those that derive from divine law.

---

[25] Canadian Conference of Catholic Bishops, Document on pornography and prostitution of April 6, 1984, "Pornogafia e prostituzione oggi," *L'Osservatore Romano*, June 9, 1984, p. 7.

[26] Erikson, Lebovici, Hesnard and Berge.

[27] In an Appendix to the book by Prof. Plinio Corrêa de Oliveira titled *Guerreiros da Virgem - A réplica da autenticidade*, Edwaldo Marques, M.D., and Miguel Beccar Varela, M.D., members of the TFP Commission of Medical Studies, made this summary of Freud's thinking on the super-ego:

"Freud divides the psyche into three different 'zones' or 'instances'

There is only one sin: evil effectively made against man. Everything else, that is, 'interior culpability,' is the fruit of the 'moral myth of sin' and is part of the 'morbid world of guilt.'

"These theses have something to offer a [Catholic] moralist: They set him on guard against the ambiguities of an archaic pre-morals of taboos and prohibitions. ...

"We think **there is a valuable lesson in psychoanalysis that keeps us from smuggling in as virtue what is only the fruit of our sensibilities.** Are we so sure this is something totally new? **Perhaps we should reread – together with Freud – our great masters of the spiritual life?**[28]

§ 21   Fr. Edward Schillebeeckx affirms that traditional Catholic Morals is "dualist" and concludes that it must be rejected:

"**In its historical and concrete application, the fundamental and continuous orientation of Christian Morals was conditioned by the logical dualism of the 'genre' and the 'specific difference.'** The affirmation of 'the soul as the form of the body' was not really an efficient antidote against it. This logical dualism constitutes the historic and contingent context, in which the fundamental and constant moral orientation was concretely explained. As a consequence, it generated ethical

---

– the *id*, the *ego* and the *super-ego*, each with its specific functions and characteristics. ... The third zone or instance of the psyche is the *super-ego*, where the idealization or sublimation of all the instinctive impulses that were repressed through the life of the individual and the species takes place. Above all, the *super-ego* is constituted by the repressed Oedipus complex and transformed by identification with one's parents into moral rules, social ethics and religion (cf. "O Ego and o Id," in *Obras psicológicas completas de Sigismund Freud*, Rio: 1970-1977, vol. 19, pp. 49-51.).

"For this reason, Morals would be the fruit of a sexual instinct repressed in the subconscious. For Freud, there is no natural law that God impresses on the soul. He states: 'We may reject the existence of an original capacity, supposedly natural, to distinguish good from evil. What is evil is often not at all what is harmful or dangerous to the ego. On the contrary, it may be something that is desirable and enjoyable to the ego. Here, therefore, there is an extraneous influence at work, which decides what is to be called good or evil,' (*O mal-estar na civilização*, vol. 21, p. 147)" (E. Marques and M. Varella, Appendix, pp. 327-329).

[28] Gianfrancesco Zuanazzi, "Freud, la morale and la colpa," in J. Tomko (ed.), *Peccato e riconciliazione*, pp. 23-24.

imperatives that were mandatory throughout the time that this anthropological doctrine, for the conscience of men, remained valid as an undisputable fact not subject to criticism. Lacking this distinction, later Scholasticism pure and simply identified biological laws and the sexual act with the absolute moral law, which provided the base for evaluating matters of sexuality.

"**By distinguishing the animal-generic dimension and the rational dimension in man, the traditional theology of marriage definitively attributed procreation to man's animal 'nature' and conjugal love to the human person. Such dualism is unacceptable to the existential and phenomenological anthropology.**"[29]

§ 22 Next, Schillebeeckx labels the moral orientation of the Church Fathers as "stoic" and "pessimist":

"The affirmations of the Fathers are profoundly biblical. However, **the stoic and Greek perspective of man [that they adopt] gives them a pessimistic orientation. The first pessimistic note, in which one senses a certain aversion for sexuality – precisely as a pleasure – could be called stoic. Not from the perspective of a Hellenistic anthropological dualism, but from a salvific conception of man as sinner: sexuality itself, above all in its element of pleasure, is understood as a consequence of original sin.**

"**A second pessimistic note** (which appears later in Patristics) **is the fruit of Aristotelianism, Platonism and neo-Platonism. For those philosophers as well as for the Christians who lived in the cultural milieu influenced by them, 'rational lucidity,' or the 'logos,' is the supreme norm of true humanism.**

"According to the Greeks, **the irrational and tactile character of the sexual experience** (termed a 'brief epilepsy' in ancient medical science), **harms and diminishes reason's capacity to judge and, for this reason, is considered an assault against human dignity.** The Greeks and **the Church Fathers could not understand that this irrational act could become the expression of that which, according to us, is characteristic of the highest human vocation: the loving gift to the other.**"[30]

---

[29] Edward Schillebeeckx, "Evolução e mudanças nas concepções cristãs do matrimônio," in V.A., *Direitos do sexo e matrimônio* (Petrópolis: Vozes, 1972), p. 50.

[30] *Ibid.*, pp. 39-40.

§ 23   In a conversation with the Author of this Volume, Msgr. Philippe Delhaye, Secretary General of the International Theological Commission and professor emeritus of Louvain University, called the sexual morals of the Church "Jansenist":

"The Church is giving a greater welcome to sexuality. ... This is why John Paul II speaks so often about youth and the Gospel in his many speeches on marriage and sexual life ... **The Church is turning away from certain interpretations of Jansenism. One can say that the 17th, 18th and 19th centuries were Jansenist centuries in [Church] teaching on sexuality."[31]**

§ 24   In another offensive instance, Fr. Antonio Hortelano considers that the distinction between good and evil or light and darkness, applied to sexual morals, to be a primitive and "morbid dualism":

"The social and ethical channelization of sexuality comes from remote times. Since ancient times, men were conscious of the fact that it was necessary to channel the impetuous force of sexuality. Without the natural control of sexuality that exists in animals ... men felt the duty to repress it with a cultural type of control. Because of ancient metaphysic-religious implications, which already appeared in the primitive peoples, **such control often was transformed into a morbid dualism. God is good; evil comes from the Devil. God is light, evil is darkness. The spirit is light; the flesh is darkness. For this reason, everything directly related to the body is dark, ugly and, finally, evil.** From this came the socio-cultural depreciation of sex and of manual work.

"Christianity reacted vigorously to the excesses of this dualism. ... Notwithstanding, **it was unable to free itself completely from the dualist intoxication.** This explains to a large extent the modern sexual revolution." [32]

§ 25   Franz Böckle, professor of Moral Theology at the University of Bonn, affirms the Church's sexual morals result from "gnostic, stoic and Manichaean influences." In a work directed by Fr. Karl Rahner, he writes:

"Gnosticism, Manichaeism ... the stoic school and Neo-Platonism instill a bitterness in Christian doctrine on

---

[31] Philippe Delhaye, in an interview granted to the Author, Louvain-la-Neuve, February 28, 1983.

[32] Antonio Hortelano, "Rivoluzione sessuale e famiglia," *Concilium* 1984/3, p. 100.

sex and matrimony and falsify it. At times **theologians** uni-laterally cite the Epistle of St. Paul to the Corinthians and **view the satisfaction of the sexual appetite only as a need. In the same way they mention – again unilaterally – the ideas of St. Augustine in order to justify conjugal love only as a means for the propagation of the species.**

"Thus, spiritual love ... and carnal love – which they con-sidered an evil to be tolerated – find themselves in opposition, **closing the way to a liberating sexuality and love, a fusion of the flesh and the spirit inherent to the human being as a whole. Neither Hugh of Saint Victor, St. Albert, St. Bonaven-ture nor St. Thomas Aquinas, none of these great men of the Church managed to fully view man's body and its sexual ap-petites in a positive manner.**"[33]

§ 26   German feminist Uta Ranke-Heinemann, in a collabora-tive essay in another book directed by Fr. Rahner, says more or less the same and agrees that the Church must overcome "sexual taboos and fear":

"The Church, today even more than in the past, must strive in her preaching and lifestyle to do away with every type of sexual taboo, fear and *feigned modesty* in her rela-tionships with others. ... Something still remains to be done to overcome gnostic-Manichaean dualistic tendencies, at least in our Central-European relations, as better explained in the vol-ume of this collection titled *The Pathology of Catholicism.*"[34]

The practical objective of this progressivist fury un-leashed against Catholic Morals – expressed in the texts we just analyzed – is to open the door to lax habits and customs. Thus, both fury and laxity count as components of the *animus injuri-andi* characteristic of the spirit of the Council.

*

---

[33] Franz Böckle, "Amor y matrimonio," in V.A., *La reforma que llega de Roma* (Barcelona: Plaza & Jares, 1970), pp. 114-115.

[34] Uta Ranke-Heinemann, "La condizione sessuale fondamentale dell'uomo," in Karl. Rahner, *Chiesa, uomo e società* (Rome-Brescia: Herder-Morceliana,1970), p. 48.

3. Church Morals on Marriage Was Founded on Taboos

This Item begins with a doctrinal explanation of Catholic moral teaching on marriage, which should make it easier for the Reader to discern the errors in the progressivist theses on the topic.

§ 27   Most progressivists believe that man should not view his body as bearing the effects of original sin. According to them, the human passions – especially the sexual instinct – are a springboard to a spiritualized love. This spiritualized love supposedly is a part of the next stage in the human evolutionary process. With this understanding of sex, it makes no sense for a married couple to follow the fundamental recommendation Catholic Morals has always given regarding carnal commerce in marriage: that the sexual act is legitimate primordially for the perpetuation of the species and, secondarily, as a remedy for concupiscence.

Instead, progressivists consider the "personal fulfillment" of the spouses based on their mutual love as the principal end of matrimony, independent of an intention to procreate. According to this concept, unwanted children are inadmissible since they would obstruct this personal fulfillment rather than help to achieve it."[35]

---

[35] By admitting only desired children, this progressivist concept of matrimony tends to slide toward unnatural practices of birth control, definitively forbidden by the Church. We cite here, for example, the condemnation of the unnatural use of matrimony by Pius XI in the Encyclical *Casti connubii* of December 31, 1930:

"But no reason whatsoever – however grave it may be – can make something that is intrinsically against nature become something conformable to nature and morally good. Since the conjugal act is destined primarily by its nature for the begetting of offspring, those who, in exercising it, deliberately frustrate its natural power and purpose, sin against nature and commit a deed that is harmful and intrinsically vicious.

"It is not surprising, therefore, that Holy Scripture bears witness that the Divine Majesty supremely hates this execrable crime and at times has punished it with death. As St. Augustine notes: 'Intercourse even with one's legitimate wife is unlawful and wicked when the conception of offspring is prevented. Onan, the son of Juda, did this and for this reason the Lord killed him' (St. Augustine, *De conjugibus*, book II, n 12; cf. Gn 38, 8-10; *S. Penitenciaria*, April 3 and June 3, 1916).

"Consistent with this, and given that some have dared recently to proclaim in public a different teaching on this question, openly straying

§ 28   The moral and social consequences stemming from this new attitude are not difficult to enumerate.

- Birth control tends to increase in proportion to the desire to engage in marital relations without the aim of procreation.

- When the wife becomes pregnant because of a misjudgment of the spouses or a failure of contraceptives, the propensity to commit the crime of abortion increases.

- If the child is born, he often does not receive the affection always given by Catholic parents, since he is viewed as an inconvenience.

- When sentimental love is the only or main foundation of marriage, it naturally provides but a precarious stability, since the fragility of all that is founded exclusively or principally on sentiment is well-known.

Notwithstanding this unstable picture that materializes as soon as Catholic Morals on marriage is abandoned, progressivist theologians assault the traditional teaching with insults as they propose their imaginary "human fulfillment."

§ 29   This is the case, for example, of Fr. Schillebeeckx, who, with subtle sophistries not difficult to refute, strives to deviate the end of marriage from the perpetuation of the species to sexual love between the spouses. He blatantly insults Catholic Morals by calling it "dualistic" and "filled with taboos." He writes:

"By distinguishing the generic-animal dimension and the rational dimension in man, the traditional theology of marriage definitively attributes procreation to man's 'nature' and conjugal love to the human person. Such dualism is unacceptable to existential and phenomenological anthropology.[36] ...

---

from the Christian doctrine taught uninterruptedly, the Catholic Church – to whom God entrusted the mission of teaching and defending the integrity and purity of morals, standing erect amidst this moral ruin to preserve the chastity of the nuptial union from being defiled by this foul stain – raises her voice and, through Our mouth, proclaims and promulgates anew: Any use whatsoever of matrimony exercised in such a way that the act is deliberately frustrated in its natural power to generate life is an offense against the law of God and of nature, and those who dare commit such actions are accountable for a grievous sin"(*Documentos Pontifícios*, n. 4, pp. 24-25).

[36] Existential anthropology is the expression adopted by certain progressivists to refer to their system of thinking. They say that in the past

"By its very make-up, corporal sexuality, considered in its specifically human quality (the only one of interest to Morals), becomes an invitation for man to express his conjugal love in bodily intimacy so that this love becomes procreative. Human sexuality is, therefore, a sign of the realization of conjugal love which, through the biological act, becomes a fecund love, surpassing the limits of both spouses in a generosity that 'creates' another person. This is collaboration to the work of God, not through a submission to (biological) 'nature,' but by raising the possibilities of this 'nature' to a perspective of a properly human possibility.

"Precisely because it is human as a sign of the realization of fecund love, sexual activity in marriage is intrinsically honest, and not only because of its compensatory value [as a remedy for concupiscence]. **It was, therefore, the dualist vision – which considered sexuality as the animal dimension of the human being – that gave rise in the past to so many taboos regarding sexuality. In the anthropological context of a conjugal love that is offered and received, there is nothing censurable about sensible pleasure** (*delectatio secundum sensum*). **On the contrary, it is the vibration of the gift of self without any egoism.** ...

"**According to this anthropological conception, the distinction between the** *finis operis* [the final goal: procreation] **and the** *finis operantis* [the immediate goal: pleasure and mutual support] **of marriage becomes obsolete. The meaning of**

Catholic theology erroneously turned to an abstract God who had little to do with human life. And even when it dealt with human problems, Catholic theology in times past did so in a "theocentric" fashion, which was also erroneous. To correct this fault of theology and to resolve the actual problems of man, existential anthropology affirms, it is necessary to see God through man. It synthesizes this inversion by citing the formula of Rabbi Abraham Heschel, so dear to Fr. Congar, which Fr. Chenu cites in an interview-book: "The Bible is not a theology for man; it is an anthropology for God" (cf. *Jacques Duquesne interroge le Pére Chenu*, pp. 83-84).

Such anthropology is existential, that is, it considers man as he exists *hic et nunc* in today's world, without attempting to connect him to past legacies or future plans. He exists, he is there: he is *Dasein*, a *phenomenon*, in the philosophical language of Heidegger and his followers (Cf. Paul Foulquié, *Dictionnaire de la Langue Philosophique*, "Être III," Paris: Presses Universitaires de France, 1962, pp. 247-248).

sexual union – understood not in its biological sense but its human meaning – **is not procreation; it is not even conjugal love. Rather it is the fundamental expression of conjugal love in sexual corporeity**, which is suitable for such expression and gives it the capacity for human procreation." [37]

§ 30   Cardinal Karol Wojtyla also aligns himself with the progressivist current by failing to point out the vile, ignoble and explosive aspect of the sexual instinct that comes from original sin. Although this vileness is greater in fornication, it is also present in the conjugal act.[38] Nonetheless, Wojtyla goes so far as to deem this act free from any stain whatsoever. As a consequence he opposes traditional Morals, which forbids sexual pleasure in matrimony independent of the intention to procreate. Wojtyla pejoratively calls Catholic Morals "rigorist."

A summary of his thinking in the book *Love and Responsibility* comes from the pen of writer Rocco Buttiglione:

"For rigorism, sexuality is justified only insofar as it is oriented to procreation; through the sexual instinct, the human body appears as a mere instrument used by God or by nature to assure the survival of the species. **What is morally permitted is only the use of man's instrumental body, emptied as much as possible of any physical and emotional enjoyment. ...**

In the correct personalist perspective, on the contrary, man freely collaborates with God and with another human person in procreation. **All the components of sexuality are harmoniously elevated to the level of the person, and in this the**

---

[37] Edward Schillebeeckx, "Evolução e mudanças nas concepções cristãs do matrimônio," in V. A., *Direito do sexo e do matrimônio*, pp. 50, 53-55.

[38] In some passages St. Thomas Aquinas refers to the wrong and ignoble aspect of the conjugal act that stems from the disorder caused in human nature by original sin:

• "The intercourse of fornication and that of marriage are of the same species as regards nature. But the intercourse of fornication is sordid in itself. Therefore, in order that the marriage intercourse not be sordid, something must be added to it to make it right and change its moral species. " (*Summa Theologiae*, Supplementum, q. 49, a. 1).

• "The turpitude that always accompanies the marriage act and always causes shame is the turpitude of punishment, not of guilt" (*ibid.*, q. 49, a. 4)

• On this topic, see also Note 23 of this Chapter.

fullest achievement of the components of enjoyment and play is found, components that are inseparable from an existentially authentic and morally good sexual life. 'The problem for sexual morals is how to enjoy sexual pleasure without treating the person as an object for use. Here is the nucleus of the sexual moral problem. ...'[39]*

§ 31   "It goes without saying that from the existential standpoint, **rigorism is incapable of ensuring a balanced evaluation of sexuality.** It separates pleasure from the objective procreative goal of the sexual instinct. **When the tendency toward pleasure is not understood positively, it is shoved into the unconscious instead of being integrated in an authentic and personal love.**"[40]

Since love between the spouses, according to progressivists, must have priority over the perpetuation of the species, it is consistent that they should defend birth control or, as they prefer to call it, natural family planning. An expressive instance of this attitude was found in the resistance made against the Encyclical *Humanae vitae,* already mentioned in another Volume of this Collection.[41]

We cite two brief examples below.

§ 32   Fr. Yves Congar, writing on the subject, concludes that the word of the Church on this matter is "strange, repressive and irrelevant":

"Regarding *Humanae vitae,* there was a rejection – or rather, a general indifference – from the average faithful who had already exercised his liberty [to use contraceptives]; there was also an acceptance. **A large number of theologians and even Bishops 'received' the Encyclical's doctrine but translated it in this way: You do not sin if you do not conform to it for serious reasons** coming from a docile and enlightened conscience. ...

---

[39]* *Amore e responsabilità* (Turin: Marietti, 1980), p. 44.

[40] Rocco Buttiglione, *Il pensiero di Karol Wojtyla*, Milan: Jaca Books, 1982, p. 119.

[41] Many Episcopal Conferences stood up against *Humanae vitae*, asserting the primacy of individual conscience over the objective norms established by the Encyclical, which was rejected by the Austrian, Belgian, Brazilian, Canadian, Dutch, French, German, Nordic and Swiss Episcopates, as well as by Bishops and theologians around the world (cf. Vol. I, *In the Murky Waters of Vatican II*, Chap. X, § 9, Note 24).

"**To many**, principally the youth, **sexual relations are an expression**, one among others, **of a personal relation** that does not depend on other ethical norms. **The word the Church may pronounce [on it] appears to them abnormal, strange, repressive and irrelevant. They pay no attention to it.**"[42]

§ 33   Fr. Heribert Mühlen, a well known theologian on pneumatology (doctrine on the Holy Spirit) and a disciple of Karl Rahner, calls the Church's condemnation of birth control a "nightmare":

"We will not bother to address here again the question of the incredible pretentiousness of Küng's comments on the encyclical *Humanae vitae*. Karl Rahner has already said everything necessary on this topic. **The origin, contents, form and modality of the promulgation [of *Humanae vitae*] were and continue to be a nightmare for the whole Church.**"[43]

In the previous Item 2 we saw Progressivism attacking Catholic Morals for its restrictions on sex; in this Item 3 we verified that this current wants to focus all Catholic Morals from the sexual perspective. Therefore, the commentaries we made in Item 2 also apply here, and are further extended to the ensemble of Morals. The *animus injuriandi* of the theologians quoted here are particularly expressive of the spirit of the Council.

4. To Forbid Homosexuality Is Brutal, Pharisaic, Biased & Anti-Christian

§ 34   Based on the supposition of love being the "fulfillment of the human person," homosexuals assert that they find such fulfillment in same-sex relationships. Church leaders increasingly are giving credence to this claim, "forgetting" that the sodomite vice is one of the four sins that cry to Heaven and clamor to God for vengeance, a vice severely condemned by the Holy Ghost in Sacred Scripture.[44]

---

[42] Y. Congar, *Eglise Catholique et France Moderne* (Paris: Hachette, 1978), pp. 199-200.

[43] Heribert Mühlen, "O teste da infalibilidade - Por que Hans Küng deve encontrar uma oposição decidida?"in K. Rahner (ed.), *O problema da infalibilidade*, p. 225.

[44] These four sins are: willful murder; sodomy; oppression of the poor, widows and orphans; denial of a just salary to working men (cf. J. Deharbe, *Kleiner Katholishcer Katechismus*, Friedrich Putest, Regensburg, n.d., p. 59; Francis Spirago and Richard F. Clarke, *The Catechism Explained* (NY: Benzinger Bros, 1921), pp. 460-461; Henry

In parallel with this "forgetfulness" of the divine con-demnations of homosexuality, the Conciliar Church has intro-duced the "homosexual pastoral," which affirms that persons with this vice should no longer be condemned and punished, but their condition should be seen as a consummate fact, an existen-tial fact, they say. Thus, the emphasis should be placed on help-ing these persons to become better rather than changing their condition.

§ 35

Thus, one of the aims of the "homosexual pastoral," as known American moralist Fr. Barnabas Ahern told the Author of this Volume,[45] is to try to eradicate the kind of promiscuity

---

Tuberville, *The Douay Catechism* (NY: P.J. Kenedy, 1649), chap. 20 "The Sins that Cry to Heaven for Vengeance Expounded."

In the **Old Testament** the Scripture refers to the heinous vice of ho-mosexuality with special severity:

• "And the Lord said: The cry of Sodom and Gomorrah is multiplied, and their sin is become exceedingly grievous" (Gen 18:20).

• "And they [the Angels] said to Lot: ... All that are yours, bring them out of this city, for we will destroy this place, because their cry is grown loud before the Lord who has sent us to destroy them" (Gen 19:12-13).

• "You shall not lie with mankind as with womankind, because it is an abomination" (Lev 18:22).

• "If any one lie with a man as with a woman, both have committed an abomination, let them be put to death: their blood be upon them" (Lev 20:13).

In the **New Testament,** St. Paul speaks strongly against the vice against nature:

• "Do not err: Neither fornicators, nor idolaters, nor adulterers, nor the effeminate, nor liers with mankind ... shall possess the kingdom of God" (1 Cor 6:9-10).

In the Epistle to the Romans, the Apostle threatens those perverted by this vice with terrible punishments already on this Earth.

• "And, in like manner, the men also, leaving the natural use of the women, have burned in their lusts one towards another, men with men, working that which is filthy, and receiving in themselves the rec-ompense which was due to their error" (Rom 1:27).

How can one fail to see a connection between these last Scriptural warnings and the pandemic of AIDS that is presently chastising homo-sexuals?

[45] Barnabas Ahern, Interview granted to the Author, Rome, March 6, 1983. Fr. Barnabas Ahern, C.P., is a member of the International Theological Commission and an adviser to the Sacred Congregation for the Cause of Saints.

where homosexuals have many different partners. Ahern thinks it would be a great "pastoral" progress if relationships between Catholic homosexuals became stable...

§ 36   An impressive description revealing the ravages caused by this homosexual "pastoral" in the United States is found in the trustworthy book by Fr. Enrique Rueda, *The Homosexual Network*.[46] In it he gives ample evidence of the connivance of Church authorities with the expansion of homosexuality.[47]

Thus we can see that *per viam facti* the grievous sin punished with fire and brimstone in the destruction of Sodom gradually is being introduced into Catholic ambiences.

§ 37   In addition to this advance by the way of facts, attempts to defend homosexuals from the doctrinal standpoint have also begun to appear. Alongside the "homosexual pastoral," and perhaps as a consequence of it, "homosexual theology" has emerged.

As we mentioned before,[48] one of the earliest attempts to make a theological defense of homosexuals was the book by American priest John McNeill, S.J., *The Church and the Homosexual.* It counted on the complaisance of the Superior General of the Company of Jesus, then Fr. Pedro Arrupe, and was supported by an *imprimatur* given by the Provincial of the New York province, Fr. Eamon Taylor. The book is an attempt to justify the sodomite vice from the theological and pastoral points of view.

---

[46]   Enrique Rueda, *The Homosexual Network* (Old Greenwich, CT: The Devin Adair Co., 1982), 680 pp.

[47]   On this topic, among the copious data provided by Fr. Rueda (pp. 299-301), see the leaflet "A Time to Speak," published by a Catholic group favorable to homosexuality. The leaflet presents a list of 16 American Bishops – including Cardinals John Krol of Philadelphia and John Francis Dearden of Detroit – who made statements favoring the homosexual movement (p. 316). Among this support a letter from Archbishop Raymond Hunthausen of Seattle stands out; in it he supports the efforts of the homosexual movement to have the House of Representatives of Washington State approve a law granting them special privileges. Also significant is a letter by Archbishop Rembert G. Weakland, O.S.B., of Milwaukee that likewise favors approval of a law defending the "basic rights" of homosexuals (cf. pp. 319-320).

[48]   See Chap. III, Note 45a of this Volume.

§ 38   Below, we will transcribe from McNeill's book statements by well-known American theologians defending homosexuality. Although the approach as a whole is highly injurious
to the natural order and Catholic Morals, we have emphasized in
bold the most offensive passages.

"In his article 'A Christian Response to Homosexuals,' in
the September 1972 issue of *U. S. Catholic*, **Fr. Henry Fahrens
testifies to the inadequacy of the Church's [traditional] pastoral policy. Based on his experiences in counseling homosexuals, he labels the traditional teaching 'brutal, pharisaic,
biased and anti-Christian.' Fr. Fahrens calls for the Church
to recognize the sexual actions of homosexuals and went so
far as to recommend "a witness of the Church to the celebration of love between two persons of the same sex.'**

"***Commonweal* was another Catholic publication to
turn to the theme of homosexuality**. Its April 6, 1973 issue
dedicated an editorial and two major articles to the question.
**The editorial urged the Church to support civil rights leg-
islation for the homosexual and observed that 'some Catholic moralists have cautiously argued** in professional journals
that, under certain circumstances, which may differ with each
individual, **a Catholic homosexual can enter an active homosexual relationship and still receive the sacraments, and lead
a life of sexual love that does not necessarily separate him
from the love of God**.

"In the same issue, **Peter Fink, S.J.**, proposed what he
calls 'a pastoral hypothesis.' ... **Fink's hypothesis is that the
Church should explore the possibility that homosexual love
is a valid form of human love and, consequently, can also
be a reflection of God's loving presence.** ... 'Homosexual love
will be sinful whenever it shows itself as destructive of the human and disruptive of man's relation with God.' **In her mission
of counseling, the Church should take the gay and lesbian
couple and their attempt to form a loving union with great
seriousness. 'All I ask here is for the Church to employ all
her resources in an honest effort to lead gay people to love, to
the human, and to God through their homosexuality.'**

"The next major publication also appeared in *Commonweal*. In its issue of February 15, 1974, Gregory Baum in his
work *Catholic Homosexuals* stated that the emergence of gay
Catholicism through their organization Dignity raised many
theological questions. ...

§ 39   "**Baum** believes it is not likely that the Catholic Church is about to change its traditional doctrine that all homosexual activity, no matter what the circumstances, is sinful. **Therefore, he thought it would be a mistake for Dignity to make an appeal to the Catholic Hierarchy for specific recognition. Rather, Baum proposes what he calls a realistic strategy: 'to create in the Catholic Church a moderate and well-founded minority position, which would be a help to vast numbers of gay people at this time, gain more pastoral experience and continue theological reflection.'"[49]**

§ 40   Moralist John Coleman of Berkeley University also believes that homosexuals should be more concerned about certain "pathologies" of their condition rather than their condition as such. Coleman endorses another insult made in passing by Fr. Matthew Fox, who called the quest for perfection "egoistic" and one of the worst sins of the modern consumer society, supposedly on par with sadomasochism. Coleman writes:

"A key source of critique focuses on the stereotyped lifestyle typical in many urban gays, the so-called 'unisex phenomenon. Others note the promiscuity of many urban gays. **Especially since the arrival of the mysterious immune system disease, the gay community has strongly discussed sexual responsibility and the search for permanent partners**.

"Finally, **many point to the ways in which homosexuals,** similar in this to other persecuted groups, **often internalize the societal stereotypes or fall prey to some of the worst sins of modern, capitalistic consumer society: 'Power over, power under, sadomasochism, consumerism, hatred of body,** inability to sustain relationships ... and **egoistic quests for perfectionism and immortality.'[50]* These pathologies, rather than the homosexual condition as such, it is argued, should govern the best moral efforts of gays.**"[51]

By calling Catholic Morals brutal, pharisaic, biased and anti-Christian, theologians and members of the Hierarchy show their complicity with the vice of homosexuality. The offenses reflect the spirit of the Council; the complicity expresses the new doctrine that has been accepted as a fruit of the Council.

---

[49] J. McNeill, *The Church and the Homosexual,* pp. 19-25.

[50]* Matthew Fox, "The Spiritual Journey of the Homosexual," in *The Challenge to Love*, p. 190.

[51] John Coleman, "Homosexual Revolution and Hermeneutics," *Concilium* 1984/3, pp. 121-122.

5. The Church's Social Morals: An Infected Moralism

§ 41   Some progressivists oppose individual salvation as an obstacle to socialization basing themselves on the principles that evolution moves faster by unifying collective groups and that grace is primarily a social phenomenon. The socialist world they seek has messianic connotations that announce a change, the next stage of mankind – its new "qualitative leap." They pretend this process of socialization is the principal "sign of the times."

§ 42   This is what can be inferred from the statements of Fr. Chenu, one of those whose inspired the opening of the Church to the modern world. Chenu offensively calls the vigilance of the Church regarding Socialism and Liberalism an "infected moralism":

"We saw socialization progressing through the 19th century parallel to the Liberalism that originated from the French Revolution. **But the Church and the Christian people in an obscure and confused way were opposed to it. Instead of acting with evangelical discernment, the Church, facing the double threat of Liberalism and Socialism, rejected the changes that were underway. The fear experienced by Christians caused a rollback in behaviors, evaluations and perspectives: Social issues were marginalized in the Christian conscience, which chose to stick to intentions as the only criterion of morality.**

"This 'moralism' still infects private consciences and official Church directives. It is satisfied with applying personal interior virtues to collective phenomena. For example, **people thought – and still think – that the reform of society would be achieved through the self-disciplined elimination of individual egoisms and that the collective transformation would be born from a transformation of individual consciences. We had to wait for the Encyclical *Populorum progressio* of Paul VI –** and the sequence of documents that came in its wake – **to find an explicit way out of the problem of individual conversion. Today it is admitted that it is an illusion to expect to transform the structures of society by a simple appeal to the conversion of the rich. ...**

"Of course, human nature is specifically personal in its intelligence, liberty, intentions and consciousness of itself. But its actions, habits, progress, perfections and happiness are included in the order of Nature with a capital N. The moral life of this person must be eminent on the personal level; but **morality**

is, permit me to say, **part of the physical order of the cosmos. For at the top, the spiritual creature**, so singular in the ensemble of nature, **is at the same time subject to Providence in a personal relation of love and to a general providence that governs his actions.** ...

"The person, whose value is absolute with regard to liberties and intentions, is nonetheless part of a whole. ... Love of God, in the radical unity of His ongoing plans, is the unifying reason for my attachment to myself and my love for my neighbor.

"Having admitted this, one understands **it is wrong to separate, as Catholics tried to do, a person's good conscience and intentions, on the one hand, and his solidarity with the universe under construction, on the other. Having admitted this, one understands that it is through this process of socialization and in this socialization that I access the truth of my being and the perfection of nature.**

"As a historian of the Church, I could also discern – beyond individual holiness and hierarchical modes of operation – **the anonymous currents which, stemming from socioeconomic determinisms, create a new climate favorable or unfavorable to the awakening of the Gospel. And, as an historian of theology, I understood ... that grace is also social.** ...

"For Pius XII and some of his advisers, everything that went beyond the family was Socialism. Society was effectively conceived as a group of families that constituted the social fabric. What **I think, however, is that the family is nothing but an element, a cell, in a body that is beyond it. The world is not a group of families. It is a community with universal dimensions.** ...

"Also, at the time of the Council [there was some confusion then between socialization and Socialism] ... I gave a lecture in Rome on socialization. The next day, the cultural page of the socialist newspaper *L'Avanti* ran this headline: 'Great French theologian opts for Socialism.' Meanwhile, **John XXIII began to introduce the word socialization into the official vocabulary of the Church with the encyclicals *Mater et magistra* and especially *Pacem in terris*. In the latter he considered the phenomenon of socialization as the most expressive sign of the times**: not only as an opportunity for man, for fraternity, for peace, but – **in the actual economy of salvation – as a predisposition and touchstone for the Kingdom of God."**[52]

---

[52] *Jacques Duquesne interroge le Pére Chenu*, pp. 103-107.

§ 43   This Messianism of socialization is correlated to the notion of man's redemption through work,[53] a concept that brings progressivists into line with communists. This is what Fr. Chenu affirms as he lambasts Catholic "moralism" in an interview:

"Christians feared ideologies that were nurtured on a scientific analysis of production [Communism], and they were more or less **consciously in solidarity with bourgeois regimes [Capitalism]. Consequently, for a long time it was common to see in catechesis old clichés ... about the arduous and penitential character of work.**

"Question: **They said it was a punishment for sin...**

"Chenu: **And that it was offered to God as expiation**. Marriage was likewise defined as a remedy for fornication and a means to tame concupiscence. It is exactly the same attitude. **Fortunately, this moralism has been surpassed; and the full meaning of the account of Genesis, where man appears as a helper of God in Creation and as a demiurge of nature, has been rediscovered**. In the 1930s, Christians rediscovered Genesis. **Since then, labor could no longer be defined primarily in relation to the good or bad intentions of workers. It was understood that it expressed the very essence of man's condition in his relation with the universe to be built."** [54]

These texts of Chenu are only one illustration of how progressivists offend the Social Morals of the Church.

*

As numerous as the insults to the honor of Catholic Dogmatics – which we saw from Chapter I to Chapter VI – are the offenses to the respect due Catholic Morals – demonstrated in this Chapter VII, which comes to its end here. Should it be necessary, a whole volume could be written only about offenses against Catholic Morals. Inasmuch as such insults are tolerated by the Vatican leadership, they constitute a fitting expression of the spirit of the Council.

* * *

---

[53] According to Marx, work creates and molds the very essence of man. In his *Economic and Philosophic Manuscripts of 1844* he expounds his thinking: "All the so-called history of the world is nothing but the self-creation of man through human labor, nothing but the transformation of nature for man" (apud Istvan Mészaros, *Marx: A teoria da alienação*, Zahar Ed., Rio de Janeiro, 1981, pp. 75-76).

[54] *Jacques Duquesne interroge le Pére Chenu*, pp. 113-114.

CONCLUSION

§ 1   On closing this Volume on the insults made by important conciliar theologians – including John Paul II and Benedict XVI – against the Catholic Faith and Morals, we consider amply exemplified the *animus injuriandi* that inspires these thinkers.

If we add to this the subject matter dealt with in the previous Volume, which presents the insults made to the institution of the Holy Roman Catholic and Apostolic Church, we have a broad picture of the affronts made to the honor of the institution and doctrine of our Religion.

Could one ever have imagined – as it is clearly shown here – that from the lips of Popes, Cardinals, Bishops, theologians and priests, we would hear so many offenses against the perennial teaching of the Church?

*

§ 2   It seems fitting here to apply to these Hierarchs and theologians the poignant lamentation of Jeremiah facing the ruins of the Temple devastated by the enemies of God: *Quomodo obscuratum est aurum... How the gold has become dim...*

How was it possible for Shepherds and theologians to have stained the seamless tunic of Faith and Morals by insulting their fundamental truths?

§ 3   Facing the insolence of Modernism that had infiltrated the Sanctuary itself, the great Pontiff St. Pius X asked himself whether the time of the Antichrist had already arrived.

"When all this is pondered," he observed, "there is good reason to fear that this great perversity of minds is a foretaste, perhaps the beginning, of those evils reserved for the last days. Such, in truth, is the audacity and the wrath employed everywhere in persecuting religion, in assailing the dogmas of the Faith, in the brazen effort to uproot and destroy all relations between man with Divinity, that the 'son of perdition' of whom the Apostle speaks (2 Thess. 2:3) may indeed have already arrived among us."[1]

---

[1] Pius X, Encyclical *E Supremi Apostolatus*, December 4, 1903, in *Documentos Pontifícios* (Petrópolis: Vozes, 1958), n. 87, p. 6.

§ 4   Along the same line of thinking, taking into account the blasphemies exposed in these two Volumes that dealt with the *animus injuriandi* of the spirit of the Council and the persecution of the true Catholic Church they reflect, we ask whether the terrible words of St. John are not applicable to our days:

"And I saw a woman sitting upon a scarlet colored beast, full of names of blasphemy. ... And the woman was clothed round about with purple and scarlet. ... And on her forehead a name was written: Mystery; Babylon the great, the mother of the fornications and the abominations of the earth. And I saw the woman drunk with the blood of the saints, and with the blood of the martyrs of Jesus. And I wondered, when I had seen her, with great astonishment" (Apoc 17:3-6).

*

§ 5   We would like to be proved that we are wrong, that the documents upon which we based ourselves are flawed, that the statements we transcribed have different interpretations than the ones we have given them. We would like it to be shown that the Author as a mere layman is unable to grasp the deepest theological meanings of the documents cited. If all this could be duly demonstrated, we would be sincerely relieved, because then all that was said and written against the Church would not have stained her perfect orthodoxy.

Unfortunately, however, we do not believe that such objections to the seriousness of this Work will even be made, since the documents upon which it is based were issued by reliable publishing houses, known to be faithful to the manuscripts in the original languages and in their translations. Moreover, many of these documents are known, tolerated or even approved by highly placed Hierarchs, if not directly by the Holy See.

The meanings of the documents also leave little room for doubt, since for the most part the texts are quite clear. Further, what we have presented and analyzed here are insults, and in the rigor of logic, an insult can be judged as such, independent of the context in which it appears. Nonetheless, throughout the Chapters we sought to show the consistency of progressivist thinking so that the Reader could see that the cited insults are not opposed to the thinking of Progressivism, but are the natural fruits of it.

Finally, the allegation that a layman is unable to analyze documents and attitudes that lie within the ready reach of any Catholic seems inconsistent; for it is to the faithful – the large majority of whom are laymen – that the teachings of the Shepherds and theologians are directed. Also, our whole analysis was founded on the *sensus catolicum* – the Catholic sense that lies within the realm of competence of the layman – rather than on elaborate theological subtleties.

*

§ 6   Adhering to the initial plan of this Work,[2] after having verified in Volume I, *In the Murky Waters of Vatican II*, that it was impossible to objectively analyze the letter of the documents of Council Vatican II because of their ambiguity, we began to ask ourselves what the spirit of the Council might be. We then dedicated Volume II, *Animus Injuriandi I*, and the present Volume III, *Animus Injuriandi II*, to the study of the purpose underlying such spirit. This provides the Reader with abundant documentation to know what the much-trumpeted spirit of Vatican II actually is.

In the two subsequent Volumes we will analyze – with the help of the *Madonna del Miracolo*, to whom we dedicate this Collection – the explicit plan of important theologians to destroy the Holy Church and the Catholic Faith.

To this we invite our Reader.

*   *   *

---

[2] Cf. General Introduction to the Collection, Vol. I, *In the Murky Waters of Vatican II*, § 5.

APPENDIX

As in Volume II, *Animus Injuriandi I* (Appendix II), we present here an ensemble of the offenses contained in the documents analyzed in each Chapter.

When the injuries against the honor due our Holy Faith are presented together, they convey more the malice of those Prelates and theologians, malice that in many ways finds its source in Progressivism, the current of thought that inspired them. Given that we are studying what constitutes the *spirit of the Council* and the *animus injuriandi* that characterizes it, presenting this summary of insults seems a valid procedure.

We call this section *Improperia* [outrages] because this is the name normally given to the series of outrages made by the Jews against Our Lord Jesus Christ that are sung in the liturgy of Good Friday during the ceremony of adoration of the Holy Cross. Analogously, the list of outrages made by progressivists expresses a similar ingratitude when they offend, ridicule and try to efface the honor due the Holy Faith. It is, therefore, this macabre "litany" what we will present in this Appendix.

The offenses will be showed in their gravest aspects and uniformly presented in the form of invocations that we have constructed and, as such, do not always appear verbatim in the texts. As the Reader has seen in this Volume, these affronts have diverse nuances that, even so, do not lessen their gravity.

For those who want to verify the objectivity of each affirmation, we will indicate alongside each offense the page where it can be found.

*　　*　　*

IMPROPERIA

IN CHAPTER I

Luther, brother in Christ (p. 23)

Luther, 'evangelist' and confessor of the theology of the cross (p. 67)

Luther, religious genius (p. 45)

Luther, misunderstood by Rome in his time (p. 46)

Luther, confessor of Christ's divinity (p. 27)

Luther, witness of the Gospel and herald of spiritual renewal (p. 49)

Luther, master of the faith (p. 49)

Luther, who sought the message of the Gospel honestly and with abnegation (p. 51)

Luther, moved by an ardent passion for eternal salvation (p. 31)

Luther, unquestionably a great personage of faith (p. 52)

Luther, whose mission was grandiose and necessary (p. 52)

Luther, illustrious reformer (p. 45)

Luther, great man of prayer (p. 45)

Luther, common master of Christians (p. 62)

Luther, common doctor of Christendom (p. 27)

Luther, similar to St. Augustine and St. Thomas Aquinas (p. 58)

Luther, similar to St. Ignatius of Loyola (p. 57)

Luther, who rethought all of Christianity (p. 56)

Luther, master for Catholics on the doctrine of justification (p. 27)

Luther, great researcher of the Gospel's truth (p. 27)

Luther, master to teach us the concept of Faith (p. 27)

Luther, master to teach us the relationship between Faith and love (p. 27)

Luther, whose unjust and dishonest portrait must be corrected (p. 24)

Luther, who would have been a conciliar *peritus* (p. 56)

Luther, whose main doctrines were accepted at Vatican II (p. 51)

Luther, whose rehabilitation is being made by the Vatican (p. 27)

Luther, whose 500th birthday anniversary portends the dawn of unity and communion (p. 34)

Lutherans, whom the Vatican treats as brothers (p. 33)

Lutherans, with whom John Paul II fraternizes and participates in worship services (p. 36)

Lutherans, whom John Paul II treats with the solicitude of a father (p. 34)

Lutherans, with whom John Paul II ardently wants to unite himself (p. 35)

Lutherans, embraced with Catholics by God the Father (p. 41)

Lutherans, united with Catholics by the Spirit of God (p. 41)

Lutherans, with whom Catholics should build bridges to establish unity (p. 43)

Luther, whose appeal invites Catholics to recognize their own infidelities (p. 49)

Luther, who was right against Rome (p. 61)

Luther, whose 500th birthday anniversary is a great event for Church unity (p. 43)

Luther, whose appeal was not rightly understood by the Church (p. 50)

Luther, whose thesis on penance must move and change today's Catholics (p. 45)

Luther, whose thesis on justification is legitimate and not a reason for division (p. 45)

Luther, from whom Catholics have much to learn (p. 45)

Luther, better understood today by new biblical studies (p. 50)

Luther, whose thinking is a legitimate form of Christian theology (p. 50)

Luther, whose demands caused the Christian faith to be better expressed (p. 51)

Luther, whose emphasis on Scripture was accepted by Vatican II (p. 51)

Luther, whose notion of People of God was accepted by Vatican II (p. 51) 30

Luther, whose view of a permanent reform in the Church was accepted by Vatican II (p. 51)

Luther, whose understanding of Church ministry as service was accepted by Vatican II (p. 51)

Luther, whose emphasis on the priesthood of all the baptized was accepted by Vatican II (p. 51)

Luther, whose demand for use of vernacular was fulfilled by Paul VI (p. 51)

Luther, whose demand for communion under two species was accepted after the Council (p. 51)

Luther, who would not have separated from Rome had he lived after Vatican II (p. 56)

Luther, studied and admired by progressivist theologians (p. 60)

Luther, the last bastion of the Pauline principle of justification by faith alone (p. 62)

Luther, lucid and courageous (p. 62)

Luther, prophet of the present doctrinal renewal (p. 58)

Luther, unjustly excommunicated by those out of touch with theological problems (p. 58)

Luther, whose protest was more than well-founded (p. 58)

Luther, who did not want a new church (p. 58)

Luther, who is no longer a heretic (p. 58)

Luther, whose appeal to the Gospel was the remedy for the sick Church (p. 61)

Luther, where would the Church be today without you? (p. 59)

Marcion of Pontus, 'first-born of Satan,' who did not want to initiate a heresy (p. 58)

Marcion of Pontus, whose followers were 'martyrs' (p. 58)

Marcion of Pontus, great confessor of the faith (p. 58)

Arius and Pelagius, confessors of the faith (p. 59)

Gottschalk and Eriugena, confessors of the faith (p. 60)

Wycliffe and Hus, confessors of the faith and great reformers (p. 61)

Zwingli and Calvin, great reformers whose zeal must be present in the Catholic spirit (pp. 42)

Giordano Bruno, confessor of the faith (p. 59)

Heretics, imbued with the feeling of God and marked by the message of the Gospel (p. 59)

Heretics, similar to the great saints (p. 59)

Heretics, who scarified everything to accomplish their task (p. 59)

Heretics, who enriched the Church with their heroism and fidelity to the truth (p. 59)

Heretics, whose good faith cannot be denied (p. 59)

Heretics, prophets of conciliar changes (p. 59)

Heretics, who open the way to progress (p. 59)

Heretics, who bring novelty into the realm of truth (p. 54)

Heretics, who should be loved for what they are (p. 54)

Heretics, what would the Church be without you? (p. 59)

Schismatics, which whom John Paul II preached unity (p. 69)

Schismatics, addressed as brothers by John Paul II (p. 70)

Schismatics, with whom John Paul II feels comfortable (p. 70)

Schismatics, whose ambience John Paul II calls a great spiritual reality (p. 70)

Schismatics, who are the second lung necessary for a Catholic to breathe (p. 70)

Schismatics, endowed with ardent faith (p. 70)

Schismatics, whose faith in the Holy Trinity is acceptable (p. 72)

Schismatics, whose faith in the Holy Ghost is acceptable (p. 72)

Schismatics, in whom the life of grace is deeply rooted (p. 70)

Schismatics, whose spirituality complements Catholic spirituality (p. 70)

Schismatics, whose faith is practically the same as the Catholic Faith (p. 70)

Schismatics, to whom John Paul II humbly pays homage (p. 75)

Schismatics, necessary for the Church of Christ to manifest her plenitude (p. 75)

Jews, whose B'nai B'rith members John Paul II calls 'dear friends' (p. 82)

Jews, whom John Paul II calls 'brothers' (p. 82)

Jews, whose differences and religious identity are profoundly respected by John Paul II (p. 83)

Jews, to whose God John Paul II renders homage (p. 83)

Jews, who must not be viewed with fear and suspicion (p. 83)

Jews, visited by John Paul II so that 'old prejudices' may be overcome (p. 101)

Jews, the favored brothers and elder brothers of Catholics (p. 102)

Jews, to whom no guilt should be attributed for the Passion of Christ (p. 102)

Jews, absolved by *Nostra aetate*, which was inspired by the Holy Spirit (p. 102)

Jews, who do not need to abandon Judaism to become Catholic (p. 87)

Jews, whom the Church may not proselytize (p. 87)

Jews, among whom the Church has no apostolic mission (p. 87)

Church, whose new relations with Judaism signify fidelity to her vocation (p. 84)

Church, finally reunited with Judaism like Jacob with Esau (p. 86)

Church, a means to accomplish Israel's vocation to take the light to the *goyim* (p. 87)

Church, a means to discover the values of Judaism and not renege them (p. 88)

Church, who received the grace to welcome the spiritual riches of the schismatics (p. 76)

Church, whose religiosity compares poorly with Protestantism (p. 58)

Church, who must reconcile with Protestants to give a true testimony of faith (p. 49)

Church, who has no plenitude that belongs by right to her (p. 58)

Church, what would you be without the heretical prophets? (p. 59)

Church, who cannot clearly establish boundaries between truth and error (p. 59)

Church, who cannot separate the faithful from heretics (p. 59)

Church, who must be welcoming toward heretics (p. 60)

Church, who after the Council looks no different from the Lutherans (p. 60)

Church, who at Vatican II took up Luther's call for a continuous penitential reform (p. 62)

Church, whose preachers recognize the Lutheran doctrine of 'justification' (p. 62)

Church, who fulfilled Luther's demand to eliminate the sacrificial character of the Mass (p. 62)

Church, who fulfilled Luther's demands regarding the eucharistic celebration (p. 62)

Church, who accepted Luther's demands for Scripture's priority

(p. 62)

Church, who must unite with heretics to know the fullness of the spirit of Christ (p. 41)

Church, who unjustly supported discriminatory practices against Jews (p. 91)

Church, who may not say that the Jews are reprobates or accursed (p. 102)

Church, whose enemies become more astute by attacking you (p. 55)

Satan, who by attacking Christianity has a more profound vision of God (p. 55)

IN CHAPTER II

God, opium of the people (p. 143)

God, immanent in the world (p. 143)

God, place of evasion (p. 143)

Yahweh, who imposes draconian laws (p. 149)

Yahweh, who makes infernal decrees (p. 149)

God, who is Calvinist (p. 149)

God, who is Jansenist (p. 149)

God, who is theist (p. 150)

God, who is stoic (p. 150)

God, who is narcissist (p. 150)

God, cold, frozen and dead being (p. 150)

God, a monstrous being (p. 150)

God, who is static and fixed, must die (p. 142)

God, who set the world in motion at the world's origin, must die (p. 142)

God, the architect and engineer of Creation, must die (p. 143)

God, who covers for the ignorance of man, must die (p. 143)

God, who guarantees the established order and *status quo*, must die (p. 143)

God, who shields authority with divine right, must die (p. 143)

God, who protects the powerful against revolutions, must die (p. 143)

God, who counsels the poor to be patient, must die (p. 143)

God, who impedes social reforms, must die (p. 143)

God, who legitimizes unjust social structures, must die (p. 150)

God, who projects himself as all powerful, must die (p. 150)

God of alienation, who Marxists rightly criticize, must be set aside (p. 144)

God, who allows creatures to suffer, must be set aside (p. 149)

God, who use sufferings for his glorification, must be set aside (p. 149)

God, who must die so that the world can live (p. 143)

God, understood in a vague and false manner (p. 144)

God, who atheists rightly criticize (p. 145)

God, conceived by atheism in a new and honest way (p. 145)

God, whom the faithful must begin to live without (p. 145)

God, who must be denied so we can live in harmony with atheists (p. 146)

God, who is more present in atheists than in Catholics (p. 146)

God, found only in earthly events (p. 144)

God, an artifice to cover social injustice (p. 150)

God, an artifice to cover self-deceptions of individuals (p. 150)

God, an abstract vision that followed the Hellenist model (p. 142)

God, whom Christians made an idol (p. 142)

God, whom Catholics transformed into a caricature (p. 142)

God, who is responsible for the suffering of innocents (p. 150)

God, who is unable to suffer or to love (p. 150)

God the Father, whose domain is Hell (p. 149)

God the Father, whose creative work has a tragic and demonic character (p. 149)

God the Father, whose creative work includes every possible decadence (p. 149)

God the Father, who judges and condemns Jesus Christ (p. 149)

God, who is Father and Mother (p. 158)

Most Holy Trinity, a teaching that means nothing to Catholics (p. 152)

Most Holy Trinity, a secondary concept (p. 152)

Most Holy Trinity, which should no longer be considered as three distinct Persons (p. 153)

Most Holy Trinity, a concept no longer licit or possible to profess (p. 153)

Most Holy Trinity, falsely and heretically interpreted (p. 154)

Most Holy Trinity, a concept that must evolve historically to avoid the tri-theist error (p. 157)

Most Holy Trinity, which can be invoked as Mother, Daughter and Holy Spirit (p. 158)

Divine Providence, a caricature of God (p. 143)

Divine Providence, nothing but rubbish (p. 143)

IN CHAPTER III

Christ, who founded a community of the condemned (p. 161)

Christ, separated from divinity by death (p. 167)

Christ, the accursed one who is cast away from God (p. 168)

Christ, the one who is sin personified (p. 167)

Christ, like a fortified city in ruins (p. 168)

Christ, rejected and cursed by God (p. 168)

Christ, whose destiny is Hell (p. 168)

Christ, abandoned by the Father to his fate of death (p. 168)

Christ, delivered by the Father to the forces of perdition (p. 168)

Christ, in whom all the black foam of sin surges (p. 169)

Christ, who gathers in himself treason and cowardice (p. 169)

Christ, who gathers in himself defiance and pride (p. 169)

Christ, who gathers in himself anguish and infamy (p. 169)

Christ, cast into Hell, the heart of the world (p. 169)

Christ, in whom Heaven and Hell clash and struggle (p. 169)

Christ, who tastes both the deepest misery and the most sublime bliss (p. 170)

Christ, abandoned by the Father, who joins His betrayers and forsakes Him (p. 170)

Christ, delivered by the Father to the flames of Hell (p. 170)

Christ, buried alive and filled with anguish (p. 170)

Christ, who gave himself to sin and the devil (p. 170)

Christ, the corpse over which vultures gathered (p. 170)

Christ, squeezed to the very dregs (p. 170)

Christ, trod upon to infinity (p. 170)

Christ, thinned into air and liquefied into an ocean (p. 170)

Christ, dissolved in totality (p. 170)

Christ, who filled the world from Heaven to Hell (p. 170)

Christ, whose restoring action took place in Hell (p. 170)

Christ, who plunged into an abyss of grief from which he could not escape (p. 172)

Christ, who should withdraw obedience to God and thus lose him (p. 172)

Christ, who cried out more terribly than a reprobate (p. 173)

Christ, whose cry of abandonment was a cry of despair (p. 173)

Christ, who lost himself in death without finding God (p. 172)

Christ, who experienced every dimension of the world to be able to judge man (p. 172)

Christ, who experienced the pain of loss (p. 172)

Christ, head of the mystical body of the wicked (p. 174)

Christ, head of the community of the condemned (p. 174)

Christ, confessor of God under the form of sin (p. 174)

Christ, who glorified God in the reprobates (p. 174)

Christ, whose mystical body is made up of reprobates (p. 174)

Christ, who has an indissoluble unity with the reprobates (p. 174)

Christ, who went down into the underworld (p. 174)

Christ, who assimilated into himself everything foreign and contrary to God (p. 174)

Christ, who assimilated Hell into himself (p. 174)

Christ, channel for the ascent of Hell into God (p. 175)

Christ, victorious for having emptied Hell (p. 175)

Christ, whose descent to the abyss became the ascent of all from Hell (p. 175)

Christ, who did away with the struggle between love and hate (p. 175)

Christ, who emptied himself to become the emptiness of Hell (p. 175)

Christ, who absorbs good and evil and makes them equal (p. 175)

Christ, who uses sin as raw material and stones for his building (p. 175)

Christ, who transforms sensual love into virginity (p. 175)

Christ, who bestows a future on the hopeless in Hell (p. 175)

Christ, who prefers prostitutes and the lawless (p. 177)

Christ, who despises those who seek after holiness (p. 177)

Christ, who calls blessed those who do not seek holiness (p. 177)

Christ, who counsels against discipline and moderating the passions (p. 177)

Christ, who calls blessed those who do not achieve self-mastery (p. 177)

Christ, who cultivates familiar relations with those on the marginalized of society (p. 177)

Christ, united with vagabonds and tramps (p. 177)

Christ, whose cherished guests are the ragged and the miserable (p. 177)

Christ, who cultivates familiar relations with prostitutes (p. 177)

Christ, who cares nothing for pious practices (p. 177)

Christ, who despises concerns about the spiritual life (p. 177)

Christ, who identifies with all 'poor devils' (p. 177)

Christ, who identifies with heretics and schismatics (p. 178)

Christ, who identifies with whores and adulteresses (p. 178)

Christ, who identifies with the politically compromised (p. 178)

Christ, who identifies and lives with the lawless (p. 178)

Christ, who forgives the godless (p. 178)

Christ, who dies on the cross like those cursed by God (p. 178)

Christ, who is contrary to and the opposite of God (p. 178)

God, who is found through Christ in darkness and scum (p. 178)

God, who is found through Christ in abandonment and marginalization (p. 178)

God, who is found through Christ among the lawless (p. 178)

God, who can only be known and found in anti-society (p. 178)

God, who can only be known and found in the poor and marginalized (p. 178)

Christ, a model for homosexuals (p. 183)

Christ, whose attributes are like those of homosexuals (p. 183)

Christ, who should not be considered heterosexual (p. 183)

Christ, masculine and feminine at the same time (p. 185)

Christ, who integrates the feminine perfectly (p. 185)

Christ, in whom the feminine was divinized and is God (p. 185)

Christ, the synthesis of man and woman (p. 185)

Christ, whose kingdom will come when there is neither man nor woman (p. 185)

Christ, the reintegrated androgynous person (p. 185)

Christ, in whom the separation between man and woman is overcome (p. 186)

Christ, archetype of both the feminine and the masculine (p. 186)

Christ, who excludes the supremacy of one sex over another (p. 186)

Christ, who is like the comic figure Don Quixote (p. 187)

Christ, whose suffering figure reveals a fool and a clown (p. 188)

Christ, whose Incarnation is an unacceptable myth (p. 195)

Christ, whose Incarnation is as ludicrous as the Dalia Lama being a reincarnation of Buddha (p. 189)

Christ, who cannot be proved to be greater than Buddha (p. 189)

Church of Love, superior to the official Petrine Church (p. 163)

Church of the wicked, preferred to the Johannine Church of love (p. 163)

St. Peter, betrayer of Christ (p 162)

St. Peter, who erred in all he did during the Passion (p. 162)

St. Peter, who presents an impossible figure (p. 187)

St. Peter, whose crucifixion was grotesque (p. 187)

St. Peter, who is like Sancho Panza (p. 187)

Judas who betrays, a symbol of the Old Covenant that is closed on itself (p. 173)

Judas who betrays, a symbol of the New Covenant representing its indignity (p. 173)

Judas, as abandoned as Christ himself (p. 173)

Judas, like Christ, suspended between heaven and earth (p. 173)

Judas, who scatters his entrails instead of shedding his blood like Christ (p. 173)

Judas who betrays, playing a role of co-redemption with his suicide (p. 173)

Reprobates in Hell, saved by the blood of Christ (p. 175)

IN CHAPTER IV

Catholic Faith, an expression that causes uneasiness (p. 196)

Catholic Faith, an oppressive burden for modern man (p. 196)

Catholic Faith, contradicting modern knowledge (p. 196)

Catholic Faith, no longer supported by philosophy (p. 196)

Catholic Faith, which finds itself in a vacuum (p. 196)

Catholic Faith, which finds no place in human thinking (p. 197)

Catholic Faith, reduced to an empty theory of no import (p. 197)

Catholic Faith, always a weak flickering flame in man (p. 197)

Catholic Faith, always the opposite of a haughty rigidity (p. 198)

Catholic Faith, which cannot determine who believes or does not believe (p. 198)

Catholic Faith, which cannot try to fathom the abyss of God (p. 198)

Catholic Faith, unbelievable if it demands man rely on something above his natural intellect (p. 201)

Catholic Faith, unintelligible if it demands man rely on something above his natural intellect (p. 201)

Catholic Faith, whose dogma on the resurrection of the dead is an illusory speculation (p. 201)

Catholic Faith, whose dogma on the resurrection of the dead is a Freudian illusion (p. 201)

Catholic Faith, whose dogma on the resurrection of the dead is based on the questionable Book of Daniel (p. 201)

Catholic Faith, which cannot be based on the words of Jesus (p. 209)

Catholic Faith, whose Revelation cannot be proved rationally. (p. 210)

Catholic Faith, whose interpretation of Jesus changes with the times (p. 210)

Catholic Faith, whose doctrine on original sin is completely irrelevant today (p. 215)

Catholic Faith, whose doctrine on original sin must be understood as our membership in society (p. 217)

Catholic Faith, whose doctrine on original sin is a collective sin – the sin of the world (p. 217)

Catholic Faith, whose doctrine on monogenism is irrelevant and can no longer be defended (p. 217)

Catholic Faith, whose doctrine on the fall is a myth (p. 217)

Catholic Faith, whose teaching that all men descend from Adam is a myth (p. 217)

Catholic Faith, whose catechesis should no longer use the term 'original sin' (p. 218)

Catholic Faith, whose use of the word 'sin' does not mean personal sin (p. 219)

Catholic Faith, whose use of the word 'sin' can only be analogical (p. 219)

Catholic Faith, whose understanding of original sin always depends on the times (p. 220)

Scriptures, whose stories of miracles are obstacles to the faith (p. 199)

Scriptures, whose Pauline interpretation of the Old Testament is unacceptable to philosophers and historians (p. 199)

Scriptures, proven by historical-critical scholarship to be a wholly human book (p. 200)

Scriptures, whose accounts about God are no longer believable today (p. 200)

Scriptures, whose accounts are not the expression of the divine word (p. 200)

Scriptures, whose recourse to the inspiration of sacred texts is disastrous (p. 200)

Scriptures, which should be open to critical discussion (p. 200)

Scriptures, whose premises should be questioned as unfounded (p. 200)

Scriptures, whose claim to be the word of God is a theological superstructure (p. 200)

Scriptures, whose claim to be the word of God is a human illusion (p. 200)

Scriptures, just a projection of our human desires (p. 201)

Scriptures, a fantastic apocalyptic literature that does not prove the resurrection of the dead (p. 201)

Scriptures, whose Book of Daniel raises more questions than it answers (p. 201)

Scriptures, whose different parts do not make an homogeneous picture (p. 205)

Scriptures, whose cosmic images are so imaginative and varied they cannot be reconciled (p. 205)

Scriptures, whose analogies drawn by St. Paul about nature are confused (p. 206)

Scriptures, whose account of the Resurrection of Christ is nothing but images (p. 206)

Scriptures, whose testimonies on the Resurrection of Christ have conflicting images (p. 206)

Scriptures, whose accounts on the Resurrection of Christ are in irreconcilable opposition (p. 206)

Scriptures, whose empty Sepulcher account results from the Jewish mentality of the time (p. 207)

Scriptures, whose empty Sepulcher account is historically dubious (p. 207)

Scriptures, whose empty Sepulcher account by St. Matthew is fraught with internal contradictions (p. 207)

Scriptures, whose empty Sepulcher account is part of the exaggerations of the apocryphal gospels (p. 207)

Scriptures, whose empty Sepulcher account by St. Mark was eliminated by the Church to impose her own opinions (p. 207)

Scriptures, whose account of the Ascension by St. Luke is a forced reaction to the times (p. 208)

Scriptures, whose words of Jesus cannot be considered as Revelation (p. 209)

Scriptures, which cannot rationally prove the divinity of Jesus (p. 210)

Scriptures, whose Gospels represent religion no better than the books of other religions (p. 210)

Scriptures, whose interpretation of Jesus is only a historical probability (p. 210)

Scriptures, which reflects the biased attitude toward women of the times (p. 211)

Scriptures, whose Epistles of St. Peter present women as the weaker sex (p. 211)

Scriptures, whose Epistles of St. Peter demand women submit to their husbands (p. 211)

Scriptures, whose mythological texts legitimate men's domination of women (p. 211)

Scriptures, whose account of the fall in Genesis must no longer be taken literally (p. 215)

Scriptures, whose account of the fall and original sin is completely irrelevant and mythical (p. 215)

Scriptures, whose inerrancy must be questioned (p. 215)

Scriptures, whose texts are confused because of presuppositions of the authors (p. 215)

Scriptures, which is better understood today than in apostolic times (p. 215)

Scriptures, whose texts on the fall story do not oblige us to believe them literally (p. 215)

Scriptures, whose account of the fall in Genesis is above all a myth (p. 216)

Scriptures, whose account of the fall is formulated in symbolic terms (p. 216)

Scriptures, whose account of Adam's nudity in paradise does not preclude sexual desire (p. 217)

Scriptures, whose account of Adam in paradise does not exclude his ability to have sexual relationships with others (p. 217)

Scriptures, whose doctrine on the fall is not about man's origins but his present and future state of evolution (p. 216)

Scriptures, whose account of Adam and Eve is just a legend and a story (p. 220)

Scriptures, whose account of the fall cannot be harmonized with natural science (p. 220)

Scriptures, whose account of the fall must be abandoned for not harmonizing with universal evolution (p. 220)

Scriptures, whose story of Paradise denies the pain and death that were already in the world (p. 220)

IN CHAPTER V

Dogma of the Trinity, a product of the Greek mind without real significance (p. 223)

Dogma of the Trinity, which no longer expresses a reality that means anything (p. 224)

Dogma of transubstantiation, an inaccessible medieval concept (p. 224)

Dogmas of original sin, the Real Presence and the Devil, simplistic beliefs (p. 225)

Catholic dogma, theological sentences that today are only bothersome (p. 224)

Catholic dogma, a language that cannot stand of itself (p. 224)

Catholic dogma, expressed in a second class language (p. 224)

Catholic dogma, whose truth is the same as other natural truths (p. 224)

Catholic dogmas, which must correspond to the concrete reality (p. 224)

Catholic dogmas, whose statements are like other human statements (p. 224)

Catholic dogmas, whose truth comes from natural conditions (p. 225)

Catholic dogmas, whose truth cannot be labeled infallible (p. 225)

Catholic dogmas, exaggerations that discredit truth when they rely on infallibility (p. 225)

Catholic dogmas, which pretentiously impose themselves when they rely on infallibility (p. 225)

Catholic dogmas, simplistic beliefs different from true tradition (p. 225)

Catholic dogmas, which must be reinserted into a more complete historic perspective (p. 225)

Symbol of the Faith, stiff, petrified formulas stripped of historicity (p. 225)

Symbol of the Faith, hampered by the biases and polemical character of the times (p. 225)

The Four Last Things, an accumulation of 'things' found somewhere beyond the curtain of death (p. 220)

The Four Last Things, wrongly studied in a physicist way (p. 220)

The Four Last Things, which wrongly viewed Heaven, Hell and Purgatory as places (p. 220)

The Four Last Things, which wrongly viewed the end of the world as an event dependent on theology (p. 220)

The Four Last Things, whose view of the cosmos must open to a new dimension (p. 220)

The Four Last Things, which became a sickly treatise (p. 231)

Heaven, which as a place is absurd (p. 232)

Heaven, which as a blessed state of pure spirit betrays the true earthly reality of man (p. 233)

Heaven, a new cosmic state reached at the end of the evolutionary process (p. 233)

Heaven, an invention that fulfilled the political needs of the Church (p. 233)

Heaven, a place invented because of Christendom's failure to manage the world (p. 234)

Heaven, imagined as an individual reward because of Christendom's social failure (p. 234)

Heaven, which as a place apart from the world shows the Church's incapacity to achieve what she preaches (p. 234)

Heaven, whose existence renders futile any attempt to overcome time (p. 234)

Heaven, whose existence favors resignation and the exploitation of the people (p. 234)

Heaven, an exalted concept with a heavy dose of Platonic dualism (p. 234)

Heaven, a concept influenced by the Stoic ideal of the spirit leaving the body (p. 235)

Heaven, which reveals a deep-set narcissism in the hope of achieving a personal reward (p. 235)

Heaven, whose classic image diminished at the end of the 20th century (p. 236)

Heaven, whose classic image was replaced by existential and interpersonal relations (p. 236)

Heaven, whose classic image was replaced by the quest for fraternity (p. 236)

Heaven, whose classic image was replaced by charismatic experiences of the Spirit (p. 326)

Heaven, whose classic image was just the fruit of a classicist culture (p. 236)

Heaven, flawed for extending the incarnate character of this finite life to the end of time (p. 237)

Heaven, flawed for separating the spirit from matter (p. 237)

Heaven, an obsolete idea since all human efforts are material (p. 237)

Hell, a dogma reflecting a fundamentally egoist spirit (p. 239)

Hell, a dogma reflecting a bourgeois and capitalist mentality (p. 240)

Hell, a dogma that excludes our solidarity with the condemned (p. 240)

Hell, an inadmissible dogma because it treats men inhumanely (p. 240)

Hell, an inadmissible dogma because no man can be condemned (p. 240)

Hell, a dogma to be understood as an inferior state rather than a place (p. 240)

Hell, a dogma that expresses the state of one who is closed in on himself (p. 240)

Hell, a dogma that has done incalculable harm through the centuries (p. 240)

Hell, a dogma born from barbarous and sadistic fantasies about the damned (p. 241)

Hell, a dogma that generated the notion of absurd torments (p. 241)

Hell, a dogma that resulted from sex and guilt complexes (p. 241)

Hell, a dogma that secures the Church's power over souls (p. 241)

Hell, a dogma that perverted Catholicism into a bloody and murderous religion (p. 231)

Purgatory, a dogma that merely reflects an encounter with God (p. 243)

Purgatory, which must not be understood as a special place (p. 243)

Purgatory, a dogma that concocted strange ideas about the poor souls (p. 243)

Purgatory, an expression that must be avoided (p. 243)

Purgatory, which should not be imagined as a place or time of purification (p. 243)

Purgatory, which is not an intermediary time between death and judgment (p. 244)

Purgatory, which was understood before Vatican II in a mythical and semi-pagan way (p. 244)

Last Judgment, a childish and mechanical conception that must be abandoned (p. 245)

Last Judgment, which denies the reality of a simultaneously private and universal judgment (p. 245)

IN CHAPTER VI

Sacrament, whose formulas and rites generate scruples and anxieties (p. 248)

Sacrament, which is nothing but a religious symbol (p. 248)

Sacrament, something that takes place only through one's interrelationship with Christ (p. 249)

Sacrament, which demands a religious commitment from the one receiving it (p. 249)

Sacrament, an 'untruthful sign' without a personal encounter with the living God (p. 249)

Sacrament, an idea that stands in the way of the appeal of the living God (p. 250)

Sacrament, a notion understood in a ritualistic and magical way (p. 251)

Sacrament, a wrongly understood notion that was a betrayal of the gifts of God (p. 251)

Baptism, a sacrament understood as a quasi-magical action (p. 255)

Baptism, a sacrament that requires faith to be valid (p. 255)

Baptism, which cannot presuppose faith as an automatic fruit of the sacrament (p. 255)

Baptism, which follows an egotistic and sterile notion of the sacraments (p. 255)

Baptism, which should not be imposed on children (p, 255)

Confession, a sacrament that demands a personal encounter with Christ to impart grace (p. 256)

Confession, a sacrament that deteriorated into an almost magical ritual (p. 256)

Confession, a sacrament that must not focus too much on telling one's sins (p. 256)

Confession, which loses its value when it is frequent (p. 256)

Confession, whose absolution as the easy answer to sin is harmful (p. 256)

Confession, a sacrament that should be celebrated as a feast for the whole community (p. 257)

Eucharist, a mystery that descends to the plane of carnal fecundity (p. 251)

Eucharist, the male seed cast by Christ in the feminine Church to impregnate her (p. 251)

Eucharist, the generating force of the New Adam in the New Eve (p. 251)

Eucharist, an invention of Christ to have human commerce with men (p. 252)

IN CHAPTER VII

Catholic Morals, which shapes a passive and childish mentality (p. 267),

Catholic Morals, which should allow acts that permit the person to freely fulfill himself (p. 267)

Catholic Morals, which stifles personal initiative, creativity and boldness (p. 267)

Catholic Morals, which must change (p. 266)

Catholic Morals, which must not allow sin to violate the notion of person (p. 269)

Catholic Morals, burdened by a false dualism that distorted Christian tradition (p. 271)

Catholic Morals, which ignores the demands of the body (p. 271)

Catholic Morals, an archaic pre-morals made up of taboos and prohibitions (p. 273)

Catholic Morals, which can learn something from Freudian psychoanalysis (p. 273)

Catholic Morals, whose teaching on sexuality was Jansenist (p. 275)

Catholic Morals, whose notions of good and evil reflected a morbid dualism (p. 275)

Catholic Morals, influenced by Gnosticism and Manichaeism (p. 275)

Catholic Morals, influenced by Stoicism and neo-Platonism (p. 275)

Catholic Morals, which falsifies the true doctrine on sex and marriage (p. 278)

Catholic Morals, wrong to consider satisfying the sexual appetite only as a need (p. 279)

Catholic Morals, wrong to consider conjugal love solely as a means to propagate the species (p. 280)

Catholic Morals, which should liberate sexuality and love (p. 281)

Catholic Morals, whose teaching on man's body and his sexual appetite were negative (p. 268)

Catholic Morals, which must do away with every taboo regarding sex (p. 279)

Catholic Morals, which must overcome Gnostic, Manichaean and Dualist tendencies regarding sex (p. 276)

Catholic Morals, dualist for separating the function of procreation and conjugal love (p. 278)

Catholic Morals, whose dualism must be rejected by existential and anthropological phenomenology (p. 278)

Catholic Morals, dualist for viewing sexuality as the animal dimension of man (p. 279)

Catholic Morals, which must affirm there is nothing censurable about sexual pleasure (p. 281)

Catholic Morals, which must state that sexual pleasure is the gift of self, without egoism (p. 279)

Catholic Morals, which must accept that the purpose of sexual union is not procreation (p. 279)

Catholic Morals, which should view sexual pleasure as the nucleus of sexual morals (p. 281)

Catholic Morals, which are rigorist and unbalanced (p. 280)

Catholic Morals, which does not understand the positive aspects of sexual pleasure (p. 280)

Catholic Morals, whose censure of birth control is strange, repressive and irrelevant (p. 282)

Catholic Morals, pretentious for condemning birth control (p. 282)

Catholic Morals, whose condemnation of homosexuality is brutal and pharisaic (p. 285)

Catholic Morals, whose condemnation of homosexuality is biased and unchristian (p. 285)

Catholic Morals, which should recognize homosexual relationships (p. 285)

Catholic Morals, which should acknowledge that the homosexual is still loved by God (p. 285)

Catholic Morals, which should present homosexuality as a valid form of human love (p. 285)

Catholic Morals, which should recognize the homosexual 'couple' and their loving union (p. 285)

Catholic Morals, which should encourage a homosexual pastoral and theology (p. 287)

Catholic Morals, which lacks perspective because of its fear of social changes (p. 287)

Catholic Morals, which errs by trying to reform society by transforming individual consciences (p. 287)

Catholic Morals, illusory for trying to transform the structures of society by converting the rich (p. 287)

*   *   *

BIBLIOGRAPHY

(AAS) ACTA APOSTOLICAE SEDIS, *Commentarium Officiale* - Vatican City: Libreria editrice vaticana, 1909- . **ABBOTT, Walter M. and GALLAGHER, J.** - *The Documents of Vatican II*, Piscataway, NJ: New Century Publishers, Inc., 1966. **AIGRAIN, René** - 'L'Espagne chrétienne" "Les Papes et l'Italie de 604 a 757," in Fliche and Martin, *Histoire de l'Église*. **ALSZEGHY, Zoltan** - See Maurizio Flick. **AMMAN, Émile** - 'Les transformations de la Chrétienté au début du IX siécle," "Les tribulations du Siége Apostolique (885-962)," in Fliche and Martin, *Histoire de 'l'Église*. **ANNIBALE, Josephus D'** - *Summula Theologiae Moralis*, Milan: Ex Typ. S. Josephi, 1882. **AUBENAS, R.** - "Hérétiques et sorciers," in Fliche-Martin, *Histoire de l'Église*. **AQUINAS, St. Thomas** - *Summa Theologiae*, Turin/Rome: Mariétti, 1948; *Super Epistolas Pauli*, Rome: Marietti, 1953, 4 vols.

BALTHASAR, Hans Urs von - *De l'Intégration – Aspects d'une theólogie de l'Historie*, Bruges: Desclée de Brouwer, 1970; *El complejo antirromano - Integración del papado en la Iglesia universal*, Madrid: BAC, 1981; *El problema de Dios en el hombre actual*, Madrid: Guadarrama, 1960; "Eschatologie," in V.A, *Questions théologiques d'aujourd'hui*; *Le coeur de la matière*, Paris: Seuil, 1976; *Le coeur du monde*, Paris: Desclée de Brouwer, 1956; *La gloire et la croix – Péguy*, Paris: Aubier-Montaigne, 1972; *Mysterium Paschale*, in V.A., *Mysterium Salutis - Compêndio de dogmática*; "O acesso à realidade de Deus," in V.A., *Mysterium Salutis*; "Sobre la dignidad de la mujer," *Communio*, October-November 1982; *Sponsa Verbi*, Brescia: Morcelliana, 1969. **BARDY, Gustave** - "Atticus de Constantinople et Cyrille d'Alexandrie," *"Les origines de l'arianisme et le Concile de Nicée* in V.A., *Histoire de l'Église*. **BARDY, G. and L. Bréhier** - "L'expansion chrétienne aux Ve. et VIe. siècles," in Fliche and Martin, *Histoire de l'Église*. **BARTOLOCCI, Giulio** - *Bibliotheca magna rabbinica*, in Felix Vernet, "Juifs et Chrétiens," in DAFC. **BECCAR VARELA, Miguel** - See Edwaldo Marques. **BELLARMINE, St. Robert** - *Opera Ommia*, Palermo/Naples/Paris: Pedone, 1872, 8 vols. **BENEDICT XII** - Instruction *Iam dudum* of 1341, in DS. **BENEDICT XIV** - Constitution *Super ad nos*, of March 16, 1743, in DS.

BERGER, Joseph - "Vatican Reveals Why It Punished Archbishop," *The New York Times, apud Jornal do Brasil*, October 29,1986. **BÖCKLE, Franz** - "Amor y matrimonio," in V.A., *La reforma que llega de Roma*. **BOFF, Leonardo** - *O rosto materno de Deus - Ensaio interdisciplinar sobre o feminino e suas formas religiosas*, Petrópolis: Vozes, 1979. **BOKENKOTTER, Thomas** - *A Concise History of the Catholic Church*, New York: Doubleday, 2004. **BONIFACE VIII** - Bull *Unam Sanctam* of November 18, 1302, in DS. **BONSIRVEN, J.** - Entry "Talmud", in *DTC*. **BOSSUET, Jacques-Bénigne** - *Oeuvres Complètes - Explication de l'Apocalypse*, Paris: Berche et Tralin, 1885. **BRÉHIER, Louis** - "La politique réligieuse de Justinien," "La querelle des images jusqu'au Concile iconoclaste de 754," "Le Concile de Constantinople et la fin du régne de Justinien," "L'Ekthesis, la fin du règne et la succession d'Héraclius (638-641)," "Les rapports entre Rome et Constantinople de l'avènement de Grégoire le Grand à la chute de Phocas," in Fliche and Martin, *Histoire de l'Église*. **BRUNELLI, Lucio** - "A via Sacra de Bartolomeu," *30 Dias*, March 1994. **BUTTIGLIONE, Rocco** - *Il pensiero di Karol Wojtyla*, Milan: Jaca Books, 1982.

CANADIAN CONFERENCE OF CATHOLIC BISHOPS - "Pornogafia e prostituzione oggi," *L'Osservatore Romano*, June 9, 1984. **CAPPELLO, Felice** - *Summa Iuris Canonici,* Rome: Universitas Gregoriana, 1955. **CAPRILE, Giovanni** - "Il Papa al tempio ebraico di Roma," *La Civiltà Cattolica*, May 3, 1986. **CARACCIOLO** - *Censura y confisco de los libros judios en los Estados da la Iglesia,* Frankfurt, 1891. **CASSIAN, John** - *Opera Omnia*, Paris: J.P. Migne, ed., 1865. *CATOLICISMO* - Excommunication formula in *Pontifical Romano,* December 1952; **CHARDIN, Pierre Teilhard de** - *Le coeur de la matiére*, Paris: Seuil, 1976; *Les directions de l'avenir*, Paris: Seuil, 1973. **CHENU, M.-D** - "The History of Salvation and the Historicity of Man in the Renewal of Theology," in V.A., *Theology of Renewal.* **CLEMENT IV** - Bull *Caeca et obdurata* of January 25, 1593, in L. Pastor, *Historia de los Papas;* Bull *Cum Hebraeorum* of February 28, 1593 and Bull *Damnabili perfidia* of July 15, 1267, in F. Vernet, "Juifs et Chrétiens." *CODE OF CANON LAW OF 1983* - Edições Loyola, São Paulo, 1983. *CODEX JURIS CANONICI* - Rome: Tipografia Poliglotta Vaticana, 1917. **CODY, Aelred** - "O Novo Testamento," *Concilium* 1979/3. **COLEMAN, John** - "Homosexual Revolution and Hermeneutics," *Concilium* 1984/3. **CONGAR, Yves** - Article in *Revue des Sciences Philosophiques et Théologiques*, 1949; *La crisi nella Chiesa e Mons. Lefébvre,* Brescia: Queriniana, 1976; *L'Église Catholique et France Moderne,* Paris: Hachette, 1978; *Jean Puyo interroge le Pére Congar,* Paris: Centurion, 1975; *La Parole et le Souffle,* Paris: Desclée, 1984; *Theology's Tasks after Vatican II*, in V.A., *Theology of Renewal - Renewal of Religious Thought* ; *Un peuple messianique*, Paris: Cerf, 1975. **COUNCIL OF TRENT** - Decrees *De Purgatorio* and *De justificatione* of 1563, in DS. **CREUSEN, Joseph** - See Arthur Vermeersch.

DEHARBE, J. - *Kleiner Katholishcer Katechismus*, Friedrich Putest, Regensburg, n.d. **DELASSUS, Henri** - *La conjuration antichrétienne*, Lille: Desclée de Brouwer, 1910, 3 vols. **DELHAYE, Philippe** - "Senso del peccato e risponsabilità personale," in J. Tomko *Peccato e riconciliazione.* **DENZINGER (D)** - **Henricus.** *Enchiridion Symbolorum,* first published 1854. **DENZINGER, Heinrich and Schonmetzer, Adolphus (DS)** - the Denzinger collection with additions by A. Schonmetzer between 1955 and 1965, Freiburg/Breisgau/Barcelona: Herder, 1965. **DEVIVIER, W.** *Curso de Apologica Christã,* São Paulo: Ed. Melhoramentos, 1925. *DICTIONNAIRE APOLOGÉTIQUE DE LA FOI CATHOLIQUE* (DAFC) - Paris: Gabriel Beauchesne, 1924, 5 vols. *DICTIONNAIRE DE THEOLOGIE*

CATHOLIQUE (DTC) - Ed. by A Vacant and E. Mangenot, Paris: Letouzey et Ane, 1923-1951. *DOCUMENTOS PONTIFÍCIOS* - Petrópolis: Vozes, 1959. **DÖPFNER, Julius** - *La Chiesa vivente oggi,* Bari: Paoline, 1972. **DUMAS, Auguste** - *Le sentiment religieux et ses aberrations,* in V. A., *Histoire de l'Église.* **DUQUESNE, Jacques** - *Jacques Duquesne interroge le Père Chenu – Une théologie en liberté,* Paris: Centurion, 1975. **DUQUOC, Christian** - "Um paraíso na terra?" *Concilium* 1979/3. **DURUY, Jean Victor** - *Histoire des Romains,* Paris: 1882.

ENCICLOPEDIA UNIVERSAL ILUSTRADA (Espasa-Calpe) - Bilbao/Madrid/Barcelona: Espasa Calpe, 1930-1956, 82 vols. (O) **ESTADO DE SÃO PAULO** - Supplement, "La sorpresa Lehmann, 1987/18. **EUGENE IV** - Bull *Cantate Domino* of November 4, 1442, in DS; Bull *Dudum ad nostram* of August 8, 1442, in F. Vernet, "Juifs et Chrétiens"; Bull *Laetentur coeli* of 1439, in D.

FAVRE, Robert - "Variações sobre o tema do céu no século das luzes," *Concilium* 1979/3. **FEDERICI, Tommaso** - "Religione e religioni oggi," in V.A., *Incontri tra le religioni.* **FERNANDO, Mervyn** - "Desafio budista ao Cristianismo," *Concilium,* 1978/6. **FERRERE, Iohannaes and Alfredus Mondria** - *Compendium Theologiae Moralis,* Barcelona: Subirana, 1953. **FESQUET, Henri** - *Le journal du Concile,* Forcalquier: Robert Morel, 1966. **FLICHE, Augustin** - *"La réforme de l'Église,"* "La Réforme grégorienne et la reconquête chrétienne (1057-1123)," in Fliche and Martin, *Histoire de l'Église.* **FLICHE, Augustin (2) and Victor Martin** - *Histoire de l'Église,* Paris: Bloud & Gay, Paris, 1946-1964, 26 vols. **FLICK, Maurizio and Zoltan Alszeghy** - *Il peccato originale,* Brescia: Queriniana, 1974. **FORCANO, B.** - *Caminos nuevos de la moral,* Valencia: EDICEP, 1973. **FOULQUIÉ, Paul** - *Dictionnaire de la Langue Philosophique,* Paris: Presses Universitaires de France, 1962. **FRANCA, Leonel** - *A Igreja, a reforma e a civilização,* Rio de de Janeiro: Livraria Catholica, 1928. *FRANKFURTER ALLGEMEINE ZEITUNG* - Nachdenken über eine neue Synode der Bistümer in der Bundesrepullik," November 12, 1983. **FREPPEL, Charles** - *Saint Justin,* Paris: 1869 *apud* F. Vernet, "Juifs et chrétiens," in *Dictionnaire Apologétique de la Foi Catholique.* **FREUD, Sigmund** - *Obras psicológicas completas de Sigismund Freud,* Rio: 1970-1977, 24 vols. **FUCHS, J.** - "Morale théologique et morale de situation," *Nouvelle Revue Théologique,* 1954.

GIUSEPPE, Alberigo et al., ed. - *Conciliorum Oecumenicorum Decreta,* Rome: Herder, 1962. **GOFFINÉ, Leonard** - *Manual do Christão,* Rio: Collégio da Immaculada Conceição, 1940. **GONZALEZ RUIZ, J.M.** - "Cristianismo: Mensagem de libertação," in V.A., *Cristianismo sem Cristo.* **GOUPIL A.** - *Les sacraments,* Laval: Imprimerie Librairie Goupil, 1955. **GREGORY XVI** - Brief of May 27, 1581, in L. Pastor, *Historia de los Papas*; Encyclical *Mirari vos* of August 15, 1832, in DS. **GRESHAKE, Gisbert** - *Stärker als der Tod, Zukunft, Tod, Auferstehung Himmel-Hölle,*

Fegefeuer, Mainz: Topos-Taschenbucher, 1976. **GUIMARÃES, Atila Sinke** - Collection: *Eli, Eli, Lamma Sabacthani?*: Vol. I, *In the Murky Waters of Vatican II*, Los Angeles: TIA, 2008; Vol. II, *Animus Injuriandi I*, Los Angeles: TIA, 2010; Vol. IV, *Animus Delendi I,* Los Angeles: TIA, 2000; Vol. V, *Animus Delendi II,* Los Angeles: TIA, 2002; Vol. VI, *Inveniet Fidem?*, Los Angeles: TIA, 2007; Vol. XI, *Ecclesia*, Los Angeles: TIA, 2009; *Vatican II, Homosexuality and Pedophilia*, Los Angeles: TIA, 2004; *We Resist You to the Face*, Los Angeles: TIA, 2000. Interviews with Fr. Barnabas Ahern, Rome, March 6, 1983; with Yves Congar, Paris, February 19, 1983; with Msgr. Philippe Delhaye, Louvain-la-Neuve (Belgium), February 28 and March 1,1983; with Fr. Joseph Fuchs, Rome, February 4, 1983; with Fr. Giovanni Caprile, Rome, February 3, 1983.

HAPPEL, Stephen - "As estruturas de nossa convivência (mit sein) utópica," *Concilium* 1979/3. **HÄRING, Bernhard** - "La speranza di Haering ... il Papa renuncerà al privilegio di nominare i vescovi," *Adista*, May 7-12, 1990. **HASLER, August.** "Lutero nei testi scolastici di teologia cattolica," *Concilium*, 1976/8. **HELLO, Henri** - *A verdade sobre a Inquisição*, Petrópolis: Vozes, 1936. **HÖFFNER, Joseph** - Speech in Worms, *Deutsche Tagespost*, November 4-5, 1983. **HONORIUS IV** - Bull *Nimis in partibus anglicanis* of November 18, in F. Vernet, "Juifs et Chrétiens". **HORTELANO, Antonio** - *Problemas Actuales de Moral,* Salamanca: Ediciones Sigueme, 1981; "Rivoluzione sessuale e famiglia," *Concilium* 1984/3, p. 100. **HUIZING, Peter** - "Vatican III: Una costituzione sulla Chiesa," in V.A., *Verso la Chiesa del terzo millenio.*

IORIO, Thomas - *Theologia Moralis,* Naples: D'Auria, 1960. **Van IERSEL, Bas** - "Son of God in the New Testament," *Concilium* (Portuguese ed.), 1982/3.

JOHN XXII - Bull *Dudum felicis recordationis* of September 4, 1320, in F. Vernet, "Juifs et Chrétiens." **JOHN PAUL I** - "Na oração, a esperança de paz," *L'Osservatore Romano*, September 17, 1978. **JOHN PAUL II** - Apostolic Letter *Euntes in mundum* of January 25, 1988; *Côdigo de Direito Canônico nico,* São Paulo: Loyola, 1983; Encyclical *Letter Redemptoris Mater*, in AAS; Insegnamenti di Giovanni Paolo II, 18 vols., Lib. Ed. Vaticana, 1983; Speeches in *L'Osservatore Romano:* Allocution at the Synagogue of Rome, April 14-15, 1986; Audience to an ecumenical group on pilgrimage to the East led by Cardinal François Marty, October 21, 1983; "Il Papa invita a lavorare per l'unione senza lasciarsi scoraggiare dale difficoltà, December 12-13, 1983; "La verità storica di Lutero alimenti il dialogo per l'unitá," June 11, 1983; Speech to the World Council of Churches in Geneva on June 12, 1984, June 14, 1984; Speech to the Federation of Protestant Churches on June 14, 1984, June 15, 1984. **JOURNET, Charles** - *L'Église du Verbe Incarné*, Bruges: Desclée, 1962. **JULIUS III.** Bull *Cum sicut nuper* of May 29, 1554, in L. Pastor, *Historia de los Papas.*

KASSNER, Rudolf - "Simon Petrus," *Neue Schweizer Rundschau*, N.F. 15, 1947-1948. **KERKHOPS, Jan** - "Diversas representações do céu," *Concilium* 1979/3. **KLOPPENBURG, Boaventura** - *A eclesiologia do Vaticano II*, Petrópolis: Vozes, 1971; *Concílio Vaticano II*, Petrópolis: Vozes, 1966, 5 vols. **KLOSTERMANN, Ferdinand** - "Principi per una riforma di struttura della Chiesa," in V.A., *La fine della Chiesa come società perfetta.* **KOKORA, Noel** - "La riconziliazione è una festa," *L'Osservatore Romano*, October 6, 1983. **KÜNG, Hans** - *A Igreja*, Lisbon: Moraes, 1970, 2 vols.; "La riforma liturgica del Concilio Vaticano II e la riunione con i cristiani separati," in V.A., *I grandi temi del Concilio; O que deve permanecer na Igreja*, Petrópolis: Vozes, 1976; *Veracidade - O futuro da Igreja*, São Paulo: Herder, 1969; *Vida eterna?* Madrid: Cristiandad, 1983.

LAIBLE, H. - *Jesus Christus im Thalmud*, Berlin: 1891. **LAPIDE, Cornelius a** - *Commentaria in Scipturam Sacram*, Paris: Ludovicum Vivês Ed., 1874-1877, 24 vols. **LASH, Nicholas** - "Filho de Deus, Reflexões sobre uma metafora," *Concilium*, 1982/3. **LAVISSE, Ernest and Alfred Rambaud** - *Histoire générale du IVe. siécle à nos jours*, Paris: Armando Colin, 1984. **LAZARÉ, Bernard** - *Anti-Semitism, Its History and Causes*, New York: The International Library Publishing Co., 1903. **LEA, Antonio Carlos** - *Em defesa dos cátaros*, in W. Devivier, *Curso de Apologica Christã.* **LEBRETON, Jules** - *Les Péres Apostoliques et leur époque, La réaction catholique*, in Fliche and Martin, *Histoire de l'Église.* **LEO X** - Bull *Exsurge Domine* of June 15, 1520, in DS. **LEO XIII** - Encyclicals *Satis cognitum* of June 29, 1896, *Ubi primum* of May 5, 1824, in DS. **LINDBECK, George A. and Martensen, H.** - "Declaration of the Catholic/Lutheran Joint Commission on the Fifth Centennial of Martin Luther," *SEDOC* 16, Petrópolis, March 1964. **LLORCA, Bernardino** - *Bulario Pontificio de la Inquisición Española*, Rome: Pontificia Università Gregoriana, 1949. **LÓPEZ AZPITARTE** - Eduardo. *Sexualidad y matrimonio hoy - Reflexiones para una fundamentación ética*, Santander: Sal Terrae, 1980. **LORSCHEIDER, Aloisio** - Interview, *O Povo* (Fortaleza), November 15, 1983. **LUBAC, Henri de** - *Athéisme et sens de l'homme*, Paris: Cerf, 1968; *Entretien autour de Vatican II*, Paris: Cerf, 1985. **LUCIA, Carlo de** - "Cari amici e fratelli ebrei e cristiani," *L'Osservatore Romano*, April 14-15, 1986. **LUGO, Joannis de** - *De Virtute Fidei Divinae - Disputationes Scholasticae et Morale*, Paris: Vivés, 1858. **LUSTIGER, JEAN-MARIE.** Interview, *Bulletin de l'Agence télégraphique juive, La Documentation Catholique*, March 1, year; Interview to the *Tribune Juive*, Le Monde, September 5, 1981.

MAISTRE, Joseph de - *Cartas sobre a Inquisição Espanhola*, Niteroi: Revista Leituras Católicas, 1949. **MALDONADO, Luis** - *Genesis del Catolicism popular*, Madrid: Ed. Cristiandad, 1979; *La violencia de lo sagrado*, Salamanca: Sígueme, 1974. **MANNA, S.** - "Il Card. Willebrands inaugura il corso dell'Instituto S. Nicola," *L'Osservatore Romano*, February 5,

1984. **MARQUES, Edwaldo and Miguel Beccar Varela** - Appendix, in Plinio Corrêa de Oliveira, *Guerreiros da Virgem.* **MARRANZINI, Alfredo** - "Identità, sviluppo dogmatico e variazioni sul sacramento della riconciliazione," in J. Tomko, *Peccato e riconciliazione.* **MARTENSEN, H.** - See George Lindbeck. **MCNEILL, John** - *The Church and the Homosexual,* Boston: Beacon Press, 1993. **MARTIN, Victor** - See Augustin Fliche (2). **MÉSZAROS, Istvan** - *Marx: A teoria da alienação,* Zahar Ed., Rio de Janeiro, 1981. **MICHEL, Albert** - Entry "Congar," in DTC. **MOELLER, Charles** - *L'élaboration du schema XIII - L'Église dans le monde de ce temps,* Tournai: Castermann. **MONDIN, Battista** - *Os grandes teólogs do século vinte,* São Paulo: Paulinas, 1979, 2 vols. **MONDRIA, Alfredus** - See Iohannaes Ferrere. **MÜHLEN, Heribert** - "O teste da infalibilidade - Por que Hans Küng deve encontrar uma oposição decidida?"in K. Rahner, *O problema da infalibilidade.*

NICHOLAS I - Letter *Proposueramus quidem* of September 28, 865, in DS.

OLIVEIRA, Plinio Corrêa de - *Em Defesa da Ação Católica,* São Paulo: Ed. Ave-Maria, 1943; *Guerreiros da Virgem - A réplica da autenticidade,* Ed.Vera Cruz, São Paulo, 1985; *O Legionário* (São Paulo Archdiocesan newspaper) articles: "Genealogy of Monsters," June 26, 1938; "What Road Is Fascism Taking?" August 7, 1938; "From Godesberg to Munich," October 2, 1938; "Twilight of the Devils," October 9, 1938; "Dawn of the Gods," October 23, 1938; "Still Fascism," January 8, 1939; "The Example of the White Russians," January 22, 1939; "Charity and Folly," May 14, 1939; "The Most Hateful of Despotisms," March 31, 1940; "Falsification," April 21, 1940; *Revolution and Counter-Revolution,* New Rochelle, NY: Foundation for a Christian Civilization, 1980. **OLIVIER, Daniel.** "Perché Lutero non é stato capito?" *Concilium* 1976/8. *L'OSSERVATORE ROMANO* - "Celebrato a Lipsia il centenario della nascita di Martin Lutero," November 13, 1983; "Conferito a padre Yves Congar il premío per l'unitâ dei cristiani, November 28, 1984; "Il Card. Willebrands inaugura il corso dell'Instituto S. Nicola," February 5, 1984; *In ocassione della visita del Pontefice Giovanni Paolo II,* Communità Israelitica di Roma: Templo Maggiore, 1986; "Solo Dio può riempire il fuoto dell'uomo d'oggi come fu per S. Agostino, September 21, 1983; "Von Baltahsar: La mi opera è abbozata più che terminate," June 24, 1984.

PALMIERI, Domenico - *Tractatus de Romano Pontifice,* Rome, 1877. **PASTOR, Ludwig** - *Historia de los Papas,* Barcelona: Gustavo Gili, 1886-1933, 40 vols. **PATROLOGIE GRECQUE (PG)** - Pub. by Paul Migne, 217 vols. More than 3 indexes. **PATROLOGIE LATINE (PL)** - Pub. by Paul Migne, Paris: Migne, 1841-1864, 161 vols. **PAUL IV** - Bull *Cum nimis absurdum* of July 14, 1555, *in* L. Pastor, *Historia de los Papas.* **PEINADOR, Antonio** - *Cursus Brevior Theologiae Moralis,* Madrid: Coculsa, 1946-1956, 4 vols. **PESCH, Otto Hermann** - "Comprensione di Lutero oggi," *Concilium* 1976/8; Lo stato attuale di comprensione e de intesa su

Lutero," *Concilium*, 1976/8. **PHILIPS, Gérard** - *La Chiesa e il suo mistero nel Concilio Vaticano II – Storia, testo e comment della Constituzione Lumen gentium*, Milan: Jaca Books, 1982. **PIGNOT, J. H.** - *Histoire de l'ordre de Cluny*, Paris: Dejussieu, 1868. **PIUS IV** - Bull *Iniunctum nobis* of 1564, in DS. **PIUS II** - Bull *Exsecrabilis* of January 18, 1460, in DS. **PIUS V** - Brief of May 3, 1569 in L. Pastor, *Historia de los Papas;* Bull *Antiqua Judaeorum improbitas* of June 1, 1581, in F. Vernet, "Juifs et Chrétiens"; Bull *Hebraeorum gens* of February 26, 1569, in L. Pastor, *Historia de los Papas.* **PIUS VI** - Bull *Auctorem fidei*, in DTC; Edicts of October 1775 and January 1793, in F. Vernet, "Juifs et Chrétiens."

PIUS IX - Allocution *Singulari quadam* of December 9, 1854, Apostolic Letter *Iam vos omnes* of September 13, 1868, Dogmatic Constitution on the Church of July 18, 1870, Epistle *Quanto conficiamur* of August 10, 1863, Encyclical *Qui pluribus* of November 9, 1846, Letter *Gravissimas inter* of December 11, 1862, in DS; Bull *Ineffabilis Deus* of December 8, 1854, in D. **PIUS X** - Apostolic Letter *Notre Charge Apostolique*, Petrópolis: Vozes, 1953; Decree *Lamentabili* of July 3, 1907, in DS; Encyclical *E Supremi Apostolatus*, December 4, 1903, in *Documentos Pontifícios;* Encyclical *Pascendi Dominici gregis* of July 3, 1907, Vozes: Petrópolis, 1959; Letter *Ex quo* of 1910, in DS. **PIUS XI.** Encyclical *Casti connubii* of December 31, 1930, in *Documentos Pontifícios.* **PIUS XII.** Encyclical *Mystici Corporis* of June 29, 1943, in DS; Letter of the Holy Office to the Archbishop of Boston, August 8, 1949, in DS. **PLINVAL, G. de** - "Les luttes pélagiennes," in Fliche and Martin, *Histoire de l'Église*

RAHNER, KARL - "Algumas observações sobre o tratado dogmático *De Trinitate*," in *O dogma repensado*; *Chiesa, uomo e società*, Rome-Brescia: Herder-Morceliana,1970; "Differenza tra morale teoretica e reale," in V.A., *La salvezza nella Chiesa*; *Escritos de teologia*, Madrid: Taurus, 1964, 23 vols.; "La resurreción de la carne," in *Escritos de Teología*; "O Deus trino, fundamento transcendente da História da Salvação," in V.A., *Mysterium Salutis*; *O problema da infalibilidade* (ed.), São Paulo, Loyola, 1976; "Qual é il messaggio cristiano? Necessità di una nuova formulazione," in V.A., *L'Avvenire della Chiesa*; *Qué debemos creer todavia?* Santander, 1980; "Sobre el sentido del dogma de la Asunción," in *Escritos de teologia*; *Teologia e Bíblia*, São Paulo: Paulinas, 1972, 2 vols.; "Théologie et anthropologie," in V.A., *Théologie d'aujourd'hui et de demain.* **RAHNER, Karl (2) and H. Vorgrimler** - *Petit dictionnaire de théologie catholique*, Paris: Seuil, 1970. **RAMBAUD, Alfred** - See Ernest Lavisse. **RANKE-HEINEMANN, Uta** - "La condizione sessuale fondamentale dell'uomo," in Karl Rahner, *Chiesa, uomo e società.* **RATZINGER, Joseph Ratzinger** - "Exame do problema do conceito de Tradição," in V.A., *Revelação e Tradição*; *Fé e futuro*, Petrópolis: Vozes, 1971; "Questioni preliminary ad una teologia della redenzione," in V.A., *Redenzione ed emancipazione; Rapporto sulla Fede*, Rome: Paoline, 1985; "Sobre la cuestión de la validez permanente de las formulas dogmaticas," in ITC., *Pluralismo teologico,* Madrid: BAC, 1976. **RATZINGER Joseph and Karl Rahner** - *Revelação e Tradição,* São Paulo: Herder, 1968. **REGATILLO, Eduardus F.** *Institutiones Iuris Canonici,* Santander: Sal Terrae, 1961. *REGNO, II* - "A outra face da Inquisição," March 16, 1986,

RICCI, Tommaso. "A luz vem do Oriente, *30 Giorni,* June 1988; "Aperte le celebrazioni per il millennio del battesimo della Rus' de Kiev," *L'Osservatore Romano* , June 6-7,1988; "Cardinal Casaroli in Moscow for the Celebrations of the Millennium of Rus," *L'Osservatore Romano,* June 9, 1988; "La visita di Giovanni Paolo II a Bari terra d'incontro d'Oriente e Occidente," *L'Osservatore Romano,* February 27/28. **ROSA, Giuseppe de.** "Ebrei e cristiani `fratelli' nel `fratelo Gesù," *La Civiltà Cattolica,* May 3, 1986. **ROUSSEAU, Olivier** - "La Constitution *Lumen Gentium* dans le cadre des mouvements rénovateurs de théologie et de pastorale des dernières décades," in V.A., *L'Église de Vatican II.* **RUEDA, Enrique** - *The Homosexual Network,* Old Greenwich, CT: The Devin Adair Co., 1982. **RUETHER, Rosemary Radford** - "Cristologia e femminismo," in V.A., *La sfida del femminismo alla teologia.*

SABAN, Giacomo - Greeting by the President of the Israelite Community of Rome, *L'Osservatore Romano,* April 14-15, 1986. **SARTORI, Luigi** - "Lo Spirito é effuso su tutti," in V.A., *Lo Spirito Santo pegno e primizia del Regno.* **SCHEFFCZYK, Leo** - "A verdade enunciada em proposições e o 'permanecer na verdade,'" in Karl. Rahner, *O problema da infalibilidade.* **Schillebeeckx, Edward** - *Cristo sacramento dell'incontro con Dio,* Rome: Paoline, 1970; "Evolução e mudanças nas concepções cristãs do matrimônio," in V.A., *Direitos do sexo e matrimônio;* "L'Etica della situazione," in V.A., *I grandi temi del Concilio;* "Les sacraments, organes de la rencontre de Dieu," in V.A., *Catholiques et Protestants;* Untitled, in V.A., *Cinco problemas que desafiam a Igreja hoje,* pp. 19-20. **SCHMALZGRUEBER, Francis** - *Jus Ecclesiasticum Universum,* Rome: Typ. Rev. Cam. Apostolicae, 1845. **SCHOONENBERG, Piet J.** - Untitled, in V.A., *Cinco problemas que desafiam a Igreja hoje.* **SESBOÜÉ, Bernard** - *O Evangelho na Igreja – A tradição viva da fé,* São Paulo: Paulinas, 1977. **SILVEIRA, A.V.X. da** - "Atos, gestos, atitudes e omissões podem caracterizar o herege," *Catolicismo,* December 1967; "Não só a heresia pode ser condenada pela autoridade eclesiástica," *Catolicismo,* November 1967. **SIPOS, Stephanus** - *Enchiridion Iuris Canonici,* Rome: Herder, 1954. **SIXTUS IV** - Bull *Intenta semper salutis* of May 31, 1484 in Llorca, Bernardino, *Bulario Pontificio de la Inquisición Española.* **SOBRINO, Jon** - "A fé de um povo oprimido no Filho de Deus," *Concilium,* 1982/3, pp. 42-43. **SPIRAGO, Francis and Richard F. Clarke** - *The Catechism Explained,* NY: Benzinger Bros, 1921. **STRACK, H. L.** - *Jesus, die Haeretiker und die Christen nach den ältesten jüdischen Angaben,* Leipzig, 1910. **SUAREZ, Francisco** - *De Fide: Opera Omnia,* Paris: Vivés, 1858, 28 vols. **SUENENS, Leo Jozef** - Cristianismo sem Deus?" in V.A., *Cristianismo sem Cristo?* **SUPREME CONGREGA-**

TION OF THE HOLY OFFICE. Instruction published on February 2, 1956, in AAS. SYNOGOGUE (Rome) - *In ocassione della visita del Pontefice Giovanni Paolo II*, Communità Israelitica di Roma: Templo Maggiore, 1986.

TANQUEREY, Adolphe - *Brevior Synopsis Theologiae Moralis,* Paris-Tornai-Rome: Desclée, 1946. TEDESCHI, John - *The Prosecution of Heresy: Collected Studies on the Inquisition in Early Modern Italy.* Medieval and Renaissance Texts and Studies, No. 78, Binghampton, NY: 1991. TERTULLIAN - *Adversus Gnosticos Scorpiace, Adversus Judaeos,* in PL. *For the Conversion of the Jews,* trans. by John Collorafi and Atila Guimarães, Los Angeles: TIA, 2007. TOMKO, J., ed. - *Peccato e riconciliazione,* Rome: Paoline, 1983. THOUZELLIER, Christine - *L'Enseignement et les universités,* in DAFC. TORNIELLI, Andres - "A moral se faz esperar," *30 Dias,* June 1993. TUBERVILLE, Henry - *The Douay Catechism,* NY: P.J. Kenedy, 1649.

URBAN VIII - Brief to the King of Spain of January 15, 1628, in L. Pastor, *Historia de los Papas.*

VAILHÉ, S. - "Constantinople" (Église de), in *DTC.* *The Washington Post,* "McNeill Leaves Jesuits," November 8, 1986.

VARIOUS AUTHORS (V.A.) - *Catholiques et Protestants,* Paris: Seuil, 1963; *Cinco problemas que desafiam a Igreja hoje,* São Paulo: Herder, 1970; *Cristianismo sem Cristo?* Paulinas: Caxias do Sul, 1970; *Direitos do sexo e matrimônio,* Petrópolis: Vozes, 1972; *I grandi temi del Concilio,* Rome: Paoline, 1965; *Incontri tra le religioni,* Verona: Mondadori, 1969; *L'Avvenire della Chiesa - Il libro del Congresso,* Brescia: Queriniana, 1970; *La fine della Chiesa come società perfetta,* Verona: Mondadori, 1968; *La reforma que llega de Roma,* Barcelona: Plaza & Jares, 1970; *La salvezza nella Chiesa,* Rome-Brescia: Herder-Morcelliana, 1968; *La sfida del femminismo alla teologia,* Brescia: Queriniana, 1980; *L'Église de Vatican II,* Paris: Cerf, 1966; *Lo Spirito Santo pegno e primizia del Regno - Atti della XIX Sessione di formazione ecumenica organizzata dal Segretariato Attività Ecumeniche (SAE),* Turin: Elle Di Ci, 1982; *Mysterium Salutis - Compêndio de dogmática,* Petrópolis: Vozes, 1974; *O dogma repensado,* São Paulo: Paulinas, 1970; *Questions théologiques d'aujourd'hui,* Paris: Desclée de Brouwer, 1965; *Redenzione ed emancipazione,* Brescia: Queriniana, 1975; *Théologie d'aujourd'hui et de demain,* Paris: Cerf, 1967; *Theology of Renewal - Renewal of Religious Thought,* Montreal: Palm Publishers, 1968, 2 vols.; *Um homem, uma obra, uma gesta - Homenagem das TFPs a Plinio Corrêa de Oliveira,* São Paulo: Edições Brasil de Amanhã, 1989; *Verso la Chiesa del terzo millenio,* Brescia: Queriniana, 1973. VALENTE, Gianni - "Bartolemeu I, a verdade está nos fatos," *30 Dias,* September 1994 "Melhor divididos que uniatas," *30 Giorni,* March 1992; "Um teatro vazio," *30 Dias,* February 1994. VERMEERSCH, Arthur and Joseph Creusen - *Epitome Iuris Canonici,* Milan-Rome: Dessain, 1946. **VERNET, Felix** - "Juifs et Chrétiens," in DAFC. **VIDAL, Pedro** - See Francisco Xavier Wernz. **VITORIA, Francisco de** - *Obras de Francisco de Vitoria,* Madrid: BAC, 1960. **VORGRIMLER, H.** - See Karl Rahner (2).

WASHINGTON POST, The - "McNeill Leaves Jesuits," November 8, 1986. **WEISS, Juan Baptista** - *História Universal,* Barcelona: La Educación, 1927. **WENGER, Antoine** - *L'Église de son temps – Vatican II – Chronique,* Paris: Centurion, 1963-1966, 4 vols. **WERNZ, Francisco Xavier and Vidal, Pedro** - *Ius canonicum,* Rome: Gregorian University, 1927. **WILLEBRANDS, Johannes** - Allocution au Comité international de liaison, *La Documentation Catholique,* January 19, 1986; Lecture delivered at the Fifth Assembly of the Lutheran World Federation, *La Documentation Catholique,* June 15, 1970.

YARNOLD, Edward - *Teologia del peccato originale,* Catania: Paoline, 1971.

ZEILLER, J. - "La persécution sous les Flaviens et Antonins," "Le siège romain," "Les premières persécutions. La législation impériale relative aux Chrétiens, "Les grandes persécutions du milieu du IIIe siècle et la période de paix religieuse de 260 à 302," in V.A., *Histoire de l'Église.* **ZUANAZZI, Gianfrancesco.** "Freud, la morale and la colpa," in J. Tomko, *Peccato e riconciliazione.*

*   *   *

SUBJECT INDEX

ANIMUS INJURIANDI (AI) – AI **exposed** in this volume: Conclusion § 1. AI against Catholic doctrine: Introduction § 1; against Faith & Morals: Introduction § 2; against *sentire cum Ecclesia*: Chap. I § 2. AI manifested by **eulogies** of heretics: Chap. I § 2. AI **similar** to the destruction of the Temple: Conclusion § 2; similar to the offenses at the time of Antichrist: Chap VII §§ 3, 4.

ARIANISM (A) – Pope Liberius adhered to A: Chap. I § 11.

ATHEISM (A) – a new **concept** of God to please A: Chap. II §§ 7, 8. A **correctly** criticizes God: Chap. II §§ 4-6, 8.

BIBLE – see *SCRIPTURES*

CALVIN, JOHN – Praised by John Paul II: Chap. I §§ 42-43; as a great reformer: Chap. I § 68. See *PROTESTANTISM, LUTHER*

CHRISTIANITY (C) – To attack C makes minds sharper: Chap. I § 58.

CHRIST (C) – **CATHOLIC PERSPECTIVE**: C went to hell to triumph over the devils and reprobates: Chap. III note 12. **PROGRESSIVIST PERSPECTIVE**: C **accursed** by God: Chap. III § 14. C an **androgynous** person: Chap. III §§ 36, 37. C. is not greater than **Buddha**: Chap. III § 40. C founded the **church of the condemned**: Chap. III §§ 1-27. *Concept* of the church of condemned: Chap. III § 6; *superior* to the official Church: Chap. III §§ 6, 7. C united with the **condemned**: Chap. III § 11; united with Judas: Chap. III § 19; united with the reprobates of hell: Chap. III §§ 16, 17, 20. C lived the **feminine** dimension: Chap. III § 35. C assimilates **hell** into himself: Chap. III §§ 22, 23. **Hell** and heaven united after C's death: Chap. III § 24. C identified himself with **heretics** and whores: Chap. III §§ 29, 30. C had **homosexual** characteristics: Chap. III § 34. C as **mad** as Don Quixote: Chap. III § 38. C was a fool and a clown: Chap. III § 38. C forms a **mystical body** with the reprobates: Chap. III §§ 21, 25. C experienced the **pain of loss**: Chap. III § 18. C. delivered himself to **sin** and the devil: Chap. III § 16. C became a **reprobate**: Chap. III §§ 13, 18. C rejects **spirituality** and asceticism: Chap. III § 28. C is not the **Son of God**: Chap. III §§ 41-43. C **subverted** the public order: Chap. III § 31. See *FAITH, CATHOLIC, GOD, TRINITY*

CHURCH (C) – C of the **condemned**: Chap. III §§ 3 – see *CHRIST*. C of **love**: Chap. III §§ 3, 5. **Petrine** church: Chap. III §§ 3, 4. Inadequacy of the classification C: Chap. III §§ 7-10. Utility of this conception to destroy the Catholic Church: Chap. III § 27. Overview of the **three Churches**: Chap. III §§ 3-13, 25, 26.

COLLEGIALITY (C) – **Concept** derived from the Schismatics: Chap. I §§ 73, 86, note 134. **Condemnations** of the supposed primacy of the synod over the Pope: Chap. I note 119c. **System** to oppose papal monarchy: Chap. I §§ 74, 86.

Communicatio in sacris – Forbidden by the Church: Chap. I note 41e.

Conciliarism – Condemned by the Church: Chap. I § 75.

Council Vatican II – **Accepted** the ideas of Luther: Chap. I §§ 27, 51, 52, 66, 70. **Opened** to liberation theology, feminist theology and homosexual theology: Chap. III § 32.

Ecumenism (E) – Authentic E, Pius IX invites heretics to **convert**: Chap. I note 58. **Common ground** tactic with heretics was condemned: Chap. I §§ 37-39; John Paul II used common ground tactic with Schismatics: Chap. I § 77.

Eschatology – Progressivist term to replace the Four Last Things: Chap. V § 8.

Evolution (E) – E changes the **concept** of God: Chap. II §§ 7, 8, note 10; replaced by God of the Above + God of the Ahead: Chap. II § 7, note 10. **Concept** of history according to E: Chap. V §§ 10, 11. **Cosmogenesis** and Christogenesis, new names for E: Chap. V §§ 9, 13 note 9. **Faith** changed to fit E: Chap. V §§ 15, 16. **Heaven** is replaced by the last phase of E: Chap. V § 9. **Original sin** was a refusal of E: Chap. IV § 35; original sin must be understood according to E: Chap. IV § 43. **Paradise** does not correspond to an evolving world: Chap. IV § 37. **Pleroma** and E: Chap. VII § 4, note 7. **Resurrection** was an evolutionary leap: Chap. IV § 23, Chap. V §§ 9, 10, 14. **Spiritualized love** and E: Chap. VII § 27.

Excommunication, Formula of – Chap. I note 65.

Existential anthropology – Chap. VII note 36.

Fast – Position of St. Peter on fast resisted by St. Paul: Chap. I § 9.

Faith, Catholic (CF) – **Catholic Perspective: Four last things**: Chap. V § 7. **Heaven** exists: Chap. V note 20. **Hell** exists and is a place: Chap. V note 35. **Purgatory** exists as a place: Chap. V note 44. **Progressivist Perspective:** CF became an oppressive burden: Chap. IV § 4; is empty: Chap. IV § 6; is a weak flickering flame: Chap. IV § 7; entered a vacuum: Chap. IV § 5; is a heavy load of indigestible doctrines: Chap. IV § 10. **Dogmas** are bothersome: Chap. V § 2; use a second-class language: Chap. V § 3; utilize an exaggerated infallibility: Chap. V § 4; must be interpreted freely: Chap. V § 6. **Dogma of Trinity** is just speculative curiosity: Chap. V § 2. **Formulae** of CF must vary: Chap. IV § 1. **Four last things,** a physicist treatise: Chap. V § 17; a sickly treatise: Chap. V § 19. **Heaven** & Hell are naïve concepts: Chap. V § 27. Heaven, Hell & Purgatory are not places: Chap. V §§ 18, 20. Heaven does not exist: Chap. V §§ 21, 22, 25, 27; it was conceived under influence of Stoicism: Chap. V § 24; hope of Heaven is narcissist: Chap. V § 25. Paradise is not necessary for an evolving world: Chap. IV § 37. There is no earthly paradise: Chap. V § 22. **Hell** does not exist or is empty: Chap. V §§ 28, 29;

teaching on hell is egoistic and bourgeois: Chap. V § 30. Hell is a psychological state: Chap. V § 32; is the fruit of sex and guilt complexes: Chap. V § 33; the fruit of perverse imagination: Chap. V § 31. To believe in hell causes perversions: Chap. V § 34. **Original sin** was a collective act: Chap. IV § 35; refers to a refusal of evolution not of morals: Chap. IV §§ 35, 43; must be replaced by the sin of humanity: Chap. IV § 37; by structures of sin or sin of the world: Chap. IV § 39; by the inhuman dimensions of human life: Chap. IV § 44. **Purgatory** is not a place or a time of purification: Chap. V §§ 35, 36; is a childish and mechanical notion: Chap. V § 38; a pagan and mythical notion: Chap. V § 37. **Resurrection** is an evolutionary leap in the process of evolution: Chap. IV § 23. See *SCRIPTURES, GOD, TRINITY, CHRIST*

FILIOQUE (F) - **Documents** defending F: Chap. I note 120a. F **maintained** in chapels of the Empire by Charlemagne: Chap. I § 16.

FOUR LAST THINGS – See *FAITH, CATHOLIC*

GOD (G) – **Catholics** should live as if G did not exist: Chap. II § 9. **Concept** of G as static and abstract is wrong: Chap. II § 3; as omnipotent is wrong: Chap. II §§ 4, 14; as a Judge is wrong: Chap. II § 4. G as providence should die: Chap. II § 3. A G who cannot suffer is a fraud: Chap. II §§ 12, 14; is a monstrous being: Chap. II § 14. G presented by Tradition is an idol & a caricature: Chap. II §§ 3, 5. **Conflict** between G the Father and G the Son: Chap. II §§ 11, 13. G the Father represents the good, G the Son saves the wicked: Chap. II § 11. The justice of G has demonic traits: Chap. II § 12; the G of the law is Calvinist & Jansenist: Chap. II § 12; G the Father's domain is hell: Chap. II § 13; this G is a devil: Chap. II § 14. G the Judge condemned Jesus Christ: Chap. II § 14. G the Father cursed Christ: Chap. III §§ 14, 15; betrayed Christ: Chap. III §§ 15, 16. G **immanent** replaced G transcendent: Chap. II §§ 7, 15, note 9; God of the Above + God of the Ahead: Chap. II § 7, note 10. G is **mother**: Chap. II §§ 23, 24. The **sacrality** of G is fraudulent: Chap. II § 14. See *TRINITY, CHRIST*

GREEK SCHISMATIC CHURCH – see *SCHISMATIC CHURCH*

HEART OF CHRIST – Different **meanings** according to Progressivism: Chap. III note 16. **Place** where hell and heaven fight: Chap. III § 15.

HERESY (H) – **Canons** against H eliminated in the 1983 Code: Chap. I note 5. **Infractions** connected with H: Chap. I note 3b. H **praised** by Catholic hierarchs: Chap. I § 2. **Suspicion of H** according to Canon Law of 1917: Chap. I § 3, note 2; types of suspicion of H: Chap. I note 2. To praise H incurs suspicion of H: Chap. I § 3. When prelates become suspect of heresy: Chap. I note 41f.

HERETIC (H) – No longer **defined** in the 1983 Code: Chap. I note 6. The modern mind is **favorable** to H: Chap. I § 56. **Heretics** were good and enriched the Church: Chap. I § 65; had great ideas: Chap. I § 68; were similar to the great saints: Chap. I § 65. Early H in the Church used "**mystery**" to hide errors: Chap. I § 93, note 150; H of the end times will use "mystery" to pervert many: Chap. I § 93, note 151. **Symptoms** that characterize the H: Chap. II § 2.

HISTORICAL METHOD OF INTERPRETING SCRIPTURES – see *SCRIPTURE*

HOMOSEXUALITY – see *MORALS, CATHOLIC; STRATEGY, PROGRESSIVIST*

HONOR OF THE CHURCH – Offenses against: Introduction § 2; Chap. I, § 1.

IMMACULATE CONCEPTION OF MARY – Documents defending it: Chap. I note 120b.

INCARNATION OF CHRIST – A myth impossible to demonstrate: Chap. III § 39.

INFALLIBILITY OF THE POPE – see *PAPAL INFALLIBILITY*

INQUISITION (I) – **Concept**: I was a mixed tribunal composed of churchmen and statesmen: Chap. I note 212b. I acted in **legitimate defense** against false conversions of Jews to Catholicism: Chap. I note 212a. The Roman Inquisition, the only exception when the Church applied temporal penalties, was a **model of moderation**, recognized by scholars: Chap. I note 212d. I did not **persecute** the Jews: Chap. I note 212. The **temporal judges** applied the laws common to their times, which were rigorous: Chap. I note 212c. The Church did not execute **temporal penalties**: Chap. I note 212b.

JEWS, JEWISH PEOPLE (J) –Crime of **Deicide**: Chap. I notes 140, 144. *Nostra aetate* tried to absolve J of Deicide: Chap. I § 91, note 144b. J **denied** the divinity of Christ: Chap. I § 88, notes 137, 140, 144. **Difference** between J as race and Judaism as religion: Chap. I note 141. J lost their **first-born** right: Chap. I § 90. Rabbi recognizes **goodness** of the Church toward J: Chap. I §§ 145, 146. Grand Sanhedrin approves report thanking the Church for her good treatment: Chap. I § 147. Church has no **racial prejudices** against J: Chap. I § 111; no temperamental or emotional prejudices: Chap. I §§ 113-147. **Symbolic character** of the J mentality: Chap. I § 162. See *JUDAISM*

JUDAISM (J) – **CATHOLIC PERSPECTIVE:** **Blasphemies** against Our Lord and Our Lady in *Talmud & Toledot Iesu*: Chap. I note 137b. Constant **conspiracy** of J against the Church: Chap. I §§ 143, 144. Catholic **dogmas** denied by J: Chap. I § 89; J is completely opposed to Catholicism: Chap. I § 89. **Direct persecution of J against Catholics** – Against the Apostles: Chap. I § 113; with the burning of Rome: Chap. I § 114, note 177; under the false messiah Barchochba: Chap. I § 116, note 180; by encouraging the Roman persecutions: Chap. I §§ 117- 120; by helping Julian the Apostate: Chap. I § 121; by instigating the persecution of King Sapor of Persia: Chap. I § 123; by leading the persecution in Ethiopia: Chap. I § 124; in Syria: Chap. I §§ 125, 127; by influencing the Caliphs in Jerusalem: Chap. I §§ 126, 129; by helping the Moorish invasion on the Iberian Peninsula: Chap. I § 127. **Documents** by Popes, councils, saints and laws combating J: Chap. I note 168. Pope **Hono-**

rius complacent with J: Chap. I § 14. **Indirect persecutions of J against Catholics** – By rejecting the Holy Trinity: Chap. I §§ 131-132; by inspiring the Alogean heresy: Chap. I § 132; by inspiring Praxeas: Chap. I § 133; by influencing Paul of Samosata and Zenobia: Chap. I § 134; by inspiring Photinus and the Arians: Chap. I § 135; by inspiring Rationalism and Theism: Chap. I § 137; by giving the foundation to Protestantism: Chap. I § 138; by influencing the French Revolution: Chap. I §§ 139, 140; by playing a part in the Communist revolutions of the 19th century in Europe: Chap. I § 141. Catholic position on J is different from **Nazism**: Chap. I § 111, note 174. Texts of **Talmud** against Catholic Church: Chap. I § 89, note 138.

JUDAISM (J) – PROGRESSIVIST PERSPECTIVE: John Paul II showed respect for **B'nai B'rith**: Chap. I § 92. To accept J is part of the **Catholic vocation**: Chap. I § 93; Catholic vocation is linked to J: Chap. I §§ 98, 99; J is intrinsic to Catholicism: Chap. I § 151. **Denial** of J is not necessary for a Jew to become a Catholic: Chap. I § 97; Catholics should not convert Jews from J: Chap. I § 98. Dialogue with J based on unclear **"mystery"**: Chap. I §§ 94, 95, 150. **Visit of John Paul II to the Rome synagogue**: Chap. I §§ 100-180. JPII appeared to **abandon** Catholic Faith and adhere to J: Chap. I §§ 148, 155. JPII pretended to **absolve** J from any curse: Chap. I §§ 159, 160. Text of the **allocution** of JPII: Chap. I § 109. Symbolic **character** of first visit in history of a Pope to a synagogue: Chap. I §§ 103, 104; end of the fight between the two religions: Chap. I §§ 101-104. **Condemnation** of the previous position of the Church: Chap. I §§ 104,105, 149; a condemnation that extends to all Catholic history: Chap. I § 106. Lack of base for this condemnation: Chap. I §§ 107, 108. JPII pretended to restore the right of **firstborn** to J: Chap. I § 152; error of this pretension: Chap. I §§ 153, 154; bad logic of JPII on J: Chap. I §§ 156-158. **Reaffirmation of the J errors** by rabbis during JPII's visit: Chap. I §§ 163-171. They reaffirmed their false faith: Chap. I §§ 167, 171; declared themselves heirs of God's promise: Chap. I §§ 163, 170, 176; insulted Catholics: Chap. I §§ 164, 169,173, 175; called Catholics enemies of God: Chap. I § 166; called Catholics guilty for Nazi persecutions: Chap. I § 168; demanded the recognition of the State of Israel: Chap. I § 174; promoted the doctrine of the eternal feminine: Chap. I § 178. Consequences of the visit: Chap. I § 172. Conclusion of the analysis: Chap. I § 179. Other **visits to synagogues** – Cologne, New York, Rome – by Benedict XVI: Chap. I § 100. See *JEWS*

JUSTIFICATION (J) – Protestant doctrine of J condemned by Trent: Chap. I note 28. Today it is considered correct: Chap. I § 50.

LUTHER (L) – **Condemned** by Pope Leo X: Chap. I § 30. L **excused** as not guilty of fracturing Christendom: Chap. I § 22. L was misunderstood: Chap. I § 47; had legitimate demands: Chap. I § 54; would not be condemned after Vatican II: Chap. I § 60, 61. The opposition between L and the Council of Trent disappeared: Chap. I § 54. L is no longer a heretic: Chap. I § 53. L recognizes his doctrine led to **moral decadence**: Chap. I note 1. L **praised** as common master of Catholics and Protestantism: Chap. I §§ 22; 24, 25, 28; as a religious genius: Chap. I §§ 21, 46; 59. L had a profound religiosity: Chap. I § 29; had lucidity and courage: Chap. I § 71; was very well founded: Chap. I § 64; was a prophet: Chap. I § 46; was a herald of renewal: Chap. I § 49; rediscovered the Gospel: Chap. I § 69; lifted up the medieval world: Chap. I § 59; would be a *perito* at Vatican II: Chap. I § 67. **New Mass** corresponds to L demands: Chap. I § 70. See *Protestantism*

Marcionism – Was good: Chap. I § 63.

Marianism, devotion to Mary – Was spurious: Chap. I § 66.

Mass, New – Corresponds to Luther's demands: Chap. I § 70.

Method of exposition of this Volume (ME) – This volume's **approach**: not to judge but to report offenses: Chap. I § 4; to see, judge, act: Chap. I § 4. **Final** dispositions of the Author: Conclusion § 5. **Problems** avoided by this ME: Chap. I § 5. Position of **resistance** of this work: Chap. I § 6; not intended to encourage insubordination: Chap. I § 6.

Militant Church, Militancy (M) – M against **Atheism** should end: Chap. IV § 8. **Divisions** between believers and non-believers should end: Chap. IV § 9. Catholics should **renounce** M: Chap. I § 48.

Modernism – **Apologetic** method condemned in *Pascendi*: Chap. I note 39. **Dogmas** can be changed: Chap. I note 39.

Monophysitism – Supported by Pope Vigilus: Chap. I § 13.

Monothelism – Supported by Pope Vigilius: Chap. I § 14.

Morals, Catholic (CM) – Catholic Perspective: **Birth control** is forbidden by the Church: Chap. VII § 27, note 35. **Concept of good egoism**: Chap. VII note 10. **Homosexuality** according to CM: Chap. VII § 34, note 44; condemnations of homosexuality in the Old and New Testaments: Chap. VII note 44; **Original sin** corrupted the sense of touch: Chap. VII § 16, note 23; this corruption is transmitted by the sexual act: Chap. VII note 23; vile aspect of the sexual act: Chap. VII § 30, note 38. **Sexual act** licit only inside marriage: Chap. VII § 27. **Vigilance** of CM regarding sex: Chap. VII note 24.

Morals, Catholic (CM) – Progressivist Perspective: Progressivist attack against good **egoism**: Chap. VII § 5. **Freud's** influence on the new morals: Chap. VII §§ 19, 20; notion of super-ego in Freud: Chap. VII § 20, note 27; CM is fruit of the sexual instinct repressed: Chap. VII note 27. **Homosexuality** according to progressivism: Chap. VII § 34; homosexuality accepted as consummated fact: Chap. VII §§ 34, 35, 36, 37. Concept of **individual morals**: Chap. VII § 6. **Nudity** of Adam & Eve reflected their ability to engage in sexual activity: Chap. IV § 34. **Offenses against – CM** is childish and puritanical: Chap. VII § 13; deforms the moral conscience: Chap. VII § 10; is dualist: Chap. VII §§ 17, 21, 29; expresses a morbid dualism: Chap. VII § 24; is egotistic: Chap. VII § 40; is falsified: Chap. VII § 11; has Gnostic and Man-

Christian religion: Chap. I note 41c. **Divisions** in P: Chap. I note 46. P doctrine of **justification** is condemned: Chap. I note 28. **Moral decadence** of: Chap. I § 2 note 1a-d, h-j. Generated scorn for **women**: Chap. I note 1g.

PROTESTANTISM (P) – PROGRESSIVIST PERSPECTIVE: Points of P **accepted** by Vatican II: Chap. I §§ 27. P should be **accepted** by the Catholic Church: Chap. I § 50. P **holds** parts of the truth: Chap. I § 57. **P praised** by John Paul II on his visit to the Lutheran temple: Chap. I §§ 33-35; on his visit to the World Council of Churches: Chap. I §§ 40-41. P is **richer** than Catholicism: Chap. I § 64. See *LUTHER, CALVIN, ZWINGLI, WYCLIFFE*

PSEUDO-REFORMATION – see *PROTESTANTISM*

REDEMPTION – New concept of: Chap. III § 26.

RELIGIOUS INDIFFERENTISM – Condemned by many Popes: Chap. I note 41d.

RESISTANCE, RESIST (R) – R **approved** by Saints & Church Doctors: Chap. I § 20. **Historic** examples of R: Chap. I §§ 8-20, note 11. **Fields** of R: the fast: Chap. I § 9; heresy §§ 11-15; liturgical rite §§ 10, 16. **Pope** who destroys the Church must be resisted: Chap. I § 7. **Right** of the faithful to resist authority: Chap. I § 6, note 9.

RITES OF THE CHURCH – Uniform rite of St. Anicetus resisted by St. Polycarp: Chap. I § 10.

SACRAMENTS (S) – **Baptism** is magical: Chap. VI § 13. Only adults should be baptized: Chap. VI §§ 13. **Eucharist** is Christ's semen: Chap. VI §§ 9-11; to receive Eucharist is coitus with Christ: Chap. VI § 11, note 14. Catholic concept of *ex opera operato*: Chap. VI § 5, note 5. **General offenses against S:** S are egotistic and sterile notions: Chap. VI § 14; are physicist operations: Chap. VI § 6; are untruthful signs: Chap. VI § 5; are symbolic and magic: Chap. VI §§ 3, 4; are "thing-ifications": Chap. VI § 7. **Holy Orders** are pagan and mythical: Chap. VI § 12. A bishop should be consecrated by the community: Chap. VI § 12. **Penance** is distressing: Chap. VI § 17; needs to become festive: Chap. VI § 17; is magical: Chap. VI §15; is mechanical: Chap. VI § 16.

SALVATION OUTSIDE OF THE CHURCH – Not admitted by the Church: Chap. I note 41d.

SCRIPTURE, SACRED (SS) – *CATHOLIC PERSPECTIVE:* Trent **condemns** changing the interpretation of SS: Chap. IV note 20. Objectivity of **Daniel'** prophecy: Chap. IV note 23. **Historical method** of interpretation condemned by St. Pius X: Chap. IV §§ 29, 30, note 42.

SCRIPTURES, SACRED (SS) – *PROGRESSIVIST PERSPECTIVE:* The account of the **Ascension** is not objective: Chap. IV § 21; Christ did not go to Heaven: Chap. IV § 22. **Historical method**, example: Chap. IV § 13. **Language** in SS is composed of legends: Chap. IV §§ 40-42; of myths: Chap. IV § 41; of mythological texts: Chap. IV § 27. **Miracles** of SS are obstacle to the Faith: Chap. IV § 11. **St. Paul's** interpretation of SS is no longer acceptable: Chap. IV § 12. SS are not **objective**: Chap. IV § 13. The account on **original sin** is symbolic, not historic: Chap. IV § 33; is irrelevant, a myth: Chap. IV § 31; gives a concept of original sin that is anachronistic: Chap. IV § 38; refers not to the sin of a couple but of an ensemble: Chap. IV § 32. The accounts on the **Resurrection of Christ** are irreconcilable: Chap. IV § 17. The accounts of the empty tomb can be doubted: Chap. IV §§ 18-20; are exaggerated: Chap. IV §§ 18, 20. **Resurrection of the dead** as reported in SS is an illusory speculation: Chap. IV § 15. The images referring to the resurrection of the dead cannot be harmonized: Chap. IV § 16. **Revelation** in the SS is only a human illusion: Chap. IV § 14. The words of Jesus are not part of revelation: Chap. IV § 24. The Gospels as revelation cannot be proved: Chap. IV § 25. See *FAITH, CATHOLIC*

SCHISMATIC CHURCH, GREEK (SC) – **Caesaropapism** dominates the SC in all countries: Chap. I note 118. **Collegiality** of SC should be adopted by Catholic Church: Chap. I § 86. SC under the influence of **Communism**: Chap. I note 118. **Condemnations** of the SC errors against the papal primacy and monarchy: Chap. I note 119; of the supposed primacy of the synod over the Pope: Chap. I note 119c. John Paul II attended **course of theology** by SC: Chap. I § 85. **Heresies** of SC: Chap. I §§ 75-77. SC denies the *Filioque*: Chap. I § 76, note 120a; denies the Immaculate Conception: Chap. I §76, note 120b. **Homage** to SC paid by John Paul II: Chap. I § 83. SC forms two lungs with the Catholic Church: Chap. I § 77-82, note 125. **Patriarchs** – of Constantinople: their historical ambition: Chap. I § 71; patriarch of Constantinople, puppet of patriarch of Moscow: Chap. I § 74. Patriarch of Moscow has more power than the others: Chap. I note 118. No equality exists among the schismatic patriarchs: Chap. I § 74, note 118. Title *primus inter pares* is not effective: Chap. I § 74. Schismatic patriarch writes *Via Sacra* for the Pope: Chap. I § 85.

SIGNS OF THE TIMES – **Concept** of: Chap. III note 42. **Liberation theology**, homosexual theology and feminist theology considered signs of time: Chap. III § 32.

SITUATION ETHICS (SE) – **Condemned** by Pius XII: Chap VII note 4. **Overview** of SE: Chap VII §§ 2, 3. **Schools** in SE: Chap. VII §§ 8, 9, note 6. **Sophism** of the partisans of SE: Chap. VII §§ 3-5, 9. See *MORALS*

SOCIALIZATION – **Introduced** by John XXIII in the Church: Chap. VII § 42. Its **messianic** aspects: Chap. VII §§ 42, 43.

SPIRIT OF THE COUNCIL – Its **complacence** with heretics: Chap. I § 2. **General plan** to study it: Introduction §§ 1-3.

SUSPICION OF HERESY, SUSPECT OF HERESY (SH) – According to **Canon Law** of 1917: Chap. I § 3, note 2. **John Paul II** became SH on his visit to the Lutheran temple: Chap. I §§ 33-35. Whoever **praises** a heretic incurs suspicion of H: Chap. I § 3. When **prelates** become suspect of heresy: Chap. I note 41f. Joseph **Ratzinger** was suspect of heresy: Chap. IV § 3. **Types** of SH: Chap. I note 2. See *HERESY*

STRATEGY, PROGRESSIVIST (S) – **Examples of S**: Regarding *homosexual theology* - Jesuit Fr. John McNeill, founder of *Dignity*, received support from his superiors to publish his book on homosexual theology: Chap. III § 33, note 45a. Head of Jesuits in the U.S. supported homosexuality: Chap. VII § 37. Archbishop Raymond Hunthausen punished by the Vatican for his support of homosexuality, was restored in all his functions through the action of American Cardinals: Chap. III note 45b. American Prelates and organizations supporting homosexuality: Chap. VII §§ 36, 38, note 47. S of homosexuals to be accepted by the Church: Chap. VII § 39. *Liberation theology* - Fr. Leonardo Boff, punished by the Vatican for his Communist approach, was defended by Brazilian Cardinals: Chap. III § 35, note 47. *Nouvelle theologie* - Joseph Ratzinger was suspect of heresy: Chap. IV § 3; he did not change his ideas: Chap. IV §§ 2, 3, notes 3, 9. Mutual support of **radicals and moderates**: Chap. I §§ 62, 63, note 97, § 72; moderates and radicals defend the same errors on interpretation of the Scripture: Chap. IV § 26. **Tricks** used by S to dodge papal condemnations: Chap. VII § 3, note 5.

TALMUD – see *JUDAISM*

TRINITY (T) – *CATHOLIC PERSPECTIVE:* **Doctrine** regarding the Trinity: Chap. II note 25. **Documents** from Tradition: note 25B; of the Church Magisterium: note 25C. *PROGRESSIVIST PERSPECTIVE:* The **dogma** of T failed to convince: Chap. II § 17; is just speculative curiosity: Chap. V § 2; does not mean anything to the faithful: Chap. II § 18. It is impossible to apply the three persons to the *kerigma*: Chap. II § 21. T should be addressed as **mother**, daughter and Holy Spirit: Chap. II § 22. **Passages** on T in the Old Testament: Chap. II note 25Aa; in the New Testament, note 25Ab. The word **person** in T should be replaced: Chap. II § 21. T is a **secondary concept**: Chap. II § 19 **Three persons** in the T means three ways of subsistence: Chap. II § 20. Three persons lead to a false and heretical interpretation of the dogma: Chap. II § 21.

VATICAN II – See *COUNCIL VATICAN II*

VIRGINITY – In its new stage of evolution does not exclude sexuality: Chap. VI note 12.

WYCLIFFE – A great reformer: Chap. I § 68. See *PROTESTANTISM*

WORLD COUNCIL OF CHURCHES (WCC) – WCC has no **authority** over its members: Chap. I note 46. WCC does not **represent** Protestant sects: Chap. I note 46. **Visit** of John Paul II to WCC: Chap. I §§ 36-40.

ZWINGLI, HULDRYCH – Praised by John Paul II: Chap. I §§ 42-43. See *PROTESTANTISM*

*   *   *

WORD INDEX

*   *   *